The regulation of standar

Manchester University Press

The regulation of standards in British public life

Doing the right thing?

David Hine and Gillian Peele

Manchester University Press

The rights of David Hine and Gillian Peele to be identified as the authors of this work have been asserted by them in accordance with the Copyright, Designs and Patents Act 1988.

Published by Manchester University Press
Altrincham Street, Manchester M1 7JA
www.manchesteruniversitypress.co.uk

British Library Cataloguing-in-Publication Data
A catalogue record for this book is available from the British Library

Library of Congress Cataloging-in-Publication Data applied for

ISBN 978 0 7190 9713 3 hardback
ISBN 978 1 7849 9267 5 paperback

First published 2016

Typeset by Out of House Publishing
Printed in Great Britain
by CPI Group (UK) Ltd, CR0 4YY

Contents

List of figures   vi
List of tables   vii
List of boxes   viii
Preface   ix
Acknowledgements   xi
List of abbreviations   xii

1   Introduction: regulating public ethics in the United Kingdom   1
2   Integrity issues: a changing agenda   30
3   Building the United Kingdom's integrity machinery: the role of the Committee on Standards in Public Life   52
4   The House of Commons: the slow erosion of self-regulation   69
5   The expenses crisis: statutory regulation and its difficulties   104
6   The House of Lords and reluctant reform   125
7   Regulation at the centre of government: the Ministerial Code   153
8   Whitehall wars: protecting civil-service impartiality   167
9   Regulating the after-life: ministers, civil servants and revolving doors   184
10   Getting to grips with lobbying: regulated office-holders, unregulated lobbies   197
11   Party funding: ambitious architecture, flawed rules   216
12   Integrity issues in local government: the rise and fall of the Standards Board for England   240
13   Integrity issues and devolution   269
14   Conclusions: higher standards, lower credibility?   292

Select bibliography   304
Index   314

Figures

1   Public trust in politicians   6
2   Public perceptions of overall standards of conduct in public life   7
3   Public estimates of *changes* in standards in public life   7
4   Assessments of changes in certain public standards (Hansard Society Audit)   8
5   Trust in MPs by party   10
6   Perceptions of MP conduct (England) 2004–2010   72
7   Procedure for handling complaints   92
8   IPSA's publication process   111
9   The growth of all-party parliamentary groups, 2003–2012   203
10   Average annual breakdown of expenditure of the three main central parties 2001–2010   221

Tables

4.1 Categories of interest of House of Commons register of
    financial interests 2015   86
4.2 Trends in complaints to the Parliamentary Commissioner
    for Standards 2007–2008 to 2013–2014   94
6.1 The rising number of Lords complaints received
    2004–2009   135
6.2 Trends in complaints received by the House of Lords
    Commissioner for Standards 2010/2011–2013/2014   145
8.1 Sources of appointments to senior (Band 2 and 3, and
    Permanent Secretary) civil-service posts reported by the
    Civil Service Commissioners, 1995/1996–2012/2013   172
9.1 Post-employment applications from Crown Servants dealt
    with directly by ACOBA 2000/2001–2012/2013   189
11.1 Income and expenditure at national level for the two
    main UK parties, 2002–2013   224
11.2 Distribution of gifts by size and party, 2001–2010   226
12.1 Complaints to the Standards Board for England,
    2002–2008   251
12.2 Source of complaints to the Standards Board for England,
    2002–2008 (% of annual total)   251
12.3 Complaints to the Standards Board for England,
    2002–2008 by type of local authority (% of total by year)   252
12.4 Complaints to the Standards Board for England,
    2002–2008: response of the Standards Board   252
12.5 Complaints to the Standards Board for England,
    2002–2008: nature of allegations referred for investigation   253
12.6 Complaints to the Standards Board for England,
    2002–2008: outcome of referrals   254

Boxes

1.1 The 7 principles of public life 16
2.1 Timeline of key changes in the integrity agenda 33
4.1 Timeline of key changes in the House of Commons standards regime 70
4.2 The House of Commons Code of Conduct 81
6.1 Timeline of key changes to the House of Lords standards regime 1974–2015 126
11.1 Timeline of party funding regulation 218

Preface

This book is about the continuing struggle to ensure that the government of the United Kingdom – its institutions, processes and political actors – adhere to high standards of probity. It is a story which concentrates on the last twenty years, although the issues it raises have a much longer pedigree. Until the early 1990s the integrity of government in the United Kingdom was widely taken for granted or at least was little discussed. Then, remarkably rapidly, the self-satisfaction was shattered by a series of colourful scandals which emerged to taint the Major governments of 1990–1997. As the word *sleaze* bedded into the national vocabulary, measures were initiated in an attempt to restore public confidence in British politicians and in British institutions. A small new body, the Committee on Standards in Public Life, set about creating regulatory machinery which could monitor ethical standards. It started at the country's constitutional heart, in Parliament, but later broadened out to cover a wide swathe of institutions. Twenty years after its first report we can see a profound transformation of the landscape of British government in the form of new regulatory institutions and processes geared to clarifying, refining and imposing appropriate values in government.

Some have questioned whether the Committee on Standards in Public Life is still needed. We think it is. Several long-standing problems remain unresolved: party funding, lobbying, and corruption in the police are clear cases. Meanwhile, in a political context sensitised by two decades of debate and controversy, new issues continue to emerge both nationally and locally; controversy over ethical issues surrounding the private delivery of public services is a clear case. The continuing salience of the Committee's work was underlined as we completed this book by arguments – violently stoked by mud-slinging during the 2015 general election – over the scale of individual donations to political parties and the enduring temptation lobbying rewards pose to politicians. When confidence in public probity is shaken by events of this sort, and by the memory of bigger ones like the MPs' expenses scandal of 2009, new matters easily get sucked into a vortex of continuing public scepticism about standards.

In short, the need for detailed analysis of acceptable standards in public life will not go away. In this book we have traced the iterative process by which values and principles have been analysed, and through which new regulatory institutions have evolved. Taken together, these institutions are an important new feature of the political system. We have concentrated on the key elements, those affecting the executive, legislature, parties, and sub-national government. There are other aspects of the public sphere – especially those on the border of public and private life – which have recently generated intense controversy, which space prevents us exploring, but which will be fruitful ground for further research. Our analysis reveals the complexity of building regulatory institutions where there is significant disagreement, not about what *constitutes* improper conduct (though sometimes there is such disagreement), but on the best way of *preventing* improper conduct. That disagreement may be about the appropriate size of the regulatory burden, the level of internal or public scrutiny office-holders should face, or the balance between self-regulation and independent regulation. On these key questions there are few easy answers, and much disagreement, sometimes honest, sometimes probably disingenuous. It is the detail and complexity of this disagreement on which we concentrate. It is the key to understanding what can work and what may not work in one of the most sensitive areas of public life. We do not claim to have definitive answers, but we believe the lessons of the last two decades need to be studied carefully because they will have to be learned and re-learned by successive generations of public office holders. We hope we have made a significant contribution to that challenge.

David Hine
Gillian Peele
Oxford

Acknowledgements

Many people – practitioners and scholars – have helped us during the writing of this book, answering enquiries and talking to us about their work. We cannot mention them all but we are extremely grateful to them for their willingness to share their expertise. In particular we would like to thank Chris Ballinger, Emily Commander, Christopher Johnson, Oonagh Gay, Robert Hazell, Robert Kaye, Sir Christopher Kelly, Brendan Keith, Sir Philip Mawer, Andrew McDonald, Maggie O'Boyle, Mark Philp, John Uhr, Hannah White and Brian Walker. We are also grateful for the comments of various anonymous reviewers.

A number of research assistants have given invaluable help. We especially thank Somer Omar and Sam Rowan. The Australian National University gave Gillian Peele a much appreciated opportunity to discuss some of these ideas with colleagues in Canberra. We are grateful also to the Department of Politics and International Relations at the University of Oxford which provided help in many ways including additional research support. David Hine is grateful to the Economic and Social Research Council's Future Governance programme: Lessons in Public Policy (grant no: L216252003), and to the Fell Fund of the University of Oxford, for financial support for parts of the research in this book, and to Christ Church, Oxford for research leave. We also gratefully acknowledge the permission to cite material used in the tables, boxes and figures from the Hansard Society and the Committee on Standards in Public Life.

Any errors are of course our own.

DJH
GRP

Abbreviations

ACA	Additional Costs Allowance
ACOBA	Advisory Committee on Business Appointments
APPC	Association of Professional Political Consultants
APPGs	All-Party Parliamentary Groups
BMRB	British Market Research Bureau
BNP	British National Party
BP	British Petroleum
CAG	Comptroller and Auditor General
CCT	Compulsory Competitive Tendering
CCTV	Closed-Circuit Television
CM	Command
CPI	Corruption Perceptions Index
CPS	Crown Prosecution Service
CRGA	Constitutional Reform and Governance Act
CSPL	Committee on Standards in Public Life
DETR	Department for the Environment, Transport and the Regions
DUP	Democratic Unionist Party
EC	Electoral Commission
ESOs	Ethical Standards Officers
ESS	European Social Survey
EU	European Union
FoI	Freedom of Information
GP	General Practitioner
GRECO	Group of States Against Corruption
HC	House of Commons
HL	House of Lords
HMRC	Her Majesty's Revenue and Customs
IPSA	Independent Parliamentary Standards Authority
IT	Information Technology
LGA	Local Government Act

LGPIHA	Local Government and Public Involvement in Health Act 2007
MP	Member of Parliament
MSP	Member of the Scottish Parliament
NAO	National Audit Office
NAW	National Assembly for Wales
NDPB	Non-Departmental Public Body
NGO	Non-governmental organisation
NHS	National Health Service
NIA	Northern Ireland Assembly
NPM	New Public Management
OCPA	Office of the Commissioner for Public Appointments
ODPM	Office of the Deputy Prime Minister
OECD	Organization for Economic Cooperation and Development
PAC	Public Accounts Committee
PASC	Public Administration Select Committee
PCRSC	Political and Constitutional Reform Select Committee
PCS	Parliamentary Commissioner for Standards
PPERA	Political Parties, Elections and Referendums Act
PRCA	Public Relations Consultants Association
SBE	Standards Board for England
SCIPSA	Speaker's Committee for the Independent Parliamentary Standards Authority
SNP	Scottish National Party
SN/PC	Standard Notes
SPAA	Standards, Procedures and Public Appointments Committee
SPCB	Scottish Parliamentary Corporate Body
SPSC	Scottish Parliamentary Standards Commissioner
SSRB	Senior Salaries Review Body
UKIP	UK Independence Party
UKPAC	United Kingdom Public Affairs Council
WSGBs	Welsh Sponsored Government Bodies

1

Introduction: regulating public ethics in the United Kingdom

The scope of the book

A major element of political life in the United Kingdom in the last twenty years has been the growing focus on integrity issues. Confidence in the probity of a country's governing arrangements and personnel is a vital part of a healthy democracy and for the most part the British political system has been seen as relatively free from corruption. Yet since the so-called 'cash-for-questions' affair erupted over John Major's government in the early 1990s a number of question marks have appeared over the traditional assumptions about the ethics prevailing in the public sector. The problem of how to sustain high standards in British public life has become a fixture of the political agenda, prompting a persistent and very wide-ranging debate involving political elites, the media and the public.

Concern about ethics and propriety has also had a profound effect on the structures of government, bringing institutional innovations into many areas of politics and administration. Much effort has gone into sharpening the values which shape public life. New legislation has been aimed at clarifying and promoting those values, and a complex new framework of ethics regulators now defines standards and monitors conduct.

However, the ethics machinery has often been controversial, and has not always prevented recurrent bouts of misconduct and impropriety. Some of these episodes, like the 2009 MPs' expenses scandal, have generated extensive media coverage with continuing consequences both for Westminster and for the public's evaluation of its politicians.[1] Others, though less spectacular in their impact, have forced the resignation of Cabinet ministers (as for example in the cases of David Blunkett and Liam Fox), revealed continuing engagement in lobbying activities by

MPs and peers in breach of parliamentary rules and highlighted, as in the loans for peerages case, the dangerous dependence of parties on individual donors. All parties have experienced embarrassing incidents of improper behaviour by their standard-bearers at national and local level. Allegations of unethical and even illegal conduct have arisen at the very heart of government, in some cases even involving the prime minister directly. There has thus been a steady drip of scandal in British public life. While rarely suggesting systemic wrong-doing or formal corruption, they have been enough to cause recurrent political controversy.

Twenty years ago integrity issues were not significant enough in public life to lead us to think that the range of institutions which regulated public ethics constituted an integrity *system*.[2] This changed with the work of the Committee on Standards in Public Life (CSPL), considered in Chapter 3. It was not itself intended to be a regulator, but through the large volume of legislation enacted after its 1995 first report it prompted extensive regulatory innovation. So extensive was the CSPL's impact that by 2007 the Public Administration Select Committee (PASC) could argue that ethics regulators constituted 'an integral and permanent part of the constitutional landscape'.[3]

This book analyses the United Kingdom's distinctive approach to regulating integrity issues. It is a study of regulatory response to the perceived problems of misconduct in public life, setting the complex new ethics machinery in the broader context of British institutions and political culture. Its main purpose is to explain the recurrent regulatory dilemmas that have emerged, and how they have been addressed. It seeks especially to understand the particular difficulties that arise in regulating public ethics where the inherently political nature of the terrain produces complicating factors not found to the same extent in other regulatory domains. Although the book is rooted in the United Kingdom, many of the conclusions have a wider relevance, not least because so many other contemporary democracies have been forced to address integrity issues.

The concept of public integrity is a broad one.[4] There is a degree of overlap with the scholarship on corruption and conflict of interest but it also intersects in important ways with the broader literature on governance and on key concepts in the study of administration such as accountability.[5] Organisational culture is also important. Although ethics regulators seek transnational standards applicable across different political systems, they also recognise that the success of a particular system will depend upon the traditions and culture of the society where it operates.[6] Later in this chapter, we consider the ways in which ethics regulation is similar to, and distinct from, regulation in other areas of commercial and public life, where culture and hard rules also interact.

This field of study is still a young one despite several new academic contributions in the last decade.[7] It is important, therefore, to be clear about the scope of this book and about what our investigation can and cannot deliver. In terms of scope we have chosen to concentrate on the key areas of British political life: Parliament and central government, local and devolved government, and the perennial questions of party funding and pressure group influence. Although the general public may think other issues such as police corruption or the treatment of tax evasion at least as, if not more important than, the ones we discuss in detail, we have inevitably had to limit our coverage. And while we necessarily take account of public disquiet about such phenomena as spin and political lying, they are not in the foreground of our analysis. We here try to understand the impact on the British political system of burgeoning ethics regulation and assess the strengths and weaknesses of the institutions and values it has generated.

It is necessary also to appreciate the limitations on our knowledge of how ethical regulation has affected governmental processes in the United Kingdom. It would be desirable if, through our analysis, we could provide an objective measure of how effective the regulatory responses to problems of ethics in the public sector have been. However, there are no easy answers to the question of effectiveness. In broad terms, it may be said to divide into two parts: the *operational* impact on office-holders and the *psychological* impact on public perceptions, in particular confidence on the part of the public that office-holders are sustaining high standards of behaviour. Both measures generate difficulties. In particular they presuppose that we can tell how much impropriety existed, and what the state of public perceptions was, before new regulatory procedures were introduced. There are two reasons why neither is possible with precision.

First, a comprehensive index of improper behaviour would need to be very broad. It would have to include various forms of corruption as defined by positive law. It would need to cover the conflicts of interest that exist in latent form but are neither reported and resolved, nor exploited for gain. And it would need to encompass the huge variety of sub-standard behaviours which, when revealed, often become controversial, but which are not strictly unlawful. Combining those into a single summary measure is a daunting task. The academic and practitioner literature tends today to describe the systems needed to address all these forms of impropriety as integrity systems. However, this approach is more a conceptual tool for thinking about the problems posed by impropriety than a precise measure for assessing a system's overall effectiveness. To evaluate the overall quality of any country's integrity system, let alone to compare it with that of other countries, a great range of indicators has to be combined into a single aggregate tool of assessment. There are measures which attempt this task.[8] The best known is Transparency International's Corruption Perceptions Index (CPI), which combines in a single comparative index the results of expert surveys – some its own, some conducted by other NGOs. In 2014 the United Kingdom was placed fourteenth out of 177 countries. Eight surveys were used for the UK itself.[9] The CPI and similar indices certainly assemble a great deal of information and are widely cited in corruption literature. However they are designed for many different contexts, including countries with high levels of criminal corruption.

While there is of course a real and growing concern about outright criminal corruption in advanced democracies, there are also concerns about two other broad categories. The first is what by some is described as 'institutionalised corruption': the multiplicity of ways in which, for example, financial institutions, taxation authorities, businesses, the police, security services, the press and other social and institutional actors gain advantages, sometimes spectacular advantages, for some groups at the expense of others. Where such behaviour may not be illegal, but is deemed highly unjust, and seems to stem from huge structural inequalities in the distribution of power in advanced societies, some scholars adapt long-standing tools used in the sociological study of power to redefine certain exercises of power as 'corruption'. Thus a recent collection of essays argues that the UK's relatively high CPI ranking is misplaced because of inherent bias towards measurement of the sorts of 'corruption' (illegal corruption) found most prevalently in less developed economies, and away from the institutionalised but mostly not illegal 'corruption' found in countries like the United Kingdom.[10] The second category, which overlaps with the first, but which is normally identified through the behaviour of individuals, rather than the structural power of institutions (though the two may be linked), is what has come to be known in the United Kingdom as 'standards in public life'. This behaviour is also controversial and in a general sense 'improper', but also falls short of hard corruption. The line between the two is clearly indistinct. Individual behaviour is more readily identified and judged. It is far easier to discuss blame in relation to individuals than entire social structures, and therefore it is the 'standards-in-public-life' dimension of non-criminal corruption that has, until recently, received most attention in public debate and public action. In relation to the United Kingdom's key political institutions, it is the focus of much of this book.

A further difficulty in assessing the impact of ethics regulation is connected to the second objective of regulation: public confidence or trust. Trust is a multi-faceted concept requiring distinctions to be drawn between its different dimensions, for example trust in institutions and trust in politicians and other public officials. In recent years, some progress has been made in measuring trust[11] but we do not have time-series data that will tell us the relevant information about public attitudes at the starting point of this study, two decades ago. Moreover, most electorates contain a mix of individuals, ranging from those who trust institutions and office-holders, to those who are less trusting, and there is likely to be no strong binary divide. The raw data that emerges from time-series data like the European Social Survey (ESS) and the Eurobarometer polls, which have long included general questions about public trust, therefore always need careful interpretation.[12] Two key ways to do so are to consider whether the democracy in question is substantially different from other democracies, and whether indicators of trust are changing over time. On the first of these, we know from ESS and Eurobarometer data that there seem to be broadly similar levels of trust in Parliament, politicians and political parties in the United Kingdom as in France and Germany. The ESS data suggests that the share of the electorate giving a positive trust rating (six or more on a ten-point scale) for politicians and parties is low in all three countries. Comparison of these states with the smaller democracies of Scandinavia and the Netherlands suggests they all exhibit levels of trust in politicians and parties about 20 per cent lower than in the smaller more cohesive democracies. But absolute levels in the larger countries do not vary greatly over the last two decades covered by the surveys.

Limiting ourselves to the UK alone, there are fairly long-standing comparisons of public trust in some classes of public office-holder, which reveal important and fairly stable differences. Judges, senior police officers and doctors tend to be trusted by above or well above 50 per cent of respondents to surveys, whereas MPs and government ministers tend to be trusted by fewer than one-third of respondents. These are well established comparisons, and have not changed since the first surveys in the 1980s.[13]

A more important question, for our purposes, is whether we can establish trends in trust in politicians *over time* that can be linked first to the impact of impropriety, and secondly to measures to prevent it. Unfortunately that information could only meaningfully arise from repeated survey research over many years, and there is very little consistent research of this type. So here we rely largely on two time-series data-sets built across the last decade: one from the CSPL[14] and the other from the Hansard Society.[15] They both began in 2004, the former publishing its most recent results in 2013, and the latter in 2014. They point to a broadly similar picture, in which from the 2004 starting point (of an already low

I Public trust in politicians

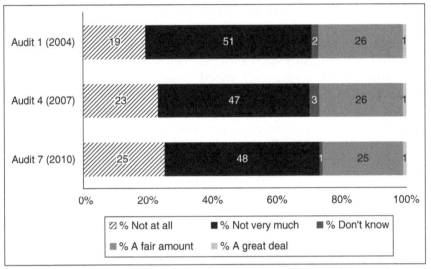

Source: The Hansard Society *Audit of Political Engagement 7: The 2010 Report*, *(Hansard Society, London, 2010) p. 8*

base of public trust) there was a significant slow widening of the negative trust deficit.

Thus (Figure 1) in 2004 in the Hansard Society's first Audit of Democratic Engagement, 70 per cent of respondents felt they could trust politicians 'not very much' or not at all, and this figure increased by 2010 to 73 per cent, with the sub-group not trusting politicians at all rising from 19 to 25 per cent. The data resulting from the CSPL survey showed a more marked shift, based on a broader question about 'overall standards of conduct of public office holders in the United Kingdom'. The question covered all office-holders and not just 'politicians' who, as we have noted, tend to rank much lower than some other office-holders; as would be expected from this, the starting point was a higher overall level of approval.

Figure 2 shows that overall those who reported a quite high or very high judgement of public standards fell from 46 to 35 per cent over five surveys from 2004–2012, while those reporting a quite, or very, low rating rose from 11 to 28 per cent.

We find a more complex pattern when respondents are asked directly whether they themselves believe there are any discernible trends.

As Figure 3 shows, just under 40 per cent in the survey conducted by the CSPL believed things had not greatly changed compared with 'a few years ago', though those who thought matters had got a lot or at least a little worse rose from 31 to 40 per cent. Those who thought matters had

2 Public perceptions of overall standards of conduct in public life

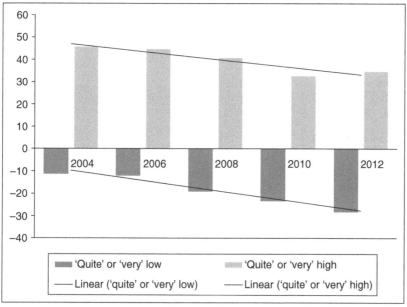

Source: Committee on Standards in Public Life *Survey of public attitudes towards conduct in public life 2012* (Committee on Standards in Public Life, London, September 2013)

3 Public estimates of *changes* in standards in public life

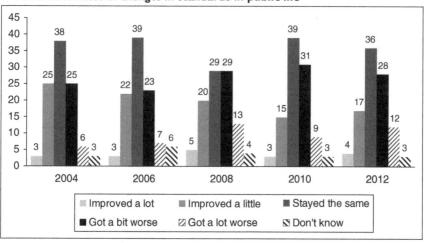

Source: Committee on Standards in Public Life *Survey of public attitudes towards conduct in public life 2012* (Committee on Standards in Public Life, London, September 2013)

improved a lot or a little fell from 28 to 21 per cent. The Hansard Audit has no comparable time-series figure, though in 2014 the Audit asked respondents (Figure 4) whether politicians were behaving 'in a more professional way than a few years ago', on which question respondents

4 Assessments of changes in certain public standards (Hansard Society Audit)

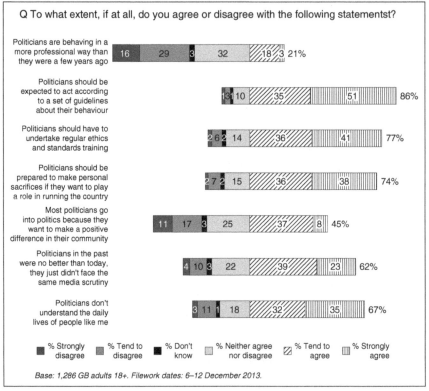

Source: The Hansard Society *Audit of Political Engagement 11: The 2014 Report, (Hansard Society, London, 2014) p. 76*

with a negative view (45 per cent) significantly outnumbered positive respondents (21 per cent). Significantly, however, when asked whether they agreed with the statement that 'politicians in the past were no better than today, they just didn't face the same media scrutiny' those who agreed outnumbered those who disagreed by 62 to 14 per cent, suggesting that when prompted towards a more considered view their negative judgements diminished somewhat.

The two surveys in question dealt with a number of other issues with varying degrees of separation from the central issue of trust, but in each case similar patterns were observed. What emerges clearly is that, as we would expect from a time period containing a dramatic episode of public controversy over the ethics of a large proportion of MPs (examined in Chapters 4 and 5) there is a significant decline in trust, though given the huge public attention the episode attracted, the impact seems to have been contained, and moreover was part of a trend already clearly in evidence before the scandal. What we have no way of establishing, however, is whether the trend is (as is popularly assumed to be the case) a direct public response to the specific chain of ethics controversies that affected UK public life from the early 1990s onwards. Alternatively, it could have been exacerbated by the public attention concentrated on public ethics as the authorities introduced more intrusive ethics regulation over the two decades thereafter, thereby attracting much media and public attention leading to *perceptions* of falling standards. Or it may, through some significant *improvement* in absolute public standards, have prevented an even worse decline in public perceptions, averted by reform processes.

Comparative survey research has thus tended to ask only general questions about trust, so the possible impact of *particular* episodes of impropriety, or of *particular* new measures to improve public ethics, is hard to deduce with certainty from the survey data. This point needs to be borne in mind in the chapters which follow. We analyse the measures that have been put in place, and we seek to assess difficulties in making them operationally effective; but we cannot lay claim to insight on their impact on public opinion. The same applies to the broader impact on British politics of the rising attention paid to ethics issues. We know from election results and survey data that the two-party share of the vote has declined over several decades, (the most rapid decline being actually back in the 1980s) and we see that share falling to an historic low (below 70 per cent) since 2010. We cannot, however, be sure what part of it, if any, to attribute to declining trust in mainstream politicians. Significantly it is evident that trust in politicians is much lower among those supporting 'challenger parties' (UK Independence Party (UKIP), the Greens, the Scottish Nationalist Party (SNP) and the British National Party (BNP)), than those supporting the three established parties. Unfortunately, we cannot be certain whether low trust in political leaders directly causes detachment from establishment politics, and increases support for radical and challenger parties, or whether there is a causal relationship running the other way. We can simply see an *association* (Figure 5) with these forms of political behaviour, so that on a seven-point scale among respondents in the British election survey, running from low trust to high trust, half or more of those reporting a vote for each of UKIP, the SNP, the BNP and the Greens reported the two lowest levels of trust, against 15, 32 and 18 per cent, respectively, for the Conservatives, Labour and the Liberal Democrats.

When seeking to understand the effectiveness of particular regulatory tools, public perceptions of corruption or of declining standards are therefore only one part of the picture. They are not a surrogate measure for absolute standards of integrity. Given the variations that result from the short-term impact of high-profile events, only a long time-series will

5 Trust in MPs by party

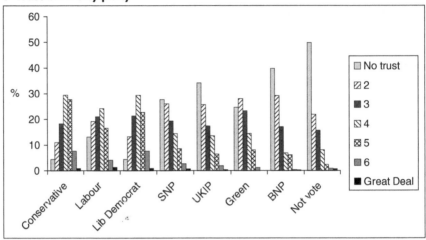

Source: British Election Study, **Panel study data** 2014 (Total respondents=29,116), saved at http://goo.gl/c0uZfq

be adequate. In any case, while the goal of public ethics certainly includes the sustaining of high levels of trust in institutions and in officials, trust may be misplaced; and mistrust may be mistaken. Public attitudes are often shallow and superficial and paradoxically may in the short term evolve in directions contrary to absolute standards.

Even after two decades of ethics re-engineering, therefore, it remains difficult to say clearly whether 'standards in public life', let alone the 'institutionalised corruption' discussed earlier, have got better or worse. Nor is it possible to say with confidence where the United Kingdom stands compared to other countries. Those who think they can confidently make such judgements are probably deceiving themselves. Office-holders are certainly more conscious of public ethics issues than they were two decades ago. They could hardly fail to be, given the burgeoning apparatus of ethics regulation we are about to explore. Rules of conduct are more precise and the media are much more engaged with ethics and integrity issues. However, the proliferation of requirements bearing on office-holders means there are more ways in which they may transgress, whether consciously or carelessly. Moreover, changes in recruitment to public life, shifts in the boundary between the public and the private sectors, alterations in the resources political parties can obtain, and developments in the opportunities available to those who leave public office, all make for a more complex ethical environment.

Beyond these factors, there is the possibility of a significant shift over time in personal standards, irrespective of the size of the temptations encountered or the pressures office-holders face. If politicians think they can survive a serious ethical controversy they may become less risk averse. A more material society may make a new generation of politicians or public servants materially greedier than its predecessors if the opportunity cost of public service seems to have risen. Controversy about the earning capacities of senior politicians and civil servants on leaving office has certainly increased in the last two decades.

There are many ways in which to get to grips with this complexity. Ours is to start with recently developed approaches to regulation. The contribution we offer in this book is an understanding of the operation of the key ethics regulators themselves, and the problems they have encountered in the different sectors of British public life. For this endeavour, we need an analytical framework giving clear hypotheses about what is distinctive about ethics regulation, how it works, how it is affected by the broader framework of institutions and institutional culture in the United Kingdom, and how it might be expected to evolve over time. We initially take the attitudinal background as a set of givens: rising public and media sensitivity to impropriety; the shift in political concerns towards valence issues such as 'fitness to govern'; and growing demands for accountability and transparency. We suspect there is a causal connection between some of the problems of setting up ethics regulators and making them fit for purpose, and the evolution of public attitudes, but for the reasons just described – mainly the absence of retrospective data – we cannot explore them in the body of the argument.

Regulation involving public ethics

If regulating public integrity is a part of a broader category of regulatory activity, we should expect many of the intellectual and academic controversies about regulation to apply to our field, albeit with variations.[16] The framework we use borrows a good deal from the regulatory literature. Much regulation involves the use of technical and scientific expertise to provide tightly-knit protections concerning safety: for example pharmaceuticals, food purity, medical practice and transport. It is distinct from ethics regulation in that it deploys specialist professional expertise, and precise technical rules as well as extensive surveillance of behaviour. Other regulatory areas focus on the consumer and on protecting the economy against structural failures, for example in banking or utility supervision. The focus there is less on the detailed surveillance of behaviour than on the general context of the market, partly through steerage and light-touch guidance, sometimes known as 'smart regulation'.

Here we get closer to our own agenda of concerns. The regulation literature seeks to capture the goals of regulation, and what makes it effective. Its sub-branches include debates on whether regulatory agencies generate perverse effects giving the regulated ways of evading the regulator's scope, and pushing a problem out beyond the initially defined area of regulation; or burdening the regulated with excessive compliance costs with negative effects on energies, talents and initiative. Certainly, one characteristic pattern of behaviour in ethics regulation that we shall observe is that governments frequently appear to legislate in haste in response to a scandal or a moral panic, without enough consideration of the issues. As we shall see, when this happens disputes over the regulatory burden, effectiveness and indeed legitimacy of ethics regulators tend to set in strikingly quickly, sometimes with damaging effects on the agencies themselves.

Regulating public ethics obviously has the greatest affinity with other forms of regulation *inside government*. In societies with a strong public-law tradition the concept of internal legal controls on all actors is very familiar. In the United Kingdom, administrative law has less well-defined roots, though few public lawyers any longer deny administrative law's force and distinctiveness. In the post-war era, furthermore, the well-studied tendency for courts to intervene to define the meaning of statute or to declare public action *ultra vires* for failing to meet legally defined standards of fairness, has expanded the opportunity for judicial review and created a further sphere of legal contention and redress, increasingly like the continental public-law tradition. Moreover, even in the United Kingdom there is a long tradition of regulation inside government which goes back well into the nineteenth century through public auditing, as in the case of the office of the Comptroller and Auditor General. More recently, quality and performance indicators for local and national public services have greatly extended the scope of this internal regulation.[17]

Regulation is therefore a fact of life in modern government, and regulation inside government (and regulation of ethics and propriety within that) seems unlikely to be scaled back dramatically in the near term. But regulation continues to be subject to debate about cost, burden and effectiveness. After the 2010 general election, that controversy increased. A key plank of Conservative local-government policy, announced immediately the new government was formed, was the abolition of the Audit Commission, on grounds of both cost-saving and audit effectiveness. Although the style of Audit Commission inquiries was sometimes controversial, the savings of replacement auditing were much disputed, as was the suddenness of the Commission's abolition.[18] Other regulators, including some in the ethics and propriety field, were also called into question after 2010. The Standards Board for England (which supervised local government ethics) was summarily abolished.

However in other areas pressures for more regulation, or new and different regulation, actually increased. There was intense debate over the effectiveness of self-regulation of the British press, following a series of scandals about hacking and other illegal activities which led to the wide-ranging Leveson Inquiry;[19] and there was debate about financial-service regulation, following extensive concern about the ethics prevalent in the banking sector. Controversy continued after the publication of the reports of the Independent Commission on Banking (the Vickers Report), and subsequently with the publication of the Parliamentary Committee on Banking Standards.[20] They brought renewed calls for stronger regulation in their respective areas. Interestingly, although both the press and the banks were private-sector operators, the source of anxiety driving the reports was not simply market disorders and imperfections but the ethical frameworks into which the actors in these sectors were socialised. The remedies were seen to lie mainly in the regulation of incentives, and the structural framework within which the sector operates. The parallel with ethics for public servants lay not simply in the need for a clearly stated code of principle-based ethical conduct, rather than simply a list of procedural requirements. It lay also in the vexed question of how best to achieve enhanced standards of behaviour. In particular, in the case of the press, despite the extreme sensitivity of suggestions of potential political interference with the press, it raised the question of whether a code of conduct and a regulator should have a minimal statutory basis.[21]

The parallel with regulation in public ethics is certainly not exact, but it is instructive. In the case of press regulation, there are contrasting considerations at work: statutory underpinning risks political interference if governments choose to interfere politically with the appointment of regulators; self-regulation without statutory underpinning risks lax and cosily inadequate standards. The risks from political interference, moreover, might be thought to run two ways: politicians might interfere with the free press through their power of appointment of regulators, or conversely the political power of the press might intimidate politicians into interfering with the regulators to make them more accommodating.

The parallel with ethics regulators is the dilemma stemming from the possibility that, without a statutory basis, public ethics regulators may lack impact and security of tenure. If, for example, they rest only on a departmental or Cabinet Office budget, they could be starved of funds or personnel, dissuaded from intervening, ignored, given inadequate operating rules, or in some circumstances summarily abolished. Equally, if there is a statutory basis, and one which emphasises independence and is separate from the political cover of a sponsoring department, that status may expose the regulator to attack from those they regulate, including the legislature and the political executive. In some extreme cases a statutory basis may actually encourage political interference if it leaves a public-ethics regulator without allies and exposed to attempts to impose excessive accountability, or to colonise or politicise its oversight board. As we shall see, these risks have been present in several of the public-ethics regulators we study in this book. The usual call in public ethics is for external and independent regulation. Internal self-regulation certainly has many pitfalls as we shall see in the case of the House of Commons, but there may also be circumstances where independence itself carries material risks.

The dilemmas raised in contemporary debates about regulation therefore certainly have relevance to the sphere of public-ethics regulation. The regulation literature raises issues about scope, purpose, proportionality, and structure. One authoritative recent work on regulation laid down five top-level criteria determining regulatory effectiveness: whether the action or regime is supported by legislative authority; whether there is an appropriate scheme of accountability; whether procedures are fair, accessible and open; whether the regulator is acting with sufficient expertise; and whether the action or regime is efficient.[22] The Committee on Standards in Public Life has similar tests for public ethics. It lists proportionality and appropriate targeting, transparency linked to accountability, consistency, sensitivity to public opinion, flexibility and use of discretion, clarity of remit, robust independence, and a range of appropriate sanctions.[23] We agree that all these are important issues, and we use them as tests in this book, though, as we have already hinted in the case of legislative authority and as we will also suggest in relation to accountability, the arguments do not always run in one direction.

We also argue that, although ethics regulation shares many features with regulation more generally, some of its aspects are unique. First, ethics regulation is very broad in scope, covering the entire public sphere, including elected assemblies, elected officials, central government departments, devolved and local government, and non-departmental public bodies. Secondly, the *goals* of public-ethics regulation are difficult to measure. A well-functioning and competitive market for products or services can be measured by market share and product- and service-price. A safe market for medicines or foods is even more self-evident. But in the case of public ethics, the apparent absence of *revealed* impropriety does not necessarily mean it is not present. Thus regulators need constantly to ask themselves how they can know they are being efficient. Moreover regulation of public ethics has two parallel dimensions: one negative, the other positive. The negative aspect (constraint of misconduct) is fairly obvious. The promotion of positive values like commitment at work, objectivity, customer service, vigilance and whistle-blowing in the face of poor performance or poor leadership, is open-ended and measures of effectiveness are more difficult to devise.[24]

Thirdly there is a possibility of perverse consequences in ethics regulation. All regulation involves a trade-off of objectives, and there are risks of externalities in the burdens it imposes. In the field of ethics, there is clearly a trade-off between the deterrence of misconduct and broader costs like loss of flexibility, initiative and public-sector entrepreneurship. There is also a risk of perverse consequences for public trust. Ethics regulation is supposed to provide public reassurance about the quality of the personnel and procedures in public life. Unfortunately, the more impropriety it discovers, the lower trust may fall.

Finally, there is a *quis custodiet?* issue, which lies in the political delicacy of the regulator's role in public ethics. Some of the offices being regulated – elected MPs, and other representatives – have their own claim to legitimacy within a democratic system and the regulators are themselves accountable to the regulated. The latter may therefore conclude that if they do not like the regulation being imposed upon them, they can replace them with other, more compliant, regulators.

Categorising the regulatory framework

Public integrity systems contain two distinct dimensions: values and principles on the one hand, and formal procedures and institutions on the other. The former propagate the basic ethos of a country's public life, mainly through their declaratory, aspirational and socialising impact rather than through legal force. The latter explain what the principles mean for particular office-holders, and define and enforce precise rules of behaviour through soft-law codes, managerial discipline or hard law.

Values and principles. In regulating ethics there is clearly a need for both values and principles and for rules and institutions.[25] Values are in practice expressed through the expression of overarching principles, such as the *Seven Principles of Public Life* adumbrated by the CSPL, which have formed a cornerstone for the development and elucidation of general values for the public service as a whole in the UK in the last two decades. Statements of values are also likely to found in special professional codes for particular parts of the public service, including the police and legal professions, education or health. Their purpose is to foster a general culture or professional ethos inside an organisation. Sustaining that ethos, and ensuring that it is internalised by individuals, is usually considered essential to the enforcement of the rules themselves. Without a value system that generates buy-in to hard rules, the rules would have to work through enforcement alone, rather than socialisation. But how such socialisation works for public servants is less clear. Explicit training and induction programmes are often offered and sometimes compulsory, though how effective self-conscious induction is, as we shall see, remains a matter of doubt.

Box 1.1 The 7 principles of public life (1995, with minor modifications to descriptors in 2013)

The Seven Principles of Public Life apply to anyone who works as a public office-holder. This includes all those who are elected or appointed to public office, nationally and locally, and all people appointed to work in the civil service, local government, the police, courts and probation services, non-departmental public bodies (NDPBs), and in the health, education, social and care services. All public office-holders are both servants of the public and stewards of public resources. The Principles also have application to all those in other sectors delivering public services.

Selflessness

Holders of public office should act solely in terms of the public interest.

Integrity

Holders of public office must avoid placing themselves under any obligation to people or organisations that might try inappropriately to influence them in their work. They should not act or take decisions in order to gain financial or other material benefits for themselves, their family or their friends. They must declare and resolve any interests and relationships.

Objectivity

Holders of public office must act and take decisions impartially, fairly and on merit, using the best evidence and without discrimination or bias.

Accountability

Holders of public office are accountable to the public for their decisions and actions and must submit themselves to the scrutiny necessary to ensure this.

Openness

Holders of public office should act and take decisions in an open and transparent manner. Information should not be withheld from the public unless there are clear and lawful reasons for so doing.

Honesty

Holders of public office should be truthful.

Leadership

Holders of public office should exhibit these principles in their own behaviour. They should actively promote and robustly support the principles and be willing to challenge poor behaviour wherever it occurs.

Codes and rules. Most parts of the public service cannot rely simply on induction programmes and socialisation into general principles. Particularly when things go wrong, the remedy is usually seen to lie in more enforcement of more firmly stated rules, not in better principles, or better socialisation. But different contexts call for different types of rules. First, there is a major difference between appointed office-holders (such as civil servants), and elected office-holders (such as MPs and local councillors). The former are usually subject to general rules about propriety, set out in a management code. For elected office-holders there are dual lines of accountability. Elected representatives need both to comply with formal rules of conduct and to be accountable to their electorate. Electoral accountability can require very punctilious forms of compliance because the elected representative involved in alleged misconduct faces a permanent potential reputational risk with electoral consequences. The introduction of recall procedures would doubtless make this risk even greater.[26] From the MP's perspective the risk of mischievous manipulation of formal accountability rules, or exploitation of minor and inadvertent non-compliance, provides a strong argument for separate arrangements for elected and non-elected office-holders.

Secondly, however specialised and technical they are, regulatory institutions are also rooted in the broader democratic arrangements of the United Kingdom and have to be coordinated with them. One recurring and difficult area for regulators – since they normally have no or only limited power of criminal sanction – is coordination with the criminal justice system in cases where investigations reveal potentially criminal activity. But there are overlaps with other processes such as parliamentary accountability, transparency requirements and financial accountability. These overlaps between the ethics institutions and broader structures of democratic governance are both a strength and weakness. The strength is that institutions at the macro- and the micro-level will reinforce each other, and the tasks of deterring misconduct in public office, and encouraging high ethical standards, will be underpinned by common understandings of such notions as responsibility, accountability and the public interest. The weakness is that the pressures of majoritarian democracy will often allow calculations of political and party interest to override considerations of ethics and propriety. In Westminster and Whitehall, where the most controversial and visible cases are likely to be concentrated, ethics controversy can easily become highly partisan. As long as they can get away with it, governments will try to deal with any issue of ethics and propriety through appeal to accountability to Parliament (where they have a majority), and through the ballot box (where ethics controversy will inevitably be diluted by the many other, possibly more salient, issues).

Some of the operating procedures of ethical regulators are, as a result, widely seen as unsatisfactory. As we shall see in Chapter 8, for example, there is a requirement on ministers and civil servants to consult the Advisory Committee on Business Appointments (ACOBA) before taking a private commercial appointment on leaving office, but no completely enforceable formal obligation to take the advice given. The general doctrines surrounding ministerial ethics, though set out in a document now called the Ministerial Code, are ultimately a matter of prime-ministerial interpretation, and depend on the willingness of the parliamentary majority to continue to support the prime minister's interpretation of its applicability in any particular case. There is also a convention governing the relationship between ministers and civil servants; but the policing of that relationship is mainly at the political discretion of a prime minister or the House of Commons.

Regulatory dilemmas: proportionality and regulatory risk

From this discussion we can begin to define a framework for analysing the establishment, operation and impact of public-ethics regulators.

There are two general dilemmas that seem more important than others in ethics regulation. These are proportionality (i.e. managing the size of the regulatory burden) and the balance between accountability and independence.

Proportionality has a significant impact on a regulator's reputation. Getting the balance right to avoid debilitating controversy over regulatory burden seems to depend on two sets of decisions: those taken by the original architects of the regulation, and those taken by the regulators themselves. Proportionality is widely recommended as a prime virtue of good regulation, but few observers have any general guidelines to offer about its meaning. Advice usually emerges in subsequent battles over instances of alleged over- or under-regulation.

Over-regulation comes from the natural tendency to guard against a low-probability event causing reputational damage to the regulator. Workplace health-and-safety regulation is a widely quoted example. The cost for employers of non-compliance is nowadays so high they generally comply, if often with bad grace, while remaining critical of the burden imposed. Regulators find it difficult to lower the compliance threshold without cover from higher political authority. Between the contrasting reputational risks of excessive zeal and regulator neglect, the regulator will prefer the former. Moreover, in the early stages of regulation, awareness of the reasons for introducing regulation is often highest. Awareness of the regulatory burden only sets in as memory of the events that led to regulation fades. A clear example of the proportionality dilemma, explored in Chapter 5, is the case of the Independent Parliamentary Standards Authority (IPSA). This body was given authority to manage the MPs' expenses regime and MPs' pay and pensions in the aftermath of the dramatic 2009 expenses scandal. Two acts of Parliament gave IPSA's board a substantial degree of discretion in defining a new, greatly more robust expenses regime than that applying before the scandal. It was robust not just against fraud by MPs but even against fairly innocent misunderstandings and mistakes and carelessness. MPs, who devolved to IPSA itself the authority to design the new arrangements, quickly regretted this decision, arguing, with serious consequences for IPSA's legitimacy, that it was guilty of regulatory overkill. Thus for example MPs argued in 2011 that the cost of reimbursing 38 per cent of their claims exceeded the size of the claim itself.[27]

Problems also arise if regulatory powers are weak. As we shall see in Chapter 11, under the Political Parties, Elections and Referendums Act 2000 (PPERA), the Electoral Commission's limited sanctions against poor reporting of income by political parties was a significant instance of weakness in the original design of the regulatory architecture.[28] Initially at least, parties were casual in their observance of the new regulations,

and found ways of avoiding them. When it was realised how little traction enforcement of the rules was having, it was not just the parties
themselves but also the Electoral Commission that suffered the reputational damage. Ultimately the fault lay in Parliament for failing to grasp
the nature of the task it was imposing on the Commission through the
founding legislation.

Closer to the heart of government, there have been instances where
the regulatory task was probably much better understood, but where
stronger regulation would have run counter to constitutional convention. This constraint applied to the regulation of relationships between
ministers and their special advisers and to the ethical conduct of ministers themselves. New rules were introduced in both areas and they
are explored in Chapters 7 and 8, but the final 'regulator' of propriety
remained essentially (and despite the emergence of a regulatory code) the
prime minister, whose decisions will rarely be seen as free from political
motivation. The result was an unsatisfactorily weak regime compared
to independent regulatory adjudication and one which has generated
continuing controversy about regulatory weakness.

When it comes to the strategies regulators themselves use to manage the regulatory burden given the hand they have been dealt by the
legislature, several different responses emerge. The first is intelligent
or so-called 'smart' accountability. For public-ethics regulators this is
less sophisticated than smart regulation in market-based regimes, but
it has some of the same strategic approach in seeking leverage through
light-touch operating procedures chosen to provide incentives for compliance. Regulators are often encouraged to be risk-based rather than
to operate regimes of full compliance, for example checking only sam-
ples of contract procedures, public appointments or expense claims. This
involves a combination of self-regulation and self-reporting for the regulated, linked to assessments by the regulator of when and if to deploy
fundamental compliance inspection in cases (categories or individuals)
where the risk of non-compliance is highest.

A second strategy presupposes a favourable initial regulatory environment: one where there is a high degree of buy-in to ethics from the targets
of regulation themselves. This strategy does not apply everywhere. In local
government, where large numbers of voluntary and unpaid individuals are
elected to public office without much socialisation into public service values, conflicts of interest are frequent, and buy-in to principles and codes
of conduct uneven. In addition to the extensive Poulson scandal of the
1970s and the Westminster 'homes for votes' scandal of the late 1980s
which we discuss in Chapter 2 there have been more recent cases of very
serious corruption. One in Doncaster, which first broke in the 1990s and

continued for over a decade, led to the conviction for fraud of twenty elected councillors. A second in Tower Hamlets in 2014 led to the government imposing commissioners to run large parts of the borough administration.[29] In contrast, at the heart of the government machine, the ethos of the United Kingdom Home Civil Service seems to be underpinned by very strong socialisation mechanisms. The regulator, in this case the Civil Service Commission through its Management Code, enjoys the fortunate circumstance that, while it has in fact a quite detailed regime of theoretical regulation, it is rarely needed and involves no special regulatory burden.

In more difficult contexts, regulators clearly have to have skins thick enough to face down claims of regulatory overkill head-on. They have to *explain*, proactively, and hope to win a rational argument. Primarily the explanation will be to those to whom the regulator is accountable but at times the battle will need to be played out with the press and public opinion. This will require vigorous appeal back to the founding legislation and regular reminders about what concerned public opinion at the time the need for regulation arose. The dependence on political sponsors that even 'independent' regulators face obviously makes this a risky strategy but as we shall see the risk is one some (such as IPSA) have been willing to take.

Finally, there is effective use of transparency. 'Openness' is one of the CSPL's Seven Principles. We discuss its strengths and limitations in more detail later.[30] Often standards-related impropriety attracts at most a censure from a regulator and nothing more because in the initial design it had been thought impossible or inappropriate to give the regulator a direct sanction. In these circumstances, the regulator may need to rely on transparency to create the threat of severe reputational damage to the miscreant and to force those higher up the scale of authority (in the case of the House of Commons, for example, the Committee on Standards in relation to the Parliamentary Commissioner for Standards) to impose a penalty *because* of what transparency has revealed. The difficulty, however, is that transparency may provide too *much* information. Transparency now operates across many different fields including party funding, interest-group access to decision-makers, politicians' personal interests, earnings and expenses payments and the income sources of officials after leaving public office. It therefore provides repeated opportunities for low-level critical comment punctuated by occasional peaks of controversy. In such circumstances, transparency may gradually lose its impact. Thick-skinned office-holders learn to tough out difficult moments; voters become inured to revelations and lose much of their capacity to target their disaffection efficiently. It is rarely argued that any particular corner of public life requires less rather than more transparency but the cumulative effect of enhanced transparency can nevertheless be perverse. Throwing a large volume of undigested information into the public domain through indiscriminate transparency requirements may be just too difficult for ordinary citizens to evaluate.[31]

A good deal of empirical trial-and-error adjustment will always be called for as regulators find the right balance between these various approaches. Few regulators get bigger budgets as time goes on. Where budgets are limited, operational experience can assist them in figuring out what is controversial and difficult, and then focusing their energies on it, even if, initially, it was not intended to be an important part of their remit. In particular, risk-based strategies that focus resources such as selective audit on the key risks can be adopted once the size of risk is understood.

Independence, self-regulation, accountability

Almost all the public bodies we examine in this study – the Electoral Commission (EC), the Standards Board for England (SBE), the IPSA, the ACOBA, even the CSPL itself – produce outputs of some sort: advice, adjudication, and sometimes services, as in the case of the IPSA's payments-provider role. They all use public resources. So while they need to be independent, they also need to be subject to some form of accountability over cost and performance, and where they have delegated authority to formulate regulatory rules, they also need to be accountable for those rules. But accountability itself has to be of a high standard. Those who exercise it must avoid deliberate and mischievous efforts to undermine its target. This problem has arisen with many regulatory agencies outside the sphere of ethics, but it is particularly serious when an agency is acting in a quasi-judicial mode and needs to be seen as authoritative and impartial. There are, of necessity, different lines of accountability, related to the different formal bases regulators have. A regulator with a statutory basis has a more direct line of accountability to Parliament, since it is Parliament that approves the initial structure and mission. An authority with NDPB status (such as the CSPL) generally relies for its sponsorship and existence directly on a government department, often on the Cabinet Office. But whatever the format, the quality of accountability needs to be high in both directions for the sake of regulator effectiveness. Judgments need to be taken in the context of the constraints of the original design; and the accountability process has to ensure that it does not undermine the operation of the regulators.

It therefore seems important that there is a hinterland of agreed support when regulators are established. This places a heavy responsibility on both government and Parliament to consider with care, and ahead of time, the balance between independence and accountability when establishing a new regulator. A proper balance is clearly best achieved if there is a settled understanding of mission, purposes, resources and duration, from the outset. If there is more work to be done on these questions after the regulator has started work, there is a serious risk of drawing it into unhealthy political controversy. Establishing a balance is more difficult to achieve than may appear because regulators have often been established hastily in response to serious ethical controversies. Important details then get postponed to subordinate legislation. Whether or not regulatory agencies are endowed with a statutory base, they should as far as possible be seen as long-term quasi-constitutional projects, in which an underpinning of prior cross-party agreement has been established. This will be vital to ensure that the proper accountability to which all regulators must be subject is not overlain by continuing political controversy. Accountability which is overlain by partisan arguments not about performance, but about the more fundamental issues of the mission and resources of the regulator, are likely to damage the regulator's effectiveness. Good-quality public servants will not commit to an organisation that may have a limited life, and is constantly facing unjustified criticism. Recruitment and retention of staff, poor morale, and endemic arguments over priorities and procedures, can seriously damage performance. Accountability takes various forms in modern democracies. The relevant forms should if possible be spelled out in founding legislation – including financial and operational accountability to appropriate parliamentary bodies. Parliament should not then depart from agreed norms lightly. Respect for some degree of separation of powers is important, and particular care should be taken of this in the early years of a new regulator's operation. As we shall see, this has not always been the case.

Analytical framework

We now draw the dilemmas we have discussed into a more formal framework for examining the United Kingdom's ethics regulators. We divide our framework into questions about the initial design, questions about regulatory implementation, and questions about accountability. Each of Chapters 3 to 9 follows this broad format. Chapters 4 to 6 cover the legislature, Chapters 7 to 9 the executive, Chapters 10 and 11 cover parties and lobbying, and Chapters 12 and 13 cover local government and the devolved systems of Scotland, Wales and Northern Ireland. We hypothesise that in any of these areas a failure at the initial design stage will have serious implications for the implementation of regulation, and for accountability. And as discussed above, accountability controversies will then feed back into operational difficulties. The indicators we use in each of these three categories require brief explanation, though they are more fully explained in the sectoral chapters which follow.

Of each initial regulatory design, we ask how far it was a version of a more general blueprint for the whole public sphere, and what its key features were, including the statutory or non-statutory basis chosen and the lines of accountability, and we assess how perfected or incomplete the framework was at the start of the agency's life. Was there more to do, especially through secondary legislation, and if so, what was the reason for deferring these choices? We consider how far the agency took over from another or filled a regulatory gap, what transfer problems were involved where there was an element of transfer, and with what consequences. And we seek to assess the extent to which there was common ground amongst all stakeholders on the need for regulation, and the form it took in the initial design. Was the agency born out of institutional consensus, or out of dissensus, and did this appear to store up operational difficulty for the future? Was it created with evidence of haste, driven by partisan politics or legislative timetable difficulties, in ways that may have compromised its operation?

As regards implementation and operation, we recognise that our assessment will be incomplete for all the reasons connected with assessing and measuring the amount of impropriety in public life more generally. Assessment has therefore to depend to a large extent on second-order measures. Clearly the emergence of new controversies, and clear signs that old pathologies continue despite the regulator's presence, are important evidence. Mostly, these issues will show up as controversies over the sufficiency of resources, over the adequacy of remit (whether too large and unfocused, or too narrow) and in changes of priority, reorganisations or, in the last resort, fresh legislation.

Lines of accountability, and accountability outcomes, are in some respects the most straightforward, since they tend to have a formal description, and they today leave a clear evidence trail. Assessing the impact of accountability is, as we have already said, far harder. Broad changes in the structure of political accountability occasionally become so obvious, as in the case of parliamentary select committees in the United Kingdom, that their impact is impossible to deny, while remaining very difficult to measure. In more circumscribed areas like the accountability of particular regulators, the judgement will be more difficult, and we have relied mainly on close textual analysis of the verbatim reports of investigation and responses of both government and regulator. It is a major innovation of openness in UK government that this evidence trail is now extensively available for analysis.

We believe that the most fundamental qualities of a regulatory regime in the sphere of public ethics are its authority and legitimacy. The rule of law can work even when judges and the police and the courts are subject to heavy criticism from politicians or others, but the sustainability of the rule of law is, under continuous criticism, eventually likely to be questioned, since many will fear that efforts are afoot to intimidate law officers. Similarly with ethics regulators, we believe that public support, and support from those being regulated, will erode if there is not a hinterland of support from those most closely involved in the original political sponsorship of regulators.

We hypothesise two contrasting paradigms of regulation:

- an optimal path, along which there is consensus over mission and resources, agreement on how a regulator should operate and how it should be audited and assessed, good public understanding of the problems in the field, and high buy-in from the leadership of institutions being regulated;
- a worst-case path in which a regulator is born without consensus, subjected to regular intense forms of accountability, threatened with abolition or replacement, starved of resources, contested by those it seeks to regulate, and brought to public attention only in the case of apparent failure.

Our task, using the tools outlined above, is to assess where ethics regulation has tended towards the one or the other. We have four main propositions. The first is that ethics regulators need a strong hinterland of broad cross-party and institutional support to establish themselves and the legitimacy of their credentials. Regulators that fail to build institutional allies, especially among those institutions and categories of public servant they regulate, will have the greatest operational difficulty. Establishing the principle and broad agency configuration of regulation, but deferring definition of its precise operational remit, poses severe risks to the agency.

Our second proposition is that principles and broad values are largely symbolic statements of top-level aspirations about public life in the United Kingdom, and that there is a natural tendency in ethics regulation to rely increasingly on detailed codes of conduct as regulation proceeds. Training for principles and values in the United Kingdom's public life is difficult to achieve and rare; compliance with detailed codes has become the norm.

Our third proposition is that, agreed mechanisms and norms of account-ability for ethics regulators having emerged only recently and unevenly, their accountability, in the United Kingdom context, depends both on the level of prevailing controversy in particular areas of regulation, and on the political sensitivity of the institutions and public-office-holders involved. The difficulty of measuring regulator effectiveness adds to its enduring controversy. Regulators are frequently required to attain unquantifiable goals, or blamed for matters that are beyond their con-trol. There is a high risk of blame avoidance in ethics regulation and the agencies of regulation have only limited tools available to avoid blame, compared to government and legislators.

Finally, we argue that the challenging task of assembling adequate resources and skill sets for effective regulation is related not just to normal issues of budget adequacy, but also to bureau-building issues, recruitment problems, the relative newness of the institutional territory, and the type of accountability to which an agency is subject.

We are clear that the testing of these ideas will not resolve any dispute beyond all reasonable doubt. The nature of the evidence we consider will be imperfect and contested. The N is small and highly varied. Our method is evaluative not quantitative. We nevertheless hope to illumi-nate and clarify issues that merit further detailed institutional analysis.

To summarise, in this chapter, we have outlined the dilemmas of ethical regulation, and the first part of a framework for examining it. In Chap-ter 2 we set the agenda of ethical regulation in historical context show-ing how the need for such regulation was acknowledged only slowly and highlight some of the ethical controversies which eventually prompted a new approach to integrity issues. In Chapter 3 we look at the impact of the CSPL – the main vehicle for setting the terms of the ethics debate that has developed since the start of the 1990s. Chapters 4 to 13 then take the regulatory dilemmas we have outlined to date to show how they affected the different sectors of public-ethics regulation in the United Kingdom. Finally in Chapter 14 we draw together our conclusions about this new but problematic area of British politics and government.

Notes

1 For an overview of the impact of the expenses scandal see van Heerde-Hudson, J., *The Political Costs of the 2009 British MPs' Expenses Scandal* (Basing-stoke: Palgrave, 2014).

2 For a definition in comparative context, see Head, B., A. Brown and C. Con-nors (eds), *Promoting Integrity: Evaluating and Improving Public Institu-tions* (Farnham: Ashgate, 2008).

3 Public Administration Select Committee, *Ethics and Standards: The Regulation of Conduct in Public Life*, HC 121 I, 29 April 2007.

4 There is now a burgeoning literature on public integrity, covered in the bibliography. For an introduction to the topic see Dobel, J., *Public Integrity* (Baltimore: Johns Hopkins University Press, 2002); also Head *et al.*, *Promoting Integrity*.

5 On corruption see Heidenheimer, A. and M. Johnston, *Corruption: Concepts and Contexts* (New Brunswick and London: Transaction Books, 2002). On conflict of interest see Trost, C. and A. Gash, (eds), *Conflict of Interest in Public Life: Cross National Perspectives* (Cambridge: Cambridge University Press, 2008).

6 For a discussion of the concept of public integrity in an international context see Huberts, L.W., J. Maesschalk and C. Jurkiewicz (eds), *Ethics and Integrity of Governance: Perspectives across Frontiers* (Cheltenham: Edward Elgar, 2008). See also the detailed work by the World Bank and the OECD including *Public Sector Integrity: A Framework for Assessment* (OECD, 2005). On the need to take specific country factors into account see Peele, G. and R. Kaye, 'Regulating conflicts of interest: securing accountability in the modern state', in I. Sandoval (ed.), *Contemporary Debates on Corruption and Transparency: Rethinking State, Market and Society* (Washington, DC: World Bank and National Autonomous University of Mexico, 2011).

7 For a survey see Lawton, A. and A. Doig, 'Researching ethics for public service organizations: the view from Europe', *Public Integrity*, 8:1 (2005–2006), 11–33.

8 See Johnson, M., 'Measuring the new corruption rankings: implications for analysis and reform', in Heidenheimer and Johnston, *Political Corruption*, pp. 865–884. On the measurement of corruption more generally see Sampford, C., A. Shacklock, C. Connors and F. Galtung, *Measuring Corruption* (Aldershot: Ashgate, 2006).

9 Transparency International, *Corruption Perceptions Index 2014* (Berlin: Transparency International, 2014). The CPI combines the survey results into a single index running from a score of 100 (corruption-free) to 0 (completely corrupt).

10 Whyte, D. (ed.), *How Corrupt is Britain?* (London: Pluto Press, 2015).

11 See Rose, J. *The Public Understanding of Political Integrity: The Case for Probity Perceptions* (London: Palgrave, 2014).

12 See respectively http://wwweuropeansocialsurvey.org/ and http://ec.europa.eu/public_opinion/archives/eb_arch_en.htm.

13 Rose, *The Public Understanding of Political Integrity*, p. 5.

14 For the latest, see Committee on Standards in Public Life, *Survey of Public Attitudes towards Conduct in Public Life*, BMRB Social Research, 2013.

15 For the latest, see The Hansard Society, *Audit of Political Engagement 11: The 2014 Report* (London: Hansard Society, 2014).

16 The literature on the role of regulation in the modern state is extensive. See Baldwin, R., M. Cave and M. Lodge, *Understanding Regulation: Theory,*

Strategy and Practice (Oxford: Oxford University Press, 2011); Baldwin, R., M. Cave and M. Lodge (eds), *The Oxford Handbook of Regulation* (Oxford: Oxford University Press, 2010); and Coglianese, C. and A. Kagan (eds), *Regulation and Regulatory Processes* (Farnham: Ashgate, 2007); Vogel, D., *National Styles of Regulation: Environmental Policy in Great Britain and the United States* (Ithaca: Cornell University Press, 1986). On the UK specifically, see Moran, M., *The British Regulatory State* (Oxford: Oxford University Press, 2003) and Hood, C., C. Scott, O. James, G. Jones and T. Travers, *Regulation Inside Government: Waste Watchers, Quality Police and Sleaze Busters* (Oxford: Clarendon Press, 1999).

17 Hood *et al.*, *Regulation Inside Government*.

18 For background on the Commission see Kelly, J., 'The Audit Commission guiding, steering and regulating local government', *Public Administration* 81:3 (2003), 459–476, and on the abolition and replacement process see Communities and Local Government Committee, *Audit and Inspection of Local Authorities*, HC 763, 7 July 2007. For a general history see Campbell-Smith, D., *Follow the Money: The Audit Commission, Public Money and the Management of Public Services* (London: Allen Lane, 2008).

19 The Leveson Inquiry, *An Inquiry into the Culture, Practices and Ethics of the Press* (London: The Stationery Office, 2012). (The executive summary, pp. 13–17, contains the main recommendations on future regulation.)

20 Parliamentary Commission on Banking Standards, *Volume I: Report, together with Formal Minutes*, HL 98, HoC 148, December 2012; Independent Commission on Banking, *Final Report*, September 2011; see also HM Treasury, *Sound Banking: Delivering Reform*, Cm 8453, October 2012.

21 Leveson recommended an independent self-regulatory system, underpinned by legislation, by which the independent code and regulator was validated by Ofcom, with the threat that if the self-regulatory system was not sufficiently robust to qualify for validation, or if some press companies refused to join, Ofcom would become the direct regulator. The Leveson Inquiry, *An Inquiry into the Culture, Practices and Ethics of the Press*, 16–17.

22 Baldwin *et al.*, *Understanding Regulation*, 27.

23 Committee on Standards in Public Life, *Standards Matter: A Review of Best Practice in Promoting Good Behaviour in Public Life*, Fourteenth Report, Cm 8519, 2013, 41–43.

24 The Committee on Standards in Public Life recently referred to this problem, noting the likelihood of a relationship between high ethical standards and high service standards, but also that it was not the job of an ethics regulator to hold office-holders to account for their use of public money. Committee on Standards in Public Life, *Standards Matter*, Fourteenth Report, 24.

25 For discussion see Head *et al.*, *Promoting Integrity*.

26 'Recall', used in some form in several advanced democracies, gives voters the chance to remove elected representatives in certain circumstances. The major parties all committed to a recall provision in the 2010 election, following the 2009 MPs' expenses scandal. As of autumn 2014, the coalition

government bill on the subject was still progressing through Parliament, with some campaigning groups dissatisfied with its contents. See, Kelly, R., C. Coleman, and N. Johnston, *Recall Elections*, House of Commons Library Standard Note 05089, 12 September 2014.

27 Arguing for example in 2011 that the cost of reimbursing 38 per cent of MPs' claims was above the size of the claim itself: Public Accounts Committee, *Independent Parliamentary Standards Authority*, HC 1426, 14 September 2011, para 2.6 (note that the PAC estimate was disputed by IPSA).

28 Committee on Standards in Public Life, *Review of the Electoral Commission*, Eleventh Report, Cm 7006, 2007, 30–36.

29 See Audit Commission, *Corporate Governance Inspection: Doncaster Metropolitan Borough Council*, April 2010 and PricewaterhouseCoopers, *Best Value Inspection of the London Borough of Tower Hamlets*, September 2014.

30 'Holders of public office should be as open as possible about all the decisions and actions that they take. They should give reasons for their decisions and restrict information only when the wider public interest clearly demands.'

31 For a general discussion of transparency see Hood, C. and D. Heald, *Transparency: The Key to Better Governance?* (Oxford: Oxford University Press for the British Academy, 2006).

2

Integrity issues: a changing agenda

Introduction

A key premise of this book is that a step change occurred in the 1990s in the way the United Kingdom handled integrity issues. Values were re-examined and defined with greater precision. The structures underpinning these values were deliberately strengthened. New ethical institutions were created and political elites were obliged to address integrity issues in a more systematic and sustained way than ever before. In this chapter we show how these changes were the consequence of the country's longer-term approach to integrity issues. We identify the drivers of change in the handling of ethical issues in British public life both historically and more recently. We argue that the United Kingdom's distinctive experience of the transition to democratic government led it to address several integrity issues at a comparatively early stage in its democratic evolution: between the mid-nineteenth and early twentieth centuries. These issues included the opportunities for political patronage, the increasing power of lobbying pressure, and the rising costs of democratic partisan competition. In response, several key institutions were reformed – albeit in a piecemeal manner – and new laws framed to tighten electoral law, prevent corruption, and reform the civil service.

With some integrity issues having been addressed at an early stage, the political elite could therefore, from the late 1920s to the 1980s, sustain a narrative that British politics was, by cross-national standards, substantially free of problems. This encouraged the authorities to treat episodes of impropriety that did arise (such as the Profumo affair or the Poulson scandal) as isolated incidents, and allowed them to dismiss suggestions that the country's integrity system needed any further substantial revision. The complacency was probably helped by broader aspects of the

British political system which, while not immediately connected to ethics and integrity, had an important bearing on how ethics was handled as a political issue. These included the high degree of centralisation in political life, a well-developed system for providing political accountability, the relative absence of localism and of clientelist politics, and the relatively low cost of politics.

By the 1990s, however, the proposition that British political life was clean was no longer so easily sustainable. The later parts of this chapter trace the social, political and cultural factors that brought about this decline of confidence in British immunity from corruption. There were shifts in both the demand for improved ethics, and in the supply side. Demand for reform was partly rooted in the effects of the Thatcherite market-based approach to public policy as well as in subtle changes in party politics and political recruitment. These factors in turn altered the incentives and opportunities facing office-holders, and in some areas increased both the *risk* of impropriety, and the *perception* of impropriety. The supply side came from developments which had implications for standards and quality assurance in governance quality more broadly, such as a new emphasis on the monitoring of performance, on policy accountability, and on governmental openness and transparency. In some cases the spill-over was direct: more robust protection against impropriety was an inherent, albeit minor, part of better performance and delivery accountability generally. In other cases the demand for reform was indirect: greater government transparency and easier access to information enabled those who had concerns about ethics and propriety, including the media, to pursue their concerns more vigorously. There were also external influences. Transnational organisations focusing on ethics and propriety were by the 1990s beginning to have a direct influence on the United Kingdom. In particular, new compliance obligations were gradually emerging from the United Kingdom's membership of bodies such as the Council of Europe and the Organization for Economic Cooperation and Development (OECD).

The interaction of historical legacy and contemporary political vulnerabilities had an important effect. A long period of inattention to integrity issues and the absence of any systematic thought about how to enhance standards in public life left a tradition of ad hoc approaches and a continuing belief in the sufficiency of self-regulation. By the 1990s, however, several new factors were changing the environment. The first was scandal, or to be more precise a series of scandals, which destabilised John Major's already weak and unpopular government and prompted it to depart from tradition by grasping the nettle of ethics and propriety at the institutional level. The response involved a technique seen in other areas of public policy in recent decades: namely the attempt to isolate decisions from routine political controversy by transferring them to new institutions operating at a distance from partisan politics.[1] Through the CSPL and a range of other new ethics bodies this technique was clearly in evidence from the 1990s onwards. As we shall see, however, the inherent political combustibility of the subject matter made the application of a neutral regulatory framework hard to achieve, underlining in particular the difficulty of reconciling the quasi-independent character of the new institutions with the centralised electoral accountability of the United Kingdom's adversarial parliamentary government.

Early approaches to integrity questions

The Victorian period saw transition from aristocratic dominance to a democratic polity and with it intense debate about the proper role of the state in managing a rapidly industrialising society. Government expanded as it took on new functions in welfare, health, education and economic regulation. The more the state extended its responsibilities, the greater the temptation for those affected by government policy to seek new and occasionally dishonest ways of influencing policy and outcomes. Pressure groups multiplied, and with them the potential for impropriety.[2] Shifts in the British economy in the late nineteenth century themselves created new ethical issues about how to balance private and public interest with dilemmas arising in business as well as government.[3] As the role of the government grew, more attention was focused on the adequacy of the state's machinery and on the tools for achieving public policy ends. In the second half of the nineteenth century the franchise was gradually broadened, and complementary reforms – the 1872 Ballot Act and the 1883 Corrupt and Illegal Practices Act – eliminated some of the system's widespread electoral malpractice.[4] Merit gradually replaced patronage in civil service recruitment following the reforms of 1870, though patronage did not completely disappear from recruitment to the civil service until well into the twentieth century.[5] Institutions for audit and oversight were established in the 1860s including notably the office of the Comptroller and Auditor General whose task was to support the Public Accounts Committee (PAC) of the House of Commons.[6] The judicial system was reformed. Professionalism became the organising principle of British society, weaving new divisions into traditional class structures.[7]

Box 2.1 Timeline of key changes in the integrity agenda

1870	Civil service reforms	Opens recruitment on merit
1872	Ballot Act	Introduces secret ballot in elections
1883	Corrupt and Illegal Practices Prevention Act	Introduces strict limit on candidates expenses
1889	Public Bodies Corrupt Practices Act	Makes bribery of public officials a crime
1906	Prevention of Corruption Act	Extends anti-corruption legislation to private sector
1912	Marconi Scandal	Ministers dealing in shares
1916	Prevention of Corruption Act	Extends range of public bodies covered and makes corruption easier to prove
1922–1925	Maundy Gregory sale of honours	Honours (Prevention of Abuses) Act 1925
1948	Belcher/Stanley scandal and Lynskey Tribunal	Minister accused of influence peddling at the Board of Trade
1963	Profumo scandal	Minister lies to House of Commons about his involvement with Christine Keeler
1972	Poulson corruption scandal breaks	Architect found to have bribed large number of contacts in government
1976	Royal Commission on Standards of Conduct in Public Life	Investigates standards in wake of Poulson affair
1994	Cash-for-Questions affair	Group of MPs found to be taking money for parliamentary activities
1994	CSPL established under Lord Nolan	Given watching brief over public ethics and power to examine standards of conduct of all holders of public office including arrangements relating to financial and commercial activities, and make recommendations which might be required to ensure the highest standards of propriety in public life

1995	CSPL issues first report	Recommends major changes in House of Commons, appointments process
1997	Labour government elected	
1997	Ecclestone affair	Political donation alleged to secure exemption from ban on tobacco sponsorship. Labour extends remit of CSPL to cover party funding
2000	Political Parties and Referendum Act	Established new regulatory regime for donations and Electoral Commission
2005	Cash for Honours	Alleged award of peerages in return for loans to Labour
2009	MPs' expenses scandal	MPs required to repay improper gains on housing benefits; five MPs convicted; IPSA established

There were also efforts to address corruption in local government and in public procurement, both increasingly fertile grounds for corruption. The 1889 Public Bodies Corrupt Proceedings Act made it a criminal offence corruptly to give or receive any gift, loan, fee or reward, in a transaction with a member or servant of a local public body.[8] The Second Boer War (1899–1902) generated several contracting scandals, some implicating ministers, and in response the Liberal administration of 1906 introduced further statutory measures designed to prevent abuses in the private and public sphere. Thus the Prevention of Corruption Act 1906 extended the statutory coverage of corruption into the private sector. The 1889 Act had mainly affected local government. The 1906 Act extended the impact to central government and to all governmental agents, whether in the public or the private sector. Further anti-corruption legislation was enacted in 1916 in response to the renewed threat of profiteering and corruption in the First World War. The 1916 Prevention of Corruption Act extended the public bodies covered and changed the burden of proof in corruption cases. Instead of the normal criminal law presumption that a guilty intention (*mens rea*) had to be proved, the 1916 legislation reversed this presumption. Henceforth, when a gift was given, those who accepted it would have to prove that the gift had *not* been given corruptly.

There was rather less action at the level of high politics. By the late nineteenth century Parliament contained growing concentrations of new vested interests. The House of Lords had historically represented the landed interest while the House of Commons – and the government itself – increasingly reflected the interests of commerce and industry.[9] Few MPs saw politics as a full time career and Parliament was widely thought to be strengthened by its members' retention of outside occupations. Sporadically there was discussion of the ethical consequences. The Select Committee on MPs' Personal Interests considered the question of conflict of interest as early as 1896. But there was little appetite for framing anything as tangible as a code of rules to govern MPs' behaviour, or even to clarify when an interest had to be declared.[10] Patronage – in the sense of appointment without open competition – remained in many posts outside the formal civil service, even if its basis shifted from the use of personal contact for securing jobs for friends and family to the use of appointment power to secure posts for party allies. Conflict of interest issues were occasionally addressed but in an incomplete way. Semi-formal rules requiring ministers to divest themselves of directorships had been in place at least since Gladstone's 1892 government but, although these restrictions eventually became consensual between the parties, they were not always seen as compelling by some of Gladstone's successors in the early years of the twentieth century.[11] During the First World War, for example, the Marconi scandal implicated senior Liberal ministers, including the Attorney General, Rufus Isaacs, and the Chancellor of the Exchequer, David Lloyd George, who had invested in Marconi shares, using insider knowledge of an imminent franchise covering telegraph facilities across the Empire.[12]

In the early twentieth century, moreover, competition for campaign funding started to push the parties into questionable practices to procure funds. Both the Liberals and Conservatives used the promise of knighthoods and peerages to potential donors, especially the newly wealthy.[13] Controversy surrounding this trafficking in honours surged during the Lloyd George coalition governments of 1916–1922. The resultant public anger reflected both the scale of the abuse and the unsavoury character of the proposed recipients, some of whom such as William Vestey had been accused of wartime food hoarding and tax evasion. The role of middlemen such as the notorious Maundy Gregory added to public concern, and eventually a Royal Commission led to the passage of the Honours (Prevention of Abuses) Act of 1925, legislation which was rarely used but was to surface again in the 'loans for peerages' scandal after the 2005 election.[14]

The unaddressed agenda

The results of the reform agenda in British politics from the 1880s to the 1920s were thus ambivalent. Important improvements were made to the integrity system – perhaps as many as in any democracy at that point – but it seemed to leave the United Kingdom with a narrative that public life was essentially free of taint, and required little further systematic attention. Self-regulation, an honour code, the rule of law, a well-run public service and a centralised accountable executive ensured that when further issues arose, they were taken to be the aberrations of individuals, rather than the symptom of a system in need of further and more fundamental regulation.

From the mid-1920s, moreover, Ramsay Macdonald, Stanley Baldwin and Neville Chamberlain seemed to set a new tone in public life. The economic struggles from 1925 to 1939, the approach to war in the late 1930s, and then the conduct of the war itself, became all-consuming of political attention. Despite isolated incidents such as the 1936 budget affair in which National Labour Secretary of State for the Colonies Jimmy Thomas was forced to resign having clearly leaked market-sensitive budget details to stock brokers, there were very few major political scandals. The 1945–1951 Labour government experienced scandal when John Belcher MP, the parliamentary under-secretary at the Board of Trade, was found to have accepted minor gifts from dubious businessmen. His behaviour became the subject of a public inquiry (the so-called Lynskey Tribunal) and he resigned in disgrace. However, the public controversy focused as much on the black market business practices involved and the appropriateness of the tribunal procedure, as on Belcher's own guilt. Few implications seemed to flow for the handling of ethics and propriety in Clement Attlee's austere government.[15]

The early years of Conservative government from 1951–1964 witnessed the trauma of the Suez invasion and the revelation that the prime minister, Sir Anthony Eden, had lied about the British government's collusion with Israel. The later period under Harold Macmillan threw up a handful of salacious sexual and espionage scandals; but even these did not raise a substantial public clamour for new regulatory institutions to deal with ethics. Macmillan's government suffered a spectacular blow when in 1963 the Minister for War, John Profumo, was exposed in an affair with a society prostitute who was herself involved with a Russian envoy.[16] At least one member of the government had evidently come uncomfortably close to an unsavoury underworld but even so the distracting circumstances – sex and security – enabled the government to dismiss the Profumo episode as a single aberrant individual, not as a cause for concern about systemic corruption.

Harold Wilson's years in office from 1964–1970 and 1974–1976 generated controversies of a rather different nature. Criticism focused especially on the behaviour of special advisers, appointments which were then relatively novel. These advisers enjoyed proximity to the inner workings of government but they seemed exempt from many of the conventions governing the regular civil service.[17] Controversy about Wilson's entourage exploded when his 1976 resignation honours list was published. The list was publicly criticised by the Public Honours Scrutiny Committee, a body established in 1922 following the Lloyd George honours abuses. The Committee's concern centred especially on the colourful character of some of the prime minister's nominees. These nominees included Lord Kagan (a textile manufacturer who had helped fund Harold Wilson's political office and who subsequently went to prison for theft) and Sir Eric Miller who committed suicide after the launch of inquiries by the Fraud Squad into his Peachey Properties Empire.[18] The fact that this was a resignation list defused the controversy, however, and like earlier post-war episodes, it passed without having much wider impact.

It was the arrest in 1973 of architect John Poulson that began to push ethics and integrity higher up the agenda. The Poulson affair involved the wide-ranging network of an ambitious architect, John Poulson, who used his contacts in local and central government to secure work for his firm. The full extent of the corruption was unveiled only when Poulson went bankrupt and his meticulous notes on his friendships and dealings were made public. Besides Poulson himself, the affair implicated councillors, civil servants, local government officers, and a small number of MPs including Sir Herbert Butcher, Albert Roberts, John Cordle and, most prominent of all, Reginald Maudling who resigned in 1972. Altogether some three hundred people were targeted for investigation.[19]

The Poulson case provoked an immediate prime-ministerial committee to examine the rules of conduct in local government (the Redcliffe Maud Committee), and further inquiries by a Royal Commission under Lord Salmon, and by a parliamentary select committee. The overall conclusion of most observers was that few substantial lessons were learned from the scandal. However the affair did force a somewhat reluctant House of Commons to agree in 1974 to set up a Register of Interests to be overseen by a Select Committee on Members' Interests.

As an investigative tool the 1976 Royal Commission on Standards of Conduct in Public Life was sadly inadequate, with imprecise terms of reference, part-time membership, no power to summon witnesses and poor administrative support.[20] Its terms of reference excluded the conduct of MPs. The Commission itself emphasised that its role was

not to act as an investigative body and its conclusions seemed com-
placent. It claimed to have heard no evidence to give the Commission
'concern about the integrity and sense of public duty of our bureaucracy as a whole or to suggest that it is common for member of the
public to offer bribes to officials of any rank or to solicit bribes'.[21] It
did highlight the need for more safeguards against malpractice and corruption but its underlying assumption was that Poulson was a one-off
case. There were no recommendations for reforming the machinery for
investigating complaints and proposals for an independent inspectorate
were rejected. Instead the Commission fell back on the existing system
of self-regulation and the public-service values of the civil service as the
main barriers to corruption. Moreover, neither its report nor that of the
Redcliffe-Maud investigation, was debated in Parliament, or effectively
linked to any wider consideration of governmental ethics. Instead, the
response was limited to local government. The Local Government Act
of 1972 redefined the grounds for ineligibility for elective office in local
government (publicly sourced conflict of interest such as paid employment directly or indirectly by the authority in question, and conviction
for an offence generating a custodial sentence of at least three months).
Part III of follow-up legislation in 1974 established the post of Commissioner for Local Government. The Commissioner was to serve as an
ombudsman to investigate complaints against local authorities. The Act
also established a *National Code of Local Government Conduct*, which,
with a modification in 1989, remained in force for almost a quarter of a
century, though as we shall see in Chapter 12, with rather little impact.[22]

The Thatcher years: changed incentives and new areas of ethical risk

Several factors combined to increase the salience of a range of
standards-related issues during the Thatcher era. Radical changes to the
role of the state began to erode traditional understandings about the
conduct of government. The celebration of wealth creation and a new
pro-business environment altered the political culture. The boundary
between the state and the market shifted and the privatisation of several
state-owned enterprises generated new opportunities for private-sector
companies. Novel approaches to public management, decentralised
decision-making within the public service, and the creation of new executive agencies, made the state a far less unified actor and complicated
processes of accountability.[23]

The Redcliffe-Maud Committee in the 1970s had identified the risk
of corruption in local government stemming from unchecked discretion

in contracting and procurement. Now, through public-service reforms which gave public-sector managers much greater freedom to manage, the risk increased at national level too. The public service was no longer a sealed and separate set of professionals but was encouraged to integrate with the private sector. There was also concern about the politicisation of core civil service appointments as Conservative ministers – sceptical about traditional public service values – advocated a new style of civil service professionalism. As we shall see in later chapters, this was a complex argument and in the 1980s the Conservatives did not in fact go far down the road of partisanship in senior civil-service appointments.[24] However, the role, culture and status of the new executive agencies provoked questioning about their vulnerability to financial and other impropriety. The closer relationships which parts of the public sector, including local government, developed with the private commercial world through contracting-out, public–private partnerships, and post-employment opportunities for former employees of public agencies raised new ethical issues. There was certainly concern that greater freedom and 'arm's length' accountability would eventually lead to problems as traditional rules and codes were eroded.

This concern was underlined by a handful of cases of administrative and financial misconduct that began to emerge as the years of Conservative dominance came to an end. Thus in 1992 the Audit Commission, a financial watchdog established in 1982 to oversee local government, warned of the risk of fraud and corruption from changes in the operation of local government services and of the National Health Service (NHS).[25] It also later uncovered the Westminster 'homes for votes' scandal in which the Conservatives in the London borough of Westminster in the late 1980s systematically manipulated council-house sales, to build up electoral support. Subsequent investigation of the council's policies led to a surcharge of £36 million on Shirley Porter, who had been in charge of the council from 1986 until 1991.[26] In 1994 the PAC identified a number of problems, partly of managerial effectiveness but also in part of ethics and propriety, in mainstream departments such as the Foreign and Commonwealth Office, the Ministry of Defence, the Department of the Environment, and in other public bodies, such as the Insolvency Service and the Property Services Agency.[27] These findings raised important questions about supervision, accountability and conflict of interest. The PAC gave notice it would henceforth pay particular attention to the ethical implications of value-for-money programmes, asking the National Audit Office to inspect all NDPBs, and recommending a check list of controls for all public-sector bodies.

There was also a significant transformation taking place within the major parties. Conservative MPs elected with the Thatcher victories of 1979, 1983 and 1987 seemed to have subtly different outlooks from previous generations of Tory parliamentarians and many became involved in the more aggressive style of parliamentary lobbying that emerged in this period.[28] Some actually ran lobbying organisations, like Westminster Communications, or were drawn into firms such as Ian Greer's – later dubbed 'the most powerful lobbying group in the land'.[29] Others took up directorships on offer through a growing number of Westminster-based consultancies. Greer himself developed extensive contacts within the Conservative Party, regularly entertained its MPs, made donations towards some of their election expenses and hired them in his campaigns. Given the prevalence of Conservative MPs with outside interests at the time, such cosy relationships initially excited little concern. By one estimate in 1991 there were 384 MPs with commercial interests, encompassing 522 directorships and 452 consultancies.[30] A decade later, another survey found that 39 per cent of the largest British firms had politicians in their executive ranks or as major shareholders, and that the United Kingdom ranked among the top five countries in the world for this type of political connection between business and politics.[31] Leigh and Vulliamy suggest that during the 1980s Conservative whips actually encouraged their backbench MPs to make money as a strategy for keeping their supporters happy and giving them strong incentives to maximise their re-election prospects and job security.[32] Julian Critchley, a liberal rebel within the Tory ranks in the 1980s, shared the view that a fundamental change in the Conservative Party had occurred in the Thatcher years, famously remarking that Margaret Thatcher had transferred control from landowners to estate agents.[33]

The need for effective party organisation had its impact on both major parties. Communication and campaigning costs were rising, as the income from traditional sources such as individual party membership subscriptions was shrinking. Political money was increasingly targeted at interests and causes. Lobbying from the private sector became more professional and more effective. It also increased across the public sector as local government and local interests attempted to influence central government's distributional decisions. The business sector itself experienced scandals. Several high-profile companies failed as result of questionable business methods leaving shareholders and others with grave financial losses These scandals included Polly Peck, a textile company which collapsed in 1990 with debts of £1 billion, a private bank (the Bank of Credit and Commerce International or BCCI) which was closed down as a result of widespread financial irregularities including money laundering, and the implosion of Robert Maxwell's publishing empire which included the *Daily Mirror*. Maxwell's business dealings were revealed to have involved extensive fraud and theft, including from pension funds.[34] Party links, in the case of Polly Peck's donations to the Conservative Party and Maxwell's Labour ties, added to the general sense of impropriety across the political landscape. Private as well as public companies seemed in need of greater monitoring encouraging a search for new strategies of regulation and corporate governance.[35]

Ethical dilemmas also emerged inside the executive as a result of Margaret Thatcher's commercial priorities and her highly personal handling of policy. The arms trade was profoundly affected by her determination to expand British arms sales even if, as one critic noted, it meant skewing them towards authoritarian regimes and accepting complex linkages and reciprocal agreements.[36] Thatcher's personal commercial diplomacy, first in the Gulf Tour of 1981 and then in securing the two Al Yamamah deals of 1986 and 1988, was highly contentious not least because of the secrecy surrounding the negotiations. Thatcher's three administrations also witnessed a systematic use of honours to reward Conservative Party donors. During her premiership, 216 peers were created, including, surprisingly, four hereditary peerages, resuming a practice apparently abandoned in 1970.

John Major and the problem of sleaze

It was, however, Margaret Thatcher's successor, John Major, who had to deal with the consequences of these changed features of British public life. Under Major's second administration, from 1992 to 1997, a torrent of scandals erupted as the press, public and Opposition cast critical scrutiny on the behaviour of MPs. Of particular concern was the willingness of some MPs to accept reimbursement for parliamentary intervention on behalf of outside groups. In 1994 a *Sunday Times* investigation revealed that two MPs (Graham Riddick and David Tredinnick) were willing to accept cash for tabling parliamentary questions.[37] Both were disciplined by the House.[38] This so-called 'cash-for-questions' affair was soon overtaken by the allegation that a number of Conservative MPs were regularly being paid by Ian Greer Associates for parliamentary work, and that Greer had built up a 'taxi-rank' of politicians to support his lobbying activities.[39] It also emerged that one Conservative MP, Neil Hamilton, had failed to disclose in the Register of Members' Interests cash payments and gifts in kind (including free stays at the Ritz Hotel in Paris) from Mohamed Al-Fayed, the owner of Harrods. Subsequent articles in the *Guardian* explored the links between MPs and lobbying, exposing some thirty MPs who had accepted donations either for themselves or their constituency parties from Ian Greer Associates.[40]

The focus of much of the cash-for-questions scandal was the campaign to secure support for Mohamed Al-Fayed. The Al-Fayeds had acquired the House of Fraser retail consortium, which included the prestigious Harrods store, in controversial circumstances, ultimately leading to the appointment of Department of Trade and Industry inspectors to scrutinise the takeover. In the complex saga of allegations and denials that followed attention focused on two MPs – Tim Smith and Neil Hamilton – who allegedly took payments both from Greer and from Al-Fayed directly.[41] Most of the MPs affected by association with Ian Greer were backbenchers but some were influential through the Conservative backbench Trade and Industry Committee. In 1992, moreover, Hamilton was given junior office in the Major government. The allegations about both Hamilton and Smith forced the Prime Minister in 1994 to commission a report from the Cabinet Secretary Sir Robin Butler.[42] The Select Committee on Members' Interests also investigated the case against Neil Hamilton in 1995 although internal divisions and procedural problems weakened its authority.[43]

Such inquiries failed to reassure the public that the matter was being taken sufficiently seriously. In a move which was to have long-term consequences for the handling of integrity issues in the United Kingdom, John Major therefore established the CSPL under Lord Nolan. It issued its first report in 1995 following a series of open meetings which surveyed the ethical landscape of British government.[44] As we shall see in the next chapter, the establishment of the Committee was a crucial turning point for the handling of ethical issues. Its recommendations led to rapid institutional innovation as its successive reports recommended new machinery and kept integrity issues firmly on the political agenda. Thus Lord Nolan's first report led directly to the establishment of a new Parliamentary Commissioner for Standards (PCS) who undertook a definitive inquiry into the allegations against some twenty-five MPs.

The results of that inquiry appeared after the 1997 general election.[45] The wrong-doing identified by the first PCS, Sir Gordon Downey, found four separate 'offences' which had been committed by a number of MPs.[46] The first was the acceptance of payment for parliamentary services, which he considered constituted a corrupt relationship. The second was a failure to register interests properly. This offence had been committed not only by Neil Hamilton and Tim Smith but by other Conservative MPs some of whom were very senior, including Lady Olga Maitland, Sir Michael Grylls, Gerald Malone and Sir Peter Hordern. Thirdly, there had been a failure by some MPs to declare an interest in relevant parliamentary proceedings and in representations to ministers or contacts with civil servants. And finally there were actions which the Commissioner deemed were not compatible with the standards 'expected of MPs'. The Commissioner did not find the highly partisan lobbying effort to promote the interests of the House of Fraser inherently objectionable; but it did become unacceptable if bribes were accepted by MPs or they made contracts which fettered their discretion or otherwise allowed their conduct to fall below the standards the House was entitled to expect of them.[47]

The cash-for-questions affair was not the only public integrity issue to arise during John Major's administrations. Many other cases broke in its wake. Jonathan Aitken MP was found to have lied about payments from an arms dealer. Revelations about their personal lives affected a number of individual Conservative politicians, including ministers David Mellor, Steve Norris and Tim Yeo.[48] For some, the 1997 general election ended their political careers. Neil Hamilton lost the safe seat of Tatton to the crusading journalist Martin Bell. Graham Riddick also lost his seat, though David Tredinnick survived in Bosworth. Michael Brown, who had received fees from Ian Greer, was defeated, along with Tory Deputy Chairman Dame Angela Rumbold, who had admitted introducing ministers to clients for a lobbying company. Jonathan Aitken (later to be imprisoned for perjury) lost his seat, as did two MPs – David Mellor and Gary Waller – who had been the subject of sexual scandals.[49] Taken together these episodes coalesced to tarnish the Conservative Party, associating it with 'sleaze', a term that entered the political vocabulary of the 1990s with a vengeance. The electoral damage to the Conservative Party was extensive. It lost the general election of 1997 by a landslide, having won the previous four. The long-term significance of the Major government's attempt to address these challenging ethical issues was profound. The establishment of the Committee on Standards in Public Life in 1994 took control of the agenda on ethics away from the government and placed it with an important and independent new actor.

The impact on Labour

Labour's landslide victory in 1997 replaced John Major's weakened government with one with a strong majority and a prime minister – Tony Blair – who initially enjoyed great personal and political popularity. Labour participated enthusiastically in the undermining of Conservative ethical credentials under John Major and the sleaze factor played a role in securing its victory. Yet Labour's response to the political changes of the Thatcher era had long-term consequences for its own capacity to deal with ethics and integrity. Frequently Blair's governments seemed to fall well below the high ethical standards promised in opposition.

The aim of the New Labour project, as conceived by Tony Blair and his advisers, was to occupy the middle ground of British politics.[50] This transformation meant identifying Labour with processes of social modernisation and accepting many Conservative policies on public ownership, economic intervention, the labour market, liberalisation, and public-service reform. Public-service modernisation indeed was accelerated, not slowed, and with minor exceptions there was no resumption of public ownership. This reorientation of Labour was engineered to destroy two key doubts about its electoral credibility: its subordinate relationship with the unions and its reputation for irresponsible fiscal management.[51]

To make these policy adaptations stick, Labour's traditional power structures had to be transformed to concentrate authority in the leadership rather than the National Executive Committee. The offices of key parliamentary leaders were staffed with individuals who could be groomed for staff-support roles when Labour assumed power. Such figures needed to interact with new clienteles beyond the traditional Labour movement and provide reassurance to overseas investors and financial markets. Thus figures like Lord Sainsbury and Lord Drayson were recruited to the Labour cause and business interests were assiduously courted, with considerable success indeed once it became apparent that the Conservatives were destined to lose the 1997 election.[52]

Labour also needed new resources. There was a compelling electoral case for reducing reliance on trade-union funding.[53] Party leaders also needed resources individually for research, networking and profile-raising. To raise these resources professional lobbyists and fund-raisers were needed. The party's diversification strategy therefore self-consciously cultivated both new donors and a cadre of intermediaries who could attract such funds: lobbyists like Derek Draper, Roger Liddell and Ben Lucas, and fund-raisers and business contacts like Jon Mendelsohn and Michael, later Lord, Levy (known as 'Lord Cashpoint' for his formidable fund-raising ability).[54] For New Labour this ability to engage with business, and recruit from business ranks, was a cause for celebration, and it contrasted its unembarrassed openness about it with Conservative Party secrecy.

In power after 1997, however, the ethical dilemmas and conflict of interest issues inherent in this new relationship with business rapidly caught up with the party. The Ecclestone affair (examined in Chapter 10) produced accusations of an improper government policy capitulation over a proposed ban on Formula 1 tobacco sponsorship and advertising. The Drayson affair, while less clear-cut, raised questions about donations by Paul, later Lord, Drayson and a contract for vaccines won by one of Drayson's biotech companies. The Draper case revealed claims made to an undercover journalist by Derek Draper, a former political adviser who worked as a lobbyist for GPC Market Access. Draper boasted of his ability to secure access to senior ministers who had been former colleagues. The proximity of Downing Street adviser Roger Liddell, a former associate of Draper at GPC, added to the complexity of the story. Finally, the Hinduja affair – the alleged intervention by Peter Mandelson in support of a passport application by Indian businessman Srichand Hinduja – led in 2001 to Mandelson's resignation from ministerial office for a second time in the space of less than three years.[55]

None of these four cases generated criminal prosecution, but they reflected poorly on Labour's links to business and lobbying groups and created a strong impression of conflicts of interest that significantly compromised Labour's reputation during its first term. Labour's pursuit of party modernity exposed the party to allegations that were difficult to refute for a government that had claimed in its campaigning that it was going to be 'whiter than white'. Labour had reinvented itself in the 1990s to win office. It transformed its image, decision-processes, and agenda, and acquired a new set of leaders and key policy-makers, many with little association with the traditional party, and closer ties with each other and with the media and business elite. But in so doing it generated new concerns about ethics and integrity that hitherto had plagued mainly the Conservatives.

Other drivers of change

As we have seen in this chapter, scandal was a significant factor forcing the United Kingdom to shed its previous complacency about standards in public life. But it was not the only driver of change. Behind the headline events, there were more subtle social, political and cultural developments changing the context and language in which such issues were discussed. Responsibility, transparency and regulatory accountability are certainly not modern discoveries, but the emphasis placed on accountability and the consciousness of regulatory demands expanded significantly during the 1980s and 1990s. Much of this changed thinking was about the accountability and liability of those who occupied positions of trusteeship in public and private sectors, and it came from a variety of sources.[56] Some of it came from a greater litigiousness in society as a whole. Some translated across from the need for much stronger forms of corporate governance and investor protection in the private sector. In an age of rapidly expanding equity markets and financial services, scandals in pension schemes, insurance syndicates and banks added to a demand for tighter commercial regulation. But demands for liability and responsibility in the public sector were growing too, and were encouraged by new governance agendas and by broad concerns about 'fitness-to-govern' and blame-avoidance strategies by those responsible for (but often not in day-to-day charge of) public-sector organisations.[57]

Over the late twentieth and early twenty-first centuries there thus emerged a new set of desiderata for both public and private sector bodies, requiring enhanced attention to transparency, inclusiveness, safety, environmental awareness, impartiality and value-for money. It became expected that organisations should be fully aware of their obligations in these areas, should monitor and account for their performance, and should be proactive in identifying potential risks.[58] The internal habits and external expectations of this culture had their impact in ethics and propriety as in other areas. And once these habits of mind set in, they ceased to be a matter of individual responsibility, and increasingly were seen as a matter of organisational risk. Such changes were encouraged by new possibilities for monitoring and accountability. Technology and much increased access to information have certainly facilitated it and its use was strongly encouraged by the new public management and new governance theories which emphasised delivery, performance and supply-side efficiency of public services.[59]

In addition to these domestic shifts there were pressures from outside the United Kingdom. Many mature democracies, even those with high ethical standards, periodically encourage extensive debate about implementing their fundamental values.[60] Specialist advocacy groups like, for example, the Institute for Democracy and Electoral Assistance and Transparency International have long pursued integrity issues within a broader governance-quality agenda, knowledge of which tends to cross borders fairly seamlessly. A common theme for agencies dealing with less-developed countries, when aid or membership of an international agency is at stake, has been explicit *governance conditionality* initiatives. Other programmes have been designed to improve institutional performance and transparency in developed countries themselves, the United Kingdom included, or to protect them from transnational corruption. Numerous agencies – the Council of Europe, the OECD, the World Bank and others – have been involved and at times the transnational activism has created an over-crowded and discordant market for initiatives forcing the United Kingdom to take notice and to participate in information transfer and a degree of peer review.

These transnational initiatives had an indirect impact on the British ethics debate and on its institutional arrangements. Whenever new arrangements are being drawn up, their architects have felt obliged, in the face of so much apparent international expertise, to refer to lessons from other jurisdictions, even if they frequently conclude that the lessons are unsuitable for the United Kingdom. Since the 1990s, the United Kingdom has been drawn into two such major integrity initiatives. GRECO – the Council of Europe's Group of States against Corruption – is an exercise in bench-marking national integrity systems through ongoing peer review. In principle, if compliance is not approved, a member-state could be removed from the agreement. Somewhat to its surprise, in the initial evaluation stage in the early 2000s, the United Kingdom found itself the subject of no fewer than twelve recommendations for improvement.[61] The second initiative was the OECD's Anti-bribery Convention. All signatories to this Convention have had to make adjustments to national legislation, including changes to the criminal law of corruption. The follow-up provisions are particularly demanding, with mutual self-evaluation for each country in turn by a Working Party on Bribery, based on a report assessing progress in enforcement. The methodology of the Convention – functional equivalence – has similarities to an EU directive (harmonisation through goals with a choice of legal means); but functional equivalence demands a holistic review of the examination of the law, the legal concept, and the wider institutional context in which it operates. Through this approach, evaluators get to grips with the niceties of the national framework, and the national authorities are forced to reflect in detail on their own systems, to compare them with other systems, and to provide a detailed justification in a range of areas (corporate liability, sanctions against corporations, information-exchange procedures within and between jurisdictions).

Conclusions

In this chapter we have outlined how integrity issues were handled over a relatively long period of British political history. We have shown that by the 1990s there was much unwarranted complacency about the standards which governed British public life, just as changes in the political culture were creating new demands and expectations domestically, and as international initiatives were raising awkward questions about the United Kingdom's approach to integrity issues. Perhaps none of these developments would have forced radical action without the peculiar situation John Major experienced in the 'cash-for-questions' crisis. But even if his decision to set up the new machinery of the CSPL was a desperate bid to defuse the sleaze question, unenthusiastically accepted by his party, it was crucial for the future handling of integrity issues. Once established, the CSPL set about identifying first principles and building a new integrity framework across the whole political system. That process was by no means straightforward; but it was a critical juncture in British public life. In a relatively short space of time across the many arenas of public life fundamental values were given expression in codes of conduct, new actors were given voice and dedicated institutions of ethical regulation were created. It is to that process that we turn in the next chapter.

Notes

1 See Oliver, D., 'The politics-free dimension to the UK constitution', in M. Quortrup (ed.), *The British Constitution: Continuity and Change* (Oxford: Hart, 2013), pp. 69–92.
2 On the development of pressure groups in the nineteenth century see Wootton, G., *Pressure Groups in Britain 1790–1970* (London: Allen Lane, 1975).
3 Taylor, J., 'Commercial fraud and public men in Victorian Britain', *Institute of Historical Research*, 78:200 (2005). For a modern survey see Clarke, M., *Business Crime: Its Nature and Control* (London: Polity, 1990).
4 O'Leary, C., *The Elimination of Corrupt Practices in British Elections, 1868–1911* (Oxford: Clarendon Press, 1962); Rubenstein, W., 'The end of "Old Corruption" in Britain 1780–1860', *Past and Present*, 101 (1983), 55–86.
5 See Bourne, J., *Patronage and Society in Nineteenth Century England* (London: Edward Arnold, 1986).
6 For further discussion of audit arrangements see White, F. and K. Hollingsworth, *Audit, Accountability and Government* (Oxford: Clarendon Press, 1999).
7 See Perkin, H., *The Rise of Professional Society, England Since 1880* (London: Routledge, 1989).
8 Dunbabin, J., 'British local government reform: the nineteenth century and after', *English Historical Review*, 92:365 (1977), 777–805.
9 Platt, D., 'The commercial and industrial interests of ministers of the Crown', *Political Studies*, 9:3 (1961), 267–290.
10 *Report of the Select Committee on Members of Parliament (Personal Interest)* 1896.
11 See Searle, G., *Corruption in British Politics 1895–1930* (Oxford: Oxford University Press, 1987).
12 See Gilbert, B., 'David Lloyd George and the great Marconi scandal', *Historical Research*, 62:149 (2007), 295–317 and for an earlier but still classic account Donaldson, F., *The Marconi Scandal* (London: Harcourt Brace, 1962).

13 Camplin, J., *The Rise of the Plutocrats: Wealth and Power in Edwardian England* (London: Constable, 1978).

14 Macmillan, G., *Honours for Sale: The Strange Story of Maundy Gregory* (London: Richards, 1954) and Cullen, T., *Maundy Gregory Purveyor of Honours* (London: Bodley Head, 1974).

15 Wade Baron, S., *The Contact Man: The Story of Sidney Stanley and the Lynskey Tribunal* (London: Secker & Warburg, 1966).

16 There is now an extensive literature on the Profumo Affair but for an overview see Lord Denning, *The Denning Report: The Profumo Affair* (London: Pimlico, 1963, 1992).

17 Blick, A., *People Who Live in the Dark: A History of the Special Adviser in British Politics* (London: Politico's, 2004).

18 Pimlott, B., *Harold Wilson* (London: HarperCollins, 1992).

19 On the affair see Fitzwalter, R. and D. Taylor, *Web of Corruption: The Story of J.G.L. Poulson and T. Dan Smith* (London: Granada, 1981) and Jones, P., *From Virtue to Venality: Corruption in the City* (Manchester: Manchester University Press, 2013), pp. 74–94; Tomkinson, M. and M. Gillard, *Nothing to Declare* (London: John Calder, 1980); Searle, *Corruption in British Politics*; Nicholls, C., T. Daniel, M. Polaine and J. Hatchard, *Corruption and Misuse of Public Office* (Oxford: Oxford University Press, 2006).

20 Pinto-Duschinsky, M., 'Corruption in Britain: the Royal Commission on Standards of Conduct in Public Life', *Political Studies*, 25:2 (1977), 274–284; Doig, A. and C. Skelcher, 'Ethics in local government: evaluating self-regulation in England and Wales', *Local Government Studies*, 27:1 (2001), 89–90.

21 Pinto-Duschinsky, 'Corruption in Britain'.

22 Committee on Standards in Public Life, *Standards in Public Life: Standards of Conduct in Local Government in England, Scotland, and Wales: Third Report of the Committee on Standards in Public Life*, Vol. 1 (London: Stationery Office, 1997); Doig and Skelcher, 'Ethics in local government', 90.

23 The literature on Thatcherism as a philosophy of public management, and as a fundamental restatement of the boundary between public and private is extensive. Among the more objective studies are Kavanagh, D., *Thatcherism and British Politics: The End of Consensus?* (Oxford: Oxford University Press, 1990); Skidelsky, R. (ed.), *Thatcherism* (Oxford: Blackwell, 1989); and for a recent reappraisal, Vinen, R., *Thatcher's Britain: The Politics and Social Upheaval of the 1980s* (London: Simon & Schuster, 2009).

24 Hennessy, P., *Whitehall* (London: Secker & Warburg, 1989); see also Campbell, C. and G. Wilson, *The End of Whitehall: Death of a Paradigm?* (Oxford: Blackwell, 1995).

25 See Audit Commission, *Protecting the Public Purse; Probity in the Public Sector: Combatting Fraud and Corruption in Local Government* (London: HMSO, 1993). For an overview see Doig, A., 'Mixed signals? Public sector change and the proper conduct of government business', *Public Administration*, 73 (1995), 191–212.

26 Hosken, A., *Nothing Like a Dame: The Scandals of Shirley Porter* (London: Granta, 2006). See also Dimoldenberg, P., *The Westminster Whistleblowers* (London: Politico's, 2006).

27 Committee of Public Accounts, *The Proper Conduct of Public Business*, HC 154, 1994.

28 Jordan, G. (ed.), *The Commercial Lobbyists: Politics for Profit in Britain* (Aberdeen: Aberdeen University Press, 1991); Grant, W., *Business and Politics in Britain*, 2nd edition (Basingstoke: Macmillan, 1993); Hollingsworth, M., *MPs for Hire* (London: Bloomsbury, 1991); Leys, C., *Market Driven Politics* (London: Verso, 2003).

29 Leigh, D. and E. Vulliamy, *Sleaze: The Corruption of Parliament* (London: 4th Estate, 1997).

30 Baston, L., *Sleaze: The State of Britain* (London: Channel Four Books, 2000).

31 Faccio, M., 'Politically connected firms', *American Economic Review*, 96:1 (2006), 369–386.

32 Leigh and Vulliamy, *Sleaze*.

33 For an overview of Critchley's views see Critchley, J. and M. Halcrow, *Collapse of Stout Party: The Decline and Fall of the Tories* (London: Indigo, 1997).

34 All of these affairs have generated analysis. See for example Greenslade, R., *Maxwell's Fall* (London: Simon & Schuster, 1992); Barchard, D., *Asil Nadir and the Rise and Fall of Polly Peck* (London: Gollancz, 1992) and Ring Adams, J. and D. Frantz, *Full Service Bank: How BCCI Stole Millions Around the World* (London: Pocket Books, 1992).

35 See Clarke, *Business Crime*, and Clarke, M., *Regulation: The Social Control of Business between Law and Politics* (London: Palgrave, 2000).

36 See Phythian, M., *The Politics of British Arms Sales since 1964: 'To Secure Our Rightful Share'* (Manchester: Manchester University Press, 2000).

37 See *Sunday Times*, 10 July 1994. See also Doig, A., 'Cash for questions: Parliament's response to the offence that dare not speak its name', *Parliamentary Affairs*, 51:1 (1995), 36–50.

38 Privileges Committee (1994–1995), HC 351.

39 See Leigh and Vulliamy, *Sleaze*, p. 32.

40 See Leigh and Vulliamy, *Sleaze* (especially ch. 6).

41 On Al-Fayed's role see Bower, T., *Fayed: The Unauthorised Biography* (Basingstoke: Macmillan, 1998).

42 See White, M., 'The sinking of Hamilton', *Guardian*, 26 October 1994.

43 See Select Committee on Members' Interests, First Report, HC (1994–95) 460.

44 Committee on Standards in Public Life, *MPs, Ministers and Civil Servants Executive Quangos* (Cm 2850) 1995.

45 See Standards and Privileges Committee, First Report (1997–1998) HC 30(1–IV).

46 Sir Gordon Downey's findings are printed as an Appendix to the Standards and Privileges Committee First Report, *Complaint from Mr Mohamed Al Fayed, the Guardian and Others Against 25 Members and Former Members*.

47 See also Gay, O. and P. Leopold, *Conduct Unbecoming: The Regulation of Parliamentary Behaviour* (London: Politico's, 1994), especially Geoffrey Lock's chapter, 'The Hamilton affair', pp. 29–58.

48 For discussion see Seldon, A., with Lewis Baston, *Major: A Political Life* (London: Weidenfeld & Nicolson, 1997).

49 See Butler, D. and Dennis Kavanagh, *The British General Election of 1997* (Basingstoke: Macmillan, 1997).

50 Gould, P., *The Unfinished Revolution* (London: Little, Brown, 1998); Nagel, J.H. and C. Wlezien, 'Centre-party strength and major party divergence in Britain, 1945–2005', *British Journal of Political Science*, 40:2 (2010), 279–304; Kavanagh, D., *The Reordering of British Politics: Politics after Thatcher* (Oxford: Oxford University Press, 1997).

51 Butler, B. and D. Kavanagh, *The British General Election of 2001* (Basingstoke: Palgrave, 2002), pp. 1–36; Heath, A.F., R. Jowell and J. Curtice, *The Rise of New Labour: Party Politics and Voter Choices* (Oxford: Oxford University Press, 2001).

52 Osler, D., *New Labour PLC: New Labour as a Party of Business* (Edinburgh: Mainstream Publishing, 2002) esp. pp. 59–84: Rawnsley, A., *The End of the Party: The Rise and Fall of New Labour* (London: Viking, 2010); Seldon, A. (ed.), *Blair's Britain, 1997–2007* (Cambridge: Cambridge University Press, 2007).

53 Ewing, K., *The Cost of Democracy: Party Funding in Modern British Politics* (Oxford and Portland: Hart, 2007), pp. 1–21. These issues are dealt with in greater detail in Chapter 11.

54 Osler, *Labour Party PLC*, pp. 62–66.

55 Butler and Kavanagh, *The British General Election of 2001*, p. 7.

56 For a useful overview as seen by the Civil Service Commissioners themselves, see: Office of the Civil Service Commissioners, *Changing Times: Leading Perspectives on the Civil Service in the 21st Century and its Enduring Values* (London, 2005).

57 On the blame avoidance literature see Hood, C., *The Blame Game: Spin Bureaucracy and Self-Preservation in Government* (Oxford and Princeton: Princeton University Press, 2011).

58 For an overview of the role of risk in government see Hood, C., H. Rothstein and R. Baldwin, *The Government of Risk* (Oxford: Oxford University Press, 2001).

59 On technology see Hood, C. and H. Margetts, *The Tools of Government in the Digital Age* (Basingstoke: Macmillan, 2007).

60 See Saint-Martin, D., 'The Watergate effect: or why is the ethics bar constantly rising?' in C. Trost and A. Gash (eds), *Conflict of Interest in Public Life: Cross National Perspectives* (Cambridge: Cambridge University Press, 2008), pp. 35–55.

61 Council of Europe: GRECO (Group of States Against Corruption) *First Evaluation Report: Evaluation of the United Kingdom, (Greco Eval I Rep (2001) 8E Final)* (Strasbourg, 2001), pp. 23–24.

3

Building the United Kingdom's integrity machinery: the role of the Committee on Standards in Public Life

Introduction

The previous chapter analysed the United Kingdom's traditional approach to integrity issues, identifying in particular the reluctance of the political class from the 1920s to the 1990s to treat the subject of ethics and integrity systematically or to learn lessons from episodes of misconduct in public life. Eventually, this approach became untenable. The eruption of the cash-for-questions scandal demanded a new strategy which began in 1994 with the establishment of the CSPL. This chapter examines the Committee's role and impact. The chief impact was clearly the new regulatory institutions of which the Committee was the main architect. The chapter does not provide a detailed description of these institutions, which are the subject of other parts of the book. Here we consider the key elements of the Committee's overall approach to ethics regulation: institutional design, implementation and accountability. The approach evolved in two distinct stages. After a first phase of extensive institution building, problems and difficulties began to emerge, as the new processes began to bite. Some critics were concerned that implementation was inadequate, others that there were shortcomings in the accountability of the new institutions. The enhanced transparency encouraged by the CSPL seemed to some observers to exacerbate negative attitudes towards office-holders. Thus the regulation of ethical issues became increasingly controversial as the CSPL had to negotiate a more complex political environment, with some of the criticism falling back on the Committee itself.

The new ethical machinery constructed since 1994 (including the CSPL itself) has also had to fit into a well-established and much larger set of institutions that help deliver accountability and audit in the United Kingdom, and combat corruption and fraud. Thus, on the formal side, the new machinery has overlapped with pre-existing parliamentary committees, ombudsmen, courts and tribunals and the specialist agencies which deal with fraud, corruption and related offences. And on the informal side it meshes with, and depends on, an attentive and vigorous media, concerned interest groups, protections for whistle-blowers, and freedom of information laws, all of which, as Nolan recognised from the beginning, are essential to uncovering and publicising wrong-doing in the public sector. That overlap has been a matter of increasing debate in recent years. Some observers have been concerned that it has resulted in a complex and less than optimal overall structure.[1]

Besides institutional fit, the Committee has also had to be sensitive to cultural context. The character and attitude of the people who implement ethics rules, and the culture they promote, are also crucial parts of an integrity system. How seriously those in authority take the goals of enhancing standards is an essential element in the transmission of values throughout the public life, so the values promoted through organisations to elected representatives and public officials are also vital to the success of any new regulatory regime.

The Committee on Standards in Public Life

The Major government's response to the sleaze crisis of the early 1990s might have been the traditional response to a problem engaging a government's honesty or competence. It could have passed the issue over to a judicial investigation or similar body, thereby buying time and diffusing attention and blame. The creation of the CSPL was a radical departure from this pattern. The CSPL was both less and more than a Royal Commission. It was less because its status was that of an advisory non-departmental body, sponsored by the Cabinet Office. It was thus initially dependent on the will of the existing government and given rather little in the way of resources to conduct its work. But it also turned out to be a good deal more. It carved out an unexpectedly robust niche for itself and despite its vulnerable status became a semi-permanent feature of the institutional landscape. Although at times it became an irritant to governments, it was a body to which prime ministers after John Major found it useful to refer difficult tasks not for delay but to endorse authoritative solutions. Examples of such use were the Blair government's 1997 referral to it of party funding and, in a slightly more complex way, the Brown government's 2009 referral of the management of parliamentary expenses. In that case the CSPL had already written to the prime minister indicating its decision to investigate the topic before Brown announced that he asked the CSPL to launch an inquiry.

The Committee's original remit ('standards of conduct of all public office-holders') was significantly extended in 1997 to include the funding of political parties. Much later, in 2013, the remit was further changed to take account of devolution, by removing the devolved governments from CSPL jurisdiction except with their agreement. In 2013 also its remit was clarified to cover all bodies with responsibility for delivering public services – for example private companies delivering government contracts. The Committee was also asked by the Cabinet Office at that time to adopt a more proactive approach to ethical issues, and to contribute to policy development through shorter investigations. Under the chairmanship of Sir Christopher Kelly (2008–2013) and his successor, Lord Bew, it started to respond more proactively to current issues, like the ethics of policing and lobbying.[2]

The CSPL is not however a direct ethics regulator, still less an 'anti-corruption' agency. Its role is to recommend strategies to improve standards of ethics and propriety. It has no power to impose them. It is non-statutory and has relatively modest resources. There is a small secretariat of three or four seconded civil-service support staff, so, as with parliamentary select committees, most of its 'input' comes from hearings of expert witnesses, though there is also a small research advisory board to supervise a modest amount of public-opinion survey work.[3] Recently the CSPL's original working model has changed and the extensive hearings of the early period have been abandoned in order to meet the 2013 Triennial Review's recommendation of short and more sharply focused inquiries.

The Committee's membership is mostly drawn from individuals with experience at senior level in public management or regulatory bodies, along with two serving MPs. They are paid only per diem allowances, and usually hold full meetings monthly with additional work through sub-committees. The lack of a statutory basis reflects continuing uncertainty about whether the CSPL should be permanent. The 1994 terms of reference suggested the CSPL might stay in existence after its initial inquiry to offer the prime minister advice as needed; but, while this turned out to be the case, it was certainly not guaranteed at the time, and there have been subsequent occasions – when the Committee's recommendations or statements seem to have not found favour with the incumbent government – when the Committee's survival has seemed in doubt.

The remit to cover 'standards of conduct' leaves a certain ambiguity over the Committee's relationship with bodies charged with addressing criminal corruption. The CSPL's remit to protect 'standards' clearly has a relationship with corruption, but corruption is at the far point of the spectrum of misconduct and there is an important analytic and practical distinction between criminal corruption on the one hand and, on the other, the conflicts of interest and sub-standard behaviour which absorb most of the CSPL's time. Although some critics such as Transparency International have argued for a centralised anti-corruption agency, responsibility for preventing corruption in the United Kingdom remains highly dispersed. The CSPL as constituted has neither the resources nor the expertise – and certainly not the remit – to take on the task of reforming or managing the criminal justice system as it relates to corruption in public life.[4] In fact there has been a clear dividing line which the CSPL (and indeed some other ethics regulators) do not cross. The criminal justice system has its own professionalised and specialised institutions to deal with many different aspects of formal corruption. These include law enforcement agencies such as the various regional police forces and the Serious Fraud Office, the Serious Organized Crime Agency and the Revenue and Customs department (HMRC) as well the investigative arms of government departments and agencies such as the NHS Counter Fraud Service. Corruption is covered by both criminal statute law and some common law offences, addressing bribery and extortion, fraud and conspiracy to defraud, securing a private gain from office, sale of office, violation of party funding and electoral law, and theft of public property, false accounting and corruption of foreign officials.[5] Reform in several of these areas has been slow, but eventually forthcoming. From the 1970s, there was ongoing controversy about corruption law reform[6] but it took almost three decades to pass the 2010 Bribery Act, forced eventually by the requirements of the OECD anti-bribery convention.[7]

Drafting corruption law to address the many different forms of criminal behaviour that officials and private individuals can use to corrupt holders of public offices has proved technically complex. It has been an unspoken premise of the remit of the CSPL that it does not contain, and shall not be given, the expertise or resources to take on the task of reforming or managing the criminal justice system as it relates to corruption in public life. Those tasks are clearly the preserve of the Home Office (and subsequently also of the Ministry of Justice) as regards policy, and the formulation of law; and the police and judicial system as regards detection and enforcement.

Initially efforts to change the CSPL's role were limited to establishing a more secure quasi-constitutional status with its independence underpinned by statute – like for example the Comptroller and Auditor General and the more recently established chair of the Electoral Commission and the Information Commissioner. A 2012 Report from the

PASC proposed the Committee should acquire the status of a full statutory regulator in the context of wider change in the regulatory framework governing post-employment rules for ministers and civil servants.[8] Earlier, in 2007, that same Select Committee had reviewed the whole landscape of the United Kingdom's ethical regulators, and proposed that the CSPL become a meta-regulator to which all the other standards regulators should be accountable.[9] But these ideas have never been taken up, and indeed were explicitly rejected by the Cabinet Office's 2013 Triennial Review of the CSPL.[10] Giving statutory protection to a regulatory body is in any case not a cast iron guarantee of survival. Both the Audit Commission and the Standards Board for England were abolished after the 2010 election despite their statutory basis. Nor is it clear that linking the CSPL more closely to Parliament would necessarily protect its independence, even if the 2007 PASC review thought it would, and even though some greater accountability to Parliament was advocated by the 2013 Triennial Review.[11]

The CSPL and Parliament

The Committee's relationship with Parliament merits special attention because of its extreme sensitivity. Elected representatives are direct representatives of voters in visible and personal ways. Voters have an expectation that an MP represents a constituency and its voters through a special bond of trust different from that with more anonymous public officials. MPs themselves appear to see this bond as one shaping the role of the modern MP.[12] Thus when MPs or ministers behave inappropriately or improperly their behaviour is more controversial than when non-elected officials are involved. In terms of the size of misappropriated public resources, voters might have cause to be more concerned about questionable lobbying or public sector contracting practices, or about corruption in the police, than about some of the parliamentary practices which have caught media attention. But elected representatives attract a special degree of public interest and are therefore particularly vulnerable to any accusation of misconduct.

A second factor making the handling of impropriety by MPs especially sensitive is the principle of parliamentary privilege which has long been a jealously guarded feature of Parliament.[13] The purpose of parliamentary privilege (which is enjoyed by each chamber of Parliament collectively and by its members individually) is to allow MPs and peers freedom to discharge their duties without external interference. Particular emphasis has traditionally been placed on the protection of freedom of speech inside Parliament (which was given statutory protection by Article IX of the 1689 Bill of Rights) and on the common law right of exclusive cognisance – effectively Parliament's right to control its own affairs. It was not intended as a mechanism to place MPs and peers above the law; although MPs and peers were historically immune from civil arrest and they could not be sued for libel in connection with proceedings in Parliament, it was never understood as a general protection against criminal prosecution. However, the precise scope of parliamentary privilege has long appeared uncertain and there has been particular disagreement about the circumstances in which an MP could be prosecuted for bribery.[14] As a result of both the ambiguities surrounding the doctrine and dissatisfaction with what appeared to be unjustified protections of MPs and peers, there has developed a demand for codification to clarify its meaning. The demand for increasingly strict regulation of parliamentary standards has imposed a particular strain on traditional understandings of parliamentary privilege. Indeed in 2010 the attempt to rely on the doctrine in criminal cases arising from the expenses scandal caused a rare exploration of parliamentary privilege in the courts and brought the issue to public attention.[15] Although, as was made clear in the *Chaytor* case, the definition and ambit of parliamentary privilege is for the courts to define, the government in 2012 published a green paper as a first step towards clarifying the situation.[16] This initiative was the first major consideration of the doctrine since a Joint Committee on Parliamentary Privilege had recommended consolidation in the late 1990s.[17] The 2012 government green paper did not however recommend consolidation, as its predecessor had done in the late 1990s; nor did the Joint Committee which looked at the 2012 green paper and whose broad recommendations against change were accepted by the government.[18]

At the time of the cash-for-questions affair in the 1990s, however, many of the subsequent criticisms of the scope and operation of parliamentary privilege had not come to light and the doctrine was still generally seen as a formidable barrier to the external regulation of parliamentary conduct.[19] Thus when the CSPL, in its First (1995) Report, addressed the issue of how to deal with MPs' financial relationships and the problems of paid advocacy presented by the cash-for-questions affair, it still put the emphasis on strengthening the House of Commons' own regulatory mechanisms:

> The public needs to know that the rules of conduct governing MPs' financial interests are being firmly and fairly enforced. There have been calls for these rules to be put into statute law and enforced by the courts. We believe that the House of Commons should continue to be responsible for enforcing its own rules, but that better arrangements are needed.[20]

The CSPL's First Report did probe in detail the issues surrounding paid advocacy on behalf of outside interests and the subtleties of the distinction between paid advocacy and paid advice. As we shall see in Chapter 4, it considered but rejected banning all forms of outside earnings and it looked carefully at the procedural issues involved in strengthening the existing parliamentary rules against paid advocacy. Throughout, however, it affirmed that these issues should be dealt with by the 'law of parliament', 'the rules of the House' and 'parliamentary procedure'.[21] Even its biggest institutional innovation, the recommendation of an independent Parliamentary Commissioner for Standards (PCS), was firmly within this system of internal enforcement. As we shall see there have been important subsequent modifications of this principle, including the establishment of IPSA as an external authority and the inclusion of lay members on the Standards Committee, the body now charged with oversight of disciplinary arrangements in the House of Commons. The PCS was to have power endowed only by House resolutions, not by statute, to investigate alleged improprieties and to report to the House. The decisions on sanctions remained firmly in the hands of MPs themselves and the rules remained part of the law of Parliament, not the criminal law.

There was however one area – the bribery of an MP – where as early as 1995 the CSPL thought that the law needed to be clarified, perhaps altering the boundary between Parliament and the courts. Bribery of an MP and the acceptance of a bribe by an MP, as the Report explained, would be a contempt of Parliament and could be punished by the House. Yet, while it was quite likely that the same behaviour would constitute a common law offence, there were, as we have seen, doubts about whether the courts or Parliament had jurisdiction in such cases. The CSPL's First Report recommended, as had the Salmon Commission in 1976, that the law be clarified.[22] This, the Report suggested, could be done in conjunction with the much delayed consolidation of the statute law on bribery which Salmon had recommended but which had not at that stage been achieved.

Common threads: principles, codes, independent scrutiny, education and training

The special position of Parliament was a strong factor impelling the CSPL in making self-regulation the key principle of ethics enforcement in the early years of the Committee's existence, but it was not the only one. From the outset there was a very clear focus in all the Committee's work on how to sustain good behaviour and high standards, rather than on how to detect and punish bad behaviour and low standards, including in areas where the sensitivities associated with parliamentary privilege did not impinge. Indeed it could be argued that the same approach was evident in its recommendations on government, the civil service and non-departmental bodies in the First Report and to local government, local spending bodies and the NHS: topics covered in the Second, Third and Fourth Reports.[23] The perspective across all these Reports was set out in what the CSPL called the 'common threads' of its approach: a set of high-level principles (the Seven Principles of Public Life: selflessness, integrity, objectivity, accountability, openness, honesty and leadership), codes of conduct for governance quality, mechanisms of independent *scrutiny* (though not enforcement), and education and training to socialise office-holders into the values that the principles and codes implied.[24]

This approach was established firmly at the start of each Report and it was a methodology still acknowledged even two decades later in the CSPL's Fourteenth Report.[25] It was based on the premise that the precise recommendations that flowed from general principles should be contained in codes of conduct for different sectors of public life. Each sector or institution should adapt their own versions of these high level codes as appropriate. Thus, while the CSPL set out the general governance quality objectives for different areas, it was not prescriptive in detail. It took expert advice about ethical risks facing different sectors and its reports discussed the most appropriate mechanisms for implementing principles in each sector. The Committee's most basic assumption, however, was that individuals and organisations should be encouraged to take responsibility for standards, and that this required the fulfilment of two key sets of conditions: the first was strong ethical leadership at all levels, effective socialisation processes, and the avoidance of top-down solutions which might encourage a mentality of minimal and defensive compliance with external requirements. The second was a high level of organisational openness: transparency and fairness in recruitment and appointments, transparency in relation to the interests of those involved in public organisations and transparency in mission, objectives and performance standards.

The Seven Principles of Public Life therefore expanded into a philosophy for government ethics generally, and an action programme in each area. Their level of generality naturally made them difficult to contest and criticism of their meaning was limited mainly to the possibility of a mismatch between the short descriptors the Committee gave them and their ordinary language meaning and resonance with the general public. Such mismatches eventually led to minor modifications of the principles in 2014.[26] The Seven Principles became widely used and were incorporated in some form into most of the codes of conduct across British public life, including elected legislatures, local government, the civil service, the Ministerial Code, and a wide range of other public organisations. They acquired a brand status and the need for a publicly declared code was rarely contested. As we shall see later, these principles also began to gain traction in the private and voluntary sectors especially where public services were being delivered.

The other two dimensions of the CSPL's strategy – independent scrutiny, and education and training – had a less uniform and less visible impact. Indeed, the evidence about education in relation to codes of conduct remains extremely patchy. Even where there are strong mechanisms for ensuring the resolution of potential conflicts of interest (for example in relation to Parliament and local government), the quality of induction and follow-up training is unclear. Similar weaknesses appear throughout the public sector. Periodically the CSPL has drawn attention to these shortcomings, especially in its Tenth Report in 2005 and in its more recent report 'Ethics in Practice' in 2014, which looked at ethical induction and training.[27]

It has been the issue of independent scrutiny which has caused by far the most controversy because the robustness of the scrutiny mechanisms introduced has turned out to vary a good deal. Independent scrutiny may involve external validation of internal processes or it may involve the creation of an external organisation with real power over internal ethics enforcement. That the CSPL did not advocate a one-size-fits-all model of independent scrutiny was not necessarily a defect. Its basic philosophy was that arrangements had to be flexible to cover the different circumstances across the public service. But the variation in the form of independent scrutiny, and the divergence of meaning of independent scrutiny in different institutional settings, were nevertheless eventually obvious, and generated numerous demands for scaling up to more robust provision. Sometimes independent scrutiny has simply involved processes which were essentially internal to the organisation with little external public transparency and a strong reliance on managerial or internal discipline. In other cases, as with many appointed and salaried public officials, managerial supervision of ethics and propriety brings severe consequences including loss of reputation or career prospects, or dismissal.

The situation is different in relation to elected office-holders. Here political partisanship is a complicating factor. Without a power to dismiss an elected office holder there is a risk that s/he may be re-elected despite any reputational sanction that may occur. Secondly, in a politically rather than hierarchically managed organisation, politics may intrude on the objectivity of the enforcement process. Self-regulation in a legislature may go wrong for several reasons including tit-for-tat exploitation of alleged ethical failures and the inherently democratic nature of power in parties where the rank and file may exercise pressure from below and the leadership may exercise pressure from above to dilute the effect of a finding. A similar malfunction may occur in the executive as well as in a legislature. As we shall see later, although mechanisms may exist for a prime minister to judge the propriety of actions by a minister, the prime minister may ignore these mechanisms if they prove politically inconvenient.

Counter-powers which make internal disciplinary processes uneven have their parallels in bureaucracies. Top level managers have to support those they manage. If the need to sustain morale involves expectations that certain practices will not be policed too heavily, the effectiveness of internal ethics enforcement may be compromised. As we shall see in a later chapter such a situation has arisen in relation to the rules governing post-employment (or so-called revolving-door) conflicts of interest.

Finally, even in the case of full external scrutiny through a statutory external compliance regime, operational failure can arise through asymmetry of information or through conflicts between the different goals of a scrutinising organisation. For example, one widely recognised contemporary regulatory failure is the banking sector. This failure has involved both asymmetry of knowledge between the regulator and the banks as well as an ambiguity of objectives: do we want safe banks or entrepreneurial banks? Later in this book we shall see there is a parallel with the external regulation of party funding. Parties and candidates clearly need external and independent scrutiny of how compliant they are with rules on permissible funding sources and on spending. However, regulators face several difficulties. There will be knowledge asymmetry. There will be a risk of compliance failure as parties which depend on volunteers find difficulty in meeting onerous reporting requirements. And there will be a risk of conflict between regulatory objectives – for example between continuing to rely on voluntary rather than state contributions and ensuring a high level of donor transparency and limiting donation size.

Thus the basic idea of independent scrutiny of ethics and propriety involves difficult and complex choices. There are many ways in which the form of such scrutiny – however well-intentioned and designed – may go wrong, and there are various meanings which can be attached to the concept of independent scrutiny itself. Such scrutiny comes in three basic forms:

General guidelines to public organisations about basic principles and codes to be established, methods of working including publicity and transparency and a general organisational accountability to a sponsoring organisation.

Statutory obligations about essentially internal processes, with legal obligations concerning their use, along with obligatory publicity and transparency of their operation and accountability to a sponsor.

Statutory obligations establishing full compliance regimes run by independent external regulators (who themselves are likely to be accountable to a further sponsor be it a legislature or a part of the executive).

It is important to note that statutory underpinning, which often involves a strong form of regulator, is compatible with both external and internal regulation. It needs to be stressed that all choices have potentially positive and negative aspects. The CSPL over its first four reports chose not to be precise in the definition of external scrutiny. However, since it was introducing a set of principles across the board for most public organisations and was largely in favour of self-regulation (albeit with 'external scrutiny') the Committee tended initially to opt for either the first or the second of the three types listed above.

Learning from doing

The goal of the CSPL in the 1990s was to create an integrity system whose values would act as a deterrent against impropriety and would foster public trust. The Major government had little option but to support the strategy of the Committee and the Labour government elected in 1997 was publicly committed to the stronger ethical regulation entailed by the establishment the CSPL. The early years of the CSPL were therefore its honeymoon period and its most constructive. The institutional infrastructure was created quickly, in the space of four years, following publication of the Committee's first five reports. The Committee's remit – how to pre-empt non-criminal impropriety by nurturing a culture of high standards – became the central narrative of the public ethics debate. Yet reliance on culture and values brought risks. Creating an ethics regime in which values were the main protection against sub-standard behaviour assumed that impropriety could be foreseen, understood and successfully deterred. And, as with all public ethics initiatives, raising the bar of ethical regulation could generate a perception that misconduct was actually increasing. Exposing episodes of misconduct could be taken as evidence of deficiencies in the programme.

The Committee's continued existence increased these risks. After the recommendations for substantive reforms of its early reports it turned increasingly to evaluating the effects of its work. From 2000 onwards most of the CSPL's work for some years was devoted to review, either through broad reports of the way the machinery was working (as in the Sixth, Tenth and Fourteenth Reports) or by revisiting areas where it had already made recommendations, as in the Eighth Report (on the House of Commons), the Ninth Report (the executive), the Eleventh Report (the Electoral Commission) and the Thirteenth Report (party finance). Indeed, after the Fifth Report on party funding in 1998, the Committee did not address a new area until it examined MPs' expenses in 2009.

The CSPL's Fifth Report in 1998, on party funding, and its Sixth Report (*Reinforcing Standards*) in 2002, marked an evolution in its understanding of the impact of its own work. The question of party funding presented the CSPL with new challenges. First, it was clear that, in this field, the strongest version of independent scrutiny – an external regulator with formal, statutory compliance powers – would be needed. Competitive parties could not be expected to constrain their behaviour simply by codes of practice and self-policed reporting systems. Secondly, party funding raised issues of principle where the right thing to do was contested and where strong partisan interests were in play. There are no self-evidently right answers to the question of what should be the level of spending by parties inside or beyond an election campaign nor about the restrictions that should be imposed on donations from individuals or organisations. Indeed there remains in 2015 no consensus about whether parties should be considered as public utilities to be funded by the taxpayer or whether they should remain self-financing voluntary organisations.

The Fifth Report therefore took the CSPL into new territory where stronger principles were required. The Sixth Report (a review of progress from the earlier reports) marked the change from enunciation of principles to evaluation of the effectiveness for ethical machinery introduced following the first four Committee reports. In this evolution there was no rethinking of the principles or, for the most part, of the meaning of the codes of conduct, and little further attention given either to education and training. But changes of approach did become identifiable in the Committee's views on mechanisms of independent scrutiny which were to lead to stronger recommendations in coming years.

Moreover as experience of how the CSPL's provisions worked started to accumulate, the attention of critics of the CSPL focused on the efficiency and accountability of the new regulators the Committee had established and on the impact of the regulatory costs and burdens. All of this created a new context for the CSPL's work which made it more controversial and led, over the next decade, to a good deal of adjustment to that machinery, some of it, such as the modifications to the Electoral Commission and to the Standards Board, requiring legislation.

The CSPL and the changing character of regulatory politics

The evolution of the CSPL's agenda inevitably changed its relationship both with Parliament and with the government. Parliament's increasingly assertive select committees, especially the PASC, interested themselves in ethics and propriety issues and, while their reports often supported the position taken by the CSPL, there was also a degree of institutional rivalry and some implied competition to be the authoritative voice in the field. Successive chairs of the CSPL found themselves summoned to select committees and sometimes questioned forcefully about the regulatory machinery the CSPL had helped design. Also, as we shall see in the next three chapters, the CSPL found itself increasingly returning to the subject of legislative ethics, a topic which did not always win it friends in Parliament. Under Sir Nigel Wicks, the committee's third chair, the CSPL expressed acute concern in its Eighth Report about the effectiveness of the predominantly self-regulatory system for dealing with misconduct in the House of Commons, despite having itself endorsed self-regulation seven years earlier.[28]

It was the relationship with the executive which generated the real tensions, however. The Sixth Report (2000) had already signalled this when it suggested that lobbying inside the executive posed greater ethical threats than lobbying in Parliament, notwithstanding the attention devoted to paid advocacy.[29] The period coincided with Labour's massive parliamentary majorities which inevitably weakened Parliament's scrutiny role, and the CSPL turned its focus onto the increasingly controversial role of ministers and special advisers in relation to lobbying. Two years later, in 2003, the CSPL took a distinctly critical approach when it revisited the relationships at the heart of the central executive, examined lobbying issues involving ministers and their special advisers, and reappraised the relationship between ministers and the permanent civil service. In the CSPL's view important characteristics of the country's public service tradition were by then coming under threat and, in tacit alliance with the PASC, it raised the need for a new Civil Service Act to protect the values it thought at risk.[30] Later in the decade, the CSPL's Tenth Report was very critical of the government's approach to ethical regulation in local government following the Local Government Act 2000.[31] Here, interestingly, the CSPL was especially critical of the highly centralising provisions of that Act and the government's slowness in introducing what became known as 'local self-determination' of conduct issues, discussed in Chapter 12. Such centralisation, the CSPL argued, worked against local government's ability to take ownership of, and responsibility for, ethics issues. In 2011, finally, the Committee again incurred the displeasure of the governing parties – indeed of all the main parties – with a new report on party finance that recommended a system of public subsidies for parties that none of the party leaders felt they could endorse.[32]

These tensions are explored in subsequent chapters. They were sometimes said to reflect a change of leadership style from the first two chairs Lord Nolan (1994–1998) and Sir Patrick (later Lord) Neill (1997–2001), both senior lawyers, to Sir Nigel Wicks (2001–2004) a retired civil servant, and Sir Alistair Graham (2004–2007), a former trade union leader and later public servant. Relations between the CSPL and the government were certainly tense during Sir Alistair Graham's tenure. Once or twice Sir Alistair, thought by some to be too ready to give his views on current ethical controversies to the media, appeared to cross the line between consideration of general ethics issues (a matter clearly within the CSPL remit) and to comment on the behaviour of individuals (which was outside it). However, some of the tensions which emerged under the Wicks and Graham leadership of the CSPL seemed close to the surface even in Lord Neill's Sixth Report in 2000.[33] It was during the 2000s that the CSPL's lack of statutory underpinning began to cause speculation that the government might simply abolish the Committee. As we have noted, although its resources were cut after 2000 to recognise that 'the framework' was now in place, the Cabinet Office's 2000 review did not recommend abolition. And once the Committee had survived the 2000 review process it became increasingly difficult to abolish later, as successive governments found themselves increasingly troubled by ethical controversies.[34]

Conclusions

This brief overview of the major components of the United Kingdom's integrity system has focused primarily on the seminal role of the Committee on Standards in Public Life as the catalyst for a new approach to the regulation of ethics in public life. After a relatively consensual start, the CSPL began to encounter difficulties and opposition to its role. The inherent complexity and intransigence of its remit was masked by the deceptive ease with which early reforms were accepted. The focus on values and socialisation, rather than on robust institutional reform, may have stored up for later difficult questions about how to react when this approach failed to work convincingly. Thus in relation to standards of conduct in the House of Commons, the CSPL had to return frequently to the subject because of flaws in the system's provision for independent scrutiny. And although the CSPL might have thought it possible to remove some topics from the mainstream of political debate and to identify shared values which would facilitate a consensual approach, the proximity of much of its subject matter to political life guaranteed political disagreement.

Over the years also the agenda of concerns altered subtly both because of external events like the expenses scandal and because of changes in the political and administrative system, including major constitutional changes such as devolution, and lower-level ones such as shifts in the mechanisms for delivering public services, which entailed evolving relationships between the public and private sector (the subject of a new report from the Committee in 2014).[35] The public's agenda of ethical concerns also altered as new issues such as the morality of the financial sector, the police or the media became causes of concern.

That said, the CSPL has self-evidently played a major and, in cross-national terms, unique role in raising the salience of ethical issues across the public sector and putting in place new institutions to regulate individual sectors. Whether there is enough logic and coherence in the institutions to justify calling it an integrity *system* is a question we shall ask throughout the remainder of the book. Certainly the incremental and somewhat incoherent pattern of the United Kingdom's ethical machinery makes it more akin to the 'bird's nest model' of integrity institutions than to the 'Greek temple' paradigm.[36] As we have already noted, part of the PASC's concern in its 2007 review of the machinery was to get rid of ad hoc approaches to ethics and standards.[37] Greater coherence, the Committee thought, could be achieved by harmonising aspects of how the various regulators worked, by mooring the institutions more firmly in Parliament and by creating a collegial structure for ethical regulators. From the perspective of 2015, although some progress has been made on harmonising (for example about terms of office for regulators), in other respects the ad hoc approach is alive and well and likely to flourish, not least because of government's interest in culling regulatory organisations. How the basic approach of the CSPL was translated into the design of regulatory arrangements for particular sectors, and the difficulties it engendered, are subjects explored in subsequent chapters, beginning with three chapters which address the ethical regime for Parliament.

Notes

1 HC 121 – I Public Administration Select Committee, *Ethics and Standards: The Regulation of Conduct in Public Life*, 2007.
2 Committee on Standards in Public Life, *Annual Report 2013–14*, September 2014, pp. 5 and 21.

3 The budget for 2012–2013 was £517,000, cut in 2013–2014 to £331,000: Committee on Standards in Public Life, *Annual Report 2013–14*, p. 22.

4 Transparency International, *Does the United Kingdom Need an Anti-Corruption Agency?* Policy Paper 4, October 2012.

5 See Nicholls, C., T. Daniel, M. Polaine and J. Hatchard, *Corruption and Misuse of Public Office*, (Oxford: Oxford University Press, 2006), pp. 15–35.

6 *Legislating the Criminal Code: Corruption* (1978).

7 Among the main recent statute changes to the three long-standing Prevention of Corruption Acts 1889–1916, discussed in Chapter 2, are the *Anti-Terrorism, Crime and Security Act* 2001, the *Money Laundering Regulation* 2001, the *Proceeds of Crime Act* 2002, the *Fraud Act* 2006, and the *Bribery Act* 2010.

8 Public Administration Committee, *Business Appointment Rules* HC 1762-1-v, 25 July 2012, 2012–2013, pp. 22–24.

9 Public Administration Committee, *Ethics and Standards: The Regulation of Conduct in Public Life*, HC 121, 29 April 2007, 2006–2007.

10 See Cabinet Office, *Report of the Triennial Review of the Committee on Standards in Public Life*, February 2013.

11 Cabinet Office, *Review of the Triennial Review of the Committee on Standards in Public Life*.

12 For an authoritative comment on the changing nature of pressures on MPs see Wright, T., 'What are MPs for?', *Political Quarterly*, 81:3 (2010), 298–308.

13 For a discussion of the doctrine and its implications in British and US history, see Chafetz, J., *Democracy's Privileged Few* (New Haven: Yale University Press, 2007). For a recent overview see Gordon, R. and M. Jack, *Parliamentary Privilege: Evolution or Codification?* (London: Constitution Society, 2014), and House of Commons Standard Notes, *Parliamentary Privilege: Current Issues*, 16 July 2013 SN 06390.

14 See for example the Salmon Commission on Standards of Conduct in Public Life which argued that statutory offences of bribery and corruption did not apply to MPs; but see also Bradley, A., 'Parliamentary privilege and the common law: *R. v Greenway* and others', *Commonwealth Law Bulletin*, 24:3–4 (1998), 1317–1324.

15 See *R. v. Chaytor and others* (2010) UKSC 52.

16 HM Government, *Parliamentary Privilege*, April 2012, Cm 8318.

17 See Joint Committee on Parliamentary Privilege Session, *Report and Proceedings*, 1998–1999, HL 43I-III and HC 214 I-III.

18 See Joint Committee on Parliamentary Privilege Session, *Parliamentary Privilege: Report of Session* 2013–2014, HL 30; HC 100; 18 June 2013. See also HM Government, *Government Response to the Joint Committee on Parliamentary Privilege*, Cm 8771, December 2013.

19 For a general overview see Gay, O. and P. Leopold, *Conduct Unbecoming: The Regulation of Parliamentary Behaviour* (London: Politico's, 1994).

20 CSPL, *Standards in Public Life: First Report of the Committee on Standards in Public Life*, 1995, p. 4.

21 The terms used vary throughout the First Report (see pp. 19–44).

22 CSPL, First Report, 1995, paras 103–104.

23 CSPL, Second Report, *Local Spending Bodies, Cm 3270, 1996*; Third Report, *Standards of Conduct in Local Government in England Scotland and Wales*, Cm 3702, 1997; Fourth Report, *Review of Standards of Conduct in Executive NDPBs, NHS Trusts and Local Public Spending Bodies*, 1997.

24 See the discussion of 'common threads' in the *First Report*, paras 13–17.

25 CSPL, Fourteenth Report, *Standards Matter: A Review of Best Practice in Promoting Good Behaviour in Public Life*. TSO, 2013, p. 14.

26 CSPL, *Standards Matter*, pp. 23–24.

27 CSPL, Tenth Report, *Getting the Balance Right: Implementing Standards of Conduct in Public Life*, Cm 6407, 2005, and Committee on Standards in Public Life, *Ethics in Practice: Ethical Standards in Public Life* (London, 2014).

28 CSPL, Eighth Report, *Standards of Conduct in the House of Commons*, Cm 5663, 2002.

29 CSPL, Sixth Report, *Reinforcing Standards*, Cm 4557, 2000.

30 CSPL, Ninth Report, *Defining the Boundaries within the Executive: Ministers, Special Advisers and the Permanent Civil Service*, Cm 5775, 2003.

31 CSPL, Tenth Report, *Getting the Balance Right: Implementing Standards in Public Life*, Cm 6407, 2005.

32 CSPL, *Political Party Finance: Ending the Big Donor Culture: Thirteenth Report of the Committee on Standards in Public Life*, Cm 8208, 2011.

33 CSPL, *Reinforcing Standards*.

34 Central Secretariat Cabinet Office, *Report of the Quinquennial Review of the Committee on Standards in Public Life*, 2001, p. 1.

35 CSPL, *Ethical Standards for Providers of Public Services*, June 2014.

36 See Brown, A.J. and B.W. Head, 'Consequences, capacity and coherence: an overall approach to integrity system assessment', in B. Head, A.J. Brown and C. Connors (eds), *Promoting Integrity: Evaluating and Improving Public Institutions* (Farnham: Ashgate, 2008).

37 Public Administration Select Committee, *Ethics and Standards: The Regulation of Conduct in Public Life*, HC 121, 19 April 2007, 2006–2007.

4

The House of Commons: the slow erosion of self-regulation

Introduction

This chapter examines the way the House of Commons regulates the conduct of its members. Until the cash-for-questions scandal of the early 1990s the regulation of parliamentary behaviour had been largely dependent upon MPs' own code of honour, underpinned by a body of precedents and rules whose content was often unclear. It was very definitely a system of *self-regulation* which relied for its enforcement on the House itself, notably through the long-established Select Committee on Privileges and the younger Select Committee on Members' Interests.[1] Cash-for-questions challenged this model, focusing public attention on paid advocacy (the acceptance of reward for promoting a cause in Parliament) and made reform of Parliament's traditional approach to disciplinary matters an urgent priority. A detailed agenda for change was set out by the newly established CSPL, created in the wake of the scandal. A new regulatory system for the House of Commons was subsequently put in place by the House. In response to the CSPL's First Report a Select Committee was appointed, the recommendations of which went even further than those of the CSPL itself. It proposed the banning of all paid advocacy and the detailed registration of outside interests.[2] (Box 4.1 gives a timeline of key changes in the House of Commons standards regime.)

This radical overhaul of the House of Commons' integrity machinery generated a Code of Conduct specifying the high-level rules which should govern MPs' behaviour, and a more detailed *Guide to the Rules* governing the registration and declaration of interests and lobbying. It also produced a new Committee on Standards and Privileges to oversee the arrangements, and a new investigating officer known as the Parliamentary Commissioner for Standards (PCS). Nevertheless vulnerabilities

Box 4.1 Timeline of key changes in the House of Commons standards regime

Date	Event
1974	Register of Interests established
1975	Select Committee on Members' Interests established
1994	Cash-for-questions scandal breaks
1994	CSPL set up by John Major
1995	First Report of the CSPL recommends new standards regime for House of Commons
1995	Sir Gordon Downey appointed first PCS
1996	Code of Conduct adopted by House of Commons
1999	Elizabeth Filkin appointed PCS
2001	Mrs Filkin decides not to reapply for her post
2002	Sir Philip Mawer appointed PCS
2002	CSPL's Eighth Report Standards of Conduct in the House of Commons
2004	Review of Code of Conduct
2007	Communications Allowance introduced
2009	Expenses scandal breaks
2009	Parliamentary Standards Act passed. Independent body (IPSA) to manage MPs' expenses body established
2009	CSPL Report MPs on Expenses and Allowances issued
2010	Constitutional Reform and Governance Act amends Parliamentary Standards Act
2010	General election. IPSA begins work
2013	Standards and Privileges Committee divided to allow participation of three lay members on Standards Committee
2014	Standards Committee reviews system of standards regulation
2015	Standards Committee recommends parity of lay members and MPs on Standards Committee
2015	House of Commons endorses parity of lay and MPs membership

remained. The new arrangements enjoyed less than wholehearted support from MPs, and were severely tested by the 2009 parliamentary expenses scandal. That scandal in turn prompted the introduction of a body (IPSA), external to Parliament, to handle expenses, pay and pensions. We examine it in detail in Chapter 5. Finally in Chapter 6 we analyse the House of Lords and evaluate its regulatory system after two decades of adjustment. First, however, we consider why the integrity arrangements of a legislature are so important.

The importance of legislative ethics

The conduct of legislators is an especially sensitive part of any country's integrity framework.[3] A legislature's collective reputation and that of its individual members can have an enormous impact both positively and negatively on the wider polity. Any suggestion of corruption, abuse of public office or simply questionable behaviour will attract intense media attention and public criticism. Even behaviour such as marital infidelity, which could be regarded as private rather than public, may bring the legislature into public disrepute. Yet legislatures find it difficult to respond effectively to ethical problems. In many Westminster-style parliaments, there is no single locus of power so that, when a scandal breaks, providing moral leadership is hard, especially if the executive is itself trying to deflect the issue. Moreover the central role of party politics further impedes the ability of legislatures to handle integrity issues swiftly and dispassionately.

Legislative ethics addresses the behaviour of individual legislators by seeking to reduce conflicts of interest, suspect relationships with outside groups, campaign fund-raising abuses, and the misuse of legislative facilities. But legislative ethics also addresses the *collective* reputation of the legislature. That reputation can be undermined by problems now common to any partisan political process: the distortion of information, 'spin', manipulation and dishonesty which are all more likely to be driven by party interest rather than that of the individual representative.

Public opinion is often critical of legislatures as institutions as well as of their individual members. The surveys of public attitudes undertaken by the CSPL suggest that in the United Kingdom the public is concerned about basic honesty, financial prudence and the need for selfless dedication to public service. The 2012 Survey suggested that on almost every measure public satisfaction with the conduct of MPs had declined since the preceding survey which had been conducted in 2010/2011 after the expenses scandal (see Figure 6).[4] Only 20 per cent of respondents in 2012 believed that MPs told the truth and a mere 28 per cent thought they were dedicated to doing a good job for the public. Such scepticism about the probity of MPs may be unfair but it is at the very least worrying. There is, as witnesses to the Standards Review Sub-Committee of the House of Commons emphasised in June 2014, a serious lack of public confidence in the integrity of MPs despite the relatively low levels of misconduct and corruption in the British Parliament.[5]

Unethical behaviour can obviously damage the legitimacy of the legislature itself and by extension that of the political class. Such damage

6 Perceptions of MP conduct (England) 2004–2010

Source: Committee on Standards in Public Life, *Survey of Public Attitudes Towards Conduct in Public Life, 2012*

is especially likely to occur if legislators and members of the public view ethical issues differently. Citizens may cease to trust their representatives to represent them or lose confidence in their integrity. Unethical conduct in a legislature also carries with it other dangers. Legislators retain privileged access to decision-makers, both elected and non-elected; and they enjoy significant opportunities to influence policy, the details of legislation, public appointments and budgetary decisions. Such influence can be exerted publicly inside Parliament itself, but it is often deployed below the radar in the private forums of party meetings, informal encounters and normal social interaction.

Types of impropriety in legislatures

The regulation of legislatures is directed towards preventing many different types of misconduct. We have already noted the important analytic and practical distinction between criminal corruption, conflicts of interest and sub-standard behaviour. These categories obviously apply to legislative misconduct. At one extreme there is wrong-doing which is sufficiently serious to attract the sanction of the criminal law, e.g. the fraudulent claiming of expenses. At the other end of the spectrum are minor breaches of the parliamentary rules.

Misconduct will be more severely judged when it is deliberate than when it is accidental. Although legislators will not escape censure simply by claiming ignorance of the rules, rules have a tendency to become dense and complex. The House of Commons' *Guide to the Rules* increased from twenty-one pages to thirty-five between 1996 and 2014.[6] Keeping abreast of all the rules is hard for busy politicians and the very process of regulating legislative behaviour risks generating more accidental 'misconduct' as a by-product, a problem which underlines the importance of inculcating the principles which underpin the rules.

Dennis Thompson's work on legislative ethics distinguishes between three broad types of threat to the integrity of legislatures:[7] general offences, conflict of interest and the abuse of the perquisites of office. General offences involve all conduct that could incur a legal sanction: including fraud and embezzlement, perjury, tax evasion, assault or theft. Parliamentary privilege has never protected MPs against criminal prosecution and, although criminal cases against MPs have been rare, five former MPs were convicted of accounting offences and imprisoned following the expenses scandal.[8] In those proceedings the Supreme Court clarified the scope of parliamentary privilege, rejecting the assertion that the submission of an expenses claim was covered by privilege.[9] Thompson's second category – conflict of interest – is a recurrent concern for a legislature. MPs bring many associations with them to their role and they sometimes combine it with outside paid employment such as directorships. Relationships with interest groups are always delicate. Even when legislative powers are relatively weak, as in an executive-dominated legislature like Westminster, interest groups may still target legislators for help. Earlier we noted that the growth of multi-client lobbying firms in the 1980s generated new ethical concerns.[10] Close relationships with lobbyists threaten the independence of legislators and their primary obligations to the public interest, their electors and their party. Yet, as we see in Chapter 10, there is also a problem for representative democracies if they seek to restrict lobbying activity. The line of acceptable behaviour for both the lobbyists and the lobbied is inevitably problematic. There are also definitional issues about what counts as lobbying, especially as so much public relations is now performed 'in house' rather than through intermediate consultancy organisations.

The leverage of lobbyists may be enhanced by open or secret payments. Such payments may be attractive for reasons apart from simple self-interest. Politicians sometimes need money for an election campaign for staffing an office or to supplement expenses especially if their constituency party is short of funds. The cash-for-questions inquiry revealed that Ian Greer had subsidised the constituency parties of a number of supportive MPs. In 2007–2008 the PCS considered a number of complaints against members of the then Shadow Cabinet who had used donations to fund their offices.[11] A related issue (which surfaced again in February 2015 when two senior politicians, Jack Straw and Sir Malcolm

Rifkind, faced accusations of being willing to lobby in return for pay-ment) is whether the job of an MP should be seen as a full-time one. Although British opinion has been shifting against combining parlia-mentary duties with other work and the then Labour leader Ed Miliband suggested capping such employment, there is as yet no consensus to ban MPs from outside occupations. The focus has thus far been mainly on transparency over the scale of payment involved.[12] The requirements became considerably stricter in July 2009, from which time MPs have had to provide detail of outside salaries as well as of the nature and amount of the work, and the employer.[13]

Abuse of the perquisites of office – Thompson's third category – is also a familiar problem for legislatures around the world.[14] Many of the claims in the expenses scandal were evidently abuses of the perqui-sites of office. There such abuses seemed largely for *personal* gain but they can also occur for *party* advantage. Fund-raising, publicity and canvassing for the party sometimes generates improper uses of such facilities as rooms, stationery and dining arrangements. Drawing a dis-tinction between a 'proper parliamentary purpose' for which House facilities may be used – usually related to the representation of con-stituents – and other purposes, whether private or party, is not always easy. It demands scrupulous attention to detail as well as training on the application of the rules. The 2007–2008 session, for example, saw stricter controls on using the House of Commons' dining rooms for direct or indirect party fund-raising events following complaints against a number of Conservatives who were sponsoring fund-raising 'Patrons Clubs' and other dinners.[15] The House also restricted the use of the Communications Allowance (introduced in 2007 but abolished in 2010) to the provision of information for constituents. Campaign-ing and partisan activity were not permissible uses of the allowance. So material on the publicly funded website had to avoid anything which promoted a party, a distinction which created enormous confusion.[16] Partisan activity, even when strictly against the rules, is however a con-stant feature of parliamentary reality. Using publicly funded parlia-mentary staff for party purposes such as by-election campaigning is often so widespread as to be hardly thought of as a breach of the rules since 'everybody does it'.

Through such attitudes MPs and the general public may thus come to exist in different ethical worlds, creating a culture which makes it dan-gerous to leave moral judgments about right conduct to an MP's own ethical sense.[17] Such a gap emerged very clearly over claiming expenses, discussed in Chapter 5. Not merely were MPs (unlike most of the pub-lic) being reimbursed for expenditure such as meals and travel to work but there was only a tenuous link between the claims and parliamentary duties. Moreover MPs were reportedly sharing with colleagues in a so-called 'tea room syndrome' the claims which had been passed by the Fees Office.

The Westminster system and the challenge of reform

Before the 1990s the regulation of parliamentary conduct in the United Kingdom depended on three elements: a code of honour, a strong belief in self-regulation, and a series of historical precedents, procedural rulings and understandings. The Strauss Committee in the 1960s had underlined the ambiguities inherent in such a loose system and in 1974, following concerns raised by the Poulson affair, a register of MPs' interests was finally introduced.[18] By the 1990s, however, this approach was clearly inadequate for a modern legislature. Self-regulation seemed increasingly anomalous when most professions and the business world had introduced independent elements into their own disciplinary arrangements. The code of honour (which depended on the ability of an MP to know intuitively whether an action was right or wrong) assumed a shared set of values which bore little relation to the reality of a rapidly changing polity and looked dangerously dependent on the individual MP's own sense of probity. The unclear status and scope of these norms also left a good deal of ignorance of their content and implications. The First Report of the CSPL, in advocating a code of conduct, observed that it was 'unreasonable to expect that the view of every MP of what is and is not acceptable' would 'produce without guidance a universally acceptable standard'.[19] Thus when the House of Commons was finally forced, by cash-for-questions, to address its standards system, the most pressing need was for a clear formal statement of parliamentary ethics. The 1996 Code of Conduct attempted to fill this glaring gap.

Changing the self-regulatory system was not straightforward, however. It encountered stiff resistance from within the House, despite the fact that there was much more critical scrutiny of MPs' behaviour and increasing scepticism about the right of the House of Commons to be the sole judge of its own affairs. This right, known technically as *exclusive cognisance of proceedings*, had long been a jealously guarded part of parliamentary privilege. Regulation which involved external or independent elements, an anathema to Westminster, was met with a strong self-narrative by MPs that their accountability was to the electorate not a body of parliamentary rules or an unelected outside regulator.

However, after the cash-for-questions scandal MPs themselves could no longer be so confident in such a narrative. Insistent demands for transparency in public life generally, answered eventually in the Freedom of Information Act 2000, together with increasingly aggressive tactics by the media, were the main drivers of change. Growing public access to Parliament's internal proceedings also changed the context in which legislators worked. Televised proceedings provided a not always edifying top-level entry point, and later internet monitoring groups such as 'My Society.org' and 'They Work for You.com' were able to log and publicise attendance records, expense claims, voting and much else. These developments came on the back of ever greater press aggressiveness. In the cash-for-questions affair both the *Sunday Times* and the *Guardian* highlighted the way in which some MPs undertook paid advocacy. The techniques employed eventually became highly controversial. Entrapment of peers and MPs appeared particularly distasteful, reaching a peak in a March 2010 sting by the *Sunday Times* and Channel 4's *Dispatches* programme which showed MPs, including some former Labour ministers, apparently agreeing to engage in improper lobbying activity.[20] But public outrage was invariably a far more powerful force than concern for fairness to MPs or peers.

Despite the crisis of the mid-1990s the changes then enacted, examined in more detail later in this chapter, seemed for some years to address the most urgent questions raised by the scandal. A number of blind spots remained however, and with public controversy over the power of lobbying growing, even the issue of paid advocacy eventually returned to prominence. The most serious problem turned out to be that of the use of parliamentary expenses. In 2007 the case of Derek Conway MP (involving the inappropriate employment of relatives on the parliamentary payroll) opened an intense new period of media investigation.[21] Again, questionable tactics were deployed, this time by the *Daily Telegraph* in its exposure of how MPs were systematically exploiting the expenses system, but the underlying reality of impropriety largely swamped concern about media tactics.[22] Ironically, had the House of Commons moved more speedily to address the issue, it might have averted the disaster that befell it. Its Members Estimates Committee – a six-member body set up in 2004 to consider matters of MPs' pay and oversee the rules on allowances – had been critical of the lax authorisation practices five years before the scandal broke, commenting that: 'viewing a gentleman's word as his bond, beyond all further challenge, belongs more to a 19th century club than to a 21st century legislature'.[23] Unfortunately, however, as a select committee established under standing order, it enjoyed parliamentary privilege and was thus exempt from Freedom of Information requests, thereby delaying for some time public access to the full implications of its work.[24] The scandal that eventually exploded in 2009 was therefore delayed and worsened, necessitating a long court battle over the limits on FoI. When the scandal did finally break, however, any remaining complacency about parliamentary standards was shattered. Permitting MPs to authorise their own expenditure claims (as had occurred in the expenses scandal) became patently unacceptable. At the same time, the scandal prompted further radical questioning not just about expenses but also about self-regulation in general, about the retention of outside interests, and about how MPs could be held accountable for their conduct.

Even after the furore over expenses, however, pockets of resistance to reform remained. Many MPs (especially those newly elected in 2010) proved reluctant to accept IPSA and the new expenses regime. IPSA (which took over management of allowances after the 2010 election) initially had to operate in a climate of bitter criticism from MPs about its ability to support them in their jobs. Equally problematic for building a new culture within the House of Commons was the limited attention given by MPs to standards issues. Thus when the three lay members who had joined the Committee on Standards in 2013 reported on their first year, they noted that the Committee suffered from a good deal of absenteeism and that on one occasion a meeting had been declared inquorate because no MPs were present.[25]

Tools of legislative ethics

Modern legislatures have developed a range of regulatory techniques to enforce standards including codes of conduct and registers of interest as well as dedicated investigative officers.

Constitutional and statutory rules. The internal arrangements of legislatures are rarely found in a constitution but the constitution may exclude certain office-holders from the legislature to avoid publicly sourced conflicts of interest. Frequent exclusions are judges, members of the armed forces and civil servants. The United Kingdom has no formal written constitution, so its rules of exclusion are statutory. The 1957 House of Commons Disqualification Act removed the incompatibility between being a public contractor and membership of Parliament, a change which occurred because, as the Strauss Committee noted, the danger of corruption from such an overlap was then deemed to be low.[26] Until

2001 there was a ban on clergy of the Church of England and of the Roman Catholic Church from sitting as MPs. Hereditary peers (who used to be excluded from the House of Commons) can now sit in the Commons since the House of Lords Act 1999 removed their right to sit in the House of Lords. The House of Commons has traditionally refused to seat bankrupts, persons who had committed electoral offences or who were detained under the Mental Health Act of 1983. However, the Mental Health (Discrimination) (No 2) Act of 2013 removed the prohibition on people with mental health conditions serving as MPs and as members of devolved legislatures.[27]

Declarations of interests. Many legislatures now require their members to register their outside interests. Such interests will include other income, investments, assets, and property and business associations but may also include non-pecuniary assets as well as liabilities and the interests of spouses, partners and close family members. Although a register of interests is a relatively modern tool of legislative ethics, there have long been conventions about declaring an interest before participating in parliamentary proceedings. Recusal – where a legislator *must* withdraw from any proceeding where a conflict of interest might occur – is also a well-established legislative convention. Conflict of interest rules and conventions vary greatly between legislatures. Thompson has urged giving more attention to calibrating the rules *within* legislatures, by adjusting them to reflect the precise role of the legislator, for example if he or she is a committee chair.[28] This issue had been addressed by the Committee on Standards and Privileges after the 2003 decision to pay select committee chairmen.[29] But the much tighter rules which followed (precluding payment for any outside activity which was a result of a select committee chairmanship) seems to have been imperfectly enforced, causing concern to both the Speaker and the CSPL. The issue resurfaced in November 2013 following the criticism of Tim Yeo, a select committee chair who referred himself to the PCS.[30] Yeo had been the victim of a sting which produced a *Sunday Times* article suggesting he had breached the rules by offering to approach ministers and civil servants on behalf of a company in which he might have expected to have a financial interest. It was also alleged that Yeo had coached a witness from a company in which he had a financial interest about giving evidence to the select committee of which he was chair. Although Kathryn Hudson, the PCS, found that Mr Yeo had not been in breach of the rules, she recommended consideration of additional restrictions on select committee chairs to avoid future potential conflicts of interest.

The Yeo case highlighted the difficulties of devising effective rules to avoid conflicts of interest. As a senior MP, he had been elected as chairman of the Energy Select Committee despite having a range of declared interests. The problem of whether special rules should apply to select committee chairs had been a concern for a decade after payment for chairs was introduced though only when a major case erupted was it tackled head on. The scope for public concern, whether justified or not in any particular case, is evident when select committee chairs maintain outside interests and is thus potentially damaging for the reputation of the House.

Codes of conduct. Codes of conduct at both national and sub-national level have become routine features of legislative life in the last two decades. There is, however, a balance to be struck between an emphasis on high level principles and detailed rules. The more such codes become specific, the more they risk micro-managing legislators' behaviour and risk being misunderstood or ignored. The effectiveness of a code will also depend on its enforcement and on whether its precepts are internalised rather than seen as a danger to be navigated or boxes to be ticked. Typically also such codes require frequent revision and systematic efforts to explain their purpose through training and induction sessions.

Internal ethics committees. Self-regulating legislatures have traditionally relied on committees of fellow legislators for their enforcement. Sitting in judgement on colleagues is, however, a thankless task, likely to be complicated by friendship, seniority and party affiliation. Few legislators enjoy serving on such committees. Investigating complex complaints may be difficult without adequate resources. A verdict from a panel of legislators sometimes lacks credibility with the public. Those accused of misconduct may find the adjudication process unfair because, even if exonerated, a legislator's reputation can be damaged. Many legislatures now reinforce regulatory machinery with an official dedicated to the investigation of complaints, to give advice on procedure and oversee the rules. The independence of such an officer depends on the design of the system but it is often difficult for such officers to operate completely autonomously both because of party considerations and because the officer may be accountable to the legislature.

Education and training. Systematic ethical training for legislators is a relatively recent innovation but some parliaments provide induction programmes covering all aspects of the job including the expected standards of behaviour and the avoidance of conflicts of interest.[31] In 2005 the House of Commons provided an information pack for newly elected MPs with material on the Code of Conduct and the rules relating to expenses. Alongside this written material there were party briefings on standards. After the 2010 election (which returned 227 new members or 35 per cent of the whole) the PCS and others devoted a good deal of time to explaining the rules of the House.[32] Nevertheless, the new induction process remained open to criticism for its neglect of ethical issues beyond the formal rules. And there was a good deal of dissatisfaction with the briefings at these induction sessions by IPSA.[33] Induction and training activity may be expected to increase, although there is scepticism about how far legislators take full advantage of it.

Regulation of lobbyists. There are broadly two approaches to the regulation of the relationship with lobbyists (discussed further in Chapter 10). One seeks to regulate the way lobbyists themselves behave, usually by requiring them to register, to adopt codes of conduct and to make public their clients. More commonly, however, the preferred approach regulates the legislators rather than the lobbyists by prohibiting paid advocacy and requiring the registration and declaration of interests. Failure to register an interest and failure to declare an interest are always likely to be significant categories of legislative misconduct. Registration alone, however, does not necessarily fully address the conflict of interest issue. Registering an interest does not mean an MP may promote it freely thereafter.

Self-regulation reformed

All of these tools have been deployed in the British Parliament's efforts to regulate ethical standards. Initially these tools were used with a light touch but that touch has been increasingly tightened and successive changes have substantially modified the system of self-regulation. And, while many of the changes have become consensual, there remain pockets of hostility to the shift in approach.

The Code of Conduct. The first such Code was adopted by resolution in 1996.[34] The Code of Conduct is short and expressed at a 'relatively high level of principle'.[35] As can be seen from Box 4.2 it sets out the public duties of MPs, the familiar Seven Principles of Public Life and eight 'high level' rules of conduct.[36] These eight rules of conduct start with a definition of conflict of interest, 'a founding provision of the code' and move on to prohibit paid advocacy and bribe taking and impose standards on MPs in their public dealings.

Box 4.2 The House of Commons Code of Conduct (2015)

I. Purpose of the Code

1. The purpose of this Code of Conduct is to assist all Members in the discharge of their obligations to the House, their constituents and the public at large by:

   (a) establishing the standards and principles of conduct expected of all Members in undertaking their duties;
   (b) setting the rules of conduct which underpin these standards and principles and to which all Members must adhere; and in so doing
   (c) ensuring public confidence in the standards expected of all Members and in the commitment of the House to upholding these rules.

II. Scope of the Code

2. The Code applies to a Member's conduct which relates in any way to their membership of the House. The Code does not seek to regulate the conduct of Members in their purely private and personal lives or in the conduct of their wider public lives unless such conduct significantly damages the reputation and integrity of the House of Commons as a whole or of its Members generally.

3. The obligations set out in this Code are complementary to those which apply to all Members by virtue of the procedural and other rules of the House and the rulings of the Chair, and to those which apply to Members falling within the scope of the Ministerial Code.

III. Duties of Members

4. By virtue of the oath, or affirmation, of allegiance taken by all Members when they are elected to the House, Members have a duty to be faithful and bear true allegiance to Her Majesty the Queen, her heirs and successors, according to law.

5. Members have a duty to uphold the law, including the general law against discrimination.

6. Members have a general duty to act in the interests of the nation as a whole; and a special duty to their constituents.

7. Members should act on all occasions in accordance with the public trust placed in them. They should always behave with probity and integrity, including in their use of public resources.

IV. General Principles of Conduct

8. In carrying out their parliamentary and public duties, Members will be expected to observe the following general principles of conduct identified by the Committee on Standards in Public Life in its First Report as applying to holders of public office. These principles will be taken into account when considering the investigation and determination of any allegations of breaches of the rules of conduct in Part V of the Code ...

V. Rules of Conduct

9. Members are expected to observe the following rules and associated Resolutions of the House.

10. Members shall base their conduct on a consideration of the public interest, avoid conflict between personal interest and the public interest and resolve any conflict between the two, at once, and in favour of the public interest.

11. No Member shall act as a paid advocate in any proceeding of the House.

12. The acceptance by a Member of a bribe to influence his or her conduct as a Member, including any fee, compensation or reward in connection with the promotion of, or opposition to, any Bill, Motion, or other matter submitted, or intended to be submitted to the House, or to any Committee of the House, is contrary to the law of Parliament.

13. Members shall fulfil conscientiously the requirements of the House in respect of the registration of interests in the Register of Members' Financial Interests. They shall always be open and frank in drawing attention to any relevant interest in any proceeding of the House or its Committees, and in any communications with Ministers, Members, public officials or public office holders.

14. Information which Members receive in confidence in the course of their parliamentary duties should be used only in connection with those duties. Such information must never be used for the purpose of financial gain.

15. Members are personally responsible and accountable for ensuring that their use of any expenses, allowances, facilities and services provided from the public purse is in accordance with the rules laid down on these matters. Members shall ensure that their use of public resources is always in support of their parliamentary duties. It should not confer any undue personal or financial benefit on themselves or anyone else, or confer undue advantage on a political organisation.

16. Members shall never undertake any action which would cause significant damage to the reputation and integrity of the House of Commons as a whole, or of its Members generally.

17. The Commissioner may not investigate a specific matter under paragraph 16 which relates only to the conduct of a Member in their private and personal lives.

VI. Upholding the Code

18. The application of this Code shall be a matter for the House of Commons, and particularly for the Committee on Standards and Privileges and the Parliamentary Commissioner for Standards acting in accordance with Standing Orders Nos 149 and 150 respectively.

19. The Commissioner may investigate a specific matter relating to a Member's adherence to the rules of conduct under the Code. Members shall cooperate, at all stages, with any such investigation by or under the authority of the House. No Member shall lobby a member of the Committee in a manner calculated or intended to influence its consideration of an alleged breach of this Code.

20. The Committee will consider any report from the Commissioner to it and report its conclusions and recommendations to the House. The House may impose a sanction on the Member where it considers it necessary.

The Code is supplemented by a *Guide* which specifies the detailed rules on such issues as the registration and declaration of interests, the advocacy rule and the complaints procedure. MPs were initially also given material about proper handling of expenses and allowances, although since 2010 IPSA has provided its own briefings on these topics.[37]

Following a report from the CSPL in 2002 it was agreed to review the Code (and the *Guide*) in each Parliament.[38] A major review occurred in 2004 and a revised Code introduced in 1995.[39] No review occurred in the 2005–2010 Parliament despite the dramatic controversies surrounding expenses and major changes introduced by the Parliamentary Standards Act 2009 and the Constitutional Reform and Governance Act (CRGA) of 2010. In November 2011 and December 2012 the Standards and Privileges Committee recommended changes to the Code and the *Guide* following proposals from the PCS. Although a number of important clarifications were made in these documents, progress in ratifying the new documents was stymied by opposition to what seemed to many MPs an extension of the Code's scope. Although it was recognised that private and personal behaviour should not *normally* be within the scope of the Code, both the Commissioner and the Committee felt that in extreme cases private behaviour could bring the House into disrepute and should fall under the Code.[40] The logic of the proposed change was the difficulty the House had in disciplining members where an alleged offence straddled the boundary between the public and the private or was so extreme as to damage Parliament. Thus in the case of Michael Hancock (who was involved in a civil suit concerning allegations of improper sexual behaviour towards a constituent) no disciplinary action could be taken against him. Initially he was suspended from the Liberal Democratic Party but then resigned from it, choosing to sit as an independent MP. Nevertheless many MPs remained wary of anything which might allow MPs to be censored for private matters and erode their privacy.

These reservations delayed consideration of revision of both the Code and the *Guide to the Rules*. Part of the reason for not pushing forward with these proposals for change was also the drawn out case of the Deputy Speaker, Nigel Evans, who was being prosecuted on a sexual offence. Although he was ultimately acquitted, the whips unsurprisingly were anxious to avoid an extension of the Code to private behaviour at this time. Nevertheless the delay was criticised by the PCS in two successive reports.[41] This failure was, she commented, 'extremely disappointing', not least because the new rules were considerably clearer on certain other issues, including some which have been the subject of inquiries that year.[42] Eventually, therefore, with further delay threatening to prevent the changes coming into effect in the 2010–2015 Parliament, the Committee on Standards and Privileges in November 2014 recommended abandoning the proposed alteration to the scope of the Code on private conduct.[43]

The registration and declaration of interests. The Register is not designed to give information about an MP's income but identifies any 'pecuniary interest or other material benefit' which 'might reasonably be thought by others', to influence an MP's actions, speeches or votes in Parliament. The Westminster emphasis is on *material* benefits – investments, property, payments, employment held by MPs or their immediate family to 'encourage transparency, and through transparency, accountability'.

The structure of the Register of Members' Financial Interests (as it was renamed in 2009) has developed with time. When a compulsory register was introduced for the House of Commons in 1974, it was opposed by some MPs, most famously by Enoch Powell who, although without outside interests, argued that it would detract from the trust that ought to exist among MPs. Few now question its legitimacy, although as we shall see later, the idea took longer to be accepted in the House of Lords. Failure to register an interest properly (even inadvertently) is a breach of the Code of Conduct and incomplete or inaccurate registration of interests is a major source of complaints against MPs.

Putting a register in place is, however, only a first step: its coverage and enforcement may be contested. In 1974 it used nine categories which, as can be seen from Table 4.1, had expanded to twelve by 2012. In April 2009 the House added the requirement for detailed information in the first three categories – directorships, remunerated employment and clients – and required the precise level of individual payments and the nature and hours of the work carried out for payment. It required the information on a monthly basis regardless of the amounts involved or whether income was the product of an MP's parliamentary status. In 2011 the rule was relaxed to exempt very small payments from registration.[44] The proposed changes to the *Guide to the Rules* brought forward in 2012 recommended reducing the number of registration categories from twelve to ten with a single employment category.

Separate registers exist for other groups whose privileged access to Westminster could produce a conflict of interest especially if they have relationships with lobbyists. There is a register for the numerous secretaries and research assistants, journalists with access to Westminster and for the all-party groups who bring together peers and MPs interested in particular subjects such as cancer or distinct geographic areas. These all-party groups are especially vulnerable to infiltration by lobbying

Table 4.1 Categories of interest of House of Commons register of financial interests 2015

	Category	Coverage
1.	Directorships	Members must register the precise amount of each individual payment made in relation to any directorship, the nature of the work carried on in return for that payment, the number of hours worked during the period to which that payment relates. Annual remuneration to be registered in bands of £5,000 (e.g. up to £5,000, £5,001–£10,000).
2	Remunerated employment office profession, etc.	All employment outside the House and any other category. Annual remuneration which do not fall clearly within any other category. Annual remuneration to be registered in bands of £5,000.
3	Clients	In respect of any paid employment registered in Category 1 and 2 any provision to clients of services. If a Member is employed as a parliamentary adviser by a firm which is itself a consultancy, he or she should register under this category any clients of that firm to which he or she has personally provided services. In addition the Member should register any clients of the consultancy known to have benefited from such advice.
4	Sponsorships	Any donation received by a Member's constituency party or association, or relevant grouping of associations which is linked either to candidacy at an election or to membership of the House; and (b) any other form of financial or material support as a Member of Parliament, amounting to more than £1,500 from a single source, whether as a single donation or as multiple donations of more than £500 during the course of a calendar year.
5	Hospitality (UK)	Any gift to the Member or the Member's spouse or partner, or any material benefit, of a value greater than 1 per cent of the current parliamentary salary from any company, organisation or person within the UK which in any way relates to membership of the House or to a Member's political activity.
6	Overseas visits	With certain specified exceptions, overseas visits made by the Member or the Member's spouse or partner relating to or in any way arising out of membership of the House where the cost of the visit exceeds 1 per cent of the current parliamentary salary and was not wholly borne by the Member or by United Kingdom public funds.

	Category	Coverage
7	Overseas benefits and gifts	Any gift to the Member or to the Member's spouse or partner, or any material advantage, of a value greater than 1 per cent of the current parliamentary salary from or on behalf of any company, organisation or person overseas which in any way relates to membership of the House.
8	Land and property	Any land or property – (a) which has a substantial value (unless used for the personal residential purposes of the Member or the Member's spouse or partner), or (b) from which a substantial income is derived. The nature of the property should be indicated.
9	Shareholdings	Interests in shareholdings held by the Member, either personally, or with or on behalf of the Member's spouse or partner or dependent children, in any public or private company or other body which are: (a) greater than 15 per cent of the issued share capital of the company or body; or (b) 15 per cent or less of the issued share capital, but greater in value than the current parliamentary salary. The nature of the company's business in each case should be registered.
10	Controlled transactions schedule 7A PPERA	Since 2006 loans and credit arrangements – 'regulated transactions' – have been controlled under PPERA and were previously reportable to the Electoral Commission (further detailed guidance on the treatment of loans is available from the Commission). When a Member is offered a loan or credit arrangement over £500 in value relating to political activities they should confirm whether it is from a permissible source (see paragraph 3 and if in any doubt consult the Electoral Commission for further information), before deciding whether to enter into it. If it is over £1,500 in value, a Member has 30 days in which to report this to the Register of Members' Financial Interests (for permissible loans). Loans over £500 in value that are from an impermissible source must not be entered into.

Table 4.1 (cont.)

	Category	Coverage
11	Miscellaneous	Any relevant interest, not falling within one of the above categories, which nevertheless falls within the definition of the main purpose of the Register which is 'to provide information of any financial interest or other material benefit which a Member receives which might reasonably be thought by others to influence his or her actions, speeches, or votes in Parliament, or actions taken in his or her capacity as a Member of Parliament', or which the Member considers might be thought by others to influence his or her actions in a similar manner, even though the Member receives no financial benefit.
12	Family members employed and remunerated through the parliamentary payroll	Members are required to register the name, relationship to them, and job title of any family members (by blood or by marriage or a relationship equivalent to marriage) employed by them and remunerated through parliamentary allowances (for casual employment, this is subject to a threshold of 1 per cent of a Member's annual parliamentary salary).

Source: http://www.publications.parliament.uk/pa/cm/cmcode.htm.

interests and there are frequent attempts to tighten the rules governing their operation.

Paid advocacy and lobbying. The House of Commons has long banned paid advocacy. Resolutions of 1695 and 1858 enshrined this ban and it was repeated in 1947 following the controversy surrounding an MP's relationship with the Civil Service Clerical Union.[45] Nevertheless various forms of linkages to lobbyists and interest groups became common and were tolerated until the cash-for-questions scandal exploded. The CSPL in its first report did not seek to ban relationships between MPs and outside interests but drew a distinction between paid advice and paid advocacy, although the line is one difficult to maintain. In November 1995 the House of Commons, in a move which was more restrictive than the CSPL recommended, amended its 1947 resolution on advocacy. The strengthened advocacy rule of 1995 asserted that:

> no Members of the House shall, in consideration of any remuneration, fee, payment or reward or benefit in kind, direct or indirect, which the member or any member of his or her family has received is receiving or expects to receive, (i) advocate or initiate any cause or matter on behalf of an outside body or individual, or (ii) urge any other Member of either House of Parliament, including Ministers, to do so, by means of any speech, Question, Motion, introduction of a Bill or Amendment to a Motion or a Bill.[46]

However this strengthened anti-advocacy rule was quickly criticised as a restriction on MPs' use of their expertise – for example by deterring an MP speaking about a country after a funded visit. The Standards and Privileges Committee therefore relaxed the advocacy rule in 2002, substituting an 'exclusive benefit rule' and renaming the advocacy rule as a rule against 'lobbying for reward or consideration'. This exclusive benefit rule, according to the PCS, would forbid MPs from seeking to confer a benefit exclusively on a body in which they have (or expect to have) a pecuniary interest. Although this narrowing of the advocacy rule was seen by some as a retrograde step, the PCS in his 2002–2003 report found the changes to be an administrative improvement and an encouragement to MPs to contribute to parliamentary proceedings.[47]

Lobbying and access remain major problems for Parliament however. In 2007 the PASC returned to the lobbying problem and in 2011 the coalition government was forced to bring forward legislation in part as a response to revelations about ministerial relations with lobbyists as well as to pressure from the CSPL. However, the scope of what became the 2014 Transparency of Lobbying, Non-Party Campaigning and Trade

Union Administration Act seemed to many critics to be inadequate not least in its definition of lobbying and its approach to what was to be registered.[48]

The Standards and Privileges Committee. Until the 1995 reforms, complaints against an MP were dealt with by the Committee on Privileges, a senior committee of the House of Commons, or by the Members' Interests Committee. The cash-for-questions scandal of the 1990s precipitated a reorganisation of these two committees and a new committee – the Committee on Standards and Privileges – was formed.

The Standards and Privileges Committee was generally regarded as an improvement on its predecessors but it was not problem free. The parties and government tried to exert influence over it. Following the Eighth Report of the CSPL, changes in its composition were made to reduce the danger of government influence. It is now chaired by a senior opposition member and even the most junior members of government (parliamentary private secretaries) are excluded from the Committee. The governing party's majority on the Committee was also removed. The expenses scandal severely strained the authority of the Committee, however, with two of its senior members including its then chairman, David Curry, incurring criticism because of their own handling of expenses.[49]

After the expenses scandal and the Twelfth Report of the CSPL, further change occurred.[50] In a radical innovation three lay members were added to the disciplinary process in 2013. The move echoed practice in other professions but it marked another breach in the principle of self-regulation. Lay members do not vote in the main committee on any matters though they can append their opinions to a report and can effectively prevent the Committee from producing an agreed report. The addition caused the Committee to be divided once again, resulting in a Committee for Privileges and a separate Committee on Standards. This move was to ensure clarity for the lay members' responsibilities and to exclude lay involvement in privileges matters.[51]

The change was not enough to restore public confidence in the efficiency of the arrangements and criticism of the handling of the Maria Miller case fed into a more general demand to review the system as a whole. In the Miller case it was alleged that the MP (who was then Secretary of State for Culture) had over-claimed on her mortgage expenses.[52] The PCS found that she had inflated interest on a mortgage which had been extended since the original purchase and ordered the repayment of £45,000. However the amount to be reclaimed was reduced by the Committee on Standards. Her case was complicated by the fact that the claims related to a previous Parliament when very different rules applied. However it was also made more problematic by an apparent failure to cooperate fully with the inquiry. The PCS called Mrs Miller's attitude to the inquiry a 'totally inadequate response'. Although David Cameron initially supported his minister, she was forced to resign. There was much press criticism of the Committee's handling of the case and of the tendency of MPs to protect their colleagues. Not surprising, one remedy increasingly canvassed was an increase in lay participation in all stages of a disciplinary case.

The lay members themselves issued reflections on the robustness of the existing system. In their 2014 observations they found the process of enforcing standards in need of overhaul, not least because of the system's incremental and piecemeal growth since 1995. They observed that a clearer view about the role of lay members was needed. The lay members were also critical of the non-attendance of elected members at what they regarded as a vital committee. And they felt that the Code of Conduct and indeed the system as a whole needed to be more integrated. As a result, a special sub-committee – the Standards Review Sub-Committee – was set up in 2014 under the chairmanship of one of the lay members (Peter Jinman) to review the existing arrangements and it reported in 2015. It urged that the Committee on Standards should develop a stronger voice for ethical leadership within Parliament, drawing on the experience of other legislatures and professions in the process.[53] It also called for equal representation of lay members and MPs, a proposal which was endorsed by the House in March 2015. The Committee on Standards will thus in future be slightly enlarged from thirteen to fourteen members, seven of whom will be MPs and seven of whom will be lay members.[54]

The Parliamentary Commissioner for Standards. One important aspect of the new regulatory landscape from 1995 was the creation of the PCS, an office seen as analogous to two other parliamentary officers, the Comptroller and Auditor General (CAG) and the Parliamentary Commissioner for Administration (PCA). The role of the PCS was to maintain the Register of Interests, to advise MPs on registration, to advise the Standards and Privileges Committee and MPs on the interpretation of the Code and on questions of propriety, to monitor the operations of any codes and registers in force and to investigate any specific matters relating to the conduct of members and to report to the Standards and Privileges Committee (Figure 7 shows the procedure for handling complaints). The new PCS was however established as a non-statutory office appointed by Parliament and responsible to it. Its existence was designed to strengthen the existing regime of self-regulation. But from an early stage there was doubt as to whether the new office had sufficient independent authority to operate effectively in a culture shaped by such a long tradition of self-regulation.[55]

7 Procedure for handling complaints

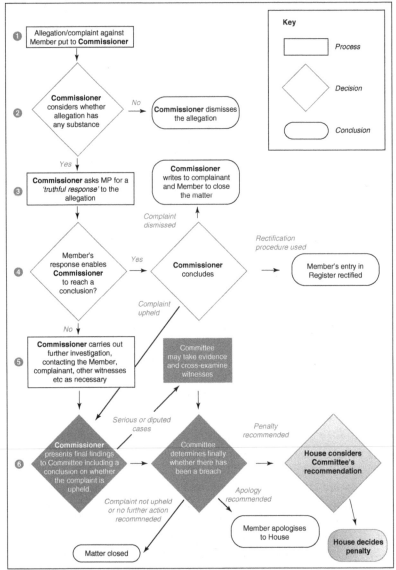

Source: Committee on Standards in Public Life, Standards of Conduct in the House of Commons, Eighth Report, Cm 5663 (TSO, Norwich, 2002) p. 21.

The office holders have shaped its role over the years. Sir Gordon Downey, the first incumbent, made an important contribution, 'chipping away at parliamentary self-regulation' and using advisory and valedictory notes to highlight issues.[56] The new system was inevitably weakened by the Commissioner's dependence on the cooperation of MPs, a factor which was acutely felt by Downey's successor, Elizabeth Filkin, between 1999 and 2001. Mrs Filkin was thought by many MPs to be too pro-active and she was publicly critical of the obstruction she encountered, especially when ministers were involved in complaints. Martin Bell observed a whispering campaign against her from 2000.[57] The decision not to renew her appointment automatically, along with a reduction in her office's resources, caused her not reapply when her initial period of appointment ended in 2001. Her treatment suggested that flaws in the standards regime remained even after the Nolan reforms. However, crit-ics of Mrs Filkin, including former Speaker Boothroyd, urged working with rather than against the grain of the House; and Mrs Filkin's succes-sors, Philip Mawer, John Lyon and Kathryn Hudson, appeared to adopt a more diplomatic tone in their dealings with MPs. Following the CSPL's recommendation in its Eighth Report the PCS is now appointed for a single period of five years to avoid the tension that was generated in the case of Mrs Filkin.

When the office of PCS was established it was assumed that it would be involved in inquiries only where complaints were lodged against an MP. Now it is possible for the PCS to consider issues without complaints being referred to her. This ability to initiate inquiries means that the Compliance Officer of IPSA can refer complaints to her.[58] And MPs may refer themselves for investigation if allegations are made in the media or elsewhere about their conduct, a course which was taken by Tim Yeo in the 2010–2015 Parliament and in early 2015 by two senior MPs, Jack Straw and Sir Malcolm Rifkind, who were caught apparently offering their lobbying services to a fictitious company.

Patterns of misconduct

Analysis of the conduct which the PCS has to investigate reflects the tightening of the rules and the successive changes to the standards regime as well, no doubt, as altered behaviour by MPs themselves. When the post-Nolan reforms were first introduced observers noticed an increase in complaints against MPs reflecting the cash-for-questions controversy, media interest and the incentive to bring charges as part of political war-fare – what has been called 'politics by other means'.[59] Taking the period since 2007–2008, however, several features of the current work of the PCS are evident (see Table 4.2). First, the number of formal complaints lodged against MPs has fluctuated; they were especially high in the period 2007–2010, peaking at 317 in 2009–2010 (the period of the expenses scandal) but subsequently dropped back from 226 in 2007–2008 to 93

Table 4.2 Trends in complaints to the Parliamentary Commissioner for Standards 2007–2008 to 2013–2014

	2007–2008	2008–2009	2009–2010	2010–2011	2011–2012	2012–2013	2013–2014
1. Formal complaints against a named MP	226	192	317	115	109	117	93
2. Complaints subject of inquiry	71	54	80	37	14	10	9
3. Complaints not inquired into	155	160	245	105	101	109	83

Source: Annual Report of the Parliamentary Committee for Standards 2014–15.

in 2013–2014. The vast majority of complaints are not taken further, frequently because they fall outside the Commissioner's remit or are vexatious. If we consider the number of complaints where further investigation has occurred the picture is rather different and an even smaller number merit a report to the Committee on Standards which may then uphold or dismiss the complaint and determines the penalty in any case upheld. In 2013–2014 there were 93 formal complaints but only nine were the subject of an inquiry. Indeed what is striking over this period is the sharp decline in complaints which were the subject of an inquiry from the 2010 Parliament.

Different kinds of alleged breaches of the rules may trigger a complaint. Errors in the registration or declaration of interests remain a major source of allegations of misconduct. The misuse of House facilities such as stationery and the dining facilities can still occur but the handling of allowances, while once a major cause of complaint, is no longer a problem for the House itself since the management of allowances has been handed to IPSA. Sometimes individual cases prompt the PCS to call for another look at the rules as occurred when a major lobbying case in 2010–2011 encouraged the PCS to add his voice to calls for a review of lobbying by MPs and former MPs.[60]

The five cases where the PCS issued memoranda to the Committee on Standards in 2013 to 2014 suggest that some MPs still engage in behaviour which breaches the rules, sometimes exacerbating the breach with a reluctance to cooperate with inquiries. Thus the PCS noted that one MP had not only failed to register payments for a television appearance but had further breached the rules by refusing to cooperate.[61] Failure to cooperate fully also occurred in the case of Maria Miller mentioned earlier.[62]

Perhaps the most serious case in 2013–2014 arose in relation to Patrick Mercer MP (discussed further in Chapter 10) who was exposed in an undercover media operation agreeing to undertake parliamentary work for reward. He was also found to have used offensive language about fellow MPs. This case was found by the PCS to be a sustained and serious breach of the rules on paid advocacy and the Committee upheld the PCS imposing a long period of suspension on Mercer. Mercer resigned his seat.

It is important however to put misconduct in perspective. Many complaints involve innocent errors and are so treated. Serious breaches of the rules are relatively rare and given the improvements to the system likely to be blatant. As Angela Eagle put it in her evidence to the review of the standards system, the vast majority of MPs do comply with the standards required, despite the attention given to the few who do not.[63] Even where evidence of wrong-doing hits the public consciousness as in the expenses scandal – the scale of the misconduct may appear relatively insignificant. Thus Greg Power noted a delegation from the Middle East regarded the expenses affair as 'piddling' and the coverage out of proportion to the misconduct discovered.[64] However, it is clear that even a small number of incidents can damage the reputation of the House of Commons. It is also clear that though the system has been progressively tightened, episodes like the Mercer case can still arise.

Conclusions

Opening his 2009–2010 report the Parliamentary Standards Commissioner John Lyon commented that 2009–2010 (which covered the expenses scandal) was 'the worst for the standing and reputation of the House of Commons in recent memory'.[65] Since the expenses scandal much effort has been directed at restoring that reputation, building on the framework of ethical regulation put in place after 1995. As this chapter has demonstrated, the House of Commons has acquired much new regulatory machinery over these two decades and has refined it to inject greater independence and some external participation in its disciplinary procedures.

How robust the system now is remains a contested question. On one level the system seems to compare well with that of comparable legislatures such as Canada, Australia, New Zealand and the United States and the enhanced power of lay members on the Committee on Standards will further strengthen it. On the other hand there are still some vulnerabilities, or cases like that of Patrick Mercer would not occur. It might be and often is argued that in the most egregious cases of rule-breaking the problem lies in the personalities of those elected rather than in the rules themselves, and indeed that unless the reputational damage an individual faces through flagrant transgression is set aggressively high, a few such cases will always occur. Screening for personality types in representative elections is never going to be foolproof, given that it primarily entails self-recommendation to selection committees and electorates! A more serious vulnerability, or at least one that can more easily be addressed, is the conduct which, although within the rules – for example some types of outside employment, or very high earnings from such employment – is still likely to damage Parliament's reputation. The number of MPs registering employment as advisers or consultants has declined dramatically, as the Committee reviewing the 2009 Parliamentary Standards Act suggested (from 41.6 per cent of MPs in 1995 before the implementation of Nolan to 11 per cent in 2005); but, as was revealed in the aftermath of the 2015 Rifkind and Straw cases, MPs still declare some £7.4 million in outside earnings.[66]

Some MPs, within the rules, retain substantial outside interests along-side their parliamentary responsibilities.[67] Some are chairmen of select committees. While the MPs involved argue that their independence is not in doubt, the appearance of a conflict is difficult to refute. Moreover the continuing presence of the all-party groups at Westminster, discussed in Chapter 10, adds a further vehicle for bringing MPs into close contact with special interests.

Further tightening of the rules – which on the basis of events since 1995 is quite likely in response to new controversy – will continue to be contested. MPs will run arguments that are difficult to refute or verify: that too much intrusion in the interests of transparency may deter individuals from standing for Parliament; that it is good to have individuals who remain 'in touch with the real world'; that too many restrictions on outside earnings or on the ability to retain professional status in, for example, medicine or the law, are also a deterrent; that added complexity is counterproductive in the effort to ensure effective compliance; or that existing procedures already raise difficult questions of fairness to Members because the media storms they raise make a fair hearing hard to guarantee.

Fairness of procedure is notably difficult to judge, especially in serious and contested cases.[68] The disciplinary procedures of the House are not intended to be a court but those who use them expect them to be fair. The CSPL in 2000 recommended a new disciplinary tribunal with a more formal appeal mechanism, possibly incorporating judicial expertise, but this suggestion was rejected by the Committee on Standards and Privileges.[69] However, there is continuing concern about whether the Committee's standards of proof – the civil law standard of 'balance of probabilities' rather than the stricter criminal 'beyond reasonable doubt' standard – is the correct one even though this standard is used in most other professional disciplinary tribunals. Many MPs questioned the fairness of retrospective inquiries of the kind involved in the Legg audit of expenses and were aggrieved that expenses claims deemed within the rules at the time should have been reopened. Others have questioned whether the procedures of the House of Commons in disciplinary matters are compliant with the European Convention on Human Rights. Indeed one MP (Geoff Hoon) did unsuccessfully challenge Parliament's disciplinary processes before the European Court on Human Rights. He alleged that they had violated his rights in several respects including denial of access to a court to challenge the decision. The application was eventually found inadmissible, and the judgement found that the procedures followed gave the applicant a fair opportunity to put his case.[70]

MPs' concerns about fairness, or about the ability of a political career to attract the best and most experienced candidates, would have more force if the one way in which the existing rules could become more effective – better education and training when MPs joined the House of Commons – were treated with greater seriousness by the House itself. Unfortunately, while the House of Commons has begun to make strides in this direction, progress has been slow, and the fault seems as much a corporate fault of the whole House as one of individual MPs.

Ultimately, however, if the House of Commons has been unable to reassure the public that the substantial range of reforms it has made are adequate, and CSPL survey data suggests that this is indeed so, the fault may ultimately lie in the failure of effective collective leadership, itself related to both partisanship and the way power on certain issues is allocated in the House of Commons. Party loyalty shapes all aspects of life at Westminster and it is accordingly difficult for MPs to treat issues of ethical misconduct entirely dispassionately.[71] The system is still liable to be swayed by Westminster's tribal politics which affects the appraisal of individual cases and attitudes to the enforcement of standards. As we have seen, party loyalty seems to come into play particularly when the reputations of ministers or senior MPs are involved. As for responsibility for maintaining ethical standards, this has been spread across different offices and independent bodies such as the PCS. Although traditionally the UK's executive is thought to dominate the House of Commons, MPs are jealous of their ability to regulate the administration of the House itself, and governments, mindful that they cannot control the backbenches by coercion alone, intrude in this particular area very carefully. When in desperation in 2009 Gordon Brown's government did, in the aftermath of the expenses scandal, try to exercise leadership, it quickly ran into difficulty, and quickly had to amend its proposals to head off rebellion. Earlier the government had given little support to the most combative of the Parliamentary Commissioners for Standards, Elizabeth Filkin. Indeed her difficulties illustrated not just this issue but the related one of the constraints which arise when a regulatory agent like the PCS is formally responsible to the body it regulates. Both these problems were present even in the operations of the new expenses regime, established to be external to Parliament. Neither the parliamentary authorities, nor the government leadership, showed the decisive leadership in support of the IPSA which might have been expected, and the reason was clearly that they had to tread a fine line between aspirations for reform, and retention of the support of easily alienated backbenchers. It is to these issues that we turn in the next chapter.

Notes

1 There has long been a select committee to deal with privilege issues in the House of Commons although it has operated under different names. In 1995 a Standards and Privileges Committee was established to replace the earlier Committee of Privileges and to absorb the work of the Members' Interest Committee (which had existed since 1975) and discharge a broader over-sight of standards issues. In 2013 it was split into two committees, the Com-mittee for Privileges and the Committee on Standards.

2 Committee on Standards in Public Life, First Report of the Committee on Standards in Public Life, *Members of Parliament, Ministers and Civil Serv-ants and Executive Quangos and NHS Bodies* (1995) Cm 2850.

3 See Dennis Thompson, *Ethics in Congress: From Individual to Institutional Corruption* (Washington, DC: Brookings Institution, 1995); Preston, N. and C. Sampford with C.A. Bois, *Ethics and Political Practice: Perspectives on Legislative Ethics* (London: Routledge, 1998); Herrick, R., *Fashioning the More Ethical Representative* (Westport: Praeger, 2003); Stapenhurst, R., R. Pelizzo and N. Johnston, *The Role of Parliament in Curbing Corruption* (Washington, DC: World Bank, 2006).

4 Committee on Standards in Public Life, *Survey of Public Attitudes towards Conduct in Public Life*, 2011.

5 See Standards Review Sub-Committee, *The Standards System in the House of Commons*, HC 383, 24 June 2014. Oral evidence of Lord Bew, Richard Thomas and Peter Riddell.

6 See Parliamentary Commissioner for Standards consultation paper, *Review of the Guide to the Rules relating to the Conduct of Members*, January 2012.

7 See Thompson, *Ethics in Congress*.

8 The recent five were David Chaytor, Elliot Morley, Jim Devine, Eric Ills-ley and later Dennis McShane. A custodial sentence of more than twelve months involves expulsion from the House of Commons (and from 2014 from the House of Lords). See also Standards and Privileges Committee, *Former Members Sentenced to Imprisonment*, HC 1215, 2010–2012.

9 See *R. v. Chaytor and others* [2010]UKSC 52 and for discussion see Lip-scombe, S., and A. Horne, 'Parliamentary privilege and the common law', in Horne, A., G. Drewry and D. Oliver (eds), *Parliament and the Law* (Lon-don: Hart, 2013).

10 See Mark Hollingsworth, *MPs for Hire* (London: Bloomsbury, 1991); Leigh and Vulliamy, *Sleaze* and Ian Greer, *One Man's Word: The Untold Story of the Cash for Questions Affair* (London: Deutsch, 1997).

11 See for example Standards and Privileges Committee, *Conduct of Mr George Osborne*, HC 560, 2007–2008.

12 CSPL, *MPs Expenses and Allowances, Supporting Parliament, Safeguarding the Taxpayer*, 2009, Cm 7724.

13 See HC Deb 30 April 2009. However, in 2011 a *de minimis* rule was intro-duced limiting this requirement to sums above 0.1 per cent of an MP's sal-ary for individual payments and 1 per cent for cumulative payments from

the same source for a year. See HC Deb 7 February 2011. See also Gay, O., *The Code of Conduct for Members – Recent Changes*, House of Commons Library Standard Notes 05127, 14 December 2012.

14 For example in 1992 a major scandal erupted in the United States when Congressmen were found to have obtained unauthorised overdrafts using House banking facilities. See Mann, T and N. Ornstein, *It's Even Worse Than It Looks: How the American Constitutional System Collided with the New Politics of Extremism* (New York: Basic Books, 2012).

15 See Standards and Privileges Committee, *Complaints about Alleged Misuse of Parliamentary Dining Facilities*, HC 431, 2006–2007; also, *Conduct of Mr Julian Brazier*, HC 682, 2006–2007, and *Handling of Future Complaints About Misuse of Parliamentary Dining Facilities*, HC 683, 2006–2007.

16 See for example two Communications Allowance cases in the 2009–2010 Session, Standards and Privileges Committee, *David Tredinnick*, HC 66 and *Mr Stephen Byers*, HC 110.

17 Mancuso, M., *The Ethical World of British MPs* (London: McGill-Queen's University Press, 1995).

18 For the Strauss Committee see Select Committee on Members Interests (Declaration) Report, HC 57, 1969–1970. For the debate on the introduction of a register of interests see HC Deb 22 May 1974 and Select Committee on Members Interests (Declaration) Report, HC 102, 1974–1975 For an overview see Doig, A. 'Full circle or dead end? Where next for the Select Committee on Members' Interests?', *Parliamentary Affairs*, 47:3 (1994), 355–373.

19 Committee on Standards in Public Life, *MPs, Ministers and Civil Servants, Executive Quangos*, Cm 2850, 1995, p. 37.

20 See Standards and Privileges Committee, *Sir John Butterfill, Mr. Stephen Byers, Ms Patricia Hewitt, Mr. Geoff Hoon, Mr. Richard Caborn, and Mr. Adam Ingram*, HC 654–1, 2010–2011.

21 See Standards and Privileges Committee, *Conduct of Mr Derek Conway*, HC 280, 2007–2008.

22 The expenses scandal is outlined in Chapter 2 and the next chapter; but for an overview see Winnett, R. and G. Rayner, *No Expenses Spared* (London: Bantam Press, 2009).

23 Members Estimate Committee, *Review of Allowances*, HC 578-I, 2007–2008, para 43.

24 House of Commons (Administration) Act 1978.

25 See Committee on Standards, *Reflections of the Lay Members on their First Year in Post January 2013–January 2014*. Published April 2014.

26 See Committee on Members' Interests (Declaration) (The Strauss Report, HC 57, 1969–1970).

27 See Kelly, R. and H. Armstrong, *Repeal of s141 of the Mental Health Act 1983*, House of Commons Library Standard Notes SN/PC 6168, 19 February 2014.

28 See Thompson, *Ethics in Congress.*

29 Committee on Standards and Privileges, *Pay for Select Committee Chairmen*, HC 1150, 2002–2003; Committee on Standards and Privileges, *Guidance for Chairmen and Members of Select Committees*, HC 1292, 2002–2003.

30 Committee on Standards, *Mr Tim Yeo*, HC 849, 2013–2014.

31 See for example the very useful article by Coghill, K., P. Holland, K. Rozzoli and G. Grant, 'Professional development programmes for Members of Parliament', *Parliamentary Affairs*, 61:1 (2008), 73–98 and Giddings, P. and M. Rush, *Parliamentary Socialization: Learning the Ropes or Determining Behaviour* (Basingstoke: Palgrave, 2011). See also *Parliamentary Affairs* special issue 63:3 (2012).

32 See Parliamentary Commissioner for Standards, *Annual Report* 2010–2011, HC 1328, 2010–2012.

33 See Fox, R. and M. Korris, 'A fresh start: The orientation and induction of new MPs following the 2010 election', *Parliamentary Affairs*, 65:3 (2012), 559–575.

34 See Resolution of the House 19 July 1995: Code of Conduct and Resolution of the House 24 July 1995.

35 *Review of the Code of Conduct for Members of Parliament: Consultation Paper*, 7 March 2011.

36 *Review of the Code of Conduct for Members of Parliament: Consultation Paper*, 7 March 2011.

37 House of Commons, *The Green Book: A Guide to Members Allowances* (revised edition July 2009). Also Standards and Privileges Committee, *Dual Reporting and Revised Guide to the Rules*, HC 2008, 2008–2009.

38 Committee on Standards in Public Life, Eighth Report, *Standards of Conduct in the House of Commons*, Cm 5663, 2002.

39 See Standards and Privileges Committee, *A New Code of Conduct and Guide to the Rules*, HC 763, 2001 and Standards and Privileges Committee, *Reviewing the Code of Conduct*, HC 472, 2004–2005. Also Standards and Privileges Committee, *Dual Reporting and Revised Guide to the Rules*, HC 208, 2008–2009.

40 Gay, O., *The Code of Conduct for Members: Recent Developments*, House of Commons Library Standard Notes 05127, January 2013. HC Deb 12 March 2012.

41 See Standards and Privileges Committee, *Review of the Code of Conduct* 2010–2012, HC 1579 and HC Deb 12 March 2012 cols 85–102.

42 'If there is disagreement with some of the Committee's proposals, MPs would be free to amend them in debate and leadership may be shown by addressing issues transparently and honestly rather than by avoiding difficult decisions.' Parliamentary Commissioner for Standards, *Annual Report*, HC 354, 2013–2014.

43 See Standards and Privileges Committee, *The Code of Conduct and the Guide to the Rules*, November 2014.

44 Standards and Privileges Committee, *Registration of Income from Employment*, HC 749, 2010–2012.

45 The case involved W.J. Brown who represented the Civil Service Clerical Association. See HC Debs 15 July 1947 Vol. 440 Cols. 284–365.

46 Resolution of 15 July 1947 as amended on 6 November 1995.

47 Parliamentary Commissioner for Standards, *Annual Report*, 2002–2003, HC 905, para 2.10.

48 See Public Administration Committee, *Lobbying: Access and Influence in Whitehall*, HC 36 I & II, 2008–2009; for the Cabinet Office consultation document see *Introducing a Statutory Register of Lobbyists* January 2012 (Cm 8233) and *Responses to the Cabinet Office's Consultation Document* July 2012 (Cm 8412).

49 See Standards and Privileges Committee, *Mr David Curry*, HC 509, 2009–2010.

50 CSPL Twelfth Report, *MPs Expenses and Allowances: Supporting Parliament, Safeguarding the Taxpayer*, Cm 7724.

51 Committee on Procedure, *Lay Members of the Standards and Privileges Committee*, October 2011.

52 Committee on Standards, *Maria Miller*, April 2014.

53 See Committee on Standards, *The Standards System in the House of Commons*, HC 383, February 2015.

54 For the debate see http://www.publications.parliament.uk/pa/cm201415/cmhansrd/cm150317/debtext/150317-0002.htm#15031763000004 (accessed 19 March 2015).

55 See the critical comments on the new regime by Oliver, D., 'Regulating the conduct of MPs: the British experience of combating corruption', *Political Studies*, 45:3 (1997), 539–558.

56 Kaye, R., *Regulating Westminster* (Oxford DPhil Thesis, 2002), p. 216.

57 Bell, M., *An Accidental MP* (London: Penguin Books, 2001), p. 178.

58 Standards and Privileges Committee, *Power of the Parliamentary Commissioner for Standards to Initiate Investigations*, HC 578, 2010–2011.

59 Ginsberg, B. and M. Shefter, *Politics by Other Means: Politicians, Prosecutors and the Press from Watergate to Whitewater* (London: Norton, 1999).

60 Parliamentary Commissioner for Standards, *Annual Report* 2010–2011, HC 1328 2010–2011 para 3.42.

61 Committee on Standards, HC 806, 2013–2014.

62 Committee on Standards, HC 1179, 2013–2014.

63 Committee on Standards, *The Standards System in the House of Commons*, ch. 3, para 54.

64 Committee on Standards, *The Standards System in the House of Commons*, ch. 2, para 13.

65 Parliamentary Commissioner for Standards, *Annual Report*, 2009–2010, HC 418.

66 Savage, M., 'Miliband calls for a limit on the outside earnings of MPs', *The Times*, 24 February 2015, pp. 6–7.

67 See Evidence to the Committee on Members Expenditure, *Review of the Parliamentary Standards Act 2009. Vol. 2.*

68 On the Browne case see Ryle, M., 'Disclosure of financial interests by MPs: the John Browne affair', *Public Law* (1990), 313–322.

69 See CSPL, *Reinforcing Standards*, 2000.

70 See *Hoon* v. *UK* ECHR Application 14832/11.

71 On this see in particular Bell, M., *The Truth That Sticks: New Labour's Breach of Trust* (London: Icon Books, 2007), especially ch. 2, which details the role of party politics inside the Committee on Standards and Privileges.

5

The expenses crisis: statutory regulation and its difficulties

Introduction: the ethical blind spot of parliamentary expenses

In the previous chapter we showed how the House of Commons since the 1990s has made adjustments to its disciplinary arrangements to maintain the essentials of self-regulation. This chapter examines the more radical outcome that followed the expenses scandal of 2009, which involved the creation of an independent extra-parliamentary body – IPSA – to handle the management of MPs' expenses and their pay and pensions.

Expenses claims are a problem in many contexts. In the House of Commons the issue was how to provide, as economically as possible, the basic necessities to allow MPs to do their jobs properly: running an office, travel, board and lodging costs away from home, and communication with constituents. Travel, office expenses and communications are relatively straightforward, but how to compensate all but London-based MPs for the costs of running two homes – one in London and the other where they live, usually in their constituency – is more difficult. The actual cost varies a good deal depending on lifestyle choices, where the main home is, and so on. Some legislatures choose simply to pay elected representatives salaries sufficient to meet their own housing needs. The House of Commons had for many years chosen instead to solve the problem through an allowance (the Additional Costs Allowance or ACA) discussed below.

The system turned out to be over-generous and easily exploitable for personal gain. The gain was not huge by the standards of corruption scandals in some overseas legislatures, but it was deeply offensive to voters. It was known to insiders for many years that MPs could make tax-free personal gains on the proceeds of property bought for the purpose of providing a second home in London or in their constituencies; but because expenses were not published it was not known how widespread or open to abuse the practice had become. Nor was it known how liberally many MPs helped themselves to a variety of other accommodation-related expenses that often had little to do with the necessities of running a modest second home. The abuse of the system was a serious ethical blind spot. No one in the House of Commons appeared to realize until too late how repugnant voters would find the arrangements if they became public. From 2005 pressure mounted for expense claims to be published, and in 2009, through leaks of expense claims to the *Daily Telegraph*, the details finally broke, with revelations that created a major political crisis.

The crisis brought a completely new way of running expenses based on an external regulator. This change proved highly unpalatable to many MPs, and difficult to operate. The difficulties stemmed from both the substance of the new regulatory framework and its form of accountability. The public sensitivity of MPs' roles made it necessary, once expenses had become controversial, to move rapidly to a transparent, receipts-based system for reimbursement rather than the earlier very lax system where receipts were not always required. The shift from permissive rules to very tough ones was sudden. It cost MPs the privileges they had enjoyed under the previous system, and became very demanding of their time and attention. A single framework suitable for everyone was difficult to devise and the high level of transparency exposed MPs to what they feared would be significant reputational damage if their expenses claims were even inadvertently inaccurate.

The question of how the new regulator itself should be held accountable was also controversial. The standard route for regulators carrying out policy tasks set by government is accountability *directly* to a government department, and then to the legislature via the government's own general accountability to Parliament. In the case of an agency regulating MPs, however, this would not work. Neither MPs nor government itself wanted the government to have direct responsibility for an agency that regulated MPs' expenses. Many years of difficulty over government intervention in the setting of MPs' salaries had already shown this. The media were ready to be highly critical of government if it was too lenient with MPs, and MPs themselves would be critical if it was too harsh. The solution chosen was therefore to make the new regulator accountable to Parliament, not to the government, though this naturally meant that the new regulator would be regulating the very MPs to whom it was itself accountable.

The expenses scandal in outline

Long before the scandal erupted, the line between MPs' expenses and remuneration had become steadily more blurred. Through the careful designation and re-designation of what was to count as a 'first' or a 'second' home (a practice known as 'flipping'), MPs could at taxpayers' expense make a handsome profit free of the capital gains tax normally payable when a second home is sold. In addition MPs could and did make claims, many of them apparently very extravagant, for household furnishing, servicing and equipment. It is clear that successive governments, embarrassed about approving higher pay for MPs, saw such practices as a way of pacifying financial discontent.

Only a small number of MPs submitted claims which were actually fraudulent, and five were eventually jailed after 2009. But a much larger number submitted claims that were within the rules but clearly manipulative.[1] Administrative arrangements in the House of Commons facilitated this. The Fees Office of the House of Commons managed the process of reimbursing costs, but was ham-strung in dealing professionally and objectively with MPs' claims. This weakness was eventually acknowledged in a report by Sir Thomas Legg, who was asked by the Members Estimates Committee to review the validity of ACA payments between 2005 and 2009. His report identified what it called a 'culture of deference' within the Fees Office. MPs were in effect self-certifying their own claims, there was no external audit, and the Fees Office officials were not acting as civil servants, with an independent duty to the public interest. Rather they had become, in the report's words, 'servants of the House and, while of course supposed to observe and apply its rules, they were also in practice expected to do so in the ways most beneficial to the MPs whom they were there to serve'.[2]

Although expenses issues might be thought to be less serious than the quasi-bribery involved in the paid advocacy cases of the early 1990s, their public impact was much greater. A far larger group of MPs was involved, and the House of Commons gave the distinct impression of having much to conceal. It fought a rearguard action against Freedom of Information requests, and against external auditing.[3] Each stage of resistance simply added to the reputational damage, lending authoritative voices to the campaign for change, and inducing the media to probe more deeply.[4] Beyond the manipulation of personal expense claims, several other issues emerged. The staffing allowance shed uncomfortable light on the questionable practice of employing family members; the London Cost Allowance was evidently drawn very arbitrarily; and the MPs' Communications Expenditure Allowance seemed to involve misuse in partisan campaigning literature.[5] Attention was also drawn to the minority of MPs who had prodigious outside earnings, while still drawing a public salary. When efforts to deny information about all these matters failed, and the House was forced to release detailed expense claims, it still tried to redact information that would allow individual MPs to be identified. The effort to redact rebounded spectacularly. The redacting team leaked. Un-redacted information had to be released anyway, but only after it had appeared in the *Daily Telegraph*.

The public impact was substantial. As a result of Sir Thomas Legg's investigation of improper claims, orders for repayment were made against no fewer than 52 per cent of the 752 MPs whose expense claims over the years since April 2004 he had inspected.[6] The crisis needed an immediate response and, although strictly the matter lay within the remit of the parliamentary authorities, finding a remedy had of necessity to be led by the government (specifically the Ministry of Justice), since the House of Commons authorities had so clearly failed to tackle the problem itself. The natural solution might nevertheless have been to refer the issue to the CSPL as in 1994. In 2009, however, under pressure from an outraged media, the government judged that there was no time for a lengthy inquiry by the CSPL. The result was an immediate move to establish a new regulatory authority, the Independent Parliamentary Standards Authority (IPSA).

To emphasise its commitment to full transparency, the government also decided to subject declarations of financial interest to outside regulation. A new procedure for the registration of MPs' financial interests was established. Strictly, financial declaration was a separate matter from expenses but, with controversy over outside earnings and interests growing, it offered an area where the Labour government, in deep political difficulties, might hope for some partisan advantage, since Conservatives were assumed to have more outside interests and earnings than Labour MPs.

However, the additional provision on financial declarations greatly complicated matters. The bill to establish IPSA was passed in just three weeks, without initial input from the CSPL. Backbenchers had reservations about almost all aspects of the proposed legislation, but were especially critical of the way breaches of the rules on financial-interest disclosure were to be handled. The new arrangements were imposed on MPs against considerable misgivings. The government had to accede to numerous amendments.[7] Eventually, at the Lords stage, opponents forced the government to offer a sunset clause to review aspects of the legislation including the provision for registration of financial interests after two years.[8] There was also uncertainty about whether any part of the new legislation would be further modified in the light of an eventual report of the CSPL. Although the government had legislated immediately in the face of extreme urgency, it had already asked the Committee to conduct an inquiry[9] and indeed somewhat ambiguously committed itself to implement the CSPL report when it eventually appeared. These commitments gave MPs some hope of an eventual rethink, but also created confusion. IPSA was to be established before the CSPL report appeared, and would in theory enjoy full statutory authority to determine the content of the new expenses scheme. So, if the CSPL recommended specific features for the scheme that IPSA disagreed with, there was potential for a clash.

The 2009 Parliamentary Standards Act and the 2010 Constitutional Reform and Governance Act

The 2009 legislation introduced a new regulator with responsibility for setting a scheme for MPs' expenses, a new procedure for administering and eventually setting the level of pay and pensions, and a new procedure for registering financial interests. IPSA itself had two elements: a regulatory board, responsible for establishing what became known as 'the Scheme for expenses' (henceforth 'the Scheme'), and an executive agency, headed by a chief executive, with a staff to operate the Scheme and disburse expenses. The initial staffing level was eighty, scheduled to drop to just half that figure over five years, as the system bedded down and became more automatic.[10] The new system was a major breach in the principle of self-regulation and, unlike the case of the Parliamentary Commissioner for Standards, did not include a mechanism for appealing IPSA decisions back to the House though, as we see in the next section, claims judged improper but not criminal, were, following complaint from an interested party, or following appeal by the MP, adjudicated by the Compliance Officer, who was under the Act technically separate from the IPSA executive.

The shift of responsibility for declarations of financial interest to the new Commissioner for Investigations was different, and there were doubts about its workability even before the 2009 Act was passed. Inside the House of Commons, the Standards and Privileges Committee and the Clerk of the House made vigorous representations to the effect that the Commissioner for Investigations' role would not only conflict with parliamentary privilege, but would become confused with the remaining functions of the PCS. MPs were especially concerned about the fairness of procedures involving investigation and sanction.[11] Under pressure, the government rethought its position, using the CSPL's Twelfth report, which appeared in November 2009, to allow it to climb down. The CSPL argued that there would be confusion between the external role of the proposed Commissioner for Investigations and the internal role of the existing PCS, and reminded the government that financial interests involved matters of parliamentary privilege, whereas expenses did not. The CSPL proposed that the new Commissioner for Investigations might *investigate* a complaint of breach of the declarations rules but should not himself impose penalties. Instead findings would still have to be reported by the Commissioner for Investigations to the Standards and Privileges Committee which would determine any penalty.[12] The CSPL also made the pragmatic argument that the *appearance* of transferring responsibility for financial declarations to an external body might undermine the 'buy-in' by MPs to standards issues more generally, including expenses, without actually adding much external regulatory authority over MPs' financial interests.

These considerations found their way into ss. 23–38 of the omnibus CRGA 2010, passed only months after the original 2009 Act, and just ahead of the 2010 dissolution. The new framework abolished the Commissioner for Investigations even before one was appointed. Responsibility for all aspects of the Code of Conduct, including financial interest declarations, remained with the PCS. Partly to offset this severe downgrading of IPSA's role (with likely consequences for the recruitment and retention of good staff) it compensated IPSA with a new power to set the level of MPs' salaries and pensions. It also it created a new officer, the *Compliance Officer*, with a more restricted role than the Commissioner for Investigations. The latter would investigate non-criminal cases of alleged overpayment and other compliance failures in relation to the expenses Scheme and have power to issue the equivalent of administrative fines in certain circumstances.

The 2010 Act also placed a new and controversial obligation on IPSA, namely that in discharging its functions 'IPSA must have regard to the principle that members of the House of Commons should be supported in efficiently, cost-effectively and transparently carrying out their Parliamentary functions'.[13] This was another concession to parliamentary disquiet, further underlining the tension in IPSA's role between regulator and service-provider and blurring that clarity of mission which is a key condition for the effective operation of an ethics regulator. In effect the CRGA 2010 was weakening IPSA's position even before it began work. IPSA was no one's child. The Brown government was unlikely to be in office after the 2010 general election and so would not have to deal with future parliamentary reactions. It was unconcerned about the administrative capacity of this new agency which, given the immediacy of the general election would have full but completely untested responsibility for the detailed operation of the scheme. MPs seeking re-election from the 2005–2010 Parliament could claim they had been kept in ignorance about how the new arrangements would operate and new MPs could claim they had had no hand in events that caused the new arrangements to be necessary in the first place.

The general election of 2010 thus wiped the slate clean as regards IPSA's paternity. There was a new House of Commons and a new government and no one had to take political responsibility for the reformed arrangements.

Implementing the IPSA scheme for expenses

By the 2010 general election IPSA was required to have designed the Scheme and established a framework for making payments worth nearly £170 million in total, covering more than 180,000 individual claims in a full year.[14] The 2009 Act gave no detailed guidelines on what forms of housing support would be permissible, nor what expenses it would continue to cover. All such matters were now decided by IPSA, which had to explain the scheme to the new House of Commons. MPs who had served in Parliament before were used to far less exacting and transparent arrangements than were now being imposed. Many new MPs had limited personal resources to bridge the gap between incurring set-up costs in their early weeks in office and receiving reimbursement.

Getting the new scheme right was a formidable challenge. IPSA could anticipate that once it had decided on what expenses were legitimate, any changes it made in the light of experience would be closely scrutinised by MPs and the media for evidence that it had made bad judgements, lacked expertise, and had been unnecessarily hard or lenient on MPs. This was exactly what happened. The original Scheme was approved by the outgoing House on 29 March 2010 but almost immediately several obvious changes were necessary and a second edition of the Scheme emerged within weeks of the election.[15] Further changes were introduced in April 2011 and thereafter revisions were made annually.

IPSA's frequently reiterated view was that its major challenge was to provide public reassurance that the manipulative behaviour that provoked the 2009 scandal would not recur. The Scheme was therefore built around the principle of a high level of transparency and a rigorous system of checks to ensure that no claim was paid without validated original receipts. It also established a formal procedure for publication of expenses that encouraged public-interest monitoring organisations like They Work for You to add a new and substantial data-bank of information on MPs to their websites. IPSA's procedures are set out in Figure 8.

The biggest departure from the old scheme was the abolition of the mortgage payments for second homes in favour of payments for rented accommodation in London for all non-London MPs. MPs could opt to rent in their constituency or in London, or could opt to stay in hotels.

8 IPSA's publication process

- **MP makes claim**
  - If approved, paid
  - Published

- **Not approved**
  - MP has 14 days to request review
  - Review process

- **Outcome**
  - Approved, paid, published
  - Rejection confirmed, published

Source: Consultation on IPSA's Publication Proposals June 2010 http://parliamentary-standards.org.uk/transparency/Our%20consultations/Publication/2010/Consultation%20-%20Publication.pdf (or http://goo.gl/ei67ce)

If they rented, the ceiling was around £20,000 per year with reimbursement for some modest communications and security costs; but the previous and highly controversial furnishings claim was abolished. Most other departures from past practice were based on the principle that all allowable expenses set out in the Scheme had to be justifiable against comparable expenses for housing, travel and staff salaries elsewhere in the public and private sectors. Thus, besides the removal of the furnishing allowance, travel costs were kept under stricter control, as regards class of travel. There were also complex new rules for relatives' travel, MPs' travel for special non-constituency purposes, office rental and equipment costs (£22–24,000 per annum for each MP), and staff costs (up to 3.5 full-time equivalents for a total of some £135,000–145,000 per annum).

Getting these details right, operating them in a timely manner, and deciding how much transparency to apply to claims, caused immediate friction between IPSA and MPs. Controversy ranged from arguments of principle about the overall cost of the regulatory burden down to matters of detail about the permissible class of travel. The system was also procedurally complex, especially at the outset when IPSA staff as well as MPs and their staff were learning how to operate the scheme, including its allegedly unfriendly IT base. The MPs' guide to procedure ran to some seventy pages of explanation. More importantly, many non-standard claims were certain to arise in almost all areas. In the past, this had been manageable given the relationship between MPs and the Fees Office staff, much assisted by the lack of public transparency.

Henceforth, under the obligations of economy, probity and transparency IPSA set, these matters were almost certain to generate friction with MPs.

The views of MPs themselves on the scheme are discussed later. Their attitudes were closely connected to MPs' experience of the early stages, during which IPSA encountered numerous operational difficulties and MPs struggled to understand the new rules. MPs' complaints included delays in dealing with claims, lost paperwork which made it difficult to submit revised claims in time, difficulty in contacting IPSA staff telephonically, and an unwillingness on the part of IPSA staff to give advice about the eligibility of particular claims. Many claims were returned to MPs for clarification, and MPs were particularly resentful of adverse publicity if such a return eventually turned into an outright rejection and appeared on the Authority's website.

IPSA quickly realised that in some areas, particularly procurement of office equipment, it needed to be flexible and leave more to the discretion of individual MPs about their needs. IPSA found, in its own words, that it was being drawn into 'micro-management of some MPs' activities … making judgements about what was and was not in support of parliamentary activity that were properly left to the MP'.[16] An early change therefore combined the office-rental allowance with the general administrative budget allowances, and removed a number of restrictions on what could be claimed under office expenses. In the April 2011 edition of the scheme, further significant changes were made to several of the rules: not just to office budgets but also to rules about personal provision and arrangements affecting MPs' family lives. MPs with families were allowed additional funding for dependent children and for family travel. The limits of the defined London Area were narrowed to permit thirty-one additional MPs to claim accommodation expenses. The London Area Living Payment was increased to recognise an unfairness in the travel costs MPs on the outer edge of London could claim; and rules on travel on parliamentary business outside constituencies were also relaxed. MPs were also permitted to decide for themselves when they need to claim for a hotel or taxi after working late in Parliament. The detail seems mundane but it was fundamental in shaping MPs' experience of the Scheme.

In 2011, the National Audit Office conducted a review of the operation of IPSA,[17] reporting to the PAC. It judged that IPSA had established a successful operation given the acute time pressure, that it had gradually increased its own efficiency, and that it had brought down the average cost of claims – a further element in MPs' criticism of the new arrangements.[18] However, the National Audit Office was critical of the balance IPSA had struck between preventing misuse of public money and supporting MPs, and recommended greater attention be paid to the costs falling on MPs by streamlining IPSA's procedures. Herein lay the inherent tension in the IPSA role between being a guardian of propriety and being a service provider for MPs. As the House of Commons started to take up the various tools available under the accountability provisions of the Parliamentary Standards Act, this tension became increasingly apparent.

IPSA's accountability: the framework

Accountability is a necessary accompaniment of independence for all regulators. Accountability in the United Kingdom goes in several directions: to the NAO for value-for-money issues; to the courts for judicial review of maladministration; to the Freedom of Information Commissioner for transparency; to the Office of the Commissioner for Public Appointments for staffing. IPSA also runs a website for public information on MPs' expense claims. Its scheme for expenses, and revisions to it, must be laid before the House of Commons. It must also produce an annual report, annual estimates for its parliamentary vote, and annual accounts in standard forms, including NAO scrutiny.

None of this is unusual. The main anomaly arises in the scrutiny IPSA receives in Parliament. Under the Parliamentary Standards Act 2009, the consultation processes demanded of IPSA were extensive. In preparing the expenses scheme, IPSA must consult:

(a) the Speaker of the House of Commons,
(b) the Committee on Standards in Public Life,
(c) the Leader of the House of Commons,
(d) any committee of the House of Commons nominated by the Speaker,
(e) members of the House of Commons,
(f) the Review Body on Senior Salaries,
(g) Her Majesty's Revenue and Customs,
(h) the Treasury, and
(i) any other person the IPSA considers appropriate.

Its main point of more general performance and budgetary accountability was the committee nominated by the Speaker, namely the Speaker's Committee for the Independent Parliamentary Standards Authority (SCIPSA), which was both the point of reference in Parliament that IPSA consulted about its scheme and in theory also its sponsoring body, speaking on its behalf in Parliament. But SCIPSA was also the filter for IPSA's budget estimate, and thus a significant scrutiniser and critic of IPSA. Two other parliamentary committees were also involved from an early stage: the PAC and the Members' Estimates Committee. The former has responsibility for value-for-money oversight. The latter (which has the same membership as the House of Commons Commission, as discussed in the last chapter) has responsibility for the budget for the administration of the House and many services to MPs. Although its scope was radically reduced with the creation of IPSA, it still covers matters like IT services and financial assistance to opposition parties (or 'Short money'). In addition a third committee (the Members' Expenses Committee) was set up in 2011 when MPs led by Adam Afriye, using new opportunities to choose topics for debate, established a committee to examine the workings of the 2009 Parliamentary Standards Act.

Moreover, even though the main relationship for monitoring the IPSA scheme and budget runs between IPSA and SCIPSA, the government itself, through the Cabinet Office Minister and the Leader of the House of Commons, retained a strong interest in the new framework. Although not strictly departmentally responsible for it in a technical sense, the Leader of the House and the Minister for the Cabinet Office (acting for the Deputy Prime Minister), along with an MP chosen as liaison officer from SCIPSA, jointly responded to parliamentary questions on IPSA, of which there was a constant flow after 2010.[19] The multiple forms of performance accountability IPSA faced through these consultation pressures were formidable. Aided by changes to the CRGA 2010,[20] MPs clearly saw IPSA primarily as a service-provider to MPs, not a regulator, and took the view that, beyond a right to be consulted on the content of the IPSA Scheme, they also had a right to hold the IPSA management to account for the quality of service it provided, since it had a direct bearing on their ability to perform their parliamentary duties.

IPSA therefore acquired an uncomfortable dual obligation to both taxpayers and MPs. The balance between the two quickly became the central focus in arguments between IPSA and MPs. Formally, IPSA was protected by statute, giving it power to set its own Scheme to meet or reject the expense claims of any individual MP. SCIPSA had only the right to be consulted. Select committees had only the power to comment through their hearings and reports. Nevertheless there were pressure points. SCIPSA had the right to approve IPSA's budget. Every three years, it had power over the terms of renewal of the board (though not the appointments themselves). And Parliament had the ultimate weapon of revising the statutory base of IPSA's role. IPSA's capacity to resist depended on the resolution of the IPSA board, how it chose to interpret the balance between its duty as service-provider to MPs, its guardianship duty to taxpayers, and the support it could summon from other quarters, including the press.

Accountability in practice

In its first two years of operation, IPSA was subject to sustained and intensive scrutiny from the House of Commons including:

- A Westminster Hall debate on 16 June 2010 obtained by David Winnick, (Labour, Walsall North), attended by some fifty (mostly Labour) MPs.[21]
- The annual budget hearings of SCIPSA. (The latter examines the IPSA draft main estimate each spring, holds a public hearing with IPSA, and meets for continuing business, including private meetings with IPSA, on average ten times per year. The non-public activity of the Committee is summarised in published summary minutes).[22]
- A House of Commons debate on a motion concerning revision of the IPSA scheme, held on 2 December 2010, moved by Adam Afriyie MP (Conservative, Windsor).[23]
- A debate under Backbench Business on a motion, moved by Adam Afriyie, that an instruction be given to the dormant Committee on Members' Allowances (the nomenclature of which was amended on 7 July 2011 to become the Committee on Members' Expenses) established under Standing Order No. 152G, to review the operation of the Parliamentary Standards Act 2009 and make recommendations.[24]
- The Report of the PAC on IPSA, considering the Report on IPSA conducted by the NAO.[25]
- The hearings and evidence of the Committee on Members' Expenses and its survey of Members' views, published in December 2011.[26]
- A debate under Backbench Business on a motion, moved by Adam Afriyie, recommending approval of the First Report from the Members' Expenses Committee.[27] (The motion in substance was not approved, having been amended on government initiative to refer the report to IPSA for consideration in its next consultation round).
- An exchange of letters running over several months during 2012 between IPSA and the Speaker, concerning the procedure for the appointment of the IPSA board at the end of the first three years.[28]

The tone of this scrutiny was overwhelmingly hostile to IPSA's performance and delivery. The first two SCIPSA budget hearings (2010 and 2011) were notably tense encounters with bitter exchanges of letters between the chair of IPSA and the Speaker revealing a sharp public disagreement over the appropriateness of certain procedures for making public appointments to the board. After the debate on IPSA in December 2010, the prime minister was widely reported as having reassured a meeting of the Conservative 1922 backbenchers' committee that if

IPSA did not change 'it would be changed'.[29] A similarly confrontational theme ran through the hearings of the PAC and of the Committee on Members' Expenses in their examinations of IPSA office-holders. Most challenging for IPSA was the decision by the House to establish the latter committee at all. The two key debates leading to this move regretted the 'unnecessarily high costs and inadequacies' and demanded a simpler and more equitable scheme cutting administrative burdens. It resolved that if these objectives were not delivered by 1 April 2011, the House should amend the Parliamentary Standards Act.[30] To that end it empowered the Members' Expenses Committee to devise a draft scheme based on various principles: value for money for taxpayers; accountability; public confidence in Parliament; the ability of Members to fulfil their duties effectively; fairness for less well-off Members and those with families; and a guarantee that the scheme would not deter Members from submitting legitimate claims.[31] These moves, and others by SCIPSA, the PAC and the Members' Expenses Committee, certainly went beyond broad-overview scrutiny. They challenged the foundations of IPSA's day-to-day operations by subjecting them to microscopic investigation, seeking justification for every policy choice and every operational practice.

There was thus a continuing fundamental disagreement about IPSA's mission. MPs pointed to the 2010 CRGA requirement that IPSA 'must have regard to the principle that members of the House of Commons should be supported in efficiently, cost-effectively and transparently carrying out their Parliamentary functions'. IPSA responded that 'have regard to' did not mean 'accord priority to', that it had been established primarily to restore public confidence and that value-for-money calculations could be constructed in terms of public confidence in the probity of expense claims.[32]

It is of interest to compare the level of criticism received by IPSA with that of another, certainly no less important, ethics innovation of the time, namely the Electoral Commission (EC). The Commission is a close comparator of IPSA for the purpose of assessing appropriate levels of scrutiny. It is involved in direct regulation of MPs' professional lives and is accountable to the House of Commons in very similar ways. It is also subject to scrutiny by the NAO, which conducts regular 'value-for-money' studies, though none, in the EC's early years, was debated by the PAC or made subject of a separate report as happened with IPSA after only a year's operation. Until 2006 no full parliamentary debate was held on the EC, whereas IPSA was the subject of four full parliamentary debates within eighteen months. Most importantly the House agreed to establish the Committee on Members' Expenses, with a remit to review the operation of the Parliamentary Standards Act 2009, in effect turning it into a full-scale investigation of IPSA itself.

IPSA, which touched MPs' interests most immediately and directly, clearly had much the hardest time, but proximity of interest was probably not the only consideration. IPSA's experience was probably also influenced by the CSPL's critique of the level of parliamentary scrutiny received by the EC itself. The CSPL argued in a 2007 report that oversight had been seriously inadequate and the EC was lacking in transparency and confused about purpose.[33] The Committee recommended that henceforth, to improve scrutiny, the Speaker's Committee deal with the EC's budget, and that operational and policy matters should be dealt with by the then Select Committee on Constitutional Affairs.[34] So by the time IPSA was created there was some momentum behind enhanced parliamentary accountability for ethics regulators of this type. The EC certainly faced nothing analogous to the Committee on Members' Expenses and it is doubtful if the CSPL had envisaged that a body like IPSA would, under enhanced scrutiny, be questioned twice in less than two years: first as a result of the CRGA 2010, and secondly by the recommendations of the Members' Expenses Committee.

Ironically, however, it was the government, which the CSPL thought should stay out of scrutiny altogether,[35] which helped save the day by intervening to shore IPSA up, despite its original inclination to keep out of arguments between IPSA and MPs. When the Members' Expenses Committee's report came before the House of Commons in December 2011, the government front bench intervened (with the cooperation of the Opposition) with an amendment to the effect that the contents simply 'be taken note of' by IPSA in subsequent consultative processes on revised schemes and a strong steer to backbenchers to stay in line, which they did. Clearly whatever it thought privately, the government had no appetite for adverse controversy by allowing expenses to be brought back under House of Commons control. For the Opposition there was little partisan gain in siding with the disaffected Tories on a publicly toxic issue.

Thus while few MPs had positive words for IPSA, the majority accepted with some bad grace that external regulation was henceforth a fact of life, perceiving that public opinion, if roused, would not easily accept repatriation of expenses inside the House of Commons. Certainly no MP called for a return to the more controversial aspects of the old Additional Cost Allowances scheme, though a minority appeared to support flat-rate allowances that MPs could use as they saw fit without receipts.[36] On the basis of two surveys in 2011 (by the NAO, answered by 325 MPs and the Members' Expenses Committee, answered by 206) it was unlikely that such a proposal would have passed even with government support. Majorities supported the principle of independent regulation, even though substantial minorities (23 per cent in the NAO survey) did not. A larger minority (32 per cent) opposed the continued publication of all MPs' claims, and 39 per cent in the Members' Expenses Committee survey opposed publication of MPs' receipts.[37] Moreover, on the matter of satisfaction with the operation of the scheme, MPs were much more dissatisfied than satisfied. On the scheme's start-up, on subsistence, accommodation and office allowances, views were overwhelmingly negative.[38] In the end, however, despite this widespread dissatisfaction, there seemed to be a realistic appraisal that making fundamental changes to the new scheme was just too risky.

Conclusions

Accountability, inappropriately used, can be highly corrosive. We argued in Chapter 1 that working relationships between regulating agencies and their sponsors (in IPSA's case the House of Commons itself) need a balance that allows the interaction to include both cooperation and accountability. If serious attempts are made to undermine the regulatory agency, as clearly happened in IPSA's case in its early years, they pose real risks to governance. In the case of IPSA, the relationship is by its nature partly adversarial in the matter of expenses claims. It is IPSA's task to ensure that the expenses procedure is transparent and fully compliant with rules which IPSA itself must set, and which are almost by definition likely to be less generous and more administratively onerous than many MPs would prefer. We also hypothesised that there is a natural tendency in ethics regulation to rely increasingly on detailed codes of conduct, rather than employ a principles-based approach. In the case of MPs this happened both for the financial-interest declarations examined in Chapter 4 and even more firmly in the case of MPs' expenses. When socialisation and self-regulation failed (for expenses it was almost non-existent) compliance with detailed codes was inevitable. The form of accountability to which a regulator is subject clearly depends both on the level of controversy in the area in question, and on the political sensitivity of the institutions and office-holders involved. Regulators may be set unquantifiable or ambiguous goals, and then blamed for matters that are beyond their control. These factors were certainly present in IPSA's case. It was established in an acutely sensitive area, and asked to be both regulator and service provider.

That does not make IPSA a failed institution. The abuses practised until 2009 have been addressed by the establishment of IPSA. With the exception of some controversy concerning repayments to the public purse of gains made on transitional relief granted under IPSA's Scheme,[39] there has been little subsequent controversy, and none comparable to that which erupted in 2009. The level of public interest in expenses, as measured by access to IPSA's website reporting MPs' claims, diminished rapidly after a brief period of interest. No cases of significant new abuse under the new system have come to light, and certainly there is no scope for the most notorious past abuses concerning housing costs.[40] Assuming the new arrangements continue to work effectively, it is therefore likely that this will work through into public consciousness and eventually erase some of the negative perceptions generated by the expenses scandal.

The main focus in this chapter, however, has been regulatory arrangements, not public perceptions. A test of those arrangements must include not only whether they stop abuse but also whether they are accepted by MPs, and whether a broad consensus has emerged about the appropriateness of the new system. On the latter, the jury remains out. The House of Commons has accepted the new settlement in the sense that vigorous efforts by MPs to return effective control to the House of Commons were unsuccessful. Nevertheless, majority dissatisfaction with the delivery of the scheme is unhealthy. For MPs it blurs boundaries. Those who are hostile to regulatory transparency in general can hide behind a claim to be defending their own functional capacity to serve their constituents. For public attitudes, this carries several risks. The strikingly high and aggressive level of scrutiny the IPSA framework encountered from the House of Commons has probably not been much noticed by the public, but it continued to be picked up at key moments by the media, sustaining a potential underlying narrative that MPs remain restive about the regulatory outcome of the expenses scandal. It also generates a permanent vulnerability for IPSA in the way described in this chapter. For a regulator to know that those it regulates are at best diffident towards it, with many openly hostile, and have counter-powers that they can deploy if mistakes are made, is corrosive of self-confidence, objectivity, and ultimately recruitment and retention of staff. The battle of attrition impeded IPSA's ability to settle down to stable operating conditions untroubled by endemic attacks from SCIPSA and select committees, and slowed the process by which MPs have become reconciled to external regulation.

One potential casualty of this difficult relationship was linked to IPSA's other role – the setting of pay and pension levels for MPs. That matter is not considered in detail in this chapter because IPSA's first review and recommendation, to apply in full after the 2015 general election, would not be confirmed until after the 2015 general election. Initially, in determining MPs' pay and pensions, for which it undertook an extensive exercise across 2013, IPSA committed itself to cautious shadowing of broader austerity-driven public-sector settlements, around the 1 per cent level.[41] Eventually, however, it grasped the long-standing nettle of comparability (with legislators elsewhere and with other professions) and concluded that higher pay (albeit tempered by a tougher pensions regime and a scaling back of generous resettlement awards for retiring or defeated MPs) was, in principle, desirable and indeed necessary. Its final 2013 determination was, subject to confirmation after the 2015 general election, to raise MPs' pay in a one-off step by 9.3 per cent (at a time of generally stagnant public-pay awards) from £67,731 to £74,000.[42] The recommendation created an outcry from politicians from Downing Street downwards for the alleged inappropriateness of its generosity. MPs rushed forward to declare they would not accept it (though they did not have to deliver on that commitment immediately, and in surveys conducted by IPSA itself, they had been in favour of rises, depending on party background, of between £77,000 (Labour) and £97,000 (Conservative)). The Prime Minister described it as 'inappropriate' and later raised the possibility of closing IPSA down if it were not to rethink. Other ministers and shadow ministers were even less restrained.[43] Given that by statute IPSA had power to impose the pay rise despite these threats, it remained to be seen whether, after the general election, a new government would allocate time to implementing them. What was clear, however, even if after 2012 the expenses issue itself seemed to have been largely if not completely resolved, was the potential for a continuing difficult relationship between IPSA and its MP stakeholders. Enduring criticism of IPSA on grounds of its competence and excessive regulatory burden looked an unsatisfactory basis from which to persuade public opinion of the need to rethink the way it recruits and rewards its political class.

Notes

1 This chapter does not examine the scandal itself, though it necessarily refers occasionally to elements of it. For the details, see *inter alia*, Winnett and Rayner, *No Expenses Spared*; Brooke, H., *The Silent State: Secrets, Surveillance and the Myth of British Democracy* (London: Heinemann, 2010); Kelso, A., 'Parliament on its knees: MPs' expenses and the crisis of transparency at Westminster', *Political Quarterly*, 80:3 (2009): 329–338; Allen, N., and S. Birch, 'Political conduct and misconduct: probing public opinion', *Parliamentary Affairs*, 64:1 (2011); Allington, N. and G. Peele, 'Moats, duck houses and bath plugs: Members of Parliament, the expenses scandal and the use of web sites', *Parliamentary Affairs*, 63:3 (2010); Riddell, P., 'In

defence of politicians: in spite of themselves', *Parliamentary Affairs*, 63:3 (2010).

2 House of Commons (2010a), Members Estimates Committee: *Review of Past ACA Payments, 348 2009–10*, 11.

3 The recommendation by the Members' Estimates Committee in favour of an external audit was overturned by the whole House in July 2009, leading the Leader of the House effectively to threaten a National Audit Review and a Committee on Standards in Public Life investigation unless external review and the abolition of the John Lewis list (see below) were accepted. See HC Deb 16 July 2008 cc31WS-32WS and Office of the Leader of the House of Commons, *Audit and Assurance of MPs' Allowances*, August 2008, Cm 7460.

4 Notably the Information Tribunal judgment of February 2008, which in justifying disclosure, referred to the 'deeply flawed' nature of the expenses system. See Gay, O., *MPs' Allowances and FoI Requests*, Standard Note SN/PC/04732 (London: House of Commons Library 2009), also Members Estimates Committee, *Review of Members' Allowances 578*, 2007–2008; and House of Commons (2008) Deb 3 July 2008 cc1061–1124.

5 Debate focused especially on the so-called 'John Lewis' list, an apparently generous tariff for second-home furnishings which emerged in 2008: see Russell, B. and N. Morris, 'Nice work if you can get it: MPs keep their perks', *Independent*, 4 July 2008; Porter, A., 'MPs vote to keep "John Lewis" list', *Daily Telegraph*, 4 July 2008. Also Brooke, *The Silent State*.

6 Members Estimates Committee: *Review of Past ACA Payments 348 2009–10*. Three MPs were asked to repay sums over £40,000, 56 sums between £5000 and £40,000, 182 sums between £5,000 and £1,000, and 149 sums below £1,000 (para 100).

7 HC Deb 30 June 2009 cols 207–240, and HC Deb 30 June 2009, cols 244–267. Gay, O., *The Parliamentary Stages of the Parliamentary Standards Bill* SN/PC/05121 (2009), pp. 4–8.

8 HL Deb 16 July 2009, col. 1317.

9 When the scandal became uncontrollable, in the early part of 2009, the government had tried to get the CSPL, which had already announced its intention to establish an inquiry into expenses, to report earlier but the Committee was clear, given the complexity of the task, and the enormous public interest in the issue, that it could not do so before the autumn. Kelly, R., *Members' Allowances – the Government's Proposals for Reform*, Standard Note SN/PC/05046 (2009), pp. 4–8.

10 Speakers Committee on the Independent Parliamentary Standards Authority, *Corrected Minutes of Oral Evidence, IPSA Draft Estimate*, Session 2012–2013, 22 May 2012, Q 23.

11 Committee on Standards in Public Life, 2009 Report 99–100; (ii) Oral evidence, 29 June 2009, paras 37–54.

12 Committee on Standards in Public Life, 2009 Report, p. 100.

13 CRGA 2010, Section 28(2).

14 Independent Parliamentary Standards Authority, *Annual Report and Accounts, 2011–12* (London: TSO, 2012), p. 5.

15 The first version was published as Independent Parliamentary Standards Authority, *The MPs' Expenses Scheme*, 29 March 2010, HC 501, 2009–2010; House of Commons, *Votes and Proceedings*, 29 March 2010, Appendix, Item 31; the second Independent Parliamentary Standards Authority, *The MPs' Expenses Scheme: Second Edition*, July 2010, HC 405, 2010–2011; House of Commons, *Votes and Proceedings*, 26 July 2010, Appendix, Item 57.

16 Committee on Members' Expenses, *Report on the Operation of the Parliamentary Standards Act 2009*, Vol. II, 6 December 2011, 'Submission of written evidence by the Independent Parliamentary Standards Authority to the Committee On Members' Expenses Inquiry into the Operation of the Parliamentary Standards Act 2009' Evidence 75, para 32.

17 Report by the Comptroller and Auditor General to the Public Accounts Committee, 'The Independent Parliamentary Standards Authority: the payment of MPs' expenses', HC 1273 Session 2010–2012, 7 July 2011.

18 Report by the Comptroller and Auditor General, *IPSA, the Payment of MPs' Expenses*, HC 1273, p. 9.

19 While maintaining that IPSA was an 'independent body' the prime minister in a written answer stated in June 2010 that the deputy prime minister would have responsibility for IPSA (HC Deb 2 June 2010 c23–24WMS), a position also confirmed by the Leader of the House (HC Deb 3 June 2010 c587).

20 As we noted earlier, a new section S.28 (2) of the Constitutional Reform and Government Act 2010 explicitly required IPSA to 'have regard to the principle that members of the House of Commons should be supported in efficiently, cost-effectively and transparently carrying out their Parliamentary functions'.

21 HC Deb Vol. 511 cols 137–210 WH, 16 June 2010.

22 Speaker's Committee on the Independent Parliamentary Standards Authority, *Corrected Minutes of Oral Evidence, IPSA Draft Estimate*, Session 2012–2013, 22 May 2012. Documentation (written evidence, estimates, exchange of letters, formal SCIPSA statements etc) related to the annual estimate process is provided on the SCIPSA website: www.parliament.uk/business/committees/committees-a-z/other-committees/speakers-committee-for-the-independent-parliamentary-standards-authority/Publications/. Documentation on the 2010–2012 session is recorded at the archived stable website: www.parliament.uk/business/committees/committees-a-z/other-committees/ speakers-committee-for-the- independent-parliamentary-standards-authority/Publications/Previous-sessions/Session-2010–12/ (both sites accessed 19 March 2015).

23 HC Deb, vol. 519/83, 2 December 2010, cols 1018–1074; 12 May 2011, and 12 December 2011, cols 944–978.

24 HC Deb, vol. 530/184, 7 July 2011, cols 1728–1736.

25 National Audit Office, Report by the Office of the Comptroller and Auditor General, *Independent Parliamentary Standards Authority: The Payment of MPs' Expenses*, 7 July 2011.

26 Committee on Members' Expenses, *The Operation of the Parliamentary Standards Act 2009*, HC 1484.

27 HC Deb, vol. 537/242, 15 December 2011, cols 944–978.

28 Eventually published first by IPSA and then by the Speaker's Office: www.parliament.uk/documents/speaker/IPSA-correspondence.pdf (accessed 19 March 2015).

29 Watt, N. and Stratton, A., 'MPs' expenses body must change or be changed, says David Cameron', *Guardian*, 15 December 2010; Brogan, B., 'David Cameron is ready to dismantle IPSA – will we let him?', *Daily Telegraph*, 16 December 2010.

30 HC Deb, 2 December 2010, cols 1018–1073.

31 HC Deb, 12 May 2011, col 1386.

32 'The Board feels it important to restate that it strikes a careful balance between the interests of taxpayers and those of MPs. We feel that your letter reflects a view which strikes a different balance, leaning more to the interests of MPs. In taking our view of the right balance, we are convinced that nothing can be more in MPs' interests and ultimately cost-effective, than the restoration of the public's confidence in MPs.' (Letter from IPSA to the Speaker about the draft Estimate 2011–2012, published 12 July2011, available at: http://goo.gl/MitMxw (accessed 19 March 2015)).

33 CSPL, Eleventh Report, *The Electoral Commission*, 2007, p. 70. These issues are discussed further in Chapter 12. The CSPL involved itself in these matters only some years after the EC became operational, when it became apparent, following the so-called loans affair during the 2005 general election, that there were complexities about the Commission's statutory role which had led to unsatisfactory elements in both the Commission's remit and in the form of its accountability.

34 CSPL, Eleventh Report, *The Electoral Commission*, 2007, p. 73.

35 CSPL, Eleventh Report, *The Electoral Commission*, 2007, p. 74.

36 National Audit Office, *Independent Parliamentary Standards Authority: Findings from the NAO's survey of MPs*, 7 July 2011, pp. 6–19.

37 National Audit Office, *Independent Parliamentary Standards Authority: Findings*, p. 6; Members Expenses Committee, *Operation of the Parliamentary Standards Act 2009*, p. 67.

38 Members Expenses Committee, *Operation of the Parliamentary Standards Act*, p. 67.

39 'Expenses: MPs cash in again', *Daily Telegraph*, 1 May 2013, p. 1 and p. 4. Transitional repayment arrangements were set out in IPSA, *Annual Review of MPs' Scheme of Business Costs and Expenses* (fourth edition, April 2012), Appendix A, pp. 46–49. The relevant information concerning the alleged un-repaid transitional capital gain is found on the IPSA publication website (www.parliamentary-standards.org.uk/, accessed 30 January 2013) where a database provided information on seventy-one MPs claiming transitional relief, only one of whom declined to make the repayment requested by IPSA. The story ran only in the *Telegraph*, and only for one day, despite its brief front-page status.

40 For 2011 and 2012, the Compliance Officer reported dealing with seventy-six cases, of which fifty-three were judged not to merit substantive investigation. See www.parliamentarycompliance.org.uk/Publications.html (accessed 30 January 2013). The remaining twenty-three were investigated. Of these, twenty were for an identical minor overclaim for the costs of a personal website which proved to contain a party logo, rendering it ineligible for reimbursement under IPSA rules. No reimbursement was however demanded in any case. The remaining cases related to different, but similarly minor matters.

41 IPSA, *Reviewing MPs' Pay and Pensions: A First Report*, January 2013.

42 IPSA, *Pay and Pensions: Final Report*, December 2013, p. 11.

43 'Pay rise for MPs triggers Westminster backlash', *Financial Times*, 13 July 2013 and 'MPs will get 10% rise', *Daily Telegraph*, 6 September 2014.

6

The House of Lords and reluctant reform

Introduction

In the last two chapters we explored the handling of integrity issues in the House of Commons and the changes made by the new arrangements for administering expenses through the IPSA. Although standards issues in the House of Lords have not generated the controversy that they have aroused in relation to the House of Commons, the regulation of conduct there has also been subject to critical scrutiny and substantial reform in recent years. Box 6.1 gives a timeline of changes to the House of Lords standards regime. As the second chamber of the United Kingdom's legislature, the House of Lords retains influence but its role is very different from that of the Commons. Until 1958 the House of Lords consisted almost entirely of hereditary peers who were often independently wealthy. The introduction of life peerages in 1958 reinvigorated the House; but is also brought to the second chamber many more members who needed to earn a living, thereby creating new potential conflict-of-interest problems between parliamentary and occupational roles. The relative absence of ethical issues from the House of Lords also reflected that body's limited legislative powers since the Parliament Acts of 1911 and 1949 subordinated it decisively to the Commons.[1] The constrained influence of the House of Lords made it less vulnerable to some kinds of lobbying activity, although peers continued to provide useful contacts for many interest groups. More recently, the tightening of the rules governing conduct in the House of Commons, together with the more flexible procedures for legislative amendment in the Lords, may have enhanced that chamber's attractiveness as a target for lobbyists. Whatever the cause, the House of Lords has in the last few years felt the need to strengthen its own ethical regulatory regime.

Box 6.1 Timeline of key changes to the House of Lords standards regime 1974–2015

Date	Event
1974	Sub-committee appointed under Lord Elwyn-Jones to consider a Register of Interests for the House of Lords
1990	House of Lords expands the interests which must be declared
1994	CSPL established
1994	House of Lords sets up its own committee of inquiry (under Lord Griffiths) to inquire into standards in the House
1995	Griffiths Report recommends a Register of Interests and a de facto Code of Conduct
1999	House of Lords Act removes rights of most hereditary peers to sit in House of Lords
2000	CSPL report on standards in House of Lords
2001	House of Lords agrees a Code of Conduct
2004	First formal complaint against a member of the House of Lords received
2008	House of Lords decides to supplement general principles of Code of Conduct. Appoints a working group to consider the rules
2008	Concern about parliamentary passes and lobbying emerges
2008	New procedure for handling complaints agreed
2009	House Sub-Committee on Lords Interests reappointed
2009	*Sunday Times* publishes story showing four peers willing to consider lobbying activity in return for reward (dubbed 'Ermingate')
2009	Leader of the House of Lords refers allegations for investigation and asks the Chairman of Committees to consider sanctions available against peers
2009	Leader's Group appointed to consider the standards regime as a whole. Recommends a new Code of Conduct and a new office (Commissioner for Standards in the House of Lords). Recommends a ban on parliamentary advice and consultancies
2009	Allegations of misuse of Lords' allowances scheme begin to surface
2010	Three peers censured for wrongly claimed allowances
2010	Committee for Privileges renamed Committee for Privileges and Conduct. Delegates investigation of conduct issues to Sub-Committee on Conduct
2010	House of Lords appoints its first Commissioner for Standards
2010	House of Lords Reimbursement scheme replaced
2014	Lord Hanningfield suspended over wrongly claimed allowances
2014	Police launch inquiry into Lord Hanningfield's wrongly claimed allowances

The unique aspect of the Lords as a legislative body – that its members are unelected and mainly sit for life – is highly controversial and there has long been a sustained, if inconclusive, debate about its reform. With the defeat of a reform plan brought forward in 2012, the prospect of immediate major change seems remote. However, more limited incremental measures to reform the upper chamber may be successful. Thus the House Lords Reform Act of 2014 made new provision for retirement from the House of Lords and for expulsion from the chamber where a peer has been sentenced to a term of imprisonment of more than one year.

The dilemma for reformers has been how to modernise the composition of the Lords (introducing some element of election) without sacrificing its expertise or independence or creating a body with the legitimacy to challenge the House of Commons more frequently. Paradoxically, the incremental reform of the Lords has in some ways energised it after the long decades of political quiescence following the 1911 Parliament Act's reduction of its powers. The removal of all but ninety-two of the hereditary peers in 1999 and the introduction of greater party balance seems to have enhanced the upper chamber's authority. There have been major defeats of government legislation since 1999 under both Labour governments and the 2010–2015 coalition.

The role and functions of the House of Lords complement those of the Commons but there are very real structural differences between the two bodies. One differentiating feature is size. Until the House of Lords Act of 1999 its potential membership was 1,326.[2] With the removal of 658 of the 750 hereditary peers the number was reduced to 670; but it rose again and stood at over 800 in 2015 – a growth which many informed critics consider dysfunctional.[3]

The process of appointing peers has frequently occasioned controversy. The practice of rewarding party donors with peerages began in the nineteenth century and in the early twentieth century much scandal was caused by the allegation that honours, including peerages, were being sold to fill party coffers. Concern about the relationship between peerages and political gifts resurfaced as an issue under Tony Blair when it was revealed that some of his nominees to the peerage had apparently loaned the Labour Party money, thereby circumventing its own campaign finance legislation. The numbers of peers appointed by Blair also occasioned comment; the period from 1997 to 2000 saw more new peers created than at any time since the initial batch of life peers were nominated under the 1958 legislation. A new non-statutory body (the House of Lords Appointments Commission) was established in 2000 to vet party nominations and to propose non-party nominees. This new body was able to block or delay nominees deemed unsuitable on grounds of propriety and it has indeed effectively vetoed or delayed a number of nominees. The Commission's goal of injecting new expertise into the House has, however, been limited by concerns about the size of House which have caused non-party nominations to be limited in number.

There are also important cultural differences between the two chambers. Life peers generally enter the legislature late in their careers and they will often bring substantial experience as well as pre-existing personal interests with them to their legislative role. Potential conflicts of interest are thus likely to occur regularly and to require careful management. In the Lords a strong code of honour was traditionally relied on to prevent impropriety. The ethos of the Lords traditionally has been voluntarism and unpaid public service, combined with a muted partisanship. There is an emphasis on courtesy and mutual respect and an implicit belief that the achievements which have led to membership of the Lords are testimony to peers' integrity.

Debate about the standards of conduct in the House of Lords has therefore to be set not merely against the background of continuing debate about its future but also against some distinctive features which make the character of the Lords very different from that of the Commons. Certainly, the development of an institutional framework for managing ethics and propriety in the House of Lords (including a Register of Interests, a Code of Conduct, and investigatory machinery) has been slower than in the House of Commons, even though the pace of change in the Lords accelerated greatly towards the end of the period under review.

Regulating standards in the House of Lords

In addition to the general features which distinguish the Lords from the Commons, the upper chamber has several specific characteristics which constrain its ability to set and enforce its standards of conduct. In the past it was difficult to see what sanctions could be applied to peers whose behaviour broke the House's rules and conventions. Peers are not subject to election. The House does not have the power, by resolution, to expel a member and until recently it did not even have the power to suspend a member temporarily. (It could, in extreme cases, expel a member by Act of Parliament.) Thus there were until recently no other sanctions, apart from naming and shaming, available to impose on peers who had flouted its rules. Partisanship, while still a factor in the life of the upper chamber, operates less rigidly than in the Commons and even where a member takes a party whip there are few sanctions or indeed incentives at the whips' disposal.[4] Peers ennobled after full-time political careers in the House of Commons are likely to feel sufficiently secure to take an independent line from that of the party leadership in the Commons. This independence is often considered a great benefit to robust deliberation but it has also until recently severely limited the sanctions that could be applied to peers even in cases of serious misconduct.

Although the composition of the House of Lords was radically changed by the addition of life peers after 1958 and by the removal of most hereditary peers in 1999, there has nevertheless been remarkable continuity in the ethos and culture of the House. Newcomers to the House have usually rapidly adopted the values and outlook of the traditional elite regarding conduct and behaviour – particularly the principle of self-regulation through an honour code. Consequently, many peers initially resisted the impetus to codify the rules governing members' conduct on lines analogous to those adopted in the Commons in the early 1990s. Nevertheless, two powerful factors shifted attitudes. The first was the effect of developments in the regulatory framework in other areas of public life. As more institutions adopted clear codes of conduct and enforcement mechanisms, it became increasingly difficult to argue that the House of Lords should be exempt from the trend. In the early 1990s some peers vehemently resisted the suggestion that Commons' initiatives (for example the introduction of a compulsory register of interests) ought automatically to be followed by the Lords. By 2010 such arguments had lost their credibility.

The second driver of change in the House of Lords' approach to ethical regulation was the eruption of scandal as a result of major breaches of the understandings about lobbying and paid advocacy and of some flagrant abuses of the system of expenses. This apparent increase in impropriety in the House of Lords in the early twenty-first century may have been in part a knock-on effect of restrictions on paid advocacy instituted in the Commons as a result of the Nolan Report. In some ways, the House of Lords is a friendly environment for pressure groups. Many peers are there because of their specialist knowledge of a particular aspect of British society. The part-time nature of service in the House of Lords and the varied occupational backgrounds of peers ensures that they will have close contact with a range of interest groups and voluntary associations. Peers often rely on pressure groups to brief them on pending legislation. Moreover, the relatively loose rules of procedure (which mean that peers' amendments are always called for debate) offer less restricted access to the legislative process than in the Commons. All this can be a strength but it can be dangerous if special interests appear to have gained too much access or peers appear to be promoting a cause for reward or gain.

Issues of conflict of interest in the House of Lords had generally stayed below the radar in the late twentieth century and the Lords' machinery for investigating integrity lapses was rarely used. Complaints against a peer were from 1995 handled by the Committee for Privileges, a sixteen-member body responsible for contested peerage claims and privilege issues, as well as allegations of misconduct.[5] (In 2010 it changed its name to the Committee for Privileges and Conduct.) Until 2004 there had been only one formal complaint against a peer. Thereafter the number of allegations of misconduct against peers rose dramatically, many as a result of complaints from MPs. In addition contingent scandals generated enhanced media interest in activities in the House. Of particular importance was the so-called 'cash for amendments' or 'Ermingate' scandal of 2009 in which the Committee for Privileges found that two peers (Lord Taylor of Blackburn and Lord Truscott) had failed to live up to the House's honour code because they were willing to use improper parliamentary influence on behalf of undercover journalists posing as lobbyists. Two other peers (Lord Moonie and Lord Snape) were cleared of breaching the Code of Conduct, but had to apologise to the House for their 'unwise' comments to the journalists.[6] This incident (which occasioned an exhaustive investigation by the Committee) also prompted a further radical review of the machinery for handling misconduct allegations.

In addition to these episodes, there were parallels to the Commons' expenses scandal as some peers were alleged to have misused their allowances. As a result the House of Lords has since 2009 revised many aspects of its regulatory procedures, including its Code of Conduct and its Register of Interests. It also radically changed its expenses system. In 2010, fifteen years after the House of Commons had introduced such an office, a Commissioner for Standards – Paul Kernaghan, a former Police Chief Constable – was appointed to this new role.

The path to the Committee on Standards in Public Life's Seventh Report

The House of Lords' approach to integrity issues evolved slowly. For a long time many peers doubted whether there was really an integrity problem in their House. The period from 1974 saw a series of decisions (or non-decisions) which effectively delayed significant change. When a compulsory Register of Interests was introduced for the House of Commons in 1974, the question naturally arose as to whether the Lords should also have one. In 1974 a large (twenty-two-member) sub-committee of the House of Lords' Procedure Committee examined the procedures for registering and declaring interests. Some peers advocated a formal register for the Lords, arguing that the Lords should follow the Commons as a matter of course and that it would prevent peers from voting on a matter without declaring an interest. Nevertheless, these arguments were countered by a robust defence of the status quo. The House of Lords was seen by many peers as qualitatively different from the House of Commons because of its unique tradition of managing its own affairs without recourse to rules of order. As the Procedure Committee put it, the House of Lords 'relies and thrives on self-discipline, and the honour of its members is the kernel of its procedures'.[7] For opponents of change, this difference of ethos from the House of Commons justified continuing without a register. Opponents of *compulsory* registration also reminded the House of Lords that there were no obvious sanctions for disciplining a peer who flouted its rules, so a compulsory register would be unenforceable and the Lords would have to recognise the limits on its ability to regulate its own members. The Lords and the Commons were seen as not comparable in another important respect. For some, membership of the House of Lords was involuntary because they had inherited their titles. To deprive such peers of their privacy could be seen as wrong in principle. Even life peers (who had accepted the burden of their position) might be reluctant to serve if stringent disclosure requirements were introduced. While these arguments have become less relevant since the 1999 House of Lords Act, they weighed heavily in the 1970s.

The 1974 sub-committee concluded that a register was 'unnecessary for the internal requirements of the House' and that a non-statutory compulsory register was not feasible. However, it left the House of Lords as a whole to decide whether the Commons' introduction of a compulsory register required it to follow suit.[8] In fact the sub-committee's report was neither published nor debated, so in the end no register, either compulsory or voluntary, was instituted. Although the Lords' approach to conflict of interest continued to rely on a declaration of interest during a debate, the procedures for policing such declarations lacked the improvements which the 1974 report had suggested.

There followed a long period in which little attention was given to integrity issues by the House of Lords, despite its continuing lack of clear rules and periodic problematic cases. In 1989, however, there were incidents in which peers seemed unsure about the significance of declaring an interest in debates.[9] There was uncertainty for example about whether declaring an interest permitted a peer to speak in a debate or whether the existing conventions and rules of the House suggested the much stricter approach of recusal.[10] Behind this question lay the broader one of how to strike a balance between forbidding peers from participating in proceedings in which they had an interest, and depriving the House of valuable expertise.

The language of the Companion to the Standing Orders covering a declaration of interest was itself ambiguous. The most relevant provision (Rule xiv) states that it is

> a long-standing custom of the House that Lords always speak on their personal honour. It follows from this that if a Lord decides that it is proper for him to take part in a debate on a subject in which he has a *direct pecuniary interest*, he should declare it. Subject to this ... there is no reason why a Lord with an interest to declare should not take part in debate. It is however considered undesirable for a Lord to advocate, promote or oppose in the House any Bill or subordinate legislation in or for which he is or has been acting or *concerned* for any pecuniary fee or reward. (*our italics*)[11]

Given the doubt about the meaning, in particular, of 'direct pecuniary interest' and about how broadly or narrowly the phrase 'concerned' should be interpreted, the Select Committee on Procedure in 1990 provided a new wording clarifying that it was 'considered undesirable for a Lord to advocate, promote or oppose in the House any Bill or subordinate legislation if he is acting or has acted personally in direct connection with it for a specific fee or reward or to vote on a private bill in which he has a direct pecuniary interest'.[12] Additionally the Committee broadened the rule to cover non-pecuniary and indirect interests, for example the interests of peers' friends and relations.[13] Putting the new rule into operation was still not altogether straightforward, however. Peers themselves remained the judge of when an interest was relevant. Making these declarations of interest also had the disadvantage of impeding proceedings, absorbing the time of the House – for example during Oral Questions. Nevertheless, the Committee thought it best to err on the side of caution and recommended that 'a Lord should make a declaration whenever he is in doubt'.[14]

The 1990 changes to the House of Lords' regulatory procedures were the last before the setting up of the CSPL under Lord Nolan in 1994, which transformed the handling of integrity issues across the United Kingdom. Lord Nolan's first inquiry was originally intended to cover both the Lords and the Commons. In December 1994, however, the House of Lords pre-empted this inclusion by setting up its own Sub-Committee of the Procedure Committee to look at the declaration and registration of interests. This committee was chaired by another law lord, Lord Griffiths. Nolan agreed to defer its inquiry into the House of Lords until after Griffiths had reported which did not happen until July 1995, two months after the Nolan Report appeared.[15]

The Griffiths Report started from two key principles – that peers should always act on their personal honour and that peers should never accept any financial inducement or reward for their influence. It also made two concrete proposals – the establishment of a voluntary register of a more modest kind than in the Commons and the imposition of some limits on lobbying. These new limits excluded peers with parliamentary consultancies or interests in a lobbying firm from participating in proceedings.

After some debate, the Griffiths recommendations were agreed and resolutions based on the proposals became a working de facto code of conduct for the Lords. These resolutions of 7 November 1995 represented a compromise between resolute opponents of reform who wanted no regulation at all or thought there was no need to rush such innovation and those who thought the House of Lords should copy the Commons.[16] But as a result of the Griffiths Report a Register of Interests *was* introduced; and most peers at that stage felt that the new system worked well. Griffiths himself in evidence to the CSPL inquiry of 2000 thought that the regulations his report had presaged went as far as was possible at the time.

The Register of Interests

The 1995 register contained three categories: consultancies and other arrangements by which peers were paid for providing parliamentary services; any financial interests by peers in businesses involved in parliamentary lobbying; and any particular interest which could affect the public perception of how peers discharged their parliamentary duties. The first two categories were mandatory (and were a bar to participation in proceedings). The third category was discretionary. But, as Patricia Leopold noted in 2000, only a very small number of peers had at that time registered in either categories 1 (where twelve peers registered) or 2 (where ten registered).[17] The discretionary category 3 was a subjective one leaving peers to decide whether an interest might affect the affect the public's view of how they would discharge their parliamentary duties. This category was much used. (Leopold noted that 408 of the 693 peers had at that time made a category 3 entry in 2000.) But the category's usefulness as a guide to *which* interests of peers might be relevant to their parliamentary activities was questionable. For the five years (1995–2000) in which this semi-voluntary register was in place there were no allegations against a peer of a failure to register an interest or of incomplete registration. The process of registration was aided by the confidential advice given by the Registrar of Lords' Interests, although such advice might be ignored by a peer who found it unpalatable. Despite its informal nature, the introduction of any register at all was a significant step which pushed the Lords a little further down the path towards a more comprehensive integrity system.

The Lords also tightened its lobbying and paid-advocacy rules. Unlike MPs, peers could continue to have financial interests in businesses engaged in parliamentary lobbying but they had to register them. Paid advice and consultancy by peers also remained permissible but again had to be registered. Parliamentary activity in return for payment was not allowed. Peers thus could still speak on behalf of interests and indeed lobby ministers but could not do so for financial reward. And peers remained free to engage in a range of outside activities.

The Committee on Standards in Public Life 2000 Report

Despite some opposition from the Lords itself, the CSPL returned to the topic of the House of Lords in 2000, not because of any scandal but because the upper chamber was one of the few public bodies which had thus far escaped a CSPL inquiry. There was also renewed interest in the House of Lords following Labour's reform which removed all but ninety-two of the hereditary peers.

While many witnesses to the CSPL inquiry reiterated the importance of personal honour in the regulation of conduct in the House of Lords, some noted the difficulty of applying it. The CSPL thought the principle of honour could provide a foundation for a more wide-ranging code of conduct. Accordingly, the CSPL recommended that the House of Lords should adopt a short code of conduct incorporating both the seven principles of public life and the resolutions adopted by the Lords in 1995 following the Griffiths Report. Those resolutions required that peers should always act on their personal honour and that Lords should never accept any financial inducement as an incentive or reward for exercising parliamentary influence. Any new code should also incorporate rules on the registration of interests.

In addition to recommending a code of conduct for peers, the CSPL report included among its twenty-three recommendations the mandatory registration of peers' relevant interests, substitution of an objective test of relevance for the subjectivity of category three in the register, tightened guidance on lobbying, enhanced induction procedures and the appointment of an ad hoc investigator to handle any allegation of serious misconduct by a peer.[18] Following publication of the CSPL report, a Leader's Group under the then Attorney General Lord Williams of Mostyn was established in the Lords to study its recommendations and report to the House. A debate in July 2001 revealed the wide range of

Table 6.1 The rising number of Lords complaints received 2004–2009

Year	Number of complaints
2004	1
2005	1
2006	2
2007	6
2008	9
2010	21

Source: Annual Report of House of Lords Commissioner for Standards 2010/2011.

thinking on standards regulation and that some peers were reluctant to accept the need for stricter procedures.[19]

Nevertheless, the Code of Conduct for the House of Lords, incorporating rules on the registration of peers' interests (both financial and non-financial), came into effect in March 2002. All relevant interests had to be registered. The register was overseen by the Sub-Committee on Lords Interests, a Sub-Committee of the Committee for Privileges, assisted by the Registrar of Lords' Interests, who also advised members of the House on whether an interest was relevant. The Register was open for public inspection. The Code was enforced by the Sub-Committee on Lords' Interests, which examined any allegations of non-compliance with the Code before deciding to investigate it further or dismiss it before reporting to the House. There was a right of appeal to the Committee for Privileges. Two of the fundamental principles set out in the Code of Conduct in 2002 were indeed the principles agreed after Griffiths that peers 'must never accept any financial inducement as an incentive or reward for exercising parliamentary influence' and 'must not vote on any bill or motion, or ask any question in the House or a committee, or promote any matter, in return for payment or any other material benefit' – the 'no paid advocacy' rule.

However, conventional wisdom remained that the Lords had no power to impose sanctions its members who did not comply with the Code of Conduct. The CSPL had noted that the 1955–1956 Swinton Committee had concluded that, while the House retained theoretical powers to imprison or fine peers, it could not suspend or expel them.[20] Although a Joint Committee on Parliamentary Privilege (the Nicholls Committee) had concluded in 1999 that the House of Lords, like the House of Commons, should have the power to suspend members, its recommendations for legislation to confirm this power were not enacted.[21] This situation was not clarified until the *Sunday Times* undercover investigation, involving four peers, in 2009.

The impact of misconduct

The new Code was introduced in 2002, but it was not until 2004 that the first formal complaint against peer was received. As Table 6.1 shows, the number of complaints rose thereafter, although it remained quite small until 2010. In 2008, however, there was much media coverage of an allegation that a member of the House of Lords had granted a parliamentary pass to a defence-industry lobbyist Robin Ashby.[22] The controversy also highlighted the role of the numerous all-party groups which bring together peers and MPs around specialised interests, but which might provide opportunities for interest groups to gain privileged access to MPs and peers.

Then in 2009 there was a cluster of decidedly headline-catching cases involving peers. The year opened with the *Sunday Times* publication of allegations against four peers – Lords Truscott, Taylor of Blackburn, Moonie and Snape – who were allegedly prepared to accept fees to amend laws in the House on behalf of business clients. Undercover reporters posing as lobbyists had apparently secured their agreement to amend legislation in return for cash, with Lord Truscott and Lord Taylor claiming they had previously secured changes in bills passing through Parliament to help clients.[23] Under the existing Code of Conduct, accepting financial inducement as an incentive or reward for exerting parliamentary influence to help amend legislation contravened the 'no paid advocacy' rules which prohibit peers from promoting the cause of paid clients in Parliament.

According to the *Sunday Times*, Lord Taylor of Blackburn offered to conduct a 'behind the scenes' campaign to persuade ministers and officials to amend legislation by discussing proposed amendments with Yvette Cooper, then Chief Secretary to the Treasury, in return for a one-year retainer of £120,000. He claimed that he had previously succeeded in changing legislation on behalf of Experian, the credit reference company.[24]

Lord Truscott, the former Labour energy minister, allegedly agreed to contact MPs, peers and civil servants, as well as John Healey, the minister in charge of the legislation, and to secure amendments in return for a fee of £72,000. He claimed that, as Minister for Energy, he had ensured that the Energy Bill was favourable to a client selling 'smart' electricity meters. The *Sunday Times* further alleged that Lord Moonie, a former defence minister, offered to amend legislation in Parliament for a fee of £30,000 a year, and that Lord Snape, a former Labour whip, indicated that he would charge £24,000 to contact ministers, civil servants and the relevant members of parliamentary committees.[25]

In the light of this scandal in January 2009 the then Leader of the House, Baroness Royall of Blaisdon, asked the Sub-Committee on Lords' Interests to investigate the allegations and at the same time asked the Lords' Committee for Privileges to review 'any issues relating to the rules of the House that arise, especially in connection with consultancy arrangements and in connection with sanctions in the event that a complaint against a Member is upheld'.[26] The backdrop to her request was Lord Moonie's alleged remark to the *Sunday Times* 'lobbyists':

> The thing with the Lords is that there's virtually nothing they can do with you, unless you break the law. Even if you don't declare (your interests), there's nothing they can do but jump up and down.[27]

The subsequent investigation revealed disagreement about the power to suspend a peer. The then Attorney General (Baroness Scotland of Asthal), echoing the Swinton Committee, advised that the power did not exist since it would conflict with the Writ of Summons but a former Lord Chancellor (Lord Mackay of Clashfern, who was also a member for the Committee for Privileges) argued that the House, as a self-regulating body, did inherently have such a power. Ultimately the Committee for Privileges relied on Lord Mackay's conclusion that the House possessed 'an inherent power to discipline its Members' and that a peer could be suspended – though for no longer than the remainder of the Parliament (that is to say until the suspension was overtaken by the issuing of a new Writ of Summons at the start of the next Parliament).[28]

The individual cases were referred to the Sub-Committee on Lords' Interests; the Sub-Committee reported to its parent committee the Committee for Privileges, to which the peers had a right of appeal. Its report cleared Lord Moonie but concluded that Lord Snape, Lord Truscott and Lord Taylor had advertised their willingness to influence Parliament in return for substantial financial inducement, thereby breaching the Code of Conduct's requirement that peers act on their 'personal honour'.[29] The House subsequently suspended Lord Truscott and Lord Taylor for the remainder of the session – the first Members to be suspended from the Lords since the 1640s.[30]

Following the press exposure of the misconduct by these peers and revelations about extensive lobbying interests in the House, there was concern that the episode indicated more general weaknesses in the Lords' ethical infrastructure. Immediately after the suspension in May 2009 the leader of the House, Baroness Royall, announced the formation of an all-party Leader's Group chaired by Lord Eames, to consider the Lords' Code of Conduct.

The Eames Report

The Leader's Group reported in October 2009. It noted a rising number of complaints against peers since 2006, and that the 2002 Code of Conduct needed further revision. Importantly, the Group interpreted its mandate broadly to cover not just the rules governing peers' conduct but related matters such as the scope of the Code, the role of the Registrar and the machinery for investigating allegations of misconduct as well as the key issue of what sanctions might be used against peers who had breached the rules. Although the Group was very aware of the expenses scandal then engulfing the Commons, the House of Lords was explicitly exempted from the Parliamentary Standards Act. Its passage nevertheless raised the possibility that its provisions for handling MPs' pay and expenses might eventually be extended to the Lords. However, the Group considered it inappropriate to introduce either a *statutory* Code of Conduct for the House or Lords, or a *statutory* Register of Financial Interests, not least because of the unsalaried nature of the House of Lords and the extent to which peers retained other occupations. The Group argued also that statutory regulation would raise the unwelcome prospect of judicial review of the House's decisions on matters of internal discipline.

The Leader's Group held thirteen meetings. In contrast to the approach of the CSPL, evidence to the Group was not published. Nevertheless its recommendations represented a significant strengthening of the Lords' machinery for regulating conduct.

First the Group proposed rebalancing the Code of Conduct, shortening it, and clarifying the principles of conduct and duties of peers, leaving the detailed rule-making to a separate *Guide*. Peers would be required to sign a formal undertaking to abide by it after taking the Oath both upon introduction to the House and at the start of each subsequent Parliament. The Code would apply to peers' conduct as parliamentarians but not to their non-parliamentary work, including any ministerial work. The Group made clear that one of the overarching principles underlying the Code was the duty to act in the public interest.

The Leader's Group realised that the requirement that peers should make a positive commitment to the Code in each parliament needed reinforcements from political parties and the Group recommended strengthened attention to induction, mentoring and refresher courses for new members.

The Leader's Group proposed a complete ban on parliamentary consultancies and on the acceptance of payment either in return for parliamentary services or for advice on how to influence Parliament. This move abolished the rather confusing distinction between parliamentary and non-parliamentary lobbying. The key distinction according to Eames was that between offering parliamentary services or advice to paying clients and thereby profiting from membership of the House (which the group thought unacceptable) and on the other hand legitimate outside employment. The group offered a new definition of paid advocacy – to the effect 'that members should not seek by parliamentary means to confer exclusive benefit on outside bodies from which they receive payment'.

The Group clarified which outside interests would be relevant for the registration process by defining them as only those interests which a reasonable member of the public might think likely to affect a member's discharge of his duties. The Group proposed simpler registration categories and sought to rein back what it called 'registration creep'.

In a highly significant innovation the Group recommended the appointment of a House of Lords Commissioner for Standards to investigate all complaints against peers for breaches of the code or of the rules governing the financial support system or for abuse of the facilities of the House. The Commissioner (who would be part-time) would establish the facts in any inquiry and report to the Sub-Committee on Lords' Interests (since renamed the Sub-Committee on Lords' Conduct). The Sub-Committee would recommend, where appropriate, a sanction. In an effort to build in procedural fairness the Group recommended retaining the existing provision for peers to appeal to the full Committee for Privileges (since renamed the Committee for Privileges and Conduct) against either the Commissioner's finding or the sanction recommended by the Sub-Committee. The House of Lords thus had an appeal mechanism in its disciplinary arrangements in marked contrast to the House of Commons.

The Report of the Leaders' Group was debated in the House of Lords in November 2009. It received support from both the government and the Opposition, as well as from Lord McNally for the Liberal Democrats and Baroness D'Souza, Convenor of the Cross Bench Peers. While recommendations for reform of the Code of Conduct were accepted on an all-party basis, a few peers such as Lord Stoddart of Swindon argued that the self-regulation procedures of the House had effectively tackled allegations of misconduct by peers for centuries; however his attempt to resist the new office of Commissioner for Standards received only minimal support.[31]

The Eames Report represented a major change in the Lords' approach to regulation. By removing much of the uncertainty which had surrounded the rules governing the Lords and by embracing more explicitly the Nolan principles, it laid the groundwork for a new approach to regulation.

Another expenses scandal

As the Eames Group was deliberating, another scandal engulfed the House of Lords. Following the 'cash-for-influence' or 'Ermingate' scandal, there emerged allegations in the press of the misuse of peers' allowances. Although peers do not receive a salary in respect of membership of the House, they have for long received tax-free allowances to cover expenses incurred as a result of their parliamentary work. By 2009 peers' could claim £174 in respect of each night spent in London if their 'only or main residence' (the location of which was self-designated) was outside London and their stay was 'for the purpose of attending sittings of the House'. Peers could also claim £86.50 for subsistence and £75 for office costs for each day they attended Parliament. During May and June 2009 the press reported that several peers had misused these allowances, mainly by claiming for overnight stays when they had either not stayed in London or in fact maintained a 'main residence' in London.[32] Thus, the *Sunday Times* alleged in May 2009 that Lord Clarke of Hampstead had claimed up to £18,000 a year for overnight subsistence when he had often stayed with friends, family or other peers free of charge or had returned to his main residence in St Albans.[33] The *Sunday Times* further alleged that more than a dozen peers had claimed hundreds of thousands of pounds in overnight allowances when they designated their main residence outside London despite owning London homes.[34] In all these cases the conduct alleged took place pre-2009 and all were therefore investigated under the pre-Eames process – without the involvement of the Commissioner for Standards.

The Lords allowances system is overseen by the House Committee, which is chaired by the Lord Speaker. Under the pre-Eames rules allegations of abuse were regarded as the responsibility of the senior official in the House of Lords, the Clerk of the Parliaments, who is Accounting Officer of the House of Lords and who reported his findings to the House Committee. From early 2009 he was able in exceptional circumstances to refer a serious or complex complaint to the Sub-Committee on Lords' Interests.

Some of the 2009 allegations of fraudulent allowances claims were sufficiently grave to warrant criminal investigation and indeed the police launched formal investigations into a number of peers causing all internal parliamentary inquiries into these cases to be halted in the second half of 2009. Subsequently (in February 2010) the Clerk of the Parliaments, then Michael Pownall, dismissed complaints of improperly claiming overnight allowances in London against nine peers who were not subject to police investigation. Pownall applied certain tests agreed by the House Committee the previous month, including that in cases where frequency of visits was an issue, peers designating a property as their 'only or main residence' outside of London, needed to visit it at least once a month while the Lords was sitting and for periods during recesses. Critics argued that this allowed peers to claim overnight allowances for living in family homes in London providing they spent a handful of days in a second property outside the capital.[35] At the same time Pownall upheld in part a complaint against one peer, Baroness Goudie, and referred a complaint against another peer, Lord Bhatia, to the Sub-Committee on Lords' Interests for more detailed investigation.

Following publication of these findings by the Clerk of the Parliaments, the DPP, Keir Starmer, dropped the criminal cases against three peers, Lord Clarke of Hampstead, Baroness Uddin and Lord Paul. The cases were then returned to the Clerk of the Parliaments and were referred by him to the Sub-Committee on Lords' Interests. These cases were hugely time-consuming for the Sub Committee on Lords' Interests during the last months of the 2005–2010 Parliament and the early part of the 2010 Parliament.

In the case of Lord Clarke, the Sub-Committee concluded that he had breached the rules governing the Members' Reimbursement Scheme in claiming for overnight subsistence for nights that he did not spend in London; but it recommended that since he had cooperated with the inquiry and had repaid money to the House he should make only a full personal apology to the House.[36] The Privileges Committee took the opportunity to confirm that, although the allowances scheme did not explicitly fall within the scope of the (pre-2010) Code of Conduct, breaches of the rules governing the scheme would be deemed to constitute failure to act on personal honour, thereby making those found to have committed such breaches liable to sanction.

The cases of Lord Paul, Lord Bhatia and Baroness Uddin came before the Sub-Committee on Lords' Conduct later – after the summoning of a new Parliament in 2010. The Sub-Committee found against all three peers, and all three appealed to the full Committee for Privileges and Conduct. In the case of Baroness Uddin a penalty of suspension until the end of the session (i.e. spring 2012) was imposed. In addition the Committee found that Baroness Uddin had wrongly claimed £125,349.10 in allowances and recommended that the Clerk of the Parliaments make arrangements for its repayment. Lord Paul was suspended for four months and Lord Bhatia for eight months. Both Lord Paul and Lord Bhatia had already repaid significant amounts of the money wrongly claimed. In the final case (that of Baroness Goudie who had been found to have breached the rules by the Clerk of the Parliaments) no further sanction was imposed since she had cooperated fully with investigation, had made a full apology and had repaid money wrongly claimed.

In the meantime the Crown Prosecution Service had launched prosecutions against two other peers (Lord Hanningfield and Lord Taylor of Warwick) accused of fraudulent misuse of the expenses scheme. Lord Hanningfield was imprisoned for nine months and on his early release he was suspended for nine months from the House.[37] Lord Taylor of Warwick was also convicted for fraudulent claims and in 2011 he was sentenced to a year's imprisonment. The House suspended him for twelve months following his release.[38]

These cases were the last episodes to be handled under the old rules. The penalties in these cases were the toughest the Lords had imposed in recent times underlining the increased awareness of how damaging such abuses were to the public standing of the House.

A new regime

The new Code of Conduct for Members of the House of Lords, based on the recommendations of the (Eames) Leader's Group, was adopted by resolution on 30 November 2009 and came into effect at the start of the new Parliament in May 2010, replacing the system which had been in operation since 2002. The new Code and the appointment of an independent Lords Commissioner for Standards, were part of a wider effort to ensure that standards of conduct in the House met public expectations of clarity, transparency and integrity. The tighter regulation of standards in the Lords now became consonant with the approach of the CSPL in 2000, and Lord Neill of Bladen claimed that the CSPL's arguments had now been accepted within the House, following greater media scrutiny of the alleged misconduct of Members.[39]

As Eames had recommended, the new Code of Conduct was shorter than before but accompanied by a detailed guide to the Code. For the first time, peers were required to sign up to the Code – any peer not on leave of absence (or disqualified from attending) who failed to sign an undertaking to abide by the Code would be considered to have breached it and referred to the Sub-Committee on Lords' Conduct.[40] The Code and its Guide would be reviewed once each Parliament by the Sub-Committee on Lords' Conduct.[41] Such a review occurred in January 2014 and resulted in some important amendments to the Code and the Guide.[42]

The new Code maintains the existing prohibition on paid advocacy – peers must not seek by parliamentary means to confer exclusive benefit on an outside body or person from whom they receive payment or reward. For example, a peer who is paid by a pharmaceutical company would be barred from seeking to confer benefit exclusively upon it by parliamentary means but would be able to speak on matters affecting the industry as a whole (as is the case in the House of Commons).[43] The Code prohibits Members from accepting payment (or other incentive or reward) in return for parliamentary advice or services to paying clients and from seeking to profit from membership of the House. This restriction bans peers from acting as paid parliamentary consultants by advising organisations or persons on how they may lobby or otherwise influence the work of Parliament. In addition, peers must not make use of their position to arrange meetings with a view to any person lobbying Members of either House, ministers or officials. However, a Member may still 'exceptionally' give parliamentary advice to an organisation or person with whom they have a financial interest, provided that they can demonstrate that they do not receive payment in return, and they may still receive payment for non-parliamentary advice and services.

Members of the House of Lords may still work for or hold financial interests in organisations such as representative bodies, trade associations or organisations involved in parliamentary lobbying on behalf of clients (such as public relations and law firms).[44] However, the new Code of Conduct reinforces the requirement on peers to register fully relevant interests, including financial interests, and to register new interests within one month of any change occurring. All interests which exceed £500 in value must be registered and the register now has ten categories: directorships; remunerated employment; public affairs advice and services to clients; shareholdings; land and property; sponsorship; overseas visits; gifts, benefits and hospitality; miscellaneous financial interests; and non-financial interests.

The Register is overseen by the new Sub-Committee on Lords' Conduct, and the Registrar of Lords' Interests advises Members about what they must register and the propriety of participation in proceedings of the House and in select committees – a workload that has inevitably increased substantially in recent years. The revised Code introduced new rules obliging Members to declare relevant interests when tabling questions and motions in the House or communicating with ministers and civil servants.[45] It notes that members with financial interests that are relevant to private legislation should exercise particular caution, and seek advice before deciding to participate in parliamentary proceedings on that legislation.[46]

In an interesting move which echoes Dennis Thompson's urging that legislatures should calibrate their ethical rules to reflect the scale of internal influence, the three salaried Officers of the House – the Lord Speaker, the Chairman of Committees and the Principal Deputy Chairman of Committees – have been made subject to stricter rules than other Members on holding outside interests.[47]

The new Code of Conduct for the first time explicitly included within its remit allowances and parliamentary facilities for Members, meaning that a breach of the rules governing allowances or facilities is a breach of the Code. However, the Code did not itself set thresholds governing the amount of financial support available.[48] These topics were addressed by a series of reports from the House Committee following a 2009 Senior Salaries Review Body report.[49] Following debate the House of Lords introduced a new expenses regime in 2010 to replace the old one.[50] This new regime was intended to be simpler and more transparent than the old one and had at its core a single daily attendance allowance of £300 full or £150 part allowance per day for unsalaried peers (i.e. those who do not receive a ministerial or office-holder's salary). The two rates allow some Members to claim a reduced allowance. Members can choose to claim no daily allowance.

While the new Code reiterated that the House of Lords would regulate its own standards, it also clarified the handling of complaints against Members alleged to be in breach of the Code. Thus the new independent House of Lords Commissioner for Standards would follow procedures similar to those used by the PCS in the House of Commons. After investigation the Commissioner would report to the Sub-Committee on Lords' Conduct whether or not he had upheld a complaint; the Sub-Committee, where appropriate, could recommend a disciplinary sanction to the Committee for Privileges and Conduct. Paul Kernaghan, former Chief Constable of the Hampshire Constabulary, was appointed the first House of Lords Commissioner of Standards in June 2010, responsible for the independent and impartial investigation of alleged breaches of the new House of Lords Code of Conduct. However he was not involved in the major inquiries relating to expenses in 2010.

Since his appointment, the Commissioner for Standards has issued annual reports and (as Table 6.2 shows) dealt with a small but rising number of complaints. In the year covered by his 2013–2014 report complaints to the Commissioner increased from sixteen to twenty-three, and the number of formal investigations remained stable at ten. Of those ten complaints seven were upheld.[51]

The fact that complaints to the Lords Commissioner for Standards are relatively few in number gives no cause for complacency however. Some of the cases which have been fully investigated recently have been serious and have cast doubt on the adequacy of the arrangements for managing misconduct. Thus the cases of Lord Mackenzie of Framwellgate

Table 6.2 Trends in complaints received by the House of Lords Commissioner for Standards 2010/2011–2013/2014

	2010/2011	2011/2012	2012/2013	2013/2014
Formal complaints received	12	10	16	23
Subject to inquiry	2	4	10	10
Not subject to inquiry	10	6	6	13

Source: Annual Reports of the House of Lords Commissioner for Standards.

and Lord Laird in 2013 underlined the continuing possibility that some peers might seek to use their position for personal gain. A sting by *Sunday Times* journalists posing as lobbyists exposed both Lord Laird and Lord Mackenzie as being willing to enter into an agreement with lobbyists to provide parliamentary services for payment. In the case of Lord Mackenzie there were also breaches of the rules relating to use of the House dining facilities. Lord Laird was at the same time subject to a separate sting by the BBC *Panorama* programme in which he also indicated willingness to provide parliamentary services in return for payment. Both peers were suspended from the House – Lord Mackenzie for six months, Lord Laird for four months.[52] The later case of Lord Hanningfield (the second involving him) raised slightly different issues. It was reported in the *Daily Mirror* that Lord Hanningfield, following his release from prison and the completion of his earlier period of suspension, had been claiming the full daily attendance allowance (of £300 per day) despite spending very little time in the Chamber. As the Commissioner for Standards found he had failed to abide by the provision of the Code of Conduct which underpinned the daily allowance by requiring members to certify that they had done appropriate parliamentary work for any day for which they claimed the allowance. He was ordered by the Committee for Privileges and Conduct to repay the wrongly claimed allowances (amounting to £3,300) and was suspended for the remainder of the Parliament (which in practice meant suspension for about a year).

When the Sub-Committee on Lords' Conduct came to review the Code of Conduct in January 2014 it recommended a strengthening of the Code to take account of the lessons of these cases especially the cases of Lords Mackenzie of Framwellgate and Lord Laird. In those cases there was an argument that a willingness to breach the Honour Code of the House should not be treated as seriously as an actual breach of the Code. However the Committee was adamant that the expression of a willingness to breach the Code (for example by negotiating an agreement for payment in return for parliamentary services) demonstrated a failure of personal honour and was itself a clear breach of the Code.[53] The Amendments also tightened the rules on staff, clarified the rules of lobbying, and lowered the threshold for the registration of gifts, benefits and hospitality given by third parties from £500 to £140.[54] The Amendments also incorporated the revised descriptions of the Seven Principles of Public Life into the Lords' Code of Conduct.

The recommendations were agreed in March 2014. A second report on the Code published in May 2014, and reflecting the findings in respect of Lord Hanningfield, recommended what it called a 'closer link' between the requirement for peers always to act on their personal honour and the system of financial support for members.[55] This strengthened link required a peer claiming financial support to certify that in making the claim they had had regard to the obligation to act on their personal honour. Two other important changes were recommended. First, following the GRECO Fourth Evaluation Round, the Committee recommended a Code of Conduct for Members' staff. As a first step in 2014 it recommended that all Members' staff in possession of a parliamentary pass should register the names of any third party also employing them. And although the House of Lords Act 2014 makes provision for a peer imprisoned for more than one year to cease to be a member of the House of Lords, the Committee recognised that any term of imprisonment of a peer could arouse public concern and recommended that it should always be deemed a breach of the Code of Conduct. Taken together these incremental changes have attempted to clarify the rules of conduct governing the Upper House and to make explicit rules which were always implicit. Thus the House, while retaining the idea of a code of personal honour at the centre, has tried to ensure that its implications are fully understood and capable of enforcement.

Conclusions: continuing concerns

Both the House of Commons and the House of Lords resisted dilution of the system of self-regulation, although the House of Lords was clearly able to protect its own system of self-regulation for longer than the Commons. Gradually however it has accepted processes of codification and a tightening of the rules in relation to conduct, although reform at each step has been sensitive to the need to maintain what the CSPL in its 2000 report termed proportionality. Until the Eames recommendations and the later round of reform, regulation in the Lords was firmly rooted in the desire to operate a light-touch regime. By the autumn of 2010, however, the touch had become noticeably weightier and the revisions of 2013–2014 strengthen the machinery further especially with respect to sanctions.[56] For the Commons the expenses scandal created a new environment in which self-regulation became increasingly difficult to defend and new machinery external to Parliament was established to handle expenses, pay and pensions.

How successful the new regimes are is debateable. Even with improvements the House of Lords remains vulnerable to efforts to promote special interests and causes. Analysis of the contemporary Register of Interests reveals a host of directorships, remunerated employment, advisory council memberships, speaking engagements, shareholdings and property ownership. The fact that these interests are now more transparent than before is a major step forward in ensuring that peers' interests are on the record. Some observers however continued to suggest that there was still room for ambiguity about what counted as a 'relevant interest' for the purposes of registration and that some peers were failing fully to register their interest.[57] There may sometimes be a misinterpretation of what is required, so that for example the Sub-Committee on Lords' Conduct in January 2014 had to correct a misunderstanding by a member of the House about the requirement to register company directorships and to make it clear that all directorships whether remunerated or not should be registered in categories 1 or 10 of the Register of Interests.[58]

Lobbying activity is inevitably a part of democratic life. Pressure groups of all stripes naturally see the House of Lords as an important target: Justice for All for example published its own guide to lobbying the upper chamber and promoted its 'pair up with a peer' strategy to amend the Legal Aid, Sentencing and Punishment of Offenders Bill. Defining the boundary between proper and improper lobbying is likely to continue to challenge peers in their daily activities. Cases of controversial individual lobbying by peers may still emerge, as with Lord Blencathra whose activities on behalf of the Cayman Islands were referred to the Lords' Commissioner for Standards.[59] Undercover journalistic activity can still flush out a willingness to engage in what will widely be regarded as improper lobbying. Indeed concern about peers abusing their position for reward was hardly allayed by a series of allegations at the end of 2013 that revealed that some peers were still willing to sell their services to lobbyists; and the sanctions (periods of suspension) imposed on two peers – Lord Mackenzie of Framwellgate and Lord Laird – appeared to some critics more like a slap on the wrist than a serious punishment. The revision of the Code of Conduct which occurred in 2013–2014, clarified the principles which should govern dealing with lobbyists and inserted

new clauses into the Code to that effect. Lobbying and the distinction
between the acceptable and the unacceptable remain high on the ethics
agenda as the recent attention given to lobbying by the CSPL and by
international agencies such as GRECO underlines.[60]

The stringent tightening of the rules on paid advocacy and lobbying have mainly been directed at peers themselves; but other aspects of
the House of Lords may be vulnerable to improper lobbying activity.
A *Guardian* report in 2011 revealed that one in five of those with members' staff passes in the House of Lords had lobbying links including to
professional lobbying organisations as well as to major interests such
British Petroleum (BP), the National Farmers Union, the Taxpayers' Alliance and sundry religious groups including the Evangelical Alliance.[61]

The House of Commons also remains vulnerable to lobbying activity
but cases such as that of Patrick Mercer have become rarer and the swift
suspension from their parties of Sir Malcolm Rifkind and Jack Straw
after lobbying allegations in February 2015 suggests a determination by
party leaders to crack down when embarrassing episodes occur. The system of financial support in both Houses has been abused and, as we saw
in the last chapter, the new machinery of IPSA has occasioned real tension between MPs and the regulator, further undermining public sympathy along the way. In the House of Lords serious abuse of the allowances
system led in two cases (Lord Taylor of Warwick and Lord Hanningfield) to criminal charges and periods of imprisonment. The House of
Lords' most recent reforms have attempted to remove uncertainty about
the rules which can occur both about claims for overnight subsistence
and the daily allowance. Whether the House has done enough to protect
itself against exploitation of the system of financial support remains to
be seen.

Although the system for handling complaints has now been thor-
oughly overhauled in both Houses, procedural fairness remains a concern. Prior to the reform of the Lords' procedures, an investigation into
Lady Uddin's claims for allowances raised several questions of fairness.[62]
These related to the reliance on hearsay evidence, the opportunities for
cross-examination of witnesses, and whether the appropriate standard
of proof should be the civil or criminal standard. Although these issues
were all carefully considered by the Committee there remains – even
after the new procedures were introduced – a concern that the proper
balance between the desire to retain an inquisitorial process and the need
to allow peers accused of serious offences the right to defend themselves
with legal representation has not been achieved. Similar worries have
emerged in relation to the Commons procedures compounded there by
the absence of an internal appeal mechanism and by the problem that

even when an MP is found not to have breached the rules the mere lodging of a complaint may be harmful to reputation.

Finally there is the issue of the sanctions available in cases of misconduct. The House of Commons has become vulnerable to the accusation that its sanctions are an insufficient deterrent; and in cases where the PCS and Committee on Standards reach different conclusions (as in the Maria Miller case) this may undermine confidence in the whole regulatory system. Traditionally the House of Lords had been thought unable to impose sanctions on peers but recent years have seen a willingness to use the penalty of suspension. In 2013 the House Committee recommended that two new sanctions (denial of access for a specific period to the system of financial support and denial of access for a specific period to the facilities of the House) be introduced.[63] Such sanctions could be contemplated because they were not tied to the writ of summons. And they would reassure the public that a peer found guilty of misconduct would not automatically be fully restored to the House after a short period of suspension. Following the passage of the House of Lords Reform Act in 2014 a peer convicted of a term of imprisonment of more than a year automatically ceases to be a member of the House of Lords, and clearly the Committee for Privileges is minded to take a much stricter line in all cases where peers are convicted of criminal offences.

Despite these continuing concerns, a remarkable degree of change has occurred in both chambers in recent years. The Commons has had an increasingly rigorous system forced upon it, although as we saw in Chapters 4 and 5, backlash against more stringent regulatory measures is always possible. After many years of resistance, the House of Lords has made rapid strides to put an integrated and effective system of ethical regulation in place. Partly that shift was forced upon it by revelations about its own members and partly it occurred as a result of public debate about second-chamber reform which required the Lords to be sensitive to its reputation. The wider national and international trends which emphasise the need to take ethical regulation seriously and public reaction to scandal have thus left a mark on both chambers, although the support for change has often been less than enthusiastic.

Notes

1 For an overview of the role of the House of Lords see Shell, D., *The House of Lords* (Manchester: Manchester University Press, 2007) and in comparative perspective Baldwin N.J. and D. Shell (eds), *Second Chambers* (London: Frank Cass, 2001). For recent studies see Ballinger, C., *The House of Lords 1911–2011* (Oxford: Hart, 2012) and Russell, M., *The Contemporary*

House of Lords: Westminster Bicameralism Revived (Oxford: Oxford University Press, 2013).

2 House of Lords Act 1999; the Constitutional Reform Act 2005 further changed the composition of the House of Lords by removing the Law Lords.

3 See Russell, M., *House Full: Time to Get a Grip on Lords Appointments* (London: The Constitution Unit, 2011) and Russell, M. and T. Stemlyn, *Enough is Enough: Regulating Prime Ministerial Appointments to the Lords* (London: The Constitution Unit, 2015).

4 On party cohesion see Norton, P., 'Cohesion without Discipline: Party Voting in the House of Lords', *Journal of Legislative Studies*, 9:4 (2003), 57–72.

5 The handling of conduct issues is now delegated to a sub-committee, the Sub-Committee on Lords Conduct.

6 Committee for Privileges, *The Conduct of Lord Moonie, Lord Snape, Lord Truscott and Lord Taylor of Blackburn*, HL 88-1 and 2, 2008–2009.

7 Committee on Procedure of the House Sub-Committee on Registration of Interests (1974) para 28 (5) quoted in CSPL, Seventh Report, *Standards of Conduct in the House of Lords*, 2000, p. 21.

8 Standards of Conduct in the House of Lords, para 41. Quoted in CSPL, Seventh Report, p. 21 with emphasis added.

9 See for example the debates cited in the CSPL report: 3 April (cols 964 and 972); on 2 May 1989 (cols 58 and 61) and 11 October 1989 (cols 403–406).

10 *Companion to the Standing Orders and Guide to the Proceedings of the House of Lords.*

11 *Companion to the Standing Orders and Guide to the Proceedings of the House of Lords.*

12 Committee on Procedure of the House 1990 para 5 reproduced as Appendix C of the CSPL, Seventh Report, *Standards of Conduct in the House of Lords*, pp. 75–76.

13 Committee on Procedure, HL 50, 1989–1990.

14 *Companion to the Standing Orders and Guide to the Proceedings of the House of Lords.*

15 Committee on Procedure of the House, 1994–1995, HL 90.

16 HL Deb, 7 November 1995.

17 Leopold, P., 'Standards of conduct in the Lords', in Gay, O. and P. Leopold, *Conduct Unbecoming: The Regulation of Parliamentary Behaviour* (London: Politico's, 2004), p. 310.

18 Committee on Standards in Public Life, *Standards of Conduct in the House of Lords*, 2000 (Cmnd 4903).

19 HL Deb, 2 July 2001.

20 *Report of the Committee on the Powers of the House in relation to the Attendance of Members*, 1955–1956, HL 66.

21 HL Paper 43-I; HC 214 1998–1999.

22 Ashby ran Defence Consultancy Bergmans. His pass was withdrawn. See Percival, J., 'Lobbyist to have security pass withdrawn', *Guardian*, 26 June 2008.

23 'Revealed: Labour lords change rules for cash', *Sunday Times*, 25 January 2009, www.timesonline.co.uk/tol/news/politics/article5581547.ece.

24 'Revealed: Labour lords change rules for cash', *Sunday Times*, 25 January 2009, www.timesonline.co.uk/tol/news/politics/article5581547.ece.

25 'Revealed: Labour lords change rules for cash', *Sunday Times*, 25 January 2009, www.timesonline.co.uk/tol/news/politics/article5581547.ece.

26 Gay, O., *Regulation of Standards of Conduct in the House of Lords*, House of Commons Library Standard Note, 04950, 7 April 2010.

27 'Whispered over tea and cake: price for a peer to break the law', *Sunday Times*, 25 January 2009, www.timesonline.co.uk/tol/news/politics/article5581570.ece.

28 See Gay, O., *Regulation of Standards of Conduct in the House of Lords*, House of Commons Library Standard Note, 04950, 7 April 2010.

29 Gay, O., *Regulation of Standards of Conduct in the House of Lords*, House of Commons Library Standard Note, 04950, 7 April 2010.

30 The last Member to be suspended from the House of Lords is believed to have been Thomas Saville for siding with King Charles I.

31 HC Deb, 30 November 2009, c 610.

32 See, for example 'Baroness claims expenses for mother's home', *Sunday Times*, 7 June 2009.

33 'Remorseful peer Lord Clarke of Hampstead says he fiddled expenses', *Sunday Times*, 31 May 2009.

34 'Remorseful peer Lord Clarke of Hampstead says he fiddled expenses', *Sunday Times*, 31 May 2009.

35 'Nine peers cleared over expenses claims', *The Times*, 10 February 2010.

36 Committee for Privileges, *The Conduct of Lord Clarke of Hampstead*, HL 112, 2009–2010.

37 Committee for Privileges and Conduct, *The Conduct of Lord Hanningfield*, 9th Report 2010–2011, 31 October 2011, HL Paper 211.

38 Committee for Privileges and Conduct, *The Conduct of Lord Taylor of Warwick*, 2010–2011, 31 October 2011, HL Paper 210.

39 HL Deb, 16 March 2010, c586–7.

40 HL Deb, 16 March 2010, c568–9.

41 *The Code of Conduct for Members of the House of Lords and Guide to the Code of Conduct*, 3rd edition HL 5 2014, www.publications.parliament.uk/pa/ld/ldcond/code.pdf.

42 Committee for Privileges and Conduct, 13th Report of Session, *Amendments to the Code of Conduct and the Guide to the Code* (HL 123) January 2014.

43 Committee for Privileges and Conduct, 13th Report of Session *Amendments to the Code of Conduct and the Guide to the Code* (HL 123) January 2014.

44 Committee for Privileges and Conduct, 13th Report of Session *Amendments to the Code of Conduct and the Guide to the Code* (HL 123) January 2014.

45 Committee for Privileges and Conduct, 13th Report of Session *Amendments to the Code of Conduct and the Guide to the Code* (HL 123) January 2014.

46 Committee for Privileges and Conduct, 13th Report of Session *Amendments to the Code of Conduct and the Guide to the Code* (HL 123) January 2014.

47 Committee for Privileges, *The Guide to the Code of Conduct*, HL 212, 2010–2012. See also Thompson, Dennis F., *Ethics in Congress, from Individual to Institutional Corruption* (Brookings Institution Press, 1995).

48 Committee for Privileges, *Code of Conduct for Members of the House of Lords and The Guide to the Code of Conduct*, HL 212, 2010–2012.

49 House Committee. *Financial Support for Members of the House of Lords*, 2010–2011; *SSRB Review of Financial Support for Members of the House of Lords*, 24 November 2009, Cm 7746; Financial Support for members of the House of Lords Report of the Ad Hoc Group HL 13 June 2010.

50 See HL Deb, 28 June 2010.

51 House of Lords Commissioner for Standards, *Annual Report 2013–2014*.

52 See Committee for Standards and Conduct, *The Conduct of Lord Mackenzie of Framwellgate*, HL 95, December 2013 and *The Conduct of Lord Laird*, HL 96, December 2013.

53 Committee for Privileges and Conduct, *Amendments to the Code of Conduct and the Guide to the Code*, HL 123, January 2014, para 7.

54 Committee for Privileges and Conduct, *Amendments to the Code of Conduct and the Guide to the Code*, paras 13 and 14.

55 Committee for Privileges and Conduct, *Further Amendments to the Code of Conduct and Guide to the Code*, May 2014.

56 See Committee for Standards and Privileges, *Amendments to the Code of Conduct and the Guide to the Code*, HL 123, 2013–2014.

57 See Wright, O. and M. Newman, 'The murky world of what peers don't think you need to see', *Independent*, 20 June 2012.

58 See Committee for Privileges and Conduct, *The Conduct of Lord Stephen*, HL 118, 2013–2014.

59 Wright, O. and M. Newman, 'Watchdog set to investigate Lord Blencathra over lobbying for the Cayman Islands', *Independent*, 18 April 2012.

60 See Committee on Standards in Public Life, *Strengthening Transparency Around Lobbying*, November 2013 and GRECO's evaluation report of March 2013, www.coe.int/t/dghl/monitoring/Greco/evaluation round4/ GrecoEval4(2012)2UnitedKingdom.EN.pdf.

61 Syal, R. and J. Ball, 'One in five staff passholders in House of Lords linked to lobbying', *Guardian*, 8 November 2011.

62 See HL Deb, 21 October 2010.

63 House Committee, *Sanctions for Breaches of the Code of Conduct*, HL 91, 2013–2014.

7

Regulation at the centre of government: the Ministerial Code

Introduction

All office-holders within the executive, whether ministers or civil servants, are subject to broad principles of good governance, such as the Seven Principles of Public Life, and must not exploit office for personal gain. They must exercise the power of executive office within the law. They are also expected to be accountable: ministers to the legislature and ultimately to voters, civil servants to their political masters or their senior managers, and for some senior civil servants also to legislatures directly. Beyond that ministers are highly visible public figures whose continuing fitness for office is from day to day judged politically, including potentially through elements of their personal and private lives. An elected politician's appeal to voters is based not just on policies, but also on perceptions of character, effectiveness and trustworthiness.

Ministers are the most high-profile of all elected office-holders. Their role in the decision-making process means that they are likely to have extensive responsibility for the detail and substance of policy in their area. When they are involved in any form of ethical controversy, even a comparatively minor one, the issue is likely to be regarded far more seriously than in the case of ordinary MPs, because ethical *leadership* is a requirement in democratic politics. And since governments generally tend to fight hard not to lose ministers over ethical controversies, and prefer denial or obfuscation to acceptance of responsibility, the stakes are often raised, and the political damage magnified, if a resignation is eventually unavoidable.

Thus although all executive office-holders, whether ministers or civil servants, have the same general obligations of office, and in many jurisdictions are formally treated in the same way, there is a significant difference in lines of accountability. Accountability to legislatures both weakens and strengthens ministers. It weakens them because attacks on their integrity can easily be politicised and will often be exaggerated out of proportion for partisan gain. It strengthens them when their integrity is justifiably under question, because, unless they have clearly broken the law, the attacks on them will be led in a partisan spirit, against which the government will generally provide a collective partisan defence.

When, as in the United Kingdom, the executive is relatively dominant over the legislature, this will have an important and potentially damaging effect on accountability mechanisms for ethics. For the most part in advanced democracies when ministers are accused of impropriety, it does not involve personal unlawfulness or criminal responsibility, even if governments are frequency challenged about the legal basis of their actions. Rather it involves behaviour which is shabby or sub-standard, where codes of behaviour and values are at stake, not hard law. But given the strong tendency of governments to circle the wagons around ministers under attack, and given that the main thrust of any attack will be political not legal, strong governments tend to be relatively effective in holding on to ministers under pressure.

The tradition in the United Kingdom of civil-service neutrality, right up to the highest levels, has added a special, and today increasingly controversial, additional narrative to ministerial ethics in recent years, that concerns minister–civil servant relationships. Attempts by ministers to alter the balance in that relationship are often seen as somehow improper, even if it is difficult to point to any hard rules that have been broken. Moreover, the presence of neutral civil servants at the heart of policy-making, and their sensitive knowledge of individuals, issues and processes, means that some of them command a market price on departure from public service that can appear at odds, and occasionally may actually be at odds with, the public-service values into which they have been socialised.

This chapter, and the next two, deal with these issues. Here we explore the way in which the ethics of ministerial behaviour have gradually been codified, but in ways that have left some observers profoundly dissatisfied with the result, since there is enduring doubt about exactly what this codification really means. The rules are often unclear, and there may be no obviously 'right' form of behaviour. In Chapter 8 we deal with minister–civil servant relationships. Here too there is a lack of clarity in the boundary between ministers and civil servants. There is a trade-off between the advantages of allowing ministers more control over their own administrative apparatus, and the risks of cronyism, inappropriate patronage and politicisation. It involves matters of efficiency and effectiveness as well as ethics and is a particularly difficult balance to strike without controversy in modern government. In Chapter 9, which deals with post-employment, we shall see that there is a similar trade-off where the risk of conflict of interest has to be balanced against restrictions so tight that they might deter many talented individuals from public service altogether.

Ethics for ministers: partisan gain and private gain

Judged by the rate of forced resignations or of controversies almost leading to a resignation, there is little doubt that the behaviour of ministers has become more controversial in the last two decades than under earlier post-war prime ministers. No prime minister until John Major suffered more than two forced resignations. Since 1990 there have been thirty-one: twelve under Major, seven under Blair, six under Brown and five under Cameron (up to summer 2014). Berlinsky *et al.* argue that under Blair the number of near-misses involving strong but unsuccessful pressure for resignation was also abnormally high compared to the past.[1]

Despite this clear evidence of increased pressure on ministers, the full disclosures of interest they are required to make on coming to office helps ensure that few ministers are involved in cases of egregious self-enrichment or are found to have unresolved conflicts of interest. Unlike MPs, ministers cannot hold outside appointments, and their official behaviour is tightly monitored. These constraints do not entirely protect against the possibility of private gain from office, but they make it more likely that controversy will be focused on partisan or policy gain, rather than private gain. In the aftermath of the 2010 general election News International's efforts to obtain regulatory approval to purchase a controlling stake in the satellite broadcasting company BSkyB ensnared two successive ministers in controversy of this type. First, Liberal-Democrat Secretary of State for Business Vince Cable was recorded (through journalist entrapment) expressing views suggesting he lacked the quasi-judicial impartiality required of him as the person ultimately required to approve the acquisition at stake. Then after responsibility for the acquisition decision was transferred to the Secretary for Culture Media and Sport (the Conservative Jeremy Hunt), it emerged, in a wider public inquiry into press ethics, that Mr Hunt's special adviser had shown a similar but opposite level of partiality through close relationships with News International.[2] Neither minister actually resigned, but both were embroiled in personal controversy even though the advantage each was seeking to gain was a partisan one, not a personal one. Likewise, under Labour, Peter Mandelson's anxiety to secure private sponsorship for the Millennium Dome project, for which he had ministerial responsibility, led to claims that he had improperly intervened over a passport application by a donor (the claim was later established to be unfounded). Earlier still under Margaret Thatcher, Leon Brittan's efforts to spin his side of the Westland helicopter policy dispute inside the Cabinet led to his forced resignation.

These cases illustrate the ambivalent and unpredictable nature of ethical controversies affecting ministers. As we shall see, cases of alleged personal gain do arise, but spin and blame displacement, improper behaviour by special advisers, and inadvertent failure to declare interests, where the real sin is the attempt to cover tracks rather than the attempt to secure a pecuniary advantage, are the more usual causes of ministerial controversy. Most compliance failures in this area have turned out to be difficult to judge against an objective standard, though as we shall see, it is not just the imprecision of rules, but the lack of an independent judge, that has been claimed to be the problem.

Making ministers accountable

By convention, ministers are formally accountable to Parliament and informally to the prime minister who appoints them.[3] In the United Kingdom's (mostly) single-party majoritarian governments, ministers almost invariably come from the governing party and hold office at the pleasure of their party leader, the prime minister. Some observers believe there is evidence that dismissing a poorly performing or controversial minister can, in the right circumstances, improve a government's electoral standing.[4] But since ministers in the United Kingdom are very much the personal choices of the prime minister, the decision to fire also rebounds on the latter, appearing as an admission of a misjudged appointment. A compact majority in the House of Commons is unlikely to allow the censure of a minister.

Governments therefore usually try hard to avoid forced ministerial resignation. Fewer than 10 per cent of the cases of in-government ministerial turnover seem to be in this category, compared to normal turnover or policy disagreement between minister and government.[5] Clearly strong prime ministers resist pressures for ministerial resignations more resolutely and effectively than weaker ones.[6] But overall, despite a rising pattern of controversy about ministerial behaviour, and despite a rise in resignations in the last two decades, pressure for ministerial resignation is mostly resisted. Not surprisingly, this has created an increasingly intense argument, with critics of existing arrangements calling for change to clarify the circumstances under which ministers should resign, and governments resolutely resisting any such clarification.

The status of the Ministerial Code

The argument was provided with considerable fuel in the early 1990s when the government made available the procedural rules under which ministers operated, which included reference to ethics and propriety. The original document (*Questions of Procedure for Ministers*) covered Cabinet procedure, access to and use of papers, parliamentary questions, issues of policy, and administrative coordination, alongside a specific though limited and fairly general section about ethics and propriety. The latter reminded ministers of the fundamental need to avoid conflicts of interest, to separate party and constituency activity from ministerial activity, and to respect the neutrality of civil servants. It laid out how to deal with offers of gifts and hospitality. It stressed that it was for ministers to determine how best to act in particular circumstances, implying that, beyond lawfulness and accountability to Parliament, ministers were expected to arrange their affairs and conduct their personal lives in ways they could be confident would be acceptable to Parliament, and by implication to the public. When published by the incoming Blair government in 1997 under the new title, *The Ministerial Code*, the document contained expanded sections on press and public relations, and policy coordination, and it incorporated the 1997 House of Commons resolution on parliamentary accountability and the CSPL's Seven Principles. The detailed section of the Code dealing with ethics and propriety retained the permissive language of its predecessor, though with some more explicit language on the central obligation to avoid potential conflicts of interest. The Code recognised a right not to dispose of all financial or commercial interests on assuming office but where assets were retained the minister could not manage them, and they were to be placed in a blind trust. Where, for reasons connected with the nature of the assets, that was not possible, the minister had to avoid any involvement in public decisions that might be seen as bearing on the value of the assets.[7] Strictly these provisions did not preclude trading-in-influence (using colleagues who take the relevant decisions to one's own ultimate benefit), though, while the protection offered under the Code looks less complete than in some other democracies, that question has never been raised as a serious matter.

However, even as a Code, the document remained advice and guidance, not a set of formal rules. Ministers, in the words of Cabinet Secretary Sir Robin Butler, were 'accountable to Parliament, not to a rule-book'.[8] More importantly, the prime minister would still have the final say in determining whether failures to follow the guidelines made a minister's position untenable. As long as the minister had not broken the law, that judgement would be a political one, not one based on the formal application of a quasi-judicial rule. In short, publication of a Code made no difference whatsoever to the constitutional position. It was now *called* a code, but it seemed to be considerably weaker than the codes of conduct gradually being introduced for the civil service, MPs, local councillors, and members of boards of public agencies.

Applying the Code in controversial cases

Publication of the Code did have one major impact, however. It changed debate about ministerial ethics, and each time a new controversy arose it created arguments about the perceived shortcomings of the Code's purportedly objective tests, and about the procedures required to apply it in a meaningful way. There have been numerous instances of this across all three prime ministers since 1997.

An early case was that of Peter Mandelson, where the issue was whether, in receiving an undeclared loan from another ministerial colleague and not declaring it in an application for a commercial mortgage on the same property, as well as in not declaring it as a personal interest, Mandelson had violated two codes – the Ministerial and the Parliamentary. Mortgages and personal housing issues arose in several other cases including Labour Minister for Culture Media and Sport Tessa Jowell,[9] Labour Home Secretary Jacqui Smith[10] and Conservative Culture Media and Sport Minister Maria Miller.[11] Tessa Jowell's case involved the question of whether she should have discussed with her Permanent Secretary, and declared under the Parliamentary Code, the background to the complex mortgage rearrangements she and her husband jointly undertook at a time when her husband was in receipt of controversial earnings arising from his role in advising on Silvio Berlusconi's tax dealings. In the case of Jacqui Smith, the issue was over the appropriateness of the designation of a room in her sister's bedroom as her main home whilst an MP and a minister. In the case of Maria Miller, the circumstances had some parallels with the Smith case, though what eventually forced her resignation was a less-than fulsome apology to the House of Commons for her excess mortgage claims while a backbench MP before taking up ministerial office. The need for an apology resulted from a reprimand from the Standards Committee over her allegedly uncooperative attitude towards the investigation of her case by the PCS.

David Blunkett, like Peter Mandelson, faced two quite separate controversies. The first was whether he or any of his departmental aides had intervened in the case of his lover's nanny's application for indefinite leave to remain in the United Kingdom, and whether evidence that there had been some acceleration of the processing of the application was evidence of ministerial intervention.[12] In the second case, the issue was whether he should have declared to ACOBA, business engagements that he undertook after his first resignation in 2004. Again he resigned, though he was later technically exonerated following an inquiry by the Cabinet Secretary. The nature of the exoneration raised significant questions about the status of the ACOBA, which are taken up in Chapter 9.

Another recurring form of alleged ministerial impropriety involves the role of special advisers. Labour Minister of Transport Stephen Byers resigned at the end of a long series of controversies marking his ministerial career, the best known of which involved the indiscretion of his personal adviser, Jo Moore, who issued an ill-judged departmental email on the day of the New York 9/11 attacks in 2001. It was, she said, a good day to bury bad news. Mr Byers did not immediately resign over the email, but his unwillingness to do so weakened him in the long term, and drew special attention to the extent to which ministers can be held responsible for the activities of their special advisers. We have already seen that Jeremy Hunt as Culture Secretary in 2011 faced similar pressures, and similarly declined to resign, even though the probability that he was personally responsible for the actions of his special adviser, Adam Smith, seemed higher than that of Mr Byers for Jo Moore.

The behaviour in each of these cases raised questions about the integrity of the individuals concerned. The misdemeanours did not involve issues of systemic corruption, or the misappropriation of substantial public resources, but they certainly compromised the moral standing of national leaders. How far the outcome – resignation, or significant damage to ministerial reputation or government reputation – was proportionate in any particular case to the size of the ethical failing, or indeed the existence of guilt at all, is a subjective matter. What did gradually become clear, however, through such cases, was that the the Ministerial Code, though much invoked by the Opposition critics of the government, did not provide a clear and consistent answer to the appropriateness of resignation in any particular case. Ultimately, the prime minister remained the interpreter of whatever guidelines the Code offered, and the prime minister's concerns were and always are necessarily political. In the face of this emerging reality, critics of the Code argued increasingly for a set of arrangements – parallel to those involved in the role of the PCS in investigating the conduct of MPs – to deal with, and in particular to investigate impartially, cases of alleged ministerial impropriety. Questions of fact, they argued, were best investigated by an independent official, and since, in controversies involving the ministers just listed, facts were often in dispute, there was a strong case for such an appointment, even if the final decision would be taken by the prime minister.

The argument that the Cabinet Secretary or a departmental permanent secretary could perform this role was regarded with scepticism by proponents of independent investigation. The Cabinet Secretary, while standing for the continuity and the non-partisan character of the public service, needs to work closely with, and retain the confidence of, the prime minister. Departmental permanent secretaries stand in a similar relationship to their ministers. In the eyes of critics of the Ministerial Code, the case for an independent adviser was further strengthened by another important aspect of the Code: namely the fact that often a case against a minister revolved around the matter of whether the minister had followed guidelines in providing information to permanent secretaries, or, if so, what advice they had received from those same permanent secretaries. The latter would therefore be key witnesses and would thus be inappropriate persons to play the role of investigation officers.

Rethinking the Code

Substantial criticisms of the Code came from House of Commons PASC and the CSPL. The PASC set out its concerns in an extensive report in 2001, returning to the argument more forcefully five years later.[13] The CSPL commented briefly in 2000, more critically in 2003, and with unusual directness in 2006 when the comments of the Committee chair, Sir Alistair Graham, offended by the Blair government's broader insensitivity to ethics issues surrounding the Deputy Prime Minister, Lord Sainsbury and Tessa Jowell, appeared to risk a head-on clash between the government and its own ethics advisory body.[14]

The argument focused on three key issues:

- 'ownership' of the Code;
- the procedure for advice when ministers come into office, or when their personal circumstances change during office;
- the procedures for investigating cases of alleged ministerial impropriety.

On the first, both the PASC and the CSPL insisted that the Code had developed 'constitutional status' and thus wanted Parliament to play a role in approving it. Their preference was to separate the procedural and administrative aspects of the Code from the ethics and propriety section, and transform the latter into a free-standing Code of Conduct for Ministers: a view the government firmly rejected.

The second issue – advice – was no easier. It covered, for example, the important matter of how ministers' financial interests should be examined when the minister came into office, how they should be recorded and perhaps publicised, and how, if necessary, potential conflicts should be resolved. The source of advice in the Ministerial Code was the minister's own permanent secretary seen by the government as the individual with an informed understanding of departmental business and civil-service procedures, and the types of interest which could cause problems. This view was resolutely challenged by 2003 Report of the CSPL, which argued that the involvement of permanent secretaries potentially compromised their neutrality, and undermined relationships with ministers.[15] It also argued that the Code itself did not absolutely require a minister to do anything specific in resolving conflicts of interest even when advised to do so, and worse that, if the permanent secretary provided advice, it exonerated the minister of the need to use his or her own independent ethical judgement and compromised a permanent secretary's ability to undertake an investigation on behalf of the prime minister in an ethics controversy involving the minister. For the Committee the answer was to relieve permanent secretaries of any advisory role and appoint an independent adviser on ministerial interests. The Committee proposed that the adviser should keep a regularly updated list of interests, consult where necessary with a minister's permanent secretary about departmental business where that expertise could clarify the likelihood of conflicts, and keep a record of action taken. The records would be made public, concealing only the size of financial interests.

On the last issue, investigation, both the CSPL and the PASC argued vigorously that an independent investigation role was necessary, and that neither permanent secretaries nor the Cabinet Secretary should play this role, for the reasons already discussed: namely that, as happened in the case of the first Mandelson resignation, and of Blunkett's second resignation and the Jowell and Prescott near-misses, the Cabinet Secretary would become involved in ways that, in the light of the close working relationship between himself and the prime minister, might not command public confidence in his impartiality. PASC, with its weather eye on enhancing the role of Parliament, wanted this done by either the PCS, or the Parliamentary Ombudsman.[16] In practice, outsiders had already been asked to investigate, as happened with Sir Anthony Hammond in the case of Peter Mandelson and Sir Alan Budd in the case of David Blunkett. The CSPL's solution was that at the start of each Parliament and in consultation with the leaders of the main opposition parties 'the Prime Minister should nominate two or three individuals as being available to carry out an investigation into an allegation of ministerial misconduct'.[17] The eventual report would go to the prime minister, who would continue to decide on the consequences, but the report would also be published.

The government rejected these proposals too, but its resistance gradually weakened as controversy mounted. Eventually in the wake of the loans for peerages issue, discussed in Chapter 5, it made a partial concession in nominating the Comptroller and Auditor General Sir John Bourn to the role of Independent Adviser on Ministers' Interests. However, the new Adviser assisted without supplanting the role of permanent secretaries.[18] The record of interests and advice remained private. The report of any investigation provided by the Adviser at the request of the prime minister also looked likely to remain hidden from public scrutiny, and would be limited to financial interests. And finally the appointment was not one made jointly with leaders of opposition parties, as many had advocated. The PASC remained concerned 'that Sir John's role is limited; inappropriately weighted in favour of an additional layer of advice over that of Permanent Secretary; and lacks a genuine investigatory dimension'.

Sir John did not stay long in office, nor undertake any investigations. When Gordon Brown became prime minister in 2007 he revised the Ministerial Code and appointed a new Independent Adviser, the former Parliamentary Commissioner for Standards, Sir Philip Mawer. The Adviser's remit was to be broader and more transparent than that of his predecessor, henceforth becoming the designated agent to investigate, rather than just one such possible agent. The Adviser would also publish 'an annual statement covering relevant Ministers' interests'. Ministers would have to provide their permanent secretary with a list of all interests potentially bearing conflicts (previously they were simply advised to do so). The PASC nevertheless remained sceptical, with the absence of a power to initiate investigations a serious weakness. It also criticised the Adviser's tenure, his dependence on the Cabinet Office for staff and funding, and 'the lack of public visibility for the post'.

Sir Philip Mawer himself investigated just one case in his three-year tenure. This was the case of Minister of Justice Shahid Malik, about claims that emerged during the *Daily Telegraph*'s revelations on parliamentary expenses to the effect that Malik had breached the Ministerial Code by failing to declare constituency property rental at preferential rates and thereby concealing an interest. The process turned out to be quite complex and Malik resigned from office temporarily during the weeks necessary to investigate. He was reinstated to a different government post when he was found not to have breached the Code.

The Ministerial Code after 2010

Controversy did not abate after the 2010 general election, even though Sir Philip Mawer made a strong case in his second and last annual report that a great deal of work during his tenure had gone into formalising the arrangements for recording ministers' interests, publishing and updating them twice yearly and developing procedures for investigation.[19] Instead two new ministerial controversies – the first concerning Defence Secretary Liam Fox, and the second the Culture Media and Sport Minister, Jeremy Hunt – raised further issues of both principle and operation affecting the Independent Adviser's role.

The first issue concerned whether a controversy gets referred to the Independent Adviser at all, since neither the Fox nor the Hunt cases was so referred. The prime minister chose instead to hold *confidential* inquiries by respectively the Permanent Secretary at the Ministry of Defence and the Cabinet Secretary. The Independent Adviser's role in providing transparency, and in avoiding a clash of interests and loyalties with permanent secretaries, was therefore ignored. However, the cases also underlined another aspect of investigation. Had the Independent Adviser been deployed, it might well have taken too much time in a fast-moving political context. The Malik case had already demonstrated that procedures could be cumbersome.[20] Malik had had to step down, which would have been particularly difficult in Fox's case (and Fox did indeed resign).[21] Admittedly, in both the Fox and the Hunt cases, the case for independent investigation was strengthened by the fact that both appeared to involve an element of concealment of interests by the minister. However, in neither case was the concealment a matter of financial interests. In the Fox case, it was an unexplained personal closeness to an individual who purported to be the minister's special adviser when he in fact was not, and who therefore was brought inappropriately close to the work of the Ministry of Defence in ways that probably broke other aspects of the Ministerial Code. In the case of Jeremy Hunt, the issue was an inappropriate closeness to an external commercial interest: both in terms of personal contact, and strong stated pre-existing support (apparently on public-interest grounds) for a policy that was also in the interests of News Corp. The argument, in short, was that Hunt had pre-judged an issue on which he was called to judge impartially as minister.

The controversial aspect of the Hunt case was essentially whether expressing a view on policy, as Hunt had clearly done to the prime minister, necessarily created an unresolved conflict of interest – a question made more poignant by the circumstantial evidence as events proceeded that both Mr Hunt and his special adviser seemed to enjoy warm and close relationships with News Corp. The issue was not resolved by the fact that the minister did not, in the end, need to sit in quasi-judicial judgement (the controversies engulfing News Corp in the United Kingdom having led to its abandoning the bid). The question was whether the minister had a conflict of interest, not whether he eventually acted on it. If he had, the prime minister knew about it, and had no need of an Independent Adviser to tell him about it. But even if it was a conflict of interest, it was not clearly one that should have been declared to the Independent Adviser on Ministerial Interests, even though the terms of reference for the role do not appear to preclude non-financial interests.[22] It was an interest generated by the minister's policy views. So to take the view that it was appropriate to refer the issue to the Independent Adviser would certainly widen the latter's terms of reference very broadly indeed, and it is far from clear where the limits would then be drawn on what would count as a conflict of interest.

Conclusion

The experience of the Ministerial Code is therefore deeply ambivalent. For the government, the Code has never been 'the public framework of rules against which conduct should be judged'.[23] It was never intended to be a justiciable code like others, and no government has accepted the pressure of the CSPL and the PASC for it to be seen in this way. Governments have also consistently argued that to provide the Ministerial Code with an independent investigatory mechanism would worsen the climate of public trust not improve it, since the public would soon see the mechanism as a means of kicking a difficult political problem into touch. If a minister's position is untenable, governments have argued, he or she will, as the Mandelson and Malik cases showed, have to go fairly quickly, even if found innocent in a subsequent investigation.

The most unsatisfactory aspect of the Code remains that there is no resolution to this problem. The Code has developed a quasi-constitutional status, but it has done so in a pragmatic and evolutionary way and the absence of an authoritative architect has left confusion. The contents of the Code were dictated by the precedent of *Questions of Procedure for Ministers*, with its curious combination of procedural description and ethical advice and as such are, it might be argued, unsuited to precise interpretation and justiciability.

Notes

1 Berlinsky, S., T. Dewan, K. Dowding and G. Subrahmanyam, 'Choosing, moving and resigning at Westminster, UK', in K. Dowding and P. Dumont (eds), *The Selection of Ministers in Europe* (London: Routledge, 2009), p. 72. See also HC 247 [2005]: *Report of the Inquiry into the Circumstances Surrounding the Death of Dr David Kelly C.M.G. by Lord Hutton*.

2 The prime minister announced a two-part inquiry, investigating the role of the press and police in the phone-hacking scandal. HC Deb, 13 July 2011, vol. 531, 311–313, resulting in the report of the Leveson Inquiry into the culture, practice, and the ethics of the press. On the specific points in this paragraph see especially: Leveson Inquiry, Transcript of morning evidence, 31 May 2012, pp. 1–107 (www.levesoninquiry.org.uk/wp-content/uploads/2012/05/Transcript-of-Morning-Hearing-31-May-2012.txt, accessed 19 March 2015).

3 For parliamentary definitions see Select Committee on the Public Services, *Ministerial Accountability and Responsibility*, HC 313, 1995–1996 and Public Administration Committee, *Ministerial Accountability and Parliamentary Questions*, HC 820, 1997–1998; see also Hansard Society, *The Challenge for Parliament: Making Government Accountable* (London: Vacher Dodd, 2001), pp. 23–34. For a case study see *Report of the Inquiry into the Export of Defence Equipment and Dual-Use Goods to Iraq and Related Prosecutions*, 5 vols, HC 115, 1995–1996.

4 Dewan, T. and K. Dowding, 'The corrective effect of ministerial resignations on government popularity', *American Journal of Political Science*, 49:1 (2005), 46–56.

5 Berlinsky *et al.*, 'Choosing, moving and resigning at Westminister', pp. 69–74.

6 Berlinsky *et al.*, 'Choosing, moving and resigning at Westminister', p. 72.

7 *The Ministerial Code, 1997*, pp. 37–39.

8 Baker, A. and P. Hennessy, *Prime Ministers and the Rule Book* (London: Methuen, 2000).

9 See *Guardian*, 3 March 2006 for the Cabinet Secretary letter, dated 2 March 2006, exonerating Tessa Jowell.

10 Standards and Privileges Committee, *Jacqui Smith*, HC 974, 12 October 2009.

11 Committee on Standards, *Maria Miller*, HC 1179, 3 April 2014.

12 *Return to an Address of the Honourable the House of Commons dated 21st December 2004 for an Inquiry into an Application for Indefinite Leave to Remain, by Sir Alan Budd*, HC 175, 21 December 2004.

13 Public Administration Committee, *The Ministerial Code: Improving the Rule Book: Report*, HC 235, 15 February 2001, 2001–2002, and Public Administration Committee, *The Ministerial Code: The Case for Independent Investigation*, HC 1457, 6 September 2006, 2006–2007.

14 Barnett, A., 'Blair critic "target of smears": parliamentary standards watchdog complains of Labour attempts to dig up dirt on him', *Observer*, 25 June 2006; Hinsliff, G., 'Blair is "ready to drop" his sleaze buster', *Observer*, 14 January 2007.

15 Committee on Standards in Public Life, Ninth Report, *Defining the Boundaries within the Executive* (Cm 5775) April 2003.

16 Public Administration Committee, *The Ministerial Code: Improving the Rule Book*, HC 235, 15 February 2001, 2001–2002.

17 Committee on Standards in Public Life, Ninth Report, *Defining the Boundaries*.

18 Public Administration Committee, *The Ministerial Code: The Case for Independent Investigation*, HC 1457, 6 September 2006, 2006–2007, 13–14.

19 Cabinet Office, *Independent Adviser on Ministers' Interests, 2010–11. Annual Report,* 2011, pp. 7–9.
20 House of Commons (2012) Public Administration Committee (2011–2012), *The Prime Minister's Adviser on Ministerial Interests: Independent or Not?* HC 1761, 17 March 2012, 2010–2012.
21 Public Administration Committee, *The Prime Minister's Adviser on Ministerial Interests: Independent or Not?* HC 1761, 17 March 2012, 2010–2012; Public Administration Committee, *The Ministerial Code: Improving the Rule Book.*
22 Cabinet Office, *Independent Adviser on Ministers' Interests, 2010–11. Annual Report* (2011).
23 Public Administration Committee, *The Ministerial Code: The Case for Independent Investigation,* HC 1457, 6 September 2006, 2006–2007, 13.

8

Whitehall wars: protecting civil-service impartiality

Administrative ethics

The administrative executive covers a broad spectrum of officialdom, including not just the core civil service but service-providers like teachers, health-care professionals, the police and armed forces, local government officials and technical specialists who do similar jobs to those found in the private sector. A good number operate in areas where there are precise and long-standing professional standards, which have always included ethics provisions. Many of these arise naturally from the sensitivities of the role, as in medicine, the police or the judiciary. For others, the growth of ethics awareness has led only in the last two decades to the addition of more precise ethics provisions in codes of conduct and management contracts.

Controversy over administrative ethics has since the 1980s been generated by significant changes to the way in which some public services are provided, involving new incentive structures, outsourcing and privatisation. Few want a public service whose workers are not incentivised to do their best, but when incentives change, and especially when material incentives increase, there is a risk that the way officials think about their job and perform their roles may also change. In the United Kingdom recent changes to funding in primary health-care provision and school education have for example led to concerns that new conflicts of interest are emerging where previously they were absent or at least less acute.[1] Performance standards for public services may also induce officials to behave unethically: the provision of crime statistics by police authorities has recently become controversial,[2] as have the responses of some teachers to pupil-performance requirements.[3] An extreme instance of this arose in UK water privatisation in 1989 where the earnings of the most senior strata of managers and directors rose dramatically in the years after privatisation and caused widespread comment that privatisation had very much served the interests of a specific class of public servants, some of whom would have provided the specialist advice that affected the terms on which privatisation was established.[4]

The ways in which public officials can be corrupted is extensive: misuse of privileged information, manipulation of data, abuse of judicial and police procedures, bribery, extortion, theft of public property, and mistreatment of staff or public-sector clients. Endemic administrative corruption among officials at all levels is common in many countries, including a few European democracies, but it cannot be said to be the case in the United Kingdom. Even Transparency International, never knowingly reluctant to draw attention to corruption, agrees that, with some exceptions, at the administrative level corruption is not marked in the United Kingdom.[5] The exceptions – the prison service and the police particularly – are hard contexts in any society, given their exposure to criminal worlds. Otherwise, however, prosecutions for administrative corruption are relatively rare. The UK Anti-Fraud Authority calculated in 2011 that annual fraud in the UK amounted to the (at first sight) formidable sum of £70 billion, of which £20 billion from the public sector, but it turned out that almost all of this was perpetrated *against* the public purse (tax evasion, benefit, housing and licensing frauds, etc.) without enablers inside the public sector helping them, suggesting that the British public may be endemically dishonest, but public administrators are not.[6] Clearly in this chapter it is not possible to trace the responses that cases of corruption and conflict of interest among officials have evoked right across the many different types of officials. Instead, given the apparent absence of low-level endemic corruption, the chapter focuses on the most sensitive area of public service: namely the senior civil service and other top managerial and directorial appointments that are closest to partisan and electoral politics.

There are two reasons for doing so. First, such roles are the most important. They set the tone for public service. The higher civil service is widely thought to be the area in which a public service ethos, providing a psychological as opposed to a material incentive to performance for public officials, is most developed. So changes to the public service that threaten it should be most visible at this level. Secondly, in the UK constitutional narrative public-service values are generally presented as a safeguard against the rampant partisanship of elected politicians. The United Kingdom does not subscribe explicitly to theories of checks and balances, but the permanence of a professional, meritocratic, non-partisan civil service is frequently seen as the embodiment of an implicit separation of powers between partisanship and procedural integrity. If this is true, a change in that relationship would potentially have consequences for public ethics. Beyond the departmental civil service, ministerial patronage has always been present, in the sense that, as we shall see, a very large number of appointments have historically been ministerial appointments. So here too any change, either because ministers are making more partisan use of ministerial patronage, or because a greater range of appointments is available, will be of significance.

The interface between politics and administration

The relationship between the partisan and the non-partisan parts of the executive lies at the heart of the Westminster/Whitehall model of parliamentary government. Its essence is that the political impartiality, centralised recruitment, training and inter-departmental mobility found in the civil service, and its strong sense of professionalism and public service, are important counter-weights to the partisanship of politicians. These features also offer important protections for civil servants themselves. Through them, civil servants exchange constitutional anonymity for managerial and career autonomy, and freedom from reprisal when they speak truth (or what they see as truth) to the power of elected politicians. As long as a civil servant's fundamental values are driven by this ethos, they stand as a check against the improprieties towards which elected politicians can be drawn: biased implementation of policy, inappropriate closeness with sectional interests that provide party funding, the manipulation of news, the improper use of privileged information, biased regulation, rigged contracts and so forth. Ministers may still periodically find ways around the civil-service barrier, and where they do, other checks and safeguards need to be deployed – most notably parliamentary and media scrutiny and high-quality public auditing – but a civil service confident in its values and in its independence makes a very strong first line of defence.

As a principle, civil service impartiality was laid down in the foundational document of the modern civil service, the 1854 Northcote-Trevelyan Report, and reaffirmed in successive reports and commentaries on the constitutional status of the service right down to the 1985 Armstrong Memorandum.[7] The Armstrong Memorandum emphasises that the civil service has no constitutional personality or responsibility separate from the duly elected government, and that civil servants serve the government of the day with disinterested loyalty. Ministers can assume that when civil servants present evidence-based argument that runs counter to their own, it comes in the spirit of honest and impartial advice. For their part, civil servants can, at least in theory, be confident that doing so will have no negative consequence for their careers. The separation of the parliamentary class from the civil service, and the large degree of self-government the civil service enjoys, underpinned by an 1884 Order in Council requiring civil servants to resign before standing for election, ensures that as long as the civil service has sound ethical foundations, it will thus exercise a powerful moral influence over the integrity of the political class. In the absence of a politicised tier of administration, ministers are largely reliant on the civil service to shape and implement the policy ideas they bring with them to office.

Alongside this constitutional principle Northcote-Trevelyan also laid down the principles of recruitment and promotion on merit, and central management. Together, they established an ethos of public service which infused the UK civil service. This ethos has always been hard to measure as a set of internalised values,[8] but it is clearly stated in successive versions of Part 4 of the modern *Civil Service Management Code*, which deals with conflicts of interest, gifts, hospitality, share-dealing, outside activities, the confidentiality of office, the proscription (later somewhat relaxed at local level from the original 1884 Order) on political activity, contracting procedures, and post-service employment.

It has been successive alleged attacks on these ideas – in particular on the pre-eminent position of the traditional civil service as adviser to government in policy-making, and as manager of the services of government – that have excited controversy over administrative ethics in the United Kingdom in the last three decades. It would be wrong to present these assaults as deliberate attempts to undermine civil-service integrity. There is no evidence that those who have criticised the service as inflexible or unresponsive, or sought to change it, have wanted lower ethical standards. What they seem primarily to have been seeking, through a series of efforts at broader civil-service reform, has been more flexible government machinery, capable of delivering policy with greater responsiveness, efficiency and effectiveness.

Opponents of such objectives would argue that the consequence has been to put at risk a central safeguard of public integrity. They would claim that the career autonomy and positional independence of civil servants are weakened, and so, with this, is their ability to serve as a bulwark against ethically questionable ministerial behaviour. Meanwhile the transformation of the policy and service-delivery element of the reform process, inherent in agency-delivery and outsourcing, would change the ethos of public servants, and increase ministerial patronage over senior appointments to service-delivery roles.

This chapter attempts to evaluate this debate. It focuses on two key issues. The first is the impact of ongoing efforts at civil-service reform, including efforts to wrest control of civil-service appointments from the service itself, and put it in the hands of ministers, allegedly resulting in better delivery of party manifestoes and voter choices. The second is the controversy over public appointments at senior level in public agencies outside the core departmental civil service.

With one clear exception – post-employment, which is dealt with separately in Chapter 9 – there is little hard evidence that relationships between the partisan world and the senior administrative world *have* actually changed for the worse in terms of ethics and propriety. At best, the changes are in the *perception* of risk, symbolised by the long-running campaign for a so-called 'Civil Service Act' which would protect the integrity and professionalism of the service and its ethos from partisan-ship. That campaign finally achieved some success in the Constitutional Reform and Government Act 2010, a measure granted by a government in its dying days, probably conscious that if it did something to bolster civil-service neutrality it might actually hamper its opponents' ability to use appointments for partisan ends when they assumed office.[9] We con-sider the effect of the Act in the last section, together with the way the coalition government responded to it. First, however, we look in greater detail at how a changing relationship between politics and administra-tion could be deleterious to ethics and propriety.

Civil service reform under Labour

There are several ways in which partisan encroachment on civil-service self-management could eventually undermine the public-service ethos. These include a change in the reservoir of recruitment that brought in large numbers of outsiders unsocialised into public-service values; the appointment of a senior tier of so-called special advisers similarly unsocialised into public-service values; ministerial encroachment on the appointment process for senior civil servants, leaving the latter in a posi-tion where, to win promotion, civil servants were forced to behave in partisan ways; and changes in the operating context of the senior civil service, shifting power away from senior civil-service management.

Where civil servants come from. The central anxiety concerning chan-ging patterns of recruitment to senior management posts in the core civil service and in public agencies is that, through the influx of outsiders from the private sector (an explicit goal of successive governments since the 1990s) public-service values will be subordinated to personal career imperatives.[10] There is no doubt that recruitment to the senior echelons of the core civil service is today considerably removed from a classical Weberian model of recruitment at the start of a career, and internal pro-motion thereafter. Different sources have used different bases to assess

Table 8.1 Sources of appointments to senior (Band 2 and 3, and Permanent Secretary) civil-service posts reported by the Civil Service Commissioners, 1995/1996–2012/2013

	Civil service	Other public sector	Private sector and other	Total
1995/1996	29	28	23 (37%)	80
1996/1997	32	37	27 (28%)	96
1997/1998	27	36	20 (24%)	83
1998/1999	32	44	31 (29%)	107
1999/2000	55	59	44 (28%)	158
2000/2001	77	98	27 (13%)	202
2001/2002	77	86	37 (18%)	200
2002/2003	29	26	42 (48%)	87
2003/2004	43	19	27 (30%)	89
2004/2005	37	17	37 (41%)	91
2005/2006	42	30	39 (35%)	111
2006/2007	35	20	35 (39%)	90
2007/2008	43	24	38 (36%)	105
2008/2009	62	13	23 (23%)	98
2009/2010	32	12	30 (41%)	74
2010/2011	21	4	7 (22%)	32
2011/2012	32	16	14 (23%)	62
2012/2013	37	31	17 (20%)	85

Source: Annual Reports of the Civil Service Commissioners, 1997/1998–2004/2005, 2009/2010, 2012/2013. The categories of appointments requiring Civil Service Commission approval were changed in 2002, reducing the number of appointments reported on. From that date, they refer to Band 2 and above. Backgrounds refer to the immediately preceding employment, so a 'civil service' background could be relatively short, following a long private-sector career, or vice versa.

this process in the United Kingdom but the picture is clear. By the 1990s at least a quarter of senior appointments in the UK civil service were normally coming from the private sector, and this did not change substantially until the drastic cutting of numbers and costs that followed the financial crisis of 2008. At that point, the greater cost of competitive compensation packages to recruit from the private sector, as Civil Service Commission data clearly show,[11] seemed to put a brake on outside appointments (see Table 8.1).

Special advisers. A second mechanism is the growth of special advisers. We have already seen in the previous chapter that special advisers have been a source of difficulty for a small number of ministers both under Labour from 1997, and more recently for the coalition government. That said, the real evidence of a basic change towards a patronage-driven system is modest. Their numbers have certainly increased, but in a far more contained way than is sometimes supposed. The main growth occurred during 1997–2001. The numbers approximately doubled from thirty-eight in the last two years of John Major's government, to eighty-one by the end of the 1997–2001 Parliament.[12] Outside Downing Street and the Treasury, however, there have remained no more than a mere two or three individuals per department. Inside Downing Street, there have been significantly more, as the prime minister's office has expanded: from eight before the 1997 election to twenty-eight by 2005 though it decreased under the coalition government after 2010.

Controversies about special advisers have varied. A 1997 Order in Council gave direct executive powers over other civil servants to up to three advisers, though in reality only two named individuals, Jonathan Powell, the prime minister's chief of staff, and Alastair Campbell, his head of communications, ever actually assumed these powers. There was no further use of that Order in Council and it was revoked in 2007.[13] A different controversy focused on press officers, arising from the 1997 Labour government's highly centralised communications strategy. The aim was to wrest management of Whitehall communications machinery away from professional (and non-partisan) civil servants and bring it under centralised Downing Street communications machinery.[14] This controversy too eventually died down and for some years – until the controversy was re-ignited by 'extended ministerial offices', discussed below – the issue appeared to be relatively settled as numbers stabilised, with only occasional episodes of alleged impropriety by particular special advisers, the most serious being, perhaps, Adam Werritty, an unofficial special adviser to Liam Fox, the first Defence Secretary in the 2010 coalition, and mainly because Mr Werritty had not actually been officially appointed to his self-proclaimed role.

Civil service reform and performance incentives. The United Kingdom civil service has been subject to successive waves of reform initiatives in the last three decades.[15] Reform has inevitably affected relations between ministers and the senior civil service, and perceptions of those relationships. The 1997 Labour government was congenitally suspicious of the capacities of the senior civil service, and determined to impose a major programme of civil-service reform emphasising public-service *delivery*.[16] That suspicion was inherited by the 2010 coalition government. For Labour it prompted a major new role for delivery units within the Cabinet Office and to some degree the Treasury, a project that, in so far as it was deliberately headed by outsiders like Michael Barber and Geoff Mulgan (both previously special advisers), Wendy Thompson (from local government) and Peter Gershon (from the private sector), was viewed with deep concern by senior civil servants. More broadly, civil-service reform, while formally worked out with the cooperation of the Civil Service Management Board (and thus also of permanent secretaries) deliberately sought to impose new forms of accountability on the service's leadership. It established performance-related pay and appraisal rewards and inevitably new definitions of leadership qualities, together with feedback loops to test and assess strengths and weaknesses of managerial capacity.[17]

There is no systematic measure of the temperature and mood of relations between the senior civil service and the political executive, though from 1997 onwards, and particularly in the wake of publication of Labour's 1999 white paper *Modernising Government*, there were frequent press reports about distrust and bad relationships.[18] The conduct of intelligence assessment and strategic planning surrounding the Iraq War added to the sourness. The Butler Review, published in the wake of the Hutton Inquiry, showed some senior public servants were uncomfortable about the precision of analysis and thinking at the top level of the policy process. Sir Robin Butler and Sir Richard Wilson, as successive Cabinet Secretaries, appeared to harbour serious concern about changes in relationships between ministers and civil servants that the Labour government had introduced.[19]

Sir Richard Wilson's replacement in 2002 by Sir Andrew Turnbull seemed to intensify efforts at public-service reform. The Cabinet Office Delivery and Reform Team included a Reform Strategy Team, a Strategy Unit, a Delivery Unit, an e-government Unit, a Corporate Development Group, and Offices for Public Service Reform and for Government Commerce. The document which launched the reform envisaged new styles of corporate board oversight in departments, and performance-partnership agreements between the centre and departments 'providing a robust internal challenge on delivery and effectiveness'. It also spoke of civil servants being 'recruited from various backgrounds, at different career stages, given better development opportunities, under more rigorous performance management, with senior postings normally limited to four years, and with progress being dependent on meeting skills and experience requirements at key "career gateways"'.[20]

In parallel with Downing Street reforms focused on delivery of joined-up government, similar changes were taking place in the relationship between the Treasury and government departments, through Public Service Agreements. Performance reviews for a limited number of departments came and went though importantly no permanent secretary was ousted. There were also reviews by Peter Gershon and Sir John Lyon concerning the overall size of the civil service and its geographical location.

By the end of Labour's second term radical intent concerning civil-service reform seemed to wane, however, with many proposals having encountered more hostility across Whitehall than the government could address. The arguments mounted by defenders of civil-service neutrality had considerable purchase and were not limited to civil-service insiders. Even former prime minister John Major came out in their support.[21] The weight of academic commentary suggests a good deal of scepticism about the overall effect even in terms of government coordination and service delivery, let alone the main issue here, which is whether there was actually an extension of political control and partisanship in senior civil-service appointments.[22]

The decision by Gordon Brown to launch his new government with *The Governance of Britain* white paper, the first two chapters of which in principle limited the powers of the executive and increased its accountability to Parliament, also suggested a change of direction in terms of civil-service reform. Although some have seen elements of continuity as regards the Brown's government's civil service objectives,[23] the environment changed with the economic crisis of 2008, so that spending reviews, rather than broader governance issues, became the key priorities. No less significant, however, was the impact of the decade-long debate about Labour's alleged designs on the impartiality of the civil service. Over time the CSPL, the PASC, the Civil Service Commission, and in government even the Cabinet Secretary from 2005 onwards, Gus O'Donnell, gradually became more exercised about the risks of politicisation, even if there was rather little evidence – other than through special advisers – of its happening in the senior levels of the civil service. Both Committees lined themselves up behind calls for a civil service act (which technically the Labour Party had also committed itself to) which would provide a statutory basis guaranteeing civil service neutrality,[24] and somewhat unexpectedly in the dying days of the Brown government legislation was finally passed to entrench the constitutional autonomy of the service.

The CRGA 2010: a victory for the traditional relationship?

Section 1 of the CRGA 2010, albeit relatively brief, constitutes an important item of legislation. It gives statutory protection to the principle that appointments to the civil service right up to the highest levels are to be made on merit, and through fair and open competition. This principle had as we have seen also applied to a civil service managed essentially under Royal Prerogative, but since 2010 it has been enshrined in law. The guarantor of this, moreover, is the Civil Service Commission, established as a body corporate, which acts as watchdog of all appointments from pay band 2 and above, chairing selection panels, and auditing the propriety of appointments at lower levels, on which it publishes an annual report. The Civil Service Code too (affirming the obligation of civil servants to act with not only integrity and honesty, but also objectivity and impartiality, and therefore acting as a further guarantee) is given statutory force. Although passed by a Labour majority in the House of Commons, the legislation had the support of the Conservatives and Liberal Democrats, and at least in principle affirmed the essence of the long-standing British model of a civil service politically neutral right up to its highest levels. On paper it was a victory for opponents of any major shift in the direction of a partially politicised top layer of the administrative executive which today exists, in one form or another, in the majority of advanced democracies.

In practice, the victory was not as complete as might have appeared. Most of the issues that had got under the skin of past governments, and especially New Labour, fairly rapidly became irritants to the coalition government formed in 2010. These included dilemmas over how to make service delivery more accountable and responsive, how to consult and coordinate better both across government and at the user interface, and most importantly how to ensure that key competencies were present across the higher reaches of the civil service, particularly in relation to project delivery and management, IT projects, and procurement. In the wake of the financial crisis the new government was inevitably concerned above all – through its *Change Programme* – with shrinking the absolute size of the government machine (by some 100,000 out of 500,000 over five years) rather than refining its delivery capacities. But this fire-storm of down-sizing itself quickly set in train a mutual 'blame-game' between ministers and civil servants for the several serious failures that subsequently manifested themselves in flawed decisions, as in the West Coast mainline fiasco, the Universal Credit IT debacle, and several other major projects.[25]

In such circumstances, ministers were fairly quickly attracted back to the narratives of their Labour predecessors: that the civil service machine was bureaucratic and unresponsive, that the centre needed greater coordinating powers; that senior civil servants should resign when implementation for which they had responsibility failed; and that ministers should have 'extended ministerial offices' (offices that to the civil service were suspiciously like French-style *cabinets ministériels*). The prime minister hugely offended everyone up to his Cabinet Secretary in 2011 when he declared that 'bureaucrats in government departments who concoct those ridiculous rules and regulations that make life impossible, particularly for small firms' were 'enemies of enterprise'. The Cabinet Office

Minister, Francis Maude, not only introduced the principle (but did not before the 2015 election pursue very far the practice) of Enhanced Ministerial Offices, but even more controversially, and contrary to the spirit of the 2010 Act, also proposed that ministers should have a greater say over the appointment of their permanent secretaries.

The result of this renewed tension, given the statutory lock on appointment enjoyed by the Civil Service Commissioners, was modest, but it showed that the problem, at least as seen from behind ministerial desks, was not solved by the CRGA 2010, even if politicians had supported its passage. On the contrary, with relationships inside the coalition (in parliament, inside the Conservative Party, and in Whitehall), more ragged as the government aged, commentators talked of a veritable Whitehall War, with relationships as bad as ever, if not worse than before.

Political patronage beyond the civil service

Thus far we have dealt with the core civil service. But under the United Kingdom system of executive prerogative ministers had historically also been responsible for appointments to a great range of public bodies beyond the civil service itself. Until the 1980s it generated little controversy. Though there is scant evidence about precisely how far, in the twentieth century (other than in the House of Lords) patronage was used in an explicitly partisan sense, the principle rarely excited much public interest or controversy.[26] However, perceptions changed in the 1980s with civil-service modernisation. The principles of new public management (NPM) greatly expanded the number of strategically important NDPBs. Around three-quarters of service and delivery civil-service staff were transferred into delivery agencies under the Next Steps programme and its successors, adding to a range of ministerial appointments that was already reckoned by some estimates to run to some 10,000.[27]

Scrutiny over this potential power of patronage was a key part of the first report of the CSPL in 1995. It recommended that all appointments to NDPBs should be subject to a code of conduct and a set of principles to ensure appointment on merit, and the achievement of a balance of skills and experience. Its central recommendation was that a Commissioner for Public Appointments be established in 1995 with a remit to develop a Code of Practice for Public Appointments, and to act as its guardian, monitoring practice, and issuing reports on compliance.[28] Indeed, every *individual* appointment should be monitored for compliance by an independent appointee on the selection board. The CSPL's 1995 recommendations, afforced by further recommendations in its fourth report in 1997, were rapidly accepted by the Conservative government.[29]

The new Commissioner's role in some respects paralleled that of the Civil Service Commission as guarantor of probity in civil-service appointments, but with the difference that the Office of the Commissioner for Public Appointments (OCPA) was simply an oversight body, making no appointments directly. Senior NPM agency appointments were made under ministerial prerogative and ministers therefore insisted on retaining a final say, selecting as in the past from a recommended list of appointable candidates. The CSPL in its 1995 report accepted the principle of ministerial prerogative. However, disagreements quickly arose over the interpretation of the rules, especially concerning a minister's right to intervene at the short-listing stage.[30] These arguments were reinforced by parallel concern about NHS appointments at lower levels, which in the late 1990s, after the 1997 general election, revealed a striking bias towards Labour Party activists, provoking formal complaints to the Commissioner by the Conservative and Liberal Democrat parties.[31]

The NHS imbalance was fairly quickly addressed, but the more general argument continued to reverberate.[32] The momentum was then taken up again by the CSPL, which proposed limiting the ministerial role to the definition, selection criteria and short-listing stages, with no say over the final candidate, and that the OCPA be transformed into a full Commission for NDPB appointments, with powers and roles analogous to the Civil Service Commission.[33] Not surprisingly, the government was unreceptive to both sets of recommendations.[34]

Thereafter, across the rest of Labour's period in office, the argument did not go away but it gradually changed in nature. The OCPA itself gradually became concerned about the quality and impact of its own procedures. It worried that the pursuit of objectivity and merit were becoming inappropriately formalised as well as cumbersome and time-consuming, with perverse effects, particularly in relation to ethnic and gender diversity on managerial boards.[35] In 2011, as part of the Coalition drive to reduce administrative costs, the role of Commissioner for Public Appointments was therefore merged with that of First Civil Service Commissioner.

Sir David Normington took on both roles with a remit to reform the OCPA code and design a more flexible, principles-driven and risk-based code. It was introduced, to little controversy, in 2012, Sir David commenting that 'the system provides visibility and independent scrutiny of the role of Ministers and no longer attracts the levels of criticism and controversy it did ten years ago'. One reason why it engendered less controversy a decade on may in fact be that – the detailed operation of the OCPA code apart – the work of the CSPL had already effected a very significant step-change in practice in 1995. Matthew Flinders argued in a 2009 study that much of the criticism of the growth of political patronage in the United Kingdom since the 1980s had been misconceived, and that there was a clear shift after 1995 (driven by the gradual extension of OCPA procedures to a wider and wider range of public bodies, and the parallel evolution of Appointments Commissions for the judiciary, the House of Lords and the NHS) from a *patronage* regime to a *public appointment* regime, backed up furthermore by steps towards the development of pre-appointment hearings by parliamentary committees for certain very high profile appointments.[36]

It has become clear over the two decades since the establishment of the OCPA that the clock is unlikely to be turned from the Next Steps revolution back towards centralised ministerial control of implementation. But it is also clear that UK governments will find it difficult to undermine the structures put in place by the oversight bodies for public appointments established since 1995. All that said, without any coordination of the NDPB universe from the executive, there would be a risk of a high degree of fragmentation of government machinery. Parliamentary oversight alone cannot fulfil this role. Even pre-legislative scrutiny of very high profile roles contains challenges, and results to date have been mixed.[37] All sides to the debate appeared gradually to recognise these realities, and this seems to have contributed to a cooling of the tone of the debate over the last few years.

Conclusion

The response to alleged threats to civil-service impartiality since the early 1990s has been formidable: the Civil Service Code; the Code of Conduct for Special Advisers; the Codes of Conduct for senior civil-service appointments; the Codes for public appointments in NDPBs; performance appraisal for appointed members of public governance bodies and civil servants; the OCPA; the new roles accorded to the Civil Service Commissioners; and the detailed scrutiny which all these new practices, codes and institutions have received from the PASC and the CSPL. It is difficult to find a public service elsewhere in the world that, not actually showing evidence of serious issues of ethics and propriety at the outset, has subjected itself to such an overhaul. Civil service ethics look much better protected in 2015 than twenty-five years ago. It remains the case, moreover, that compared to all other advanced democracies – Westminster dominions included – the level of partisanship at senior levels of both the civil service and NGOs seems extremely low. Special advisers are still a small group mainly concentrated in No 10 and the Treasury, and ministers have shown little appetite for the rampant colonisation of public bodies, or the parking of political colleagues, that occurs in NGOs in many democracies.

This is not to argue that the intense debates were not worth having, or that the measures were not important. Nor indeed is it to argue that those in the political class who remain unhappy that too high a priority is still accorded to the preservation at all costs of civil-service 'virtue', are necessarily wrong. Whether virtue is preserved at the expense of a civil service that is fit for purpose is a serious argument, and as we have seen, one that continues to run. What is clear is that the administrative ethics debate in the United Kingdom has largely been a second-order debate; it has not been about impropriety itself, but about the *potential* for impropriety under changing conditions. And it has been conducted at elite level. Occasionally there is some public controversy, but compared to ethics for elected politicians, parties and lobbyists, it has rarely had public visibility. Those engaged in the debate have never been fully differentiated from each other, either as ministers versus civil servants, or in partisan terms. An ongoing and quite sophisticated ethical seminar has been conducted over a long period, in an extensive round of reports and responses, in a remarkably calm atmosphere.

As for non-civil service appointments, the conclusion seems to be that in the 1990s, the United Kingdom woke up rather suddenly to the perceived risk of partisanship in administrative and oversight appointments, and conducted a public argument about how to deal with the issue, but without any real knowledge of how serious the problem really was. The headline number of 'thousands' of ministerial appointments is not helpful. Ministers can only concern themselves with a small number of key appointments, and in these areas OCPA-type procedural safeguards will work in some instances, and ways will be found around them in other cases. Appointments certainly need oversight, but as the first iteration of the OCPA code showed, form can empty it of real meaning. It is therefore likely that the argument will recur periodically, both about ministerial involvement in public appointments and the best form of protection against it, though without there being any clear principles that can resolve that argument definitively.

Notes

1 For an example see the PAC's report on conflicts of interests in academy-school funding: Committee of Public Accounts, *Education Funding Agency and Department for Education Financial Statements*, HC 1063-I, 10 June 2014, 2013–2014: 'We were concerned that individuals with connections to both academy trusts and private companies may have benefited personally or their

companies may have benefited from their position when providing trusts with goods and services. The Agency has reviewed 12 cases of related-party transactions, when a conflict of interest could arise; but it is likely that many more exist and have gone unchallenged by the Agency' (pp. 6–7). See also NHS Commissioning Board, *Code of Conduct: Managing Conflicts of Interest where GP Practices are Potential Providers of CCG-Commissioned Services*, 2012.

2 Public Administration Select Committee, *Caught Red-Handed: Why We Can't Count on Police Recorded Crime Statistics*, HC-760, 9 April 2014, 2013–2014.

3 See, *inter alia*, Wolf, A., *Review of Vocational Education – The Wolf Report* (London: Department for Education, 2011), the recommendations of which were immediately acted upon by the Secretary of State to address perverse incentives.

4 Treasury and Civil Service Select Committee, *The Role of the Civil Service*, 1993–1994, HC 27 November 1994, 1993–1994. Data on post-privatisation directorial earnings in the water industry is found in: House of Commons Library Research Paper 98/117, 10 December 1998, *Water Industry Bill 1 [1998/99]*, p. 50.

5 Transparency International, *UK Corruption Report Overview and Policy Recommendations*, 2011, p. 8.

6 National Fraud Authority, *Anti-Fraud Indicators*, March 2012.

7 The Memorandum is recorded in a written answer by the Prime Minister to a Parliamentary Question on 26 February 1985, and was reissued in amended form in December 1987 (HC Deb, Written answers 572, 2 December 1987). Most of the early reports (Haldane, Tomlin, and the 1936 Treasury Committee Report) are described in detail in the 1968 Fulton Report: *The Civil Service – Report of the Committee 1966–1968, Chairman Lord Fulton, Vol 1 appendix B*. Cmnd 3638 June 1968, 108–131. See also the Salmon Commission Report Cmd *Royal Commission on Standards in Public Life* (The Salmon Commission), 1976, 164–172. The Northcote-Trevelyn Report, a revealing commentary on the state of public ethics in the United Kingdom in the mid-nineteenth century, is reprinted in *Public Administration*, 32:1 (1954), 1–16.

8 See Public Administration Committee, *The Public Service Ethos*, HC 263-I, 13 June 2002, 2001–2002. On empirical measurement of the public service ethos see Rayner, J., H. M. Williams, A. Lawton and C.W. Allinson, 'Public service ethos: developing a generic measure', *Journal of Public Administration Research Theory*, 21:1 (2011), 27–51.

9 The CRGA 2010, Part 1, established (among many other governance provisions) for the first time a statutory basis for management of the civil service.

10 Treasury and Civil Service Committee, *The Role of the Civil Service*; Public Administration Committee, *The Public Service Ethos*.

11 Civil Service Commission, *Annual Report and Accounts 2012–13*, pp. 16–17.

12 Committee on Standards in Public Life, *Defining the Boundaries within the Executive: Ministers, Civil Servants and Special Advisers*, Cm 5775, 2003, p. 50.

13 Select Committee on the Constitution, *The Cabinet Office and the Centre of Government*, HL 30, 2009–2010, p. 20.

14 CSPL, *Defining the Boundaries*, p. 19.

15 Boviard, T. and K. Russell, 'Civil service reform in the UK, 1999–2005: revolutionary failure or evolutionary success?', *Public Administration*, 85:2 (2007), 301–328.

16 Powell, J., *The New Macchiavelli: How to Wield Power in the Modern World* (London: The Bodley Head, 2010); Blair, T., *A Journey* (London: Random House, 2010).

17 See Cabinet Office, Performance and Innovation Unit, *Better Policy Delivery and Design: A Discussion Paper by Geoff Mulgan and Andrea Lee*, January 2001.

18 Boviard and Russell, 'Civil service reform'.

19 *Review of Intelligence on Weapons of Mass Destruction* ('the Butler Review') HC 848, 14 July 2004, pp. 146–148, and *The Chilcott Inquiry*, Minutes of Evidence (Lord Wilson of Dinton, 25 January 2011, pp. 1–25). See also Meyer, C., *DC Confidential* (London: Phoenix, 2005), chs 19–20.

20 Cabinet Office, *Civil Service Reform: Delivery and Values*, 2004; see also Hennessy, P., 'Rulers and servants of the state: the Blair style of government 1997–2004', *Parliamentary Affairs*, 58 (2005), 6–16.

21 Major, J., *The Erosion of Parliamentary Government* (London: Centre for Policy Studies, 2003).

22 Page, E. 'Joined up government and the civil service', in V. Bogdanor (ed.), *Joined Up Government* (Oxford: Oxford University Press, 2005).

23 Evans, M., 'Gordon Brown and public management reform: a project in search of a "big idea"?', in M. Beech, *The Brown Government: A Policy Evaluation* (Oxford: Routledge, 2010).

24 Committee on Standards in Public Life, *Reinforcing Standards (Sixth Report)*, January 2000, ch. 5; Public Administration Select Committee, *A Draft Civil Service Bill: Completing the Reform*, HC 128-1, January 2004, 2003–2004; Public Administration Committee, *Constitutional Renewal: Draft Bill and White Paper*, HC 499, 2007–2008, Oral evidence, 28 April 2008.

25 On blunders and blame more generally see King, A. and I. Crewe, *The Blunders of Our Governments*, (London: Oneworld, 2013).

26 Goldston, R., 'Patronage in British government', *Parliamentary Affairs*, 30:1 (1977), 80–96.

27 Cabinet Office, 1996, *Public Bodies 1996*, Stationery Office, 165 and Cabinet Office, 2000, *Public Bodies 2000*, Stationery Office, 168. By 2012 the number of NDPBs had fallen to 8700: Cabinet Office, 2012, *Public Bodies 2012*, Stationery Office, 166. The Public Administration Committee in 2003 estimated there were over 65,000 such appointments at national level.

28 Committee on Standards in Public Life, *Standards in Public Life*, 1995, paras 4.22–4.31.

29 Committee on Standards in Public Life, 1997, *Review of Standards of Conduct in Executive NDPBs, NHS Trusts and Local Spending Bodies*, November 1997; see also Flinders, M., 'The politics of patronage in the United

Kingdom: shrinking reach and diluted permeation', *Governance*, 22:4 (2009), 555.

30 Committee on Standards in Public Life, Tenth Report, 2005, *Getting the Balance Right*, pp. 21–47.

31 See Office of the Commissioner for Public Appointments, Third Report of the Commissioner for Public Appointments, 1997–1998, pp. 3–5 and Office of the Commissioner for Public Appointments, Sixth Report of the Commissioner for Public Appointments, 2000–2001, p. 4.

32 See Wright, T., *Beyond the Patronage State* (London: Fabian Society, 1995); Viney, J. and J. Osborne, *Modernising Public Appointments* (London: Demos, 1995); Wilson, D., 'Quangos in the skeletal state', *Parliamentary Affairs*, 48:2 (1995), 181–91; Greve, C., M. Flinders and S. Van Thiel, 'Quangos – what's in a name? Defining quangos from a comparative perspective', *Governance*, 12:2 (1999), 129–146; Skelcher, C., *The Appointed State* (Oxford: Oxford University Press, 1998).

33 Committee on Standards in Public Life, Tenth Report, *Getting the Balance Right*, 2005, p. 123. In making this shift, moreover, the Committee was endorsing a very similar set of proposals made by the Public Administration Committee two years earlier. See Public Administration Committee, *Government by Appointment. Opening up the Patronage State*, HC 165, 26 June 2003, 2002–2003.

34 The government declined to support the proposal, however, also rejecting the idea of giving the OPCA a 'full-whistle-blowing power' to alert Parliament to perceived difficulties in the operation of the Code (see government response). *The Government's Response to the Tenth Report of the Committee on Standards in Public Life*, Cm 6723, December 2005, p. 2.

35 The Commissioner for Public Appointments, *Review of the Public Appointments System: A Consultation Document*, June 2011, p. 9.

36 Flinders, 'The politics of patronage'.

37 Maer, L., 'Parliamentary involvement in public appointments' (House of Commons Library Research Paper 08/39, 2008); Waller, P. and M. Chalmers, *An Evaluation of Pre-Appointment Scrutiny Hearings Prepared for the House of Commons Liaison Committee and the Cabinet Office* (London: UCL, The Constitution Unit, 2010).

9

Regulating the after-life: ministers, civil servants and revolving doors

Post-employment conflicts of interest

For ministers and civil servants departure from office does not necessarily mean retirement. Ministers, and certainly special advisers, mostly find themselves out of office well before retiring age. Many civil servants too leave office in mid-career, or come into public service only for short intervals in a longer career in the private sector. This mobility inevitably generates a well-established concern about the potential post-employment conflicts of interest that arise when individuals move from public service to the very areas of private enterprise they have been regulating, or contracting with, and where they have gained special commercially sensitive knowledge.

Individuals cannot be stopped from earning a living after public service. Harm only arises where post-employment gives an improper advantage to the new employer. The risk of this moreover needs to be balanced against the danger of segmenting labour markets so rigidly that segmentation becomes a serious disincentive to recruitment to public service in the first place. Nevertheless, evidence of a well-trodden path between, for example, regulatory agencies and the businesses they regulate will always provoke controversy. Even where claims about impropriety are speculative or unfounded the persistence of such claims can be harmful, and issues of public confidence in the integrity of big-spending departments of government, or regulatory agencies, may be so significant that some restrictions on employment become unavoidable.

Post-employment conflicts of interest are hard to pin down. It is certainly difficult to establish whether an office-holder, anticipating an eventual private-sector opportunity, has, while in public service, shown bias in favour of a potential future employer. It is harder still to show conclusively that an individual who goes to work for that employer really is behaving improperly in that new role. If procedures to ensure proper contracting and public procurement cannot identify impropriety when someone is in office, it is unlikely that wrong-doing can be proved retrospectively once the individual has left public service. So the risk of post-employment conflicts of interest usually has to be dealt with in terms of the balance of perceived risk *ahead* of an individual taking up private-sector employment.

Doing this is not easy. It raises questions about who should take on this supervisory task, with what resources and what powers. The decision to approve a private-sector appointment, to block it, or to impose conditions (for example a ban on lobbying for a fixed period, or a ban on the use of privileged information acquired in office) may need to be taken quickly, since offers of employment will not realistically remain for long. But it also has to be an informed decision that may demand significant investigation and staff resources. After approval has been given, if any special conditions are imposed the approving authority needs to be confident its conditions are being met. Unless non-compliance becomes a matter for the criminal law, which seems unlikely except in the case of official-secrecy provisions, there is a further question of what other sanctions are available for non-compliance. Reputational damage may not be a disincentive. For public servants who were previously in a contractual relationship with a public authority, the contract can in principle lay down the terms of some of these issues, with the ultimate sanction being loss of pension rights. For ministers, who since the 1970s have also received defined-contribution pensions in addition to their parliamentary pensions, a similar principle could theoretically apply.[1] But bringing a case for deprivation of pension rights against a minister, or indeed a senior civil servant, seems improbable.

Awareness of post-employment issues in the United Kingdom

Until the 1990s, post-employment issues were rarely controversial in the UK. They were considered to apply only to civil servants, and they were handled discretely through civil-service management. There was little controversy over what ministers did after leaving office, and there were no efforts to restrict it. From 1975 the civil service was advised by a committee – the Advisory Committee on Civil Service Appointments – consisting of former senior civil servants, business figures and politicians. It received requests to take up post-employment positions from permanent and deputy secretaries and later from a wider group including diplomats and military personnel. The committee's name was changed to the Advisory Committee on Business Appointments (ACOBA) in 1995, when, for the first time, ministers were also included in its remit, and the Committee's work became more transparent, with annual public reports on its individual decisions. ACOBA's remit was also modified to monitor the treatment of a sample of applications by lower level staff – applications which were decided on by departments and the Cabinet Office – to ensure parity of treatment across the whole system. In all civil-service cases, the government retained the final decision, though until 2003 there were no cases of ACOBA's recommendation being overruled by the government.[2] Moreover, the Committee was not, as it frequently pointed out when facing external criticism, given a principles-based remit, and asked to formulate its own detailed rules. Rather its rules were given to it by the Cabinet Office, and remained the prerogative of the government through successive rule-changes in 2011 and 2014.

The inclusion of ministers created an anomaly, however. The CSPL recommended in its First Report in 1995 that ministerial post-employment should be vetted by the Advisory Committee, though the procedure for ministers included neither a proviso that the final decision lay with government, nor powers to allow ACOBA itself to impose a veto. In effect, ministers were only being 'advised' by ACOBA, though for almost a decade this did not cause any difficulties. Only a small minority of cases led to ACOBA advising any special conditions on taking up proposed appointments and, having dealt with an exceptionally large number of applications (covering 175 appointments) around the time of the 1997 change of government, and despite noting that many ministers were unaware of the new rules until they were written to on leaving office by the chair of the Advisory Committee, the chair could nevertheless comment in the Committee's 1996–1998 Report that the system worked well; that none of the 175 proposed appointments was unsuitable (indeed not even the subset of thirty-seven that had been taken up without prior advice from the Committee!); and that of the thirty-four where the Committee was minded to advise conditions (mostly concerning waiting periods or non-disclosure of privileged information) such advice had apparently been happily and amicably accepted by the applicant.[3] In its Second Report in 1999, ACOBA again reported in reassuring terms.[4]

However, in 2006 the case of David Blunkett's directorships of outside companies (where as Home Secretary he had had some responsibility) drew significant public attention to the rules, which, as we shall see below, were already – as regards the civil service – attracting the attention of the PASC in the House of Commons, and of the CSPL. As a minister who had already returned to office after having resigned once before (over a different ethical issue) David Blunkett's alleged failure to observe the rules (initially he did not seek advice over the directorships) was bound to raise the profile of the issue. Thereafter ACOBA's tone in its annual reports became markedly more critical of alleged disregard for the rules among both ministers and civil servants.[5] Faced with a new round of significant ministerial turnover at the end of the Blair premiership, it proposed increasingly strict restrictions on ministers. In the period 2006/2008, it received sixty applications for post-employment advice from thirty-two former ministers, advising twelve-month lobbying bans on forty-one.[6] Meanwhile the high-profile posts taken up by ministers on leaving office, culminating in the unprecedentedly lucrative consultancies taken up by Tony Blair with Zurich and J.P. Morgan, prompted a substantial degree of adverse press comment, and a growing interest in post-employment generally, as well as in the apparent freedom of ministers to ignore ACOBA's advice if they really wished to. As incoming prime minister in 2007, Gordon Brown issued a new version of the Ministerial Code stressing that 'on leaving office, Ministers must seek advice ... [and are] expected to abide by the advice', raising the bar, though still not specifying what the sanction was for failing to follow the advice. An episode just ahead of the general election of 2010 suggested that at least some former ministers were unmoved by efforts to make the system more effective. Three departing ministers – Stephen Byers, Geoff Hoon and Patricia Hewett – who had served in Labour governments under Blair and Brown, and who were leaving the House of Commons in 2010 were trapped by *Sunday Times* journalists posing as potential lobbyists seeking to hire them to exercise influence. The claims they were alleged to have made about the extent of their influence were much disputed, but the Labour Party took the issue seriously enough to suspend the three from the party when the case came to light.[7]

The issue of post-employment ethics was driven by public interest in the destinations of ministers, whose visibility, compared to senior civil servants, made them ready targets for criticism from both the media and political opponents. Of the two main parties, the Conservative Party – more closely connected to business and finance – had always had a higher number of ministers for whom post-employment questions would be relevant when demitting office. But Labour was changing, as we saw in Chapter 2, and towards the end of the Blair/Brown years, as its ministers gradually left office, many of them were not only desirous but capable of selling their expertise in the private sector. The two key peaks for this process were obviously the changes of governing party in 1997 and 2010. But in one important respect the risk of impropriety was greater when a minister left office, but his or her party stayed in power. In those circumstances, the opportunities for lobbying were higher, so that what happened *between* 1997 and 2010 was thus no less significant than what happened at the end. Moreover the fact that now former ministers from *both* parties were engaged in behaviour considered to be ethically questionable brought the nature of the problem into even sharper relief.

A changing civil service

The ministerial anomaly introduced by the CSPL proposal in 1995 did not just affect ministers, however. It also helped provoke a more general tension between ACOBA and the Labour government, which fed back to the way the Advisory Committee looked at requests from senior civil servants. From around 2001 onwards, without any change in the rules ACOBA was asked by the Cabinet Office to apply, the Committee significantly increased the imposition of special post-employment conditions on civil servants. It argued that these restrictions were necessary because of the growing interpenetration of careers between the public and private sector: more senior appointments from outside the service, more civil servants on fixed-term contracts, and more resignations from public service ahead of retirement age.[8]

ACOBA's response to the increased risk of impropriety in the public sector was to tighten its interpretation of the rules and impose more conditions on applicants, banning especially their lobbying of their former departments. This restriction had been imposed in relatively few cases until 2000, but thereafter became a much more common sanction. In 2000/2001, as Table 9.1 shows, it was used in around 15 per cent or fewer of the applications ACOBA received. It then rose steadily to reach 85 per cent by 2011/2012. The Committee expressed particular concern at the situation in the Ministry of Defence, where a combination of factors had led to what was termed 'traffic' between the Ministry and contracting firms. It cited the young age of military retirements, the attractiveness of those with military experience to defence suppliers, and the inevitably close relationship between Ministry and commercial suppliers as all contributing to this situation. Of the possible consequences of this traffic on serving officers and officials, it noted that civilian counterparts of serving officers might enter their final postings with a hope or expectation of post-retirement employment with companies with which they would be dealing officially.[9]

That, under unchanged rules, over which the government in principle had complete control, outcomes as adjudicated by ACOBA could change strikingly had important implications for the Committee's standing. From a position of almost complete public invisibility, and from a stance which, to those few critics who took the trouble to look, could easily

Table 9.1 Post-employment applications from Crown Servants dealt with directly by ACOBA 2000/2001–2012/2013

	Applications	Approved without condition	Conditions	% with conditions
2012–2013	124	6	118	95.2
2011–2012	56	7	48	85.7
2010–2011	63	20	43	68.3
2009–2010	62	12	50	80.7
2008–2009	179	53	126	70.4
2007–2008	79	35	54	68.3
2006–2007	88	37	51	58.1
2005–2006	79	45	34	43.1
2004–2005	71	31	40	56.3
2003–2004	49	16	33	67.3
2002–2003	38	25	13	34.2
2001–2002	33	24	9	27.3
2000–2001	93	80	13	14.1

Source: successive Annual Reports of the Advisory Committee on Business Appointments (2000–2001 (Fourth Report) to 2012–2013 (Fourteenth Report)).

seem like an almost cosy relationship with government and the civil service, the Committee quickly found itself drawn into an adversarial relationship with government. Its toughening stance was quickly rejected by the Blair government, which responded by commissioning a report from Sir Patrick Brown, a former civil servant, on the future of the business appointment rules in their entirety.[10] The Brown Report proposed a major simplification of procedures, a single standard sanction in the case of perceived conflict of interest between the last civil service role and the new private-sector role, and the winding up of ACOBA.[11] It generated little support, however, and the choice of Sir Patrick (a civil servant with an earlier business background who himself held business appointments after leaving public life) was criticised as inappropriate from within the PASC.[12] In any case, the government seemed to lack the energy to pursue its case. The Advisory Committee delivered a vigorous rebuttal of its arguments, claiming in its Eighth Report in 2006 that Brown's fundamental assumptions were misconceived.[13] The Committee argued that the existing framework worked well, and that the risks of lobbying were real. The CSPL, the First Civil Service Commissioner and the PASC (to which the government eventually referred Sir Patrick's report) also supported ACOBA and the government buried the issue as the Blair government entered its final year. The PASC's unsupportive response was published in 2007, shortly before Gordon Brown became prime minister. Its fundamental conclusion was that the Advisory Committee worked satisfactorily: 'we see little benefit in changing [ACOBA's] composition, or its way of working'.[14] In October, the new government issued a response to the Select Committee in which it effectively agreed.[15]

ACOBA under scrutiny

Surviving the Brown Report, however, did not draw a line under the controversy, in part because the issue of lobbying – itself closely connected to one aspect of post-employment ethics – was being pursued by the PASC, and, as we see in Chapter 10, was to become a significant matter in the 2010 Parliament, once the Coalition Agreement committed the new government to legislate on lobbying. More importantly, while the *principle* of independent scrutiny of ministerial and civil-service post-employment had been reaffirmed from the events surrounding the Brown Report, the debates around 2006/2007 had drawn attention to growing concerns about the way ACOBA operated. Despite the Advisory Committee's clash with the Blair government, not everyone was persuaded that the apparent toughening of its position towards post-employment applications after 2000 was adequate.

Even the broadly supportive 2007 Select Committee on Public Administration Report had revealed concerns within the Committee about whether ACOBA was any longer adequate for the task it had been set. In the debate that followed, running across both the Brown and Cameron governments, three fundamental issues were present. The first was about the credibility of ACOBA itself, given its composition; the second was about the Committee's working methods; and the third was whether ministers' and civil servants' commitments to abstain from lobbying and from use of privileged information when being given conditional approval to take up appointments could be relied upon, or indeed enforced.

Anecdotal evidence of vigorous lobbying through inappropriate post-employment – discussed below – emerged from various investigative press actions where former ministers, members of the House of Lords and former defence staff officials were entrapped by fictitious offers of consultancy involving political lobbying roles. This evidence suggested that several such individuals were likely, if offered real consultancy roles, to take a fairly casual attitude to the constraints imposed on them by ACOBA rules. In this atmosphere, however, ACOBA itself came under scrutiny not just for its effectiveness, but also for the appropriateness of its membership, with Lord Lang, the incoming chair of the Committee in

2009, facing a torrid hearing before the PASC. The hearing focused both on the lack of a full and formal pre-appointment confirmatory hearing, and on the concern by some members of the Committee who thought his appointment straightforwardly unsuitable, *inter alia* because they considered Lord Laing himself had shown less than perfect judgement in his reaction to a fictitious attempted lobbying consultancy offer.[16]

The new coalition government quickly sought to address some of these concerns by changes to the rules on which ACOBA decisions were based.[17] The key change was a new blanket two-year lobbying ban for ministers, director generals and permanent secretaries, together with a new and clearer definition of lobbying. Special advisers were also henceforth required to make applications to the Committee on leaving their roles. There were also concerns about procedures, at lower levels of the civil service, where applications to take up post-employment offers were handled inside individual departments. Permanent secretaries were henceforth to have formal responsibility for decisions on all applications from staff at director level and below, but ACOBA was henceforth to conduct compliance assurance checks on departments to ensure that arrangements for handling applications were firmly applied and consistent.

The significance of the last provision can be seen from the fact that whereas, in Table 9.1 above, we noted a dramatic increase in the rate of conditionality imposed on applicants whose requests were dealt with by the Advisory Committee during the years after 2000, there was no comparable increase in the rate of conditionality imposed where the approvals were given directly by the departments. One interpretation of this disparity was that senior officials in departments were confident in the robustness of the internal process.[18] Unfortunately, comparison of ACOBA approvals and departmental approvals was no longer possible after 2008/2009 since ACOBA Annual Reports no longer provided data on approvals made within departments after that date. Between 2001 and 2009 the latter rose only from 22 to 38 per cent (compared with a rise from 5 to 70 per cent for ACOBA-approved applications).

The reason for the disparity is not clear. Given the complexity of contracting for long-term projects in areas such as defence or health, or the complexity of corporate tax-liability negotiations in HMRC cases, many key decisions are likely to be signed off by individuals below the grades dealt with by the ACOBA process. Individuals below the ACOBA scrutiny level may have significant responsibilities for contracting decisions which may generate possible post-employment conflicts. But without some very major scaling up of the ACOBA machinery, the system could not cope if all post-holders who might in theory bear a post-employment conflict risk had to be scrutinised by ACOBA itself.[19] The system was not designed for this in the 1970s, and the ACOBA capacity did not change greatly in the 1990s when it was made more public, and its rules were made more explicit. It was designed to monitor a small elite, and the difficulties even of making the new monitoring procedures work following the rule-changes in 2011 appear to testify to this. Given the level of the Committee's resources, and the size of the departmental universe ACOBA is expected to monitor, these realities seem difficult to avoid. Departments will have their own imperatives and their own long-standing self-narratives about exposure to ethics and propriety risk. In these, expectations about post-employment patterns and opportunities may well have become internalised over long periods, and disruptions may have consequences for staff morale and recruitment and retention. ACOBA makes no secret of the fact that it has no real power to monitor or enforce the recommendations it makes.[20] Whether individual civil servants really comply with lobbying bans would in any case be an exceptionally difficult matter to determine. In short, whatever rules are in place a legally enforceable framework looks difficult to establish without an intrusive detection mechanism, and without complex, costly and uncertain litigation. There is no obvious answer to this problem, unless by giving ACOBA or an agent the power to conduct random compliance investigations. This almost certainly requires ACOBA to be placed on a statutory footing with additional costs and resources.

A parliamentary ally lost

Mounting doubts about the robustness of the ACOBA regime eventually persuaded the PASC to issue a report in 2012 recommending that ACOBA be abolished. The rules, it argued, were on one side inadequate, and on the other, precisely because they did not engender public confidence, failed to deter unfair and damaging allegations against individuals after they took up post-employment positions that had been approved.[21] The 2012 report proposed to replace ACOBA with an independent ethics commissioner with legal powers of investigation and enforceable statutory penalties, backed up by a clear code of conduct. Moreover, the independent ethics commissioner was to replace not only ACOBA, but the CSPL. It therefore sought to combine in one body two quite different roles in ethics management: a contemplative and reflective role for the public sphere as a whole, as carried out hitherto by the CSPL, and a quasi-judicial enforcement role in the limited area of post-employment, as carried out, albeit with extremely limited power, by ACOBA. Targeting both ACOBA and the CSPL for abolition (in the CSPL's case for alleged excessive ambition; in the ACOBA case for alleged under-achievement) was a bold move, but seemed to have been little prepared through any consultation with government.

Unsurprisingly, the government's response was long delayed, and eventually largely negative.[22] It proposed small modifications to the rules for civil servants (but not ministers) and limited itself to a better definition of lobbying:

> Lobbying in the context of these Rules means that the former civil servant should not engage in communication with Government (including Ministers, special advisers and officials) with a view to influencing a Government decision or policy in relation to their own interests, or the interests of the organisation by which they are employed, or to whom they are contracted. In certain cases, due to the nature of the proposed appointment or employment, the Advisory Committee may, at its discretion, recommend that the lobbying ban need not prevent communications with Government on matters that are an integral part of the normal course of business for the organisation concerned. The model application form prompts applicants to provide the relevant details about the proposed employment or appointment that will assist with the formulation of an appropriate lobbying condition.[23]

In this sense, the 2012 PASC report, through its lack of clear focus, was a missed opportunity. It was evident from the events surrounding Lord Lang's appointment itself, from the business destinies of retiring members of the defeated Labour government, and from further revelations of lobbying turned up by the press and parliamentary select committees in the first two years of the 2010 coalition government, that controversy and public concern had not been fully addressed by the new rules. ACOBA itself had also lost the confidence of the PASC, which in the past had been an important ally. Meanwhile the fundamental difficulty remained that enforcement of the rules continued to depend on an honour code. Once a public servant was out of public service and employed by a commercial organisation, there was no guarantee that assurances given to gain approval under the above paragraph would actually be adhered to, and if not, how departments or ACOBA could know they were not being adhered to.

Conclusion: searching for consensus around a weak ethics institution

The experience of managing post-employment ethics in the United Kingdom in the last two decades is a low-profile but important object-lesson in the difficulties of creating appropriate regulators. It is an area where evidence of malfeasance is extremely difficult to assemble, but where the suspicion of it has become quite strong, even if the most egregious examples have come from journalist entrapment. The consequence has been that the institutions have been created in many respects *ahead* of proven cases, and not surprisingly in a low-key way. For this reason, and in parallel with some other regulatory enterprises dealt with in this book, the main difficulty has been that of winning support from all those involved and reaching a settled consensus on the size of the problem. At different stages the government, and some in Parliament, have appeared to lose confidence in the ACOBA solution, exposing public disagreement over a set of arrangements that require a tight consensus if they are to work well.

The ACOBA solution has evolved in a piecemeal way, deprived of the resources necessary to restore confidence. Originally, it was designed for a small elite, its philosophy being that fellow-members of that elite should act as guarantors of each other. When individuals of unimpeachable integrity and worldly experience can say that an appointment is free of compromising baggage from the past, this alone is supposed to be a sufficient guarantee all is well. But gradually the context changed in important ways. The range of actors ACOBA was asked to regulate increased: first to ministers, and then to a group of civil servants too large for it to monitor without a major scaling up of the organisation, and for whom, therefore, ACOBA could only act as a sort of light-touch quality-controller. Secondly, the robustness of what was effectively an honour code looked increasingly questionable. When those seeking approval gave their reassurances that they would not exploit their contacts and knowledge for lobbying purposes, or make use of privileged commercial intelligence, it stretched credulity too far that at least some individuals, in a large and growing universe of former office-holders of many different types, would not exploit the absence of checks and controls for their own benefit.

Ultimately ACOBA's credibility is under threat on two fronts: capacity and composition. It is too small for the range of tasks it confronts, and its own members resemble too closely, in social extraction, career experience, and in the way they have themselves benefitted from combining public-sector and private-sector careers, those whose motives and sincerity they are asked to judge. None of this is to imply that the ACOBA model is definitively broken, or that there is a better way by doing away with ACOBA entirely, as, in their different ways, both Sir Patrick Brown's Report in 2005, and that of the PASC in 2012, have advocated. But what is clear is that an institution which was designed especially for its capacity to give the public confidence has found that central task a harder and harder call.

Notes

1 Djuna Thurley, *Pensions of Ministers and Senior Office Holders*, House of Commons Library Standard Note, SN 04586, 14 March 2014.

2 Cabinet Office, The Advisory Committee on Business Appointments, *Seventh Report 2003–4*, COI, 2004, pp. 14–15.

3 Cabinet Office, The Advisory Committee on Business Appointments, *First Report 1996–98*, COI, 1998, p. 10.

4 'We had, nevertheless, no serious reservation about any of them [the applications received from Ministers], and in no case did we think it necessary to advise a former Minister to wait before taking up an appointment'. Cabinet Office, The Advisory Committee on Business Appointments, *Second Report 1998–1999*, COI, 1999, p. 8.

5 In its Ninth Report the Committee reported that: 'We have noted with concern that during the period covered by this report some appointments about which we were consulted had been accepted before our advice on them was sought or given. In other instances we were given little time to carry out the enquiries we need to make in order to give advice. We recognise that some offers of employment may materialise suddenly and that they may be subject to an early risk of withdrawal. Nevertheless, we urge that in the interests of public confidence every effort should be made to seek our advice in good time.' Cabinet Office, The Advisory Committee on Business Appointments, *Ninth Report 2006–2008*, COI, 2006, p. 9.

6 Cabinet Office, The Advisory Committee on Business Appointments, *Ninth Report 2006–2008*, COI, 2006, pp. 19–24.

7 Wintour, P. and A. Stratton, 'Stephen Byers and other ex-ministers suspended from Labour party over lobbying allegations', *Guardian*, 23 March 2010.

8 Cabinet Office, The Advisory Committee on Business Appointments, *Seventh Report 2003–4*, COI, 2004, paras 23–24.

9 Cabinet Office, The Advisory Committee on Business Appointments, *Seventh Report 2003–4*, COI, 2004, paras 9–10.

10 The remit announced by the Prime Minister, *Hansard*, 22 July 2004, Col. 462, was 'To review the Business Appointment Rules to ensure that they are compatible with a public service that is keen to encourage greater interchange with the private and other sectors which is essential for effective delivery in today's public service. The review will consider the operation of the system, taking account of practice overseas. It will also consider the current machinery for dealing with applications and the necessary resources'.

11 *Review of the Business Appointment Rules*, Dep 05/1677 25 February 2005. The Review was never formally published other than through deposition in the House of Commons Library, but is summarised in various documents, in particular HC 651 House of Commons, Public Administration Select Committee, *The Business Appointment Rules*, HC 651, 14 June 2007.

12 Public Administration Committee, *Minutes of Evidence*, Sir Patrick Brown, KCB, HC 884-ii, Thursday 9 February 2006, 70–125.

13 Cabinet Office, The Advisory Committee on Business Appointments, *Eighth Report 2005–2006*, COI, 2006, pp. 9–10.

14 Public Administration Committee (PASC), *The Business Appointment Rules*, HC 651, 14 June 2007, p. 17.

15 PASC, *The Business Appointment Rules: The Government's Response to the Committee's Sixth Report of Session 2006–7*, HC 1087, 18 October 2007, 2006–2007.

16 PASC, *Selection of the Advisory Committee on Business Appointments*, HC 42-I, 27 November 2009, 2009–2010, p. 4: 'We are satisfied that Lord Lang has the professional competence and personal independence required for the post of Chair of the Advisory Committee on Business Appointments as it is currently constituted. However, we have serious concerns about the appointment of a former Cabinet Minister with business appointments of his own to a role that needs the perception of independence if it is to attract public confidence. We ask the Commissioner for Public Appointments to take account of our concerns when reviewing the appointment process.'

17 Advisory Committee on Business Appointments, *Twelfth Annual Report*, 2010–2011, pp. 20–22, 42–50.

18 Under the new 2011 rules, all decisions at SCS2 were to be scrutinised by permanent secretaries. ACOBA was required to undertake informal compliance-assurance checks on departments' arrangements for handling applications. As of December 2013, however, when the Fourteenth Annual Report was published, this scrutiny had not been completed, or at least was not reported on. The Thirteenth Report stated that during the year the Secretariat had completed its visits to departments to advise on how its compliance monitoring would operate, but the Report itself contained no account of the outcome of that monitoring.

19 In 2008/2009, ACOBA reported 121 such applications in the sector. An FoI request reported by the *Sunday Telegraph* stated that, in 2009/2010, 326 MoD officials or military officers 'were cleared to join the private sector' (of which 240 were to defence sector employers). 'A scandal worse than lobbying?', *Sunday Telegraph*, 11 December 2011, 24. Lord Lang gave further data in his PASC written evidence in spring 2011. See House of Commons, Public Administration Select Committee, Business Appointment Rules: written evidence by Lord Lang (http://goo.gl/0QqLKB, accessed 19 March 2015).

20 PASC, Business Appointment Rules: written evidence by Lord Lang (http://goo.gl/0QqLKB, accessed 19 March 2015).

21 PASC, *Business Appointment Rules*, HC 404, 17 July 2012, 2011–2012.

22 PASC, *Business Appointment Rules, Government Response to Committee's Third Report of Session*, HC 563, 17 July 2014, 2012–2013.

23 PASC, *Business Appointment Rules, Government Response*, HC 563, 17 July 2014, 2012–2013, p. 14.

10

Getting to grips with lobbying: regulated office-holders, unregulated lobbies

Introduction

Lobbying is an inescapable feature of modern democracy yet the term is often used with negative connotations. To lobby is not necessarily to exercise improper influence, and there is a strong case in a democracy for tolerating lobbying unless it contravenes the law, for example through outright bribery. But while the ability to advance political claims through lobbying is considered an important democratic freedom, much of what goes on, while not illegal, often looks at the least undesirable, and causes public concern.

There are two main critiques of modern lobbying. The first, as E.E. Schattschneider wrote half a century ago in questioning the pluralist view of democracy, is that interest-group resources are unevenly spread.[1] Some interests lobby vigorously; others, with fewer resources or less immediate interest, may not be able to lobby at all. The second, more general, critique is that while it may be difficult to establish that lobbying is intended to make public officials depart improperly from the obligations of their roles, the circumstances surrounding it often suggest that some kind of improper personal exchange of benefits might be involved. Such inducements may not be straightforward financial bribery but they can involve help with campaign finance, side benefits like entertainment or travel, or a job on leaving office, all of which look almost as unacceptable as bribery itself.

Even without an identifiable inducement to public officials, lobbyists may capture the office-holder's attention and beliefs in an inappropriate way. This can happen when the lobbyist has special knowledge or expertise that is selectively shared with the office-holder. The sub-contracting to the non-governmental arena of regulatory functions over professional registration or product standards are obvious examples. A substantial literature has arisen on regulatory capture in law, economics and political science, though it has generated little agreement on how influence is to be measured, or exactly how interests capture office-holders by setting the frames within which policy is understood.[2] Further problems arise with so-called public–public lobbying. Most academic literature on lobbying deals with private actors who influence public ones, though increasingly lobbying by public bodies is also of concern. Doctors, teachers, members of the military, universities and local authorities all lobby central government for outcomes favourable to their interests. When a public organisation lobbies government, it is seeking to alter decisions that the public may be said to have chosen through their elected representatives at a higher and more authoritative level. If public employees in one area of government become decision-makers in another (for example as local councillors, or trustees of schools or arts organisations), reciprocal partisan obligations can take on a potentially incestuous quality.[3]

These complexities have altered the lens through which lobbying and interest groups are seen by academics and other third-party observers. While once the focus was on the contractual power of major producer groups like business and unions as mutually antagonistic corporate interests,[4] more recently concern has shifted to the activities of many different *individual* groups inside but also beyond these corporate interests.[5] The methods used by lobbyists have come in for closer critical scrutiny.[6] Political scientists have recognised that compared to the modest structures through which parties make policy, the lobbying universe operates on a much larger scale, so that lobbyists generally have far better and more detailed knowledge of areas of policy than either party politicians or their official advisers and civil servants.

Estimates of the size of the interest-group universe in the United Kingdom are however difficult to calculate with precision, which is one reason why lobbying is difficult to regulate.[7] Most lobbying is based on in-house resources: in companies directly, in representative associations of business sectors, or in trades and professions. Large businesses have their own corporate public relations departments.[8] Separate budgetary information about spending on lobbying is therefore rarely provided. The UK's Public Affairs Council[9] in its evidence to a 2012 government consultation paper on lobbying, tried to estimate how many organisations and individuals would have to register if formal registration of lobbying were to be introduced.[10] The Council was reported as believing that a register would cover around 100 specialist public affairs companies (i.e. professional lobbyists who lobby *on behalf* of third-party clients) and that about 60 large corporates with in-house specialist teams would also need to register, along with a further 100+ professional groups and third-sector organisations (charities and unions).[11] In the same exercise, the Cabinet Office and the House of Commons Political and Constitutional Reform Select Committee (PCRSC) thought the figure much higher. The PCRSC Report quoted evidence provided by one witness of 3,500–4,000 lobbyists (consultants and in-house) operating in the UK.[12] Whatever the real figure, it is clear that spending on lobbying dwarfs the amount of money and effort spent annually by political parties on the details of policy-making, and more importantly that it has grown very rapidly over the last thirty years.

Where to intervene?

Lobbying potentially affects most areas of politics and as we have seen in various chapters of this book, efforts to regulate it have long had an impact on holders of public office, including MPs, ministers, and civil servants and their equivalents at regional and local level. In other words, most regulation involved the public-office *targets* of lobbying, rather than those doing the lobbying. Until recently that was the United Kingdom's only approach. The approach was rather fragmented, and did not define lobbying as a general phenomenon, or see it as something precise enough for regulatory or criminal-enforcement purposes. Improper lobbying is thus addressed through, for example, the law of bribery, but hitherto, with a few exceptions, not by making certain categories of lobbyist subject to special transparency regulations, or by restricting the amount of access to office-holders that lobbyists can obtain. This contrasts in particular with the United States, which has made serious efforts to regulate those who do the lobbying, as well as the office-holders who are on its receiving end.[13]

Since around 2008 however there has been increasingly intense debate about whether the line should be drawn differently, to bring lobbyists into the regulatory area, as well as whether existing controls aimed at office-holders are sufficient. This change has occurred in large part because of revelations about lobbying and a growing concern about its methods and goals. Greater public scrutiny has started to shift change attitudes about what is acceptable.

These concerns were captured remarkably frankly by the then Leader of the Opposition, David Cameron, just ahead of the 2010 general election when in what quickly became a landmark quotation, he said that lobbying was the 'next big scandal' waiting to explode: 'It's an issue that crosses party lines and has tainted our politics for too long ... an issue that exposes the far-too-cosy relationship between politics, government, business and money. I'm talking about lobbying – and we all know how it works. The lunches, the hospitality, the quiet word in your ear, the ex-ministers and ex-advisors for hire, helping big business find the right way to get its way.'[14] David Cameron's warning quickly came back to haunt his party once in power, repeating a pattern from the early years of Tony Blair's government after 1997. In both cases, governments came to power bringing, as special advisers, individuals who were closely linked to strong interests or lobbying firms. The two governments also came into office significantly indebted to interests that had made major financial contributions to electoral campaigns, and with a powerful incentive to secure new party donations to pay off overdrafts from campaigning.[15] In the Conservative case, over the space of six months from October 2011 to March 2012 no fewer than four major lobbying scandals broke over the party:

- In October 2011 the ambiguous status and role of Defence Minister Liam Fox's special adviser, Adam Werrity, led directly to the minister's resignation.[16]
- In December 2011 a multi-client lobbying firm BPP was caught in an entrapment case by the *Independent* boasting of highly dubious practices by which the company assisted questionable regimes overseas, and of its special and privileged access to the UK government for lobbying purposes.[17]
- In March 2012 Conservative Party co-Treasurer Peter Cruddas resigned having also been caught by entrapment offering access to Downing Street in return for party donations.[18]
- In April 2012 Frederic Michel, a News Corporation lobbyist, was revealed – in connection with his company's bid for BSkyB – as having been in regular close contact with officials at Jeremy Hunt's Department for Culture, Media and Sport, notably through Mr Hunt's special adviser Adam Smith. The latter resigned.[19]

There have also been episodes of questionable probity by those leaving, or already departed from, public office. Just ahead of the 2010 general election three retiring former Labour ministers, Stephen Byers, Geoff Hoon and Particia Hewitt, were recorded confirming their availability for hire as lobbyists.[20] In October 2012 several senior retired armed forces staff were recorded making similar offers.[21]

These episodes have brought to a head concern that has long been brewing. As we saw in Chapter 4, developments in the lobbying industry in the 1980s were at the heart of the cash-for-questions scandal of the early 1990s. The reforms introduced in response to that scandal were directly largely at the rules governing MPs and paid advocacy. As more attention was paid to sources of party finance, and as awareness grew of the career connections between public-relations firms, lobbyists and elective office, the focus has shifted towards the activities of lobbyists themselves, and especially to one part of the lobbyist universe: the 100 or so multi-client lobbying firms that lobby in the United Kingdom on behalf of paying clients.

Awareness of these issues was also fostered by the ethical watchdogs that have taken it on themselves to monitor aspects of lobbying behaviour as part of their wider brief – particularly the CSPL, the Commissioner for Parliamentary Standards, the ACOBA and some parliamentary select committees. Open-source information-campaigning organisations like They Work for You and Who's Lobbying have also been active in scrutinising lobbying, offering web-based data giving a first port of call for journalists and others probing particular cases.[22] Taking their cue from cases of malpractice exposed in the media, these various organisations have gradually formed a caucus promoting more rigorous analysis of the issues surrounding lobbying.

Scrutiny of those activities was also helped by the changing pressures on office-holder relationships with lobbies and interests. Given the UK's strong central government and cohesive parliamentary majority, the key target of the lobbyist was historically the executive. As we have already seen in Chapters 7–9, civil servants and ministers have been required to follow increasingly scrupulous rules of procedure in recording whom they meet and in what circumstances. Rules governing relationships between lobbyists and officials have long been included in *Questions of Procedure for Ministers*, later the *Ministerial Code*, and in the *Civil Service Code* and the *Civil Service Management Code*. We have also seen, however, that it is difficult to close all possible loopholes. The difficulties have included the extent to which transparency rules concerning ministers' meetings with lobbies are adequate, and the extent to which party-funding provides special access to decision-makers, and untraceable influence over them. And for both ministers and senior civil servants there has been concern, as we saw in Chapter 9, over the adequacy of the post-employment rules managed by the ACOBA.

Developing a broader approach

Potential weaknesses in regulating office-holders have gradually created pressure for a wider and more holistic approach to regulating lobbying, dealing directly with lobbyists themselves. One intermediate step in this direction has taken place at parliamentary level. As the distinctiveness of strong executive leadership in the UK has diminished through the effects of electoral volatility and coalition government, the issue of lobbying in other arenas, notably the legislature, has assumed growing importance. The conflict of interest threshold for MPs is generally higher than that applying to ministers, civil servants, judges, the police or regulators. This is because, in the UK as in most democracies, it is seen as a legitimate part of the democratic process to lobby the legislature. Moreover MPs in the United Kingdom do not have to divest themselves of interests while in office (they only have to declare them), they can accept parliamentary sponsorship, and they can take roles as parliamentary advisers to interest groups, as long as they do not actively lobby for these interests, either covertly or publicly. Because there is a resistance to the idea of lifetime professional politicians, they can also continue in careers, professions or businesses that may benefit from public policy and legislative choices. Exposure to conflicts of interest is taken more loosely than for members of the executive. MPs in this sense are special. The assumption is that the elected representative is resistant to improper lobbying and that the public interest will be safeguarded by the processes of socialisation, honour, the rules on transparency, declarations of interest, and ultimately the need for re-election.

We have already explored in Chapter 4 in relation to the House of Commons what these transparency and declarations safeguards consist of and how adequate they are. However, there is potentially another side to this question, where the relationships are more ambiguous. This is the area of so-called All-Party Parliamentary Groups (APPGs). These are cross-party specialist subject groups which are recognised and minimally regulated by the parliamentary authorities. Normally no resources, other than parliamentary accommodation, are provided for them. Their ostensible purpose is to allow MPs and peers to engage in effective and orderly non-partisan or cross-party study of specific policy issues, or of specific countries or regions of the world, and at the same time to interact with outside experts, specialists and interest groups.[23] Their relevance to lobbying is that they offer a channel of access for lobbyists. Even though APPGs have semi-official status, a practice has grown up by which outside interests provide support, in money or in kind, to assist their work. In 2006 a report by the Hansard Society reported that around 170 APPGs were in receipt of administrative or financial support from named individuals, trade organisations, charities, or not-for-profit organisations.[24]

Despite this controversial financial aspect of APPGs, however, it has generally been assumed that to close off the potential parliamentary pathway to lobbying they provide would drive the interaction further out of public sight.[25] Without APPGs, Parliament would either be less well-resourced or would have to substitute public funds for private

9 The growth of all-party parliamentary groups, 2003–2012

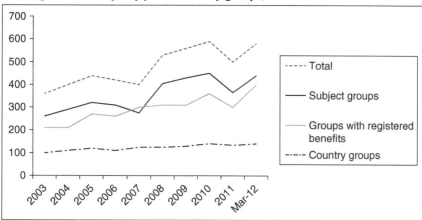

Source: Speakers' Working Group on All-Party Groups, Report to the Speaker and Lord Speaker, June 2012, available at: http://www.parliament.uk/documents/speaker/Speakers-Working-Group-on-APGs-report.pdf

ones. This would bring APPGs into the official circuit of parliamentary administration and change their nature significantly, probably increasing majority-party control over their agendas.

Clearly APPGs are not the only route to lobby Parliament, but all others are regulated by rules bearing solely on MPs and peers. Regulation of APPGs is the earliest example – other than criminal laws of bribery and corruption – where efforts have been made which also impact on the lobbyist. This change has come about slowly over three decades, but at an accelerating rate since 2006, when *The Times* reported an investigation into a group of APPGs, six of which it believed had broken the minimal rules then governing registration.[26] Since that time, other newspapers and transparency-oriented pressure groups have taken up the issue, producing monitoring reports drawing attention to the links between APPGs and external lobbying organisations covering a broad range of large businesses, trade associations, PR companies, and multi-client lobbying companies, as well as many other cause-group interests and charitable organisations.[27]

There are two striking and related aspects to the case of APPGs as an object lesson in regulating lobbying. The first is the huge growth of APPGs over a fairly short period of time. In 1986 there were 148, by 2006 there were 442, and in 2014 there were 611 (see Figure 9).[28]

The second is the impact and effectiveness of transparency. Transparency is particularly weakened where there is uncertainty over who exactly is doing the lobbying on behalf of whom. The key concern expressed by MPs and the parliamentary authorities is the potential lack of transparency in the transmission process from lobbyist to public official and on into the policy-making circuit. Underlying this concern has been the issue of the 'ultimate client' driving some of the best-resourced APPGs. As we shall see in the next section, this worry has applied not just to APPGs themselves but to debates about where the emphasis on lobbying regulation should lie more broadly. Where the support provided to an APPG comes from multi-client lobbying firms, which can in principle conceal the source of their own clients and which operate under different incentive structures from those who lobby directly, the risks to propriety are particularly marked. *The Times* reported in 2006 that thirty-six APPGs were financed by external lobbying organisations[29] and in 2011 the *Guardian* reported that some forty-five groups had been given assistance by lobbying companies including Quiller Consultants, Luther Pendragon and Bell Pottinger Public Affairs.[30] The register of financial donations maintained by the EC showed that a number of the seventy-three consultancies listed on the membership list of the Association of Professional Political Consultants (APCC) and of the 308 consultancies listed on the broader-based Public Relations Consultants' Association (PRCA) were direct donors to parties, whether at central-party level, local level, or to individual candidates.[31]

Multi-client professional lobbyists therefore have important implications for lobbying transparency in the legislature. The lobbying firm with access and contacts is potentially a knowledgeable and engaged intermediary in its own right, selecting the interests of paying clients over those who do not pay (in areas of public procurement, for example) and certainly developing its own status as an informed player with its own network of contacts. It can then develop an independent role in the selection and transmission of issues and views to Parliament as well as helping fund their dissemination inside Parliament. The prolific growth of all-party groups, and within them, the important role of multi-client lobbying firms, therefore seems to represent a significant change in parliamentary culture, generating new opportunities for external interests to influence agenda-setting. Any particular APPG may sit at the end of a chain where the real activities take place in the sponsoring organisation outside Parliament, and the APPG itself is an appendage. The learning process from which parliamentarians benefit through the APPG system thus has the potential to be seriously one-sided if a lobbying group, with particular paying clients behind it, is the source of administrative or financial support.

The House of Commons has tried over many years to develop tools for the orderly and transparent registration and publication of the range of APPGs. The rules have included a requirement to show how each group is linked to outside interests, particularly as regards funding and staffing. Yet with a 600-page register being published every few weeks, the sheer volume of information makes it quite difficult for any member of the public or the electorate to make up-to-date judgements about the resistance of the legislature to lobbying pressure. Indeed, despite all this transparency, for the most part APPGs work well below the public radar, and there is almost no public awareness of them. This means that when there is controversy, the impact on public opinion can be very limited. The public is likely to be unclear what the fuss is about. Moreover, since the main tool for understanding public life is partisan controversy, as is the main tool for meting out sanctions, the fact that such groups are, by definition, cross-party in nature makes voter sanction very difficult.

For most MPs registration and transparency requirements will be a strong constraint on their susceptibility to lobbying, whether through APPGs or any other routes. Circumstantial evidence has gradually mounted that APPG safeguards need to be tightened however. The consequence has been a long, if rarely decisive, series of investigations by the parliamentary authorities. The House of Commons (Services) Committee looked at the issue as long ago as 1983. The Select Committee on Members' Interests looked again in 1985. The Administration Committee revisited the issue in 2006, based on an inquiry by the PCS. There were further reports by the Committee on Standards and Privileges in 2009 and by the Parliamentary Commissioner in his 2012 mid-term review of the *Guide to the Rules*.[32] In the 2010–2015 Parliament, scrutiny became particularly intense. In 2011 the Speaker and the Lord Speaker created a joint working party under chairmanship of Jack Straw, a former leader of the House, which reported back in June 2012.[33] It dealt with broadly the same core group of questions that each of its predecessors had been concerned with: the influence of such groups, the risks of improper access, relations with outside organisations, finance, proper registration, the means by which the work of such groups could be kept distinct from full parliamentary committees, and the use of Palace of Westminster resources and facilities. Then in 2013, following the separation of the former Committee on Standards and Privileges into two distinct committees, the Standards Committee undertook a new inquiry, resulting in a further overhaul of the rules governing APPGs, some of which came into effect in September 2014, with the remainder operative from after the 2015 general election.[34]

While the Committee was investigating, moreover, a new and particularly egregious case arose, underlining the difficulties of making the rules governing APPGs stick in the face of really determined efforts to undermine them. Patrick Mercer, Conservative MP for Newark, was caught through press entrapment offering to sell his parliamentary position to work for the readmission of the government of Fiji to the Commonwealth. One part of the case against him was the attempt to create an All-Party Parliamentary Group to further that cause. The Commons Standards Committee was particularly concerned about this aspect of the affair.[35] Concluding that the Mercer case was among the worst cases its members had encountered, the Committee suspended Mr Mercer for the unprecedentedly long period of six months, forcing him to resign his seat.

Following the episode, all APPG staff passes were withdrawn immediately and the system of passes for such staff was later ended permanently. When the Standards Committee report eventually appeared in November 2013, it brought further changes to procedure. The new rules required a stronger and tighter structure for groups, a chair directly accountable to the Commons for compliance with parliamentary rules (ruling out peers as sole chairs), proper internal elections, regular meetings (at least two per year including an AGM), a meeting quorum of five MPs, and compliance with the rules on registering financial benefits. As regards the financial benefits provided by outside lobbies, groups receiving in excess of £12,500 per year would henceforth be required to produce proper accounts identifying external sources of funding. There were also tighter rules on publication and communication. Publications had to make clear that they had not been officially approved by either House, that views expressed were simply those of the group involved, and that, where outside help was provided to research or write a report, this must be acknowledged.[36]

Through these various efforts to stiffen the rules, the transparency requirements bearing on APPGs have gradually strengthened, and yet the number of APPGs continues to grow. Between £1.5 and £2 million annually is flowing from private sources into the servicing of the formal structures that for practical purposes affect the information flows on which the work of MPs depends. That is only the start of potentially risky financial flows: much larger risks lie behind them in terms of political donations, directorships, networks of contact and employment after officials leave office.[37] This might suggest that the more open and resistant to centralised party discipline parliamentary parties become, the more lobbies will think their efforts will pay off. For this reason, alongside rules governing APPGs and other lobbying directly on Parliament, attention gradually turned to regulating lobbying firms directly, starting with the multi-client lobbying firms that act as a form of political filter in their own right. It is to that wider extra-parliamentary lobbying world that we now turn.

Regulating lobbyists beyond Parliament

Any regulation of lobbying is a potential threat to political liberty. Most direct regulation is therefore based more on transparency than on restraint, with restraint reserved for a self-enforced code of conduct with associated sanctions. That approach was at the heart of the recommendations emerging from the inquiry into lobbying by the PASC in 2009.[38] The Report recommended a statutory register of lobbying activity, independently managed, combining in one place information about both the lobbyists and the lobbied, covering names and organisations, both directly and via third-party lobbying organisations. It called for disclosure of the names of the ultimate clients of third-party lobbyists, and for information to be published concerning: any public office a lobbyist had previously held; the private interests of ministers, senior civil servants and senior public servants being lobbied; and their career histories outside the public service. It also sought diary records and minutes of meetings of all contact between lobbyists and public officials.

Initially the then Labour government resisted this proposal, preferring instead a voluntary register.[39] Subsequently it relented, promising a statutory register along the lines proposed.[40] This was included in Labour's 2010 Manifesto and also figured in the 2010 Coalition Agreement, though it took a further eighteen months for even a consultation document to emerge on what was to become the Transparency of Lobbying, Non-party Campaigning and Trade Union Administration Act 2014. That appeared in January 2012.[41] Even then, the proposal was limited to the easiest and most justifiable target. The real issue was presented as transparency, and the least transparent lobbyists were identified as the multi-client lobbying companies. The coalition government's proposal argued – looking back to the broader ambition of the 2009 Select Committee Report – that since ministers had started to publish details of their meetings with lobbyists, there was no need to regulate the activities of in-house lobbyists since their activities could already be monitored from these publicly available sources. To go beyond multi-client lobbying forms, and to include, alongside the statutory register, a code of conduct, would, for a government seeking to cut the costs of regulatory burdens to both business and taxpayers, be complex and expensive. Initially the government also argued that this would draw in not only in-house lobbyists, but many other organisations such as charities and public-sector organisations. As finally passed, however, the Act ignored this drawback, at least for charities, and included them in its registration requirements, leading many to argue that really the government had only trade unions in its sights.[42]

Certainly, as professional agents for the claims of others, multi-client lobbying companies operate in a highly competitive market. If there are methods that will deliver success they will be tempted to use them, and the reputational damage they suffer will be less than for their ultimate client. Tough tactics may actually enhance a group's reputation for leaving no stone unturned. Multi-client companies are also an attractive haven for post-employment, especially for the least regulated parts of the political class: special advisers and party officials. All this applies not only to overtly commercial companies but think tanks too, where the nature of the operation may be quasi-commercial, and de facto financial reliance on what is effectively a commercial client or clients may be concealed.[43]

Nevertheless, the view that multi-client companies should be the real target of lobbying reform did not go uncontested. A forceful critique emerged from the PCRSC. Its report in July 2012 it reworked much of the ground covered by the PASC in 2008/2009, and took issue with several of the basic premises of the government's position. Its main case was that multi-client companies were not the most urgent issue and that the overwhelming majority of contacts between office-holders and lobbyists were direct rather than via third-party lobbyists. Without a register including *all* significant lobbyists, including in-house ones, the Report argued, the government's proposals would have little impact.[44] The Committee was also concerned about the absence of a code of conduct. Under the government's proposal, there was no statutory code. Lobbying companies were encouraged towards a voluntary code operated by one or more of the peak associations of which lobbying companies might (but might not) be members. The industry has three principal associations: the Chartered Institute of Public Relations, which represents individual practitioners, the PRCA, which sees itself as a trade body for the public relations body as a whole, including teams, agencies and individuals, and the Association of Professional Political Consultants (APPC). The APPC (which is a more specialised public affairs grouping) used to be based on corporate membership but now allows participation from trade associations, in-house lobbyists and individuals. In 2010 the three organisations came together to develop a system of joint voluntary self-regulation through a new body the United Kingdom Public Affairs Council (UKPAC). However by December 2011 the PRCA withdrew from UKPAC, commenting that it no longer thought a voluntary register under UKPAC supervision credible and the government proposal of a statutory register under an independent registrar was the best way forward for the industry.[45]

Not surprisingly much of the public relations industry was deeply critical of the government's Transparency of Lobbying Bill not so much because of its use of a statutory register but because of lack of breadth.

As the PCRSC pointed out, in fact, even though the government proposal involved only light-touch regulation with no code of conduct and little transparency, it did not actually have the wholehearted support of the multi-client lobbying firms themselves. Indeed the government's consultation process seemed to unite two potentially opposing sides of the main argument: lobbying organisations and transparency organisations. The former believed the proposal would at best have no impact, and the latter feared it might even drive firms that had previously joined one or more of the three peak associations, and would therefore be required to resister, and pay an association fee, to disaffiliate and escape both regulation and fee.

The PCRSC argued strongly that if there was to be regulation, it had to go much further than the government's bill. It called for a broader definition of lobbying, disclosure of issues being addressed, a statutory or hybrid (industry-run) code of conduct, and coordination with data provided by ministers and civil servants about meetings with lobbyists.[46] Heavier regulation than this (including more disclosure on money earned and spent by lobbyists, and penalties of a financial or even criminal nature for non-compliance), would in the PCRSC's view be better still, but it acknowledged its political and economic impracticality in the short term, and therefore recommended the medium-regulation solution. It also argued that existing practice on publishing information on ministers' and civil servants' meetings with lobbies and interests should be improved with more timely and detailed information, and on websites and in forms that made transparency monitoring far easier and more effective than was currently the case.

The Act as finally passed also covered 'third-party' campaigning by non-party organisations that campaign on behalf of particular candidates or parties. Organisations campaigning only on policy issues were not included. Its claimed objective was to shed light on the way third parties interact with the political system and to help take 'big money' out of politics by limiting campaign spending during an election year to prevent unregulated spending by vested interests. Organisations were limited to £390,000 across the UK in any defined election period. Expenditure on these campaigns must be recorded and disclosed for transparency. One avowed aim was to prevent undeclared paid full-time campaign staff, and in particular trade unions running banks of telephone canvassers and other systematic campaign efforts.

The Act provoked a vigorous protest by charities undertaking non-party political activity which, according to the existing charity law, had been permissible where the trustees could show it supported their purposes and would be an effective use of their resources. The law already prohibited charities from engaging directly in party politics, party campaigning, supporting particular political candidates or undertaking political activity unrelated to the charity's purpose. The initial version of the Bill appeared to change this but following concerns raised by the charitable sector, the government altered the wording to ensure that controlled expenditure remained as defined under existing legislation. Charities could thus still support specific policies advocated by political parties if it would help achieve their charitable purposes. Only expenditure 'which can reasonably be regarded as intended to promote or procure electoral success' is included.

Conclusion: can transparency be enough?

The debate on lobbying has undoubtedly moved on over the last decade with profound changes in the lobbying industry itself, greater appreciation by government of the need for intervention, and of course the recurrence of scandals. Certainly the 2014 Act incurred extensive criticism because of its limited scope in relation to the industry as a whole. Although the machinery has been set up with a registrar with criminal and civil sanctions for non-compliance the legislation will almost certainly need to be revisited. Nevertheless discussion of lobbying has become much more informed, fuelled by professional organisations, a host of voluntary organisations and advocacy groups. That debate seems capable of providing a perspective on lobbying that finally begins to integrate the related aspects of the problem. It looks unlikely that a transparency-driven solution can be made workable without integrating the sources of information that exist on both sides of the lobbying relationship: that of the lobbyist as well as the office-holder. It also appears, given the size and complexity of lobbying, that effective technology and well-integrated data-sources are required to make the range of information potentially available on lobbying relationships manageable to those who wish to use it.

There must remain doubt, however, that simply shedding light – however comprehensively – on the subject matter, timing and content of meetings, or even the financial rewards to lobbying companies that flow from it, will ever get ahead of public and media scepticism about the purpose and the effects of lobbying. The regulation of lobbying envisaged imposes largely procedural constraints but does not curtail the exercise of influence itself. With time and effort, all lobbyists can comply, but continue to lobby much as before. Whether the public is likely to respond with such deep and lasting disapproval that this affects lobbying relationships and behaviour is more doubtful except in the most contumacious cases of impropriety. A rise in use of information about lobbying, therefore, will probably not create any parallel rise in public trust and confidence.

What is clear is that although the coalition government acknowledged the problem and eventually brought forward legislation, that measure is unlikely to end debate. The government's claim that the statutory register to be introduced in 2015 will make a significant advance in addressing the problems associated with lobbying is unlikely to convince critics who think the legislation is inadequate, coverage too limited and that special interests have too much leverage in policy-making. The Scottish Parliament, which is at the time of writing promoting its own legislation on lobbying, has expressed a determination to avoid the weaknesses of Westminster's approach and may be able to develop a different and more consensual strategy. Even if it does so the controversy surrounding lobbying will certainly not be eradicated completely from UK politics.

Notes

1 Schattschneider, E., *The Semi-Sovereign People: A Realist's View of Democracy in America* (Austin: Holt, Rinehart and Winston, 1960).

2 Baumgartner, F., J. Berry, M. Hojnacki, D. Kimball and B. Leech, *Lobbying and Policy Change: Who Wins, Who Loses and Why?* (Chicago: University of Chicago Press, 2009); see also Beyers, J., R. Eising and W. Maloney, 'Researching interest group politics in Europe and elsewhere: much we study, little we know?', *West European Politics*, 31:6 (2008), 1103–1128.

3 Doig, A., 'No reason for complacency? Organisational change and probity in local government', *Local Government Studies*, 21:1 (1995), 99–114.

4 Hall, P. (ed.), *Governing the Economy: The Politics of State Intervention in Britain and France* (Oxford: Oxford University Press, 1993); Hall, P. and D. Soskice (eds), *Varieties of Capitalism: The Institutional Foundations of Comparative Advantage* (Oxford: Oxford University Press, 2001).

5 Jordan, G. (ed.), *The Commercial Lobbyists: Politics for Profit in Britain* (Aberdeen: Aberdeen University Press, 1991); Grant, W., *Business and Politics in Britain* (New York: Palgrave Macmillan, 1993), and 'Pressure politics: the changing world of pressure groups', *Parliamentary Affairs*, 57:2 (2004), 408–419.

6 See Hollingsworth, M., *MP's for Hire* (London: Bloomsbury, 1991), Leigh, D. and E. Vulliamy, *Sleaze: The Corruption of Parliament* (London: Fourth Estate, 1997), and also Leys, C., *Market Driven Politics* (London: Verso, 2003). See also the recent brief survey of lobbying, undertaken by the Hansard Society: Parvin, P., *Friend or Foe? Lobbying in British Democracy: A Discussion Paper* (London: Hansard Society, 2007), which concluded that lobbying organisations were 'occupying an increasingly central role not only in the development of policy, but also in its delivery'.

7 But see 'PR today: the economic significance of public relations' (London: Centre for Economic and Business Research Ltd, 2005) and Maloney, K., *Rethinking Public Relations: PR Propaganda and Democracy* (London: Routledge, 2006). p. 2 Quoted in Parvin, *Friend or Foe?* p. 10.

8 A Chartered Institute of Public Relations survey reported by Dinan and Miller claimed that 47,800 people worked directly in the PR sector defined in the broadest possible terms (of which 80 per cent were in-house), with a turnover of £6.5 billion. Miller, D. and W. Dinan, *A Century of Spin: How Public Relations became the Cutting Edge of Corporate Power* (London: Pluto Press, 2008), pp. 102–104.

9 The Council was formed in 2010 – in response to moves towards greater regulation of lobbyists – by the three main representative organisations, the Chartered Institute of Public Relations, the Association of Professional Political Consultants, and the Public Relations Consultants Association (though the latter subsequently withdrew). There is significant overlap between memberships of the three.

10 Her Majesty's Government, *Introducing a Statutory Register of Lobbyists: Consultation Paper*, January 2012, Cm 8233.

11 *Introducing a Statutory Register of Lobbyists: Consultation Paper – Impact Assessment (1A)*, Cabinet Office, 27 November 2011 (http://goo.gl/5jWiE2, accessed 19 March 2015).

12 Political and Constitutional Reform Committee, 2nd Report, *Introducing a Statutory Register of Lobbyists*, Vol. I, HC 153, 2012, p. 12.

13 Lobbying is directly regulated through, *inter alia*, the *Ethics in Government Act, 1975*, the *Lobbying Disclosure Act 1995*, and the *Legislative Disclosure and Transparency Act 2006*. Lobbyists must reveal the issues they seek to affect, their expenditure and details of gifts, trips, meals, campaign finance, etc. that may be thought to help lobbying. Political finance and Political Action Committee activity is also extensively regulated. See Baumgartner, F. and B. Leech, *Basic Interests: The Importance of Groups in Politics and Political Science* (Princeton: Princeton University Press, 1998); Cigler, A. and B.A. Loomis (eds), *Interest Group Politics* (Washington, DC: CQ Press, 2007), especially the chapters by Kersh and Currinder *et al*. See also Chari, R., G. Murphy and J. Hogan, 'Regulating lobbyists: a comparative analysis of the United States, Canada, Germany and the European Union', *The Political Quarterly*, 78:3 (2007), 422–438.

14 Political and Constitutional Reform Committee, *Introducing a Statutory Register of Lobbyists*. The Cameron speech is available at: http://goo.gl/jIL70Y (accessed 19 March 2015).

15 In Labour's case two special advisers – one, Roger Liddle, a member of the No. 10 team, another, Derek Draper, formerly a member – were alleged to have offered special access to Downing Street, a matter compounded by Draper's move to a lobbying-firm role. Strongly denied by the Prime Minister, the denial was nevertheless accompanied by a commitment to tighten safeguards against inappropriate access by lobbyists. Prime Minister's Questions,

Hansard, 8 July 2008, cols 1065–67. The Conservative case, after the 2010 election, involved both the alleged influence of an unaccredited special adviser to the Minister of Defence, Liam Fox, which provoked the latter's resignation after only a few months in office, and the offer by the co-Treasurer of the Party, Peter Cruddas, of 'premier league' access to the Prime Minister himself. Cruddas too immediately resigned, though in both cases, as in the Draper and Liddle affairs in 1998, it was denied that anything improper had occurred.

16 Cabinet Office, 'Allegations against Rt Hon Dr Liam Fox MP Report by the Cabinet Secretary', October 2011. Available at: http://goo.gl/Ppxy1z (accessed 19 March 2015).

17 Newman, M. and O. Wright, 'Caught on camera: top lobbyists boasting how they influenced the PM', *Independent*, 6 December 2011.

18 Insight Team, 'Cash for Cameron', *Sunday Times*, 25 March 2012.

19 The Leveson Inquiry, *An Inquiry into the Culture, Practices and Ethics of the Press: Report [Leveson]*, ch. 6.5 'December 2010 – July 2011: The Rt Hon Jeremy Hunt and the Department for Culture, Media and Sport' (London: TSO, 2012), pp. 1351–1407.

20 Select Committee on Standards and Privileges, *Sir John Butterfill, Mr Stephen Byers, Ms Patricia Hewitt, Mr Geoff Hoon, Mr Richard Caborn and Mr Adam Ingram*, 9th Report, Vol. 1, HC 654-II, 7 December 2010.

21 Insight Team, 'Arms firms call up "generals for hire"', *Sunday Times*, 14 October 2012.

22 Political and Constitutional Reform Committee, *Introducing a Statutory Register of Lobbyists*, HC 153, 13 July 2012, para 80 and 'Written evidence by Rob McKinnon', (Ev 122).

23 In late 2014 there were 611 recorded APPGs, of which 137 section 1 (area) groups and 474 section 2 (subject) groups. They are registered by the office of the Commissioner for Parliamentary Standards, on whose website are found both the nature and purpose of the groups, and registration details for each group. www.publications.parliament.uk/pa/cm/cmallparty/register/contents.htm.

24 Parvin, *Friend or Foe?*

25 'There is a longstanding dilemma about the regulation of APPGs: they are essentially informal groupings, established by individual Members, yet the more restrictions and requirements that are placed on them, the more they appear to be endorsed by the House. Work of this sort would continue whether or not APPGs were regulated; there would simply be less transparency about it.' Committee on Standards, Sixth Report of Session 2013–2014, *All-Party Parliamentary Groups*, HC 357, 13 November 2013, p. 3.

26 Coates, S., 'How business pays for a say in Parliament', *The Times*, 13 January 2006; Editorial section, 'Dirty little secret', 13 January 2006.

27 Ball, J., 'Coalition urged to act over lobbyists who use party groups "to buy influence"', *Guardian*, 24 February 2011.

28 Data drawn from: (i) House of Commons, Committee on Standards and Privileges, *Lobbying and All Party Groups*, Ninth Report of Session

2005–2006, Report and Appendix, House of Commons, 23 May 2006, London: The Stationery Office Limited, appendix para 9; and (ii) Parliamentary Commissioner for Standards, *Annual Report 2011–12*, House of Commons 21 June 2012, HC 311, London: The Stationery Office Limited. (Updated from the PCS website for 2014).

29 Coates, 'How business pays'; Editorial section, 'Dirty little secret'.

30 Ball, 'Coalition urged to act'.

31 From searches on the EC donor database, 30 November 2012: https://pefon-line.electoralcommission.org.uk/search/searchintro.aspx.

32 Kelly, R. and S. Yousaff, *All-Party Groups*, House of Commons Library Standard Note SN/PC/06409, 30 August 2012.

33 Speakers' Working Group on All-Party Groups: report to the Speaker and Lord Speaker, 19 March 2015, available at: www.parliament.uk/documents/speaker/Speakers-Working-Group-on-APGs-report.pdf.

34 See, for the report and the new rules: Committee on Standards, Sixth Report of Session 2013–2014, *All-Party Parliamentary Groups*, HC 357, 13 November 2013, and for the new rules: Committee on Standards, *From the Rt hon Kevin Barron MP, Changes to the Rules for All-Party Groups*, 2 July 2014 (http://goo.gl/S1nhxk, accessed 19 March 2015).

35 Committee on Standards, Eleventh Report of session 2013–2014, *Patrick Mercer*, HoC 1225, 1 May 2014, 'He offered to procure a pass for a member of staff of that APPG. While he warned that he could not guarantee a "satisfactory" report from the APPG, he was quick to reassure his client that it was likely that such a report would achieve their aims. In addition to his actions in tabling questions and in setting up an APPG, identified by the Commissioner, the transcripts make clear Mr Mercer also volunteered to make approaches to a Minister and host the "*Friends of Fiji*" in the House of Commons … **The Commissioner [for Parliamentary Standards] concludes that Mr Mercer's particular choice of Fiji for an APPG and the attempts to influence positively the UK government's attitude towards his readmissions [*sic*], "is closely linked to the financial reward that was being offered to himself and that which he was seeking on behalf of his associate [a Mr Paul Marsden]." We agree'** (emphasis in original report), pp. 5 and 8.

36 Committee on Standards, Sixth Report of Session 2013–2014, *All-Party Parliamentary Groups*, HC 357, 13 November 2013

37 Beleaga, T., 'Donations to all-party parliamentary groups', *Guardian*, 10 April 2012. The *Guardian's* reports in 2011 and 2012 depend on simply summing donations declared in the House of Commons register. They make no estimate for donations-in-kind, so the real figure is much higher. The Commissioner for Parliamentary Standards does not make any official estimate of these sums, nor has any of the House of Commons' own reports.

38 Public Administration Select Committee, *Lobbyists: Access and Influence in Whitehall*, 5 January 2009, HC 36-1, 2008–2009.

39 Public Administration Committee, *Lobbying: Developments since the Committee's First Report of Session 2008–09: Government Response to the*

Committee's Fifth Report of Session 2009–10, HC 393, 3 March 2010, 2009–2010.

40 See HC Deb, 22 March 2010, cc25–26.

41 Her Majesty's Government, *Introducing a Statutory Register of Lobbyists: Consultation Paper*, January 2012, Cm 8233, along with an impact assessment, *Introducing a Statutory Register of Lobbyists: Consultation Paper – Impact Assessment (1A)*, Cabinet Office, 27 November 2011 (http://goo.gl/5jWiE2, accessed 19 March 2015).

42 *Introducing a Statutory Register of Lobbyists*, p. 9.

43 The growth of think-tanks in the last two decades has been almost as prolific as that of APPGs: Policy Exchange, the Centre for Policy Studies, the Institute for Public Policy Research, the Adam Smith Institute, the John Smith Foundation, Demos, Civitas, Politea, the Institute for Government and the New Local Government Network are all relatively recent arrivals, competing in a crowded space for funding and commissions.

44 Political and Constitutional Reform Committee, *Introducing a Statutory Register of Lobbyists*, HC 153, 13 July 2012 paras 17–48.

45 See Singleton, D., 'Lobbying blow as PRCA withdraws from UK Public Affairs Council', *PR Weekly*, 9 December 2011.

46 Political and Constitutional Reform Committee, *Introducing a Statutory Register of Lobbyists*.

11

Party funding: ambitious architecture, flawed rules

Introduction: public interest beyond public office-holders

Parties present special problems for ethics regulators. Parties are not official public institutions, so party office-holders are not technically public
office-holders. Yet there is clearly a public interest in what they do, how
they are organised and how they raise money. In modern democracies
there is usually at least some light legal regulation of parties, but it mainly
concerns public registration and transparency about who is legally
responsible and about where money comes from. Regulating the internal
lives of parties is less common. Much party activity is voluntary, and the
rewards are often non-material ones. The more accountable and compliant party volunteers have to be, the more the personal rewards may be
diluted, and the more volunteers may be deterred from participating.

The issue of finance is especially difficult. Parties need money to operate. Funding must not come from corrupt exchanges, but most people
who donate money or voluntary effort hope for a return of some sort,
whether through broad policy outcomes, or more specific benefits. The
more specific the return, the more the exchange can look questionable,
and the more it will raise public concern. However, deciding where
acceptable electoral exchange ends and corruption begins is controversial. First, a party official who takes money on a party's behalf from a
special interest is not normally the individual who provides a favourable policy or decision in return. Such a 'reward' will be returned by a
party representative in public office. So a collusion which might reveal
that an improper exchange has occurred will often be hard to establish.
In most democracies, unless the law requires parties to operate exclusively on a combination of membership fees and public subsidies, funding comes to some degree from interest groups, business and private
individuals. Secondly, there can be controversy over *access*, as well as
over direct policy concessions. From the politician's perspective, selling

access for contributions to party funds might seem legitimate as long as the politician retains a completely free hand to decide policy. From the public-interest perspective this assumption is more questionable. The credibility of that 'free hand' will be tarnished. So if access to current or prospective government officials has a market value, it is questionable whether it should be marketed at all. Yet ministers cannot be isolated from civil society. The best that can be achieved is transparency about who they meet and what is said, and even that is difficult because ministers act in a public, a party and a private capacity, and their special advisers can meet anyone they wish on their behalf.

Regulating the finances of political parties has therefore to be about creating a climate of public confidence as well as outlawing specific acts of impropriety. That climate is delivered by ensuring that the money which enables parties to operate comes from acceptable sources, in agreed amounts, and that the public in principle has access to information about these matters. When wrong-doing is established, it will usually be about compliance with these requirements – transparency, donation size or spending limits – rather than about corruption per se. The burden of proof required to demonstrate outright corruption, as opposed to a procedural compliance failure, will result in many smoking guns, but few successful prosecutions.

All this is fine in theory but hard to achieve in practice. Agreeing rules on party finance is unusually difficult. Decisions are not taken behind a veil of ignorance about party advantage. Parties, as members of legislatures that draft ethical rules, normally come to such decisions with long-established links to interests and sources of income. Changing the rules on party finance may jeopardise important funding streams. Parties will differ over the need for transparency of funding sources, permissible donors, spending limits, and how third-party campaigners (including charities and issue-campaigning organisations) should be treated. The rights and wrongs of these questions are not self-evident, and parties with strong and diverging interests will struggle to agree, leaving the legitimacy of the rules in question. Parties that are short of resources will also struggle to meet the compliance requirements in relation to finance and may be tempted to ignore the rules, perhaps because they suppose their higher purposes justify what they are doing. They may be tempted to disguise the real source of a donation, or conceal its true size by breaking it down into a series of smaller donations subject to lower transparency requirements. They may even ignore the letter of the law because the penalties for non-compliance are low or non-existent. As we shall see, these considerations have had a fundamental impact on the regulation of party finance in the United Kingdom in the last two decades.

Party finance in the United Kingdom

Box 11.1 Timeline of party funding regulation

1883 Corrupt and Illegal Practices Act (limits on constituency spending in elections)

1925 Honours (Prevention of Abuses) Act criminalises sale of peerages or honours

1974 'Short Money' public financial aid for opposition parties in the House of Commons

1976 Houghton Committee recommends extending public finance to parties outside House of Commons

1983 Representation of the People Act further legislation on candidate spending in elections

1994 Home Affairs Select Committee recommends code of practice for political parties. Minority Labour seeks stricter disclosure rules

1997 CSPL inquiry into party funding established

1998 Committee report recommends full donation disclosure, limit on campaign expenditure and tax relief on small donations

2000 PPERA establishes the EC as the regulator of political party finance: central reporting, publication of donations, national spending limits

2006 The Electoral Administration Act makes loans subject to same rules as donations

2007 Phillips Review proposes cap on donations and additional public funding

2009 Political Parties and Elections Act: additional limits on pre-election spending by candidates outside regulated campaign. New sanctions for EC

2011 Further CSPL inquiry into party funding recommends major restrictions on donations, and major new provisions on public subsidies for parties, but is rejected by parties

Source: Committee of Standards in Public Life, *Political Party Finance: Ending the Big Donor Culture*, Thirteenth Report (Cm 8208 London, Nov 2011), p. 105, plus authors' elaborations

---

Until the 1980s the sources of funding for the two major British parties were stable and simple. The organic link between Labour and the unions made trade-union money crucial to Labour's finances. Individual trade-union members paid affiliation fees to the Labour Party via their unions and, although there was provision for individuals to opt out of the system, it produced large aggregate funds which unions gave to Labour. The Conservatives relied to a considerable degree on business, both through direct company contributions and front organisations such as the British United Industrialists (BUI).[1] British politics was relatively low-cost as a result of the ban on TV advertising, long-established limits on candidate expenses,[2] and the centralisation of power in parliamentary parties which curtailed the locally rooted factionalism which has driven up costs in some other countries.[3]

Against the background of a differentiated party duopoly, the two parties criticised each other's funding sources, but overall party funding costs stayed low. The party funding regime until the late 1990s consisted to a large extent of the TV advertising ban and the constituency-candidate spending rules in elections. In the 1970s and 1980s there were a few efforts to broaden the debate about party finance but with little effect. The 1976 Houghton Committee on Financial Aid to Political Parties led to a limited form of public funding for the Opposition parties, known as 'Short Money',[4] but efforts in the 1980s by the Hansard Society and others to raise the issue of corporate donations and shareholder rights made little progress.[5]

The perception of sleaze in politics that developed under John Major accelerated change and put a number of key issues concerning party finance on the public agenda. In 1994 Labour's minority report to the Home Affairs Select Committee advocated wide-ranging reform: the publication of all donations over £5,000, caps on election spending, a ban on foreign donations, an independent electoral oversight body and legislation to put regulations governing corporate donations on a par with trade-union donations. The Select Committee split along party lines. The majority (Conservative) report supported publication and independent audit of party accounts, but rejected compulsory disclosure of sources of gifts. It also opposed more state funding or restrictions on foreign donations, and rejected capping of donations or increased shareholder control over corporate donations.[6] By 1994 the debate had thus begun to broaden and also to open up partisan division.

It was also apparent that traditional sources of funding were coming under strain. The social composition of each party was more differentiated than in the past, and the two major parties sought to broaden their financial bases. The Conservatives began to find that large businesses, with institutional shareholders and public reputations that could be damaged by close identification with Conservatism, were becoming wary of making donations, especially in an atmosphere of greater public openness. Labour's modernisation made its new leaders anxious to reduce reliance on the unions. There was also growing debate about the decline of party membership subscriptions, though in reality individual membership dues were never the major source of central funding for parties in the United Kingdom, compared to union block transfers and business donations. For the Labour Party, individual membership fees accounted for just under 12 per cent of revenue over the period 1992–1997. For the Conservative Party similar calculations are more difficult because for a long period it did not collect constituency membership figures, and individual subscriptions to the local party varied. However the so-called constituency quota (a voluntary tax on local associations to fund the central party) produced just under 5 per cent of central revenue between 1992 and 1997.[7]

A more important development was an emerging change in spending patterns. The costs of campaigning rose significantly in the 1980s and 1990s. Spending by the two major parties in the acutely competitive 1997 general election rose to £54.3 million (from only £21.4 million in 1992 and a mere £5.8 million in 1983). Even allowing for inflation, the CSPL estimated this as a real-terms increase over fourteen years of 329 per cent for the Conservatives, and 550 per cent for Labour.[8] A further element was the need to spend not just on elections but also *between* elections. While parliamentary candidates rarely ever spent up to the individual constituency limits during campaigns, the central parties were increasingly conducting a national campaign between elections in marginal constituencies. For the two major parties, as Figure 10 shows, general running costs were by the turn of the century far outstripping campaign costs. The costs of party leadership also rose. In the 1990s senior Labour figures in Opposition developed their own personal offices and financed them independently of the formal party budget. Think tanks close to parties also grew, encouraging the tendency of senior Labour figures in Opposition to test out personal staff, with a view to their later employment as special advisers in government. The pattern was to be repeated for the Conservatives in the years after 1997.

The solution: the Political Parties, Elections and Referendums Act 2000

Some form of new framework to regulate party funding was therefore increasingly likely by the later 1990s. However, party finance had not been part of the initial remit of the CSPL, since it did not, strictly

10 Average annual breakdown of expenditure of the three main central parties, 2001–2010

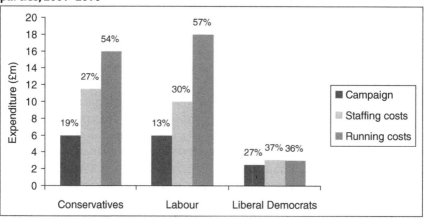

Source: Central parties' statement of accounts and the Thirteenth Report of the Committee on Standards in Public Life, 2011

speaking, involve public office-holders and Labour did not at first see non-partisan recommendations of the sort that would emanate from the Committee as a necessary first step to legislation. However, although the Labour Party had made party funding transparency an election commitment in its 1997 manifesto, it quickly found itself caught in its own party-funding scandal. It emerged that Formula 1 owner Bernie Ecclestone had given Labour a £1million donation ahead of the 1997 election. The incoming Labour government's decision to give Formula 1 a limited exemption from an imminent ban on tobacco advertising in sport thus looked highly controversial. The affair was damaging for Labour: it eventually had to return the money, while upholding the exemption. To save face it added party funding to the CSPL's formal remit and asked it to produce an immediate report, which it did, in 1998.

The CSPL's Report recommended banning foreign donations, making all donations above a certain size transparent, subjecting corporate donations to shareholder approval, making tax breaks for party donations, and limiting campaign expenditure by national parties.[9] The result was the Political Parties, Elections and Referendums Act (PPERA) 2000, which established a new agency, the Electoral Commission, whose core tasks were to register political parties, publicise details of where parties and candidates got money from and how they spent it, manage electoral registration, run elections, encourage electoral participation and registration, and conduct referendums.[10]

The most important impacts of the legislation were on party donation sources, the transparency to be attached to donations, and the rules on expenditure during election campaigns. The PPERA 2000 defined 'permissible donors' and, above a threshold of £200 per annum (raised to £500 in 2009), it banned funding by foreigners. It defined the registration and reporting requirements on parties, and defined so-called 'third parties' (organisations other than their own party campaigning in support of candidates). Donations exceeding £5,000 in a calendar year to the party headquarters and £1,000 to local accounting units had to be reported on a quarterly basis – thresholds that were raised to £7,500 and £1,500 in 2009. Donors were required to provide minimum information about themselves to the recipient parties for onward transmission to the EC. Companies registered under the Companies Act and conducting business in the United Kingdom needed shareholder permission for gifts to parties. Parties had to report under three main heads: quarterly donation returns (increased in frequency to weekly during elections); an annual Statement of Accounts; and spending in any particular Westminster, devolved-assembly, or European election. From 2006 parties were also required to make quarterly returns on loans. The Act also placed limits on national campaign expenditure by registered political parties during a regulated 'relevant election period' – a period of one year up to the poll date. This new national limit complemented existing restrictions on local campaign spending by candidates at constituency level.

The EC's powers under PPERA were underpinned by both criminal and civil sanctions. Illegal donations could be forfeited and false statements or failure to reveal donations or to mislead could lead to a year's imprisonment. Civil sanctions could be imposed for late returns on a sliding scale. The EC was given power to seek a Court Order to enforce payment, but itself had no direct power to fine or prosecute. There were therefore quite detailed compliance requirements in the new regulatory environment, although not much thought was given to the possibility that compliance failures might result from lack of party resources, internal disorganisation, and individual maverick behaviour, rather than deliberate deceit by those running the central party organisations. Nor was much thought given to whether the EC itself had the resources to manage a complex set of tasks, including some – such as managing elections and promoting electoral participation – that went beyond regulating party finance. Such resources included not just manpower, but also political backing when the Commission had to act in politically controversial circumstances.

The consequences

During the 1990s, the main parties gradually came to agree that escalating competitive spending in election campaigns was undesirable, and that there needed to be more transparency over donations. In this sense the PPERA 2000 appeared to solve the key problems of political finance. The estimate of the likely costs of election campaigns made by the CSPL, which was incorporated into the PPERA 2000, turned out, for reasons connected to Labour's electoral supremacy in the period, to be initially unproblematic. In neither the 2001 general election nor the more competitive 2005 campaign did either major party's central organisation spending come up against the PPERA expenditure ceilings.

However, while the PPERA restricted spending during election campaigns it did not do so outside them. In 2006, the Select Committee on Constitutional Affairs discovered from data reported to the EC that over the period 2001–2005 80 per cent of total party spending had actually been devoted to items not falling within the regulated expenses headings of the campaign periods, mainly on general staffing and running costs.[11] It also noted a decline in party income from traditional sources, leaving a growing funding gap between party income and expenditure. The problem therefore was not just that campaign expenditure limits were ineffective when looked at in a longer time horizon, but also that while (non-campaign-regulated) spending was rising, income was falling. Overall, in fact, party spending was continuing to rise well ahead of income sources, with parties running especially big deficits around election years between 1997 and 2005. Worse, the funding gap was increasingly being filled from large private donations and by loans. Both sources undermined the credibility of the new regulatory regime.

The gap between national party income and national party spending between 2001 and 2010 can be seen in Table 11.1. Labour and the Conservatives both spent far in excess of income for much of this period. The accumulated deficit of the two major parties over the years from 2001 onwards was £9.7 million for the Labour Party and £21 million for the Conservatives. Not unexpectedly, the three election years were the peak years for expenditure for the two main parties, and they racked up large deficits.

Until after the 2010 general election, spending did not drop back sufficiently below income in the other years to compensate. In Labour's case, however, the party was clearly experiencing severe cash flow constraints by the end of the decade. Its spending at the general election of 2010 was under 50 per cent of the permitted ceiling set by the Act, suggesting the party's credit rating had diminished drastically,[12] as might be expected for an unpopular party facing election after a long period in power.

The funding gap during these years was increasingly filled by dependence on high-value donors. In 1998 the CSPL had had few concerns of principle about this. It required high-value donations to be *transparent*

Table 11.1 Income and expenditure at national level for the two main UK parties, 2002–2013

Conservative	2002	2003	2004	2005	2006	2007	2008	2009	2010	2011	2012	2013
Income	9.8	13.6	20.0	24.2	30.9	33.5	32.4	42.0	43.1	23.7	24.2	25.3
Expenditure	10.5	16.0	28.2	39.2	26.7	31.9	31.9	37.2	49.2	23.0	23.3	23.5
Assets	3.0	13.4	14.3	13.9	36.3	16.4	16.3	16.2	9.8	9.2	9.0	8.4
Liabilities	8.5	11.4	11.5	32.0	45.3	24.1	23.8	19.0	19.1	17.9	16.8	14.3
Labour	2002	2003	2004	2005	2006	2007	2008	2009	2010	2011	2012	2013
Income	21.2	26.9	29.3	35.3	25.8	32.4	34.0	26.8	36.3	31.3	33.0	33.3
Expenditure	22.1	24.3	32.1	49.8	26.6	24.8	26.2	24.7	33.8	30.3	30.2	27.9
Assets	12.1	13.3	13.4	14.6	7.9	14.1	16.8	15.0	16.6	13.3	13.7	17.2
Liabilities	19.0	13.2	11.2	41.8	32.8	30.0	28.9	31.6	24.0	18.7	15.6	15.5

Source: Party accounts registered at Electoral Commission (Electoral Commission website last accessed 19 March 2015: http://www. electoralcommission.org.uk).

but rejected the argument for capping.[13] Over the period 2001–2010, however, the fifty largest donors turned out to be providing £191 million of the total reported in donations by the two major parties: about 44 per cent of all donations.[14] The importance of individual donations compared to organisational or corporate donations rose dramatically over the period 2001–2010. In each of the years from 2001 to 2010, taking all parties together, individual donations of over £100,000 constituted between 33.6 per cent of the total donation income in the lowest year, reaching 50.4 per cent of the value in the highest year.

Between Labour and Conservatives there were certain differences in the pattern of high-value donations, the Conservatives raising donations from a wider pool of individuals. The Conservatives also did better than Labour in the lower bands of the four high-value categories themselves. Labour relied on a significantly smaller base of individuals within the category of high-end donors and thus got much of its income in larger donations (see Table 11.2). Overall, however, high-value donations constituted a significant proportion of the income streams for both major parties.

How greatly that dependence had increased over the late twentieth century is difficult to tell, since there is no reliable data on the period before compulsory registration began in 2001. The transparency brought to party funding by the PPERA 2000 suggested the strong possibility that a small number of wealthy individuals was exercising a growing and disproportionate influence over the financial health of the main parties even before 2000.

Once the PPERA was in place, moreover, reliance on high-value donors increased incentives to evade the transparency aspect of PPERA rules by resort to unrecorded loans. For donors, loans had two advantages for donors. As long as they were on commercial terms (or what could plausibly pass for commercial terms) they did not have to be registered. Secondly, they could be called in if the donors subsequently felt dissatisfied, in theory at least giving greater leverage than a simple gift. This issue eventually exploded in the middle of the 2005 election campaign when the Conservatives were revealed as using non-commercial-term loans to sustain their heavily debt-laden finances. Later, Labour's own use of unregistered soft loans triggered allegations that several of those lenders had been promised peerages in return for the loans. Under the Honours (Prevention of Abuses) Act 1925 it was a criminal offence to seek to 'sell' peerages. The allegations were examined in a long police investigation in 2006/2007, eventually dropped on grounds of insufficient evidence; but given the difficulty of effectively enforcing the 1925 Act, the suspicion remained strong that peerages were being awarded for large donations, generating a new and damaging element of the controversy surrounding party funding.

Table 11.2 Distribution of gifts by size and party, 2001–2010

	Conservative Party		Labour Party		Liberal Democrats	
	Total number	Total value	Total number	Total value	Total number	Total value
£0–999	437	£228,078.57	3,181	£1,556,824.50	507	£349,161.35
£1000–9,999	6,545	£22,683,764.87	6,872	£18,473,138.88	5,036	£11,284,716.79
£10,000–49,999	2,238	£38,452,241.85	1,025	£18,764,669.70	346	£5,772,095.80
£50,000–99,999	566	£31,437,163.20	121	£7,493,217.77	38	£2,146,203.63
£100,000–249,999	195	£25,327,596.49	144	£23,640,842.94	35	£4,960,141.96
£250,000–499,999	62	£18,534,680.44	138	£44,666,781.11	10	£2,930,850.00
£500,000–999,999	21	£11,993,184.98	29	£17,389,737.14	1	£632,000.00
£1M +	10	£18,733,865.85	20	£29,800,646.30	1	£1,536,064.80
Total	10,074	£167,390,576.25	11,530	£161,785,858.34	5,974	£29,611,234.33

Source: Electoral Commission donations register, 2011.
Note: Donation totals exclude public funds given to parties.

Regulatory overstretch

The 2005 loans affair was a serious breach of the spirit, if not the letter, of the PPERA. It led quickly to the Electoral Administration Act 2006 which tightened the regulations on non-commercial loans, required parties to declare future and outstanding borrowings, strengthened reporting requirements on parties both for timeliness and transparency, and introduced tougher penalties for breaches of the legislation.[15] However, it was by no means the only difficulty with the original legislation. The EC itself was concerned from its inception about the breadth of its regulatory remit, and about the resources and sanctions it had to carry that remit out. Some of its allotted tasks lacked clear and effective enforcement powers, even on the regulatory front. Moreover, a ban on use of staff with hands-on experience of contemporary political parties in the Commission's own rules (eventually relaxed in the 2009 Political Parties and Elections Act) denied the Commission essential expertise in developing effective relationships with the parties it was supposed to regulate. Some roles performed by the Commission also seemed to be in conflict with others. On the one hand the Commission was supposed to offer advice to parties; on the other hand it had to inspect them. But its sanctions for compliance failure were modest. It had power to name and shame, but no direct power to fine. It could denounce offenders to the Crown Prosecution Service (CPS) but this was a drastic weapon to use against parties which were essentially voluntary organisations, varying in robustness from area to area, and on whose cooperation the EC of necessity depended.

The dilemma of how heavy a regulatory burden to impose on organisations that were at times barely coping soon emerged as a serious issue, especially given the Commission's own concerns about declining political participation, party membership and turnout. It had to impose regulation on activity that had previously gone largely unregulated. Party officers and candidates at both national and local level suddenly found themselves forced to conduct themselves according to new protocols in relation to what they had previously regarded as perfectly legitimate private activities. Even among the great majority not seeking contumaciously to float the Act, or to find creative ways to defy its spirit, there were probably many who remained unfamiliar with its requirements, and others who regarded it as, at best, general guidance to be followed as time allowed. Others found its demands prohibitively expensive. These practical considerations, alongside the Act's complexity and considerable doubt about its enforceability, had a major impact on implementation, with extensive late and inaccurate reporting: a serious flaw for a system in which timely transparency was supposed to assist voters make judgements.[16]

As early as 2003, the Commission produced a report dealing with the burden on parties imposed by the PPERA's reporting requirements – especially the costs to smaller parties of registration and weekly reporting requirements during a general election. It was also acutely aware of the difficulties of securing compliance from the larger parties, and recommended a wider range of penalties for non-compliance than the stark options of seeking criminal prosecution or civil action. The Commission also wanted its own power to fine.

In 2004, the Commission published a further wide-ranging report arguing in favour of legislation providing tighter overall controls on spending. On donations it spelled out clearly its concern that transparency might not be enough. Disclosure and enhanced transparency requirements, it argued, had not diminished public unease about the role of large political donations which were being made to central party offices, but distributed down in targeted fashion to marginal constituencies.

The Commission was also worried about loopholes in the law. One concerned the problem of identifying who was a foreign donor after it emerged that overseas donors could channel funding into British parties through locally based subsidiaries. A second problem in a number of cases was that of identifying who was the real donor. Private donations from companies continued to flow into the parties – especially the Conservative Party – but the majority of these were from privately owned companies, where there were no transparency obligations to shareholders. It was thus difficult to assess who stood behind such donations, especially when donations were directed to constituency party associations and targeted on marginal seats.

A further problem concerned third parties: organisations external to electoral parties that actively supported particular candidates. These organisations had long been regulated as regards spending by candidates in elections. However, under the PPERA they became an effective vehicle by which national parties could spend in individual constituencies in advance of the regulated period for elections. This was because at constituency level spending was limited initially only in the period from the formal announcement of an election until the poll. Anything spent beforehand did not count. Third-party organisations were therefore subject to transparency requirements about who they supported and how much they gave but they provided a mechanism for evading candidate election expenses and for concealing the true source of funding going into the parties. The number of registered third parties tripled between 2001 and 2005. During this time sixty-three Conservative constituency associations received significant pre-electoral injections of funds from a third party known as Bearwood Corporate Services Ltd.[17]

The dysfunctions caused by operational overload, and the controversies which arose as the ambiguities of the PPERA became clear, had an equally serious impact on the credibility of the EC itself. However little responsibility it bore for the choices made in its own founding legislation, it was certain to be drawn into controversy about those choices once controversy had set in. One way this happened was through the priorities the Commission set, faced with the complex set of tasks given it by the Act. Alongside the PPERA, the Representation of the People Act 2000 had introduced measures to increase the availability of postal voting to boost turnout. This initiative soon generated claims of lax registration in which abuses and electoral fraud would go unpunished. Since the electoral system (outside Northern Ireland) had hitherto been considered largely free of electoral malpractice, even a few high-profile prosecutions could discredit the new procedures.[18] In fact later research undertaken by the Commission itself suggests that claims of a wave of cases of electoral malpractice were a serious misreading of data on police files, so the fear of widespread electoral fraud may have been exaggerated. However, such findings did not prevent a great deal of public speculation about the Commission's role and competence.[19]

Political and constitutional underpinnings

Some of the difficulties with the operation of the EC in the years from 2001–2010 were eventually addressed in the 2009 Political Parties and Elections Act. The Act provided the Commission with a more proportionate range of sanctions to apply than it had previously enjoyed, and gave it new investigatory powers and new civil penalties where previously its only real sanction had been to refer cases to the police for criminal investigation. The range and difficulty of the tasks imposed by the PPERA on the EC nevertheless clearly threatened the Commission's credibility whenever controversy arose.

The 2006 Electoral Administration Act and the 2009 Political Parties and Elections Act have not fundamentally altered the Commission's vulnerability. That vulnerability was thrown into sharp relief in the aftermath of the loans affair. The CSPL investigated the lessons for party-funding regulation of the loans affair, and made the focus of its critique less the behaviour of the parties in taking out hidden loans than the operational performance of the Commission in countering that behaviour. The CSPL concluded that the Commission had shown an excessively cautious approach to its regulatory obligations and was sharply critical of the Commission's leadership and operating style.[20] The Report urged the Commission to adopt a more risk-based approach to its supervision of party finances which would enable the Commission to anticipate problems and be ready to intervene even at delicate moments such as the middle of election campaigns.

However, the Report's recommendations went beyond operational style to the fundamental question of accountability. The accountability relationships for the Electoral Commission are very similar to those examined in Chapter 5 for the IPSA, and indeed were, as we have seen, the model for IPSA's relationship with the House of Commons. The Electoral Commission is financially accountable under Schedule 1 of the PPERA to the Comptroller and Auditor General in the normal way for public bodies, and is therefore also accountable to Parliament through the PAC. It produces a five-year plan approved by the Speaker's Committee, chaired by the Speaker of the House of Commons and submits its annual estimates for supply to Parliament through the Speaker's Committee. The model thus does at least something to avoid the dilemmas likely to arise had the Commission been made directly accountable to a government department. The Speaker's Committee stands between government and the EC and therefore guarantees the Commission's independence. Independence is further bolstered by the fact that members of the Commission hold office for up to ten years. They can be removed on address to the Crown for failure to discharge the functions of the office, though the government and the House of Commons would clearly have to use this power very cautiously.

The fundamental issue for the EC is whether this combination of partial accountability and partial independence provides it with sufficient authority and political support. This support is especially important for issues that are too delicate to address without political cover, or require decisions which can only be taken by politicians. Loans, and very large private donations, both fall into this category.[21] Indeed, the EC's capacity to enforce its mandate relies not only on its formal powers, but also on a supportive culture of lawfulness and compliance to ensure timely reporting. In promoting such a culture, party support in the House of Commons is vital.[22] Formally, that support comes through the Speaker's Committee. However the Committee enjoys little public recognition and has no minister to speak for it. Crudely this means the natural bedrock of majority-party support in the House of Commons that ministerial sponsorship brings is absent. According to its first chair, Sam Younger, the robust support the EC needed to secure compliance from national party organisations (whether on loan compliance or on regular and timely submission of records) risked being compromised by the loans affair essentially because there was no one to put a strong case on behalf of the Commission at the highest level. That problem was rooted not only in the inadequacies of the PPERA legislation, but also the neglect of their own obligations by the parties. These arguments were not heard effectively in Parliament, Younger argued, to a large extent because Parliament lacked an effective and public forum for debating these issues.[23]

Although it was critical of the Commission over its handling of loans, the CSPL took a similar view about the need for more engagement with the Commission by parties in Parliament. It made a strong plea for a division of labour between the Speaker's Committee and the Constitutional Affairs Select Committee, whereby the former would act as the Commission's parliamentary sponsor for budget issues, while the latter would engage with the Commission on a more regular basis than hitherto with the substantive questions of policy, including regulatory burden and compliance problems.[24]

In reality, however, little changed as a consequence of the loans affair other than the more precise definition of loans contained in the 2006 Act. The Constitutional Affairs Select Committee did not take up the CSPL recommendation to become a major interlocutor for the EC on policy matters, and the annual parliamentary debates on the work of the Commission recommended by the CSPL have not taken place either.

Discussion of party funding issues in Parliament was put on hold through 2007 and 2008 as the Phillips Review (a review set up to try to secure intra-party agreement on reform) grappled with the bigger question of controlling large private donations. When this Review failed, the 2009 Act – essentially a tidying up exercise – was pushed through ahead of the general election to supplement the hasty response of the Electoral Administration Act three years earlier. In the meantime, however, the vulnerability constituted by the reliance of the two main parties on large private donations increased, and with it, potentially, the vulnerability of the EC's reputation. The contribution of the business and financial sector grew significantly ahead of the 2010 general election. An analysis by the *Financial Times*, based on EC data, showed, for example, that hedge-fund donations grew from around 1 per cent of the total donations to the Conservative Party in the years 2001/2003 to 13.92 per cent (£3.8 million) in 2009 and 10.82 per cent (£3.5 million) in 2010. In these two years, the great majority of these sums were provided by just four individuals.[25] If the regulatory system's main impact was to regulate and make transparent increasing dependence on high-value donors, it did not seem to be deterring it through transparency. As long as overall spending was not capped, or new sources of spending found, party competition seemed bound to generate pressures to seek out new funds. The EC itself could only regulate what it was empowered to regulate. The two major parties had to be willing to see further measures enacted.

The donations stalemate: the Phillips Inquiry and the 2011 Committee on Standards in Public Life Report

Although there was evidence of their willingness to accept a cap on both donations and overall expenditure, the major parties were still in 2010 divided on how new restrictions should operate and despite numerous efforts failed to find agreement throughout the following five years. A cap on donations threatened Labour more than the Conservatives, since Labour received very large donations from the trade unions in affiliation fees and additional discretionary gifts. To avoid exceeding a donations cap, therefore, affiliation fees would have to be treated as individual donations and monitored more stringently than hitherto; they could not be processed as the combined contributions of individual members. So Labour was disinclined to accept a cap unless this problem could be resolved.

In the absence of a cap on overall spending, moreover, any significant limitation on the size of individual donations would risk leaving both parties with a serious long-term funding gap, putting them under more pressure to find other sources of income. The dilemma emerged starkly in the review chaired by Sir Hayden Phillips, set up following the loans scandal in 2006. That Review differed from previous exercises in that it largely eschewed commissions, reports, and investigations, opting instead for a direct inter-party negotiating table. It published its own analysis of the problem and delivered an interim report, but the heart of the process was built on talks between the two key parties. The main proposals were: a cap on donations at £50,000; a cap on expenditure which would apply to the whole Westminster electoral cycle of £150 million; two schemes of extended public funding; and a strengthening of the EC to make it a more robust, proactive and investigative body.[26] In August 2007 negotiations took place between the three major parties on Sir Hayden's draft agreement but by October 2007 it became clear that the three parties could not agree over how to handle trade union donations in particular, and talks were suspended indefinitely.

The Labour government then published its own white paper which, in the absence of agreement about capping and expenditure limits, announced proposals (later enacted in the Political Parties and Elections Act 2009) to strengthen the governance and powers of the EC and give it new powers to impose civil sanctions. The Act made small changes to the donation and loan thresholds and strengthened transparency requirements for donations and loans over £7,500. Additional restrictions on candidates' spending were also imposed so that in addition to the restrictions which under PPERA came into force once a dissolution had been announced, limits were also set for a longer campaign period.

However, the 2009 Act still did not address the fundamental issue of dependency on donations and loans. Ahead of the 2010 general election each of the three major parties included some commitment to party funding reform in its manifesto and the Coalition Agreement in 2010 pledged the government to 'a detailed agreement on limiting donations and reforming party funding in order to remove big money from party politics'; but despite further face-to-face negotiations between party leaders no broad inter-party agreement could be reached, notwithstanding regular expressions of optimism by front-bench government spokesmen. The government did permit the CSPL to return to the issue after the election, and late in 2011 the Committee produced an unexpectedly trenchant report that sought to grasp the joint nettle of union affiliation fees and donations with a solution heavily dependent on public subsidies for the parties. A further key element of the 2011 CSPL Report was the radical step of a cap of £10,000 on donations. The cap would apply to donations from individuals and organisations including trade unions, unless individuals made a positive decision to opt-in to the affiliation fee. The level of permissible campaign spending before an election would be cut by 15 per cent. The inevitable damage to party income would be compensated by a major increase in public subsidy calculated on a pence per vote basis, and the introduction of tax relief on small donations.

The CSPL report was rapidly side-lined by the coalition government. In any case, it was largely doomed by its inability to command unanimity among its members. Both the political representatives (Margaret Beckett and Oliver Heald), submitted minority reports on key issues which stressed the continuing differences between the two major parties, especially over the level at which the cap on spending should be set. From a Conservative perspective, at £10,000 per donor, it was too low; from Labour's too high. They also continued to disagree over the way in which trade-union affiliation fees would be transmitted to parties.[27] Heald proposed that unions would be obliged to collect affiliation fees on behalf of all parties, not just the Labour Party, given that evidence suggested that in 2010 only 40 per cent of union members identified themselves with the Labour Party. Beckett, in contrast, was concerned that the administrative and institutional implications of the Report's proposals would be damaging for both the Labour Party and the Co-operative Party, and that the proposed cap on individual affiliation fees was too low.

Although neither minority note of dissent made much of the issue of public subsidies (Margaret Beckett simply expressed doubt about its acceptability in the existing economic climate) the issue of public subsidy, on which the Report's viability clearly depended, was a further stumbling point, even if an unacknowledged one. The government's response, through the Office of the Deputy Prime Minister, was rapid and terse:

> The Government believes that the case cannot be made for greater state funding of political parties at a time when budgets are being squeezed and economic recovery remains the highest priority ... the Government accepts in principle the Committee's recommendation that donations to political parties should be capped. But the level of a cap will need to be considered with reference to other elements of a reform package, in particular the impact on the ability of parties to continue to raise sufficient funds and the absence of any additional support from the state ... a new party funding settlement must include genuine reform in respect of trade union donations ... Reform is best achieved as far as possible by consensus. To that end we plan to continue cross-party discussions based on the principles identified by the Committee and the Government's reform commitments.[28]

Public money has of course long been used to supplement private sources both in the form of cash grants to the opposition parties for research and policy-making purposes, and to subsidise specific campaign communication activities such as postal costs and broadcasting. The 2011 Report noted the importance of public funding to the parties and underlined in passing the impact coalition had had on the Liberal Democrats as it lost opposition-status funding. However, the parties and party leaders, and (depending on how the issue was presented) some of the public, would clearly find it difficult. The question was a complex one. The CSPL 2010 Public Attitudes Survey found that large donations by activist pressure groups, large companies, trade unions and individuals also caused public concern, and the 2011 Report argued that there were indications that it might be possible to persuade the public of the merits of enhanced public subsidy.[29] Some academic commentators took the same view,[30] as did a Rowntree State of the Nation survey in 2010 in which 72 per cent of respondents were worried by party dependency on large donations and 52 per cent supported public subsidies to reduce this dependency, with only 15 per cent actively opposed (30 per cent held no view).[31]

Return to partisanship

The failure of cross-party talks and the rejection by both parties of the proposals by the CSPL seemed to spell the end of a cross-party approach. The Political and Constitution Affairs Select Committee continued to work at the issue, and in 2013 a cross-party group called Funding Democracy, sponsored by a Labour and a Conservative MP and a Liberal

Democrat peer, published a widely-publicised draft bill setting out a comprehensive plan to deal with all aspects of the issue – donations, spending controls, third-party campaigning and public funding of parties – which took its cue from the CSPL Report.[32] Without parliamentary time and government support, however, this proposal made no progress.

In the absence of a broad and comprehensive agreement, the coalition instead focused on the limited issue of third-party campaigning. There was no doubt this was a real issue. The EC reported that between 2005 and 2010 there had been a significant increase in organisations campaigning nationally on behalf of specific parties, and in the amount they spent (up from £1.8 million to £2.8 million over the five years – compared with £31 million spent by the parties in total in the campaign).[33] The measure introduced by the government, inserted as section 2 of the Transparency of Lobbying, Non-Party Campaigning and Trade Union Administration Act 2014, dealt with the limits set for spending by each third party in the UK and the definition of expenditure considered to count as campaign expenditure. The measure was vigorously contested inside Parliament and beyond as a partisan and hastily assembled measure. The Labour Party saw it as aimed primarily against trade unions (along with the third section of the Act which toughened the legal requirements placed on trade unions to keep their membership lists updated). The chair of the PCRSC argued that the third-party provision of the Bill should have been subject to consultation with affected parties – most notably charities – and to pre-legislative scrutiny. Perhaps most tellingly for its workability in the face of the burdens it would place on some organisations, the EC, in a long Briefing Note, expressed reservations about how it would work.[34] The Bill was eventually amended significantly as regards the spending thresholds that third-party campaigners needed to exceed before they were subject to registration and reporting provisions, and ominously for confidence in what might happen in its first trial – the 2015 general election – a provision was inserted for a full review of the Act after the election.

Conclusion

The lesson of ethical regulation generated by new party-funding controls in the UK since 1997 is that regulatory architecture, and with it confidence in regulatory intent and fairness, will suffer if the underlying rules are controversial. The operational performance of the EC has not itself been flawless, but compared to democracies that rely solely on electoral administration managed by an Interior Ministry, underpinned exclusively by the criminal law, the *design* implemented through the PPERA 2000 does not appear to be the major problem. In comparison with what was in place before 2000, indeed, it looks like a very significant advance.

The PPERA 2000 brought party funding under a complex regulatory framework, generating a systematic and reasoned effort to define rules of fairness and transparency. An essential fact of modern democratic politics was acknowledged: that parties cannot simply be ignored as if they were private actors having no bearing on public life. They need to have legal personalities and public responsibilities. Access to them, through money, is not a matter on which the public can remain indifferent. Parties are key intermediaries, selecting personnel and packaging policies. Where they obtain resources affects what voters can expect of them in power. Because parties and party systems are 'sticky' and institutionalised, parties will not go away just because doubt is raised about who might be supporting them. The electoral marketplace is highly imperfect, voters' memories are short, and voters' knowledge is limited. And voters themselves are easily distracted by other issues. They cannot be relied upon, unaided, to police the propriety of party finance through the ballot box.

For a society to recognise these issues is not to solve them, however. The politics of party finance is very similar to the politics of the other major topics of partisan advantage in democratic politics such as lobbying, electoral rules and constituency boundaries. The latter have rarely been approached without partisan advantage in mind.[35] If partisanship can occasionally be abandoned, this normally comes from a political crisis so profound that there are no partisan advantages left to get in the way. That has not been the case in the United Kingdom in the last two decades. There have certainly been limits to partisanship. Neither Conservative governments before 1997, nor the 2010–15 Coalition, felt it politically wise or possible to launch a full attack on Labour's source of trade-union funding through the affiliation fee. Labour, as we saw, did claw away at *some* Conservative interests – particularly overseas donors – when it came to power in 1997 in implementing the PPERA 2000. However, it chose not to place very radical limits on the size of donations even though it started to advocate them when – as its hold on power slipped – its own sources of large donations started to fall well behind those of the Conservatives.

Negotiating a way through mutually opposed partisan interests is therefore difficult. Sir Hayden Phillips almost did so during a moment of mutual weakness in both partisan camps, but the moment passed. The Conservatives felt strong enough to raise the demands they were making on trade-union affiliation fees, and their demands were unacceptable to the Labour Party. The elections of 1997 and 2005 both brought short term crises – the Ecclestone affair and the loans affair – which resulted in partial and partisan solutions to the issue of party funding. The one thing that was not partisan for most of the period down to the 2010 election was the need to rely on large donations, and the two major parties therefore had an interest in keeping in place the most sensitive and risky aspect of party finance law: the absence of a cap on donation size. Given the disparity in funding between the two major parties in the 2010 election, and the extent to which the Conservative Party's funding sources began to tilt towards financial-sector sources in 2008–2010, the Conservative Party was fortunate that the election did not immediately generate a fresh scandal. Instead, despite the further information that trickled out after the election, there was no single new drama and throughout the subsequent Parliament the coalition was able to rebuff the pleas of the CSPL to address the problem anew. As almost everyone recognised, however, this state of affairs was unlikely to last. Together, the fragility of the EC's authority, the reliance of the parties on donations and loans, the growing complexity of legislation, and the growth of third-party campaigning, offered fertile ground for fresh eruptions in the future.

Notes

1 Pinto-Duschinsky, M., *British Political Finance, 1830–1980* (Washington, DC and London: American Enterprise Institute for Public Policy Research, 1981); Ewing, K., *The Cost of Democracy: Party Funding in Modern British Politics* (London: Hart, 2007).

2 Parliamentary candidates were limited to a constituency spending ceiling of £30,000, plus a capitation figure per voter, which in practice set a spending limit of some £35,000–40,000 per candidate.

3 For comparative political finance costs see International Institute for Democracy and Electoral Assistance, Reginald, A. and M. Tjernström (eds), *Funding of Political Parties and Election Campaigns* (Stockholm: IDEA, 2003) (see especially the chapter by Nassmacher, pp. 33–54) which also reports on past efforts to compare costs (Heard, 1960, and Heidheimer, 1963 and 1970) all of which place the UK at the foot of the scale in transnational cost comparisons. See also Ewing, K. and S. Issacharoff (eds), *Party Funding and Campaign Financing in International Perspective* (Oxford: Hart, 2006); Grant, A., 'The reform of party funding in Britain', *The Political Quarterly*, 76:3 (2005), 381–392.

4 Houghton Report, *Financial Aid to Political Parties* (Cm 6601, 1976).

5 Hansard Society Commission, *Paying for Politics* (1981).

6 Home Affairs Select Committee, *Funding of Political Parties*, 16 March 1994 (HC 301, 1993–1994).

7 Committee of Standards in Public Life (CSPL), *Standards in Public Life: The Funding of Political Parties in the United Kingdom, Report*, Cm 4057-I Oct (1998) pp. 30–31. On the quota scheme see Pattie, C.J. and R.J. Johnston, 'Paying their way: local associations, the constituency quota scheme and Conservative Party finance', *Political Studies*, 44:5 (1996), 921–935.

8 Committee on Standards in Public Life, Fifth Report: *The Funding of Polit-ical Parties in the United Kingdom* (1998), p. 49.

9 Committee on Standards in Public Life, Fifth Report: *The Funding of Polit-ical Parties in the United Kingdom* (1998), pp. 1–14.

10 The idea of tax-incentives for donations (which might have encouraged small gifts) was the one significant issue where the CSPL and the eventual legislation differed; the government flatly overruled the idea.

11 Constitutional Affairs Select Committee, *Party Funding: First Report of Ses-sion 2006–07*, House of Commons London 2007; Committee on Standards in Public Life, *The Funding of Political Parties in the United Kingdom*, The Stationery Office, London, 1998, p. 17.

12 Watt, P. and I. Oakshott, *Inside Out: My Story of Betrayal and Cowardice at the Heart of New Labour* (London: Biteback Publishing, 2010).

13 CSPL, *Standards in Public Life: The Funding of Political Parties* (1998), pp. 78–80.

14 Electoral Commission, *Party Funding: The Electoral Commission's Submis-sion to the Committee on Standards in Public Life*, October 2010, p. 22. The fifty broke down as follows: twenty-three individuals, twelve companies, eleven trade unions and four other organisations.

15 Episodes of alleged impropriety nevertheless continued to emerge. In 2007, the Labour Party found itself in serious difficulty for apparently having been complicit in the efforts of a wealthy businessman, David Abrahams, to give it £380,000 through the use of proxy donors who concealed his identity. *The Times*, 27 November 2007. A year later, George Osborne, then Shadow Chancellor, received unfavourable publicity for allegedly seeking to channel Russian money to the Conservative Party through a British-based company. *Daily Telegraph*, 22 October 2008.

16 In 2005, the Commission revealed that only 60 per cent of party income reports were submitted on time. Electoral Commission, *Annual Report and Accounts 2004–2005* (London, 2005), p. 15.

17 Ewing, K., *The Cost of Democracy: Party Funding in Modern British Politics* (Portland: Hart Publishing, 2007).

18 See Wilks-Heeg, S., *Purity of Elections in the UK: Causes for Concern* (York: Joseph Rowntree Trust, 2008).

19 This came back to haunt the Commission on a further occasion in the gen-eral election of 2010, when an apparent shortage of polling stations seemed to lead to long queues. With a late surge just before the close of polling, some voters claimed to have been excluded from voting.

20 CSPL, *Review of the Electoral Commission* (Cm 7006, 2007), pp. 35–47.

21 CSPL, *Review of the Electoral Commission* (Cm 7006, 2007), pp. 35–47.

22 Younger, S., 'Regulation: the state as regulator', in Emmott, W., J. Howell, E. Kamarck, A. Langlands, J. Lloyd, G. O'Donnell, O. O'Neill, H. Phil-lips, U. Prasha, D. Savoie, D. Turnbull, S. Younger, J. Anoon and B. For-rester, *Changing Times: Leading Perspectives on the Civil Service in the 21st Century and its Enduring Values* (London: Office of the Civil Service

Commissioners, 2005), pp. 119–132. Younger made similar observations in his evidence.

23 Younger, 'Regulation', p. 127.

24 CSPL, *Review of the Electoral Commission* (Cm, 7006, 2007), pp. 69–74.

25 Rigby, E., 'PM's fundraiser quits over cash for access', *Financial Times*, 25 March 2012. The data was assembled by the *Financial Times* following a *Sunday Times* revelation that the Conservative Party treasurer, Peter Cruddas, had offered confidential access to senior Conservatives including the Prime Minister in return for 'premier league' donations of £250,000. See *Sunday Times*, 25 March 2012. Cruddas immediately resigned and ironically was replaced by one of the four major hedge fund donors.

26 See Review of the Funding of Political Parties, *An Interim Assessment* (London, 2006) and *Strengthening Democracy: Fair and Sustainable Funding of Political Parties* (London, 2007). Also Phillips, H., 'The funding of political parties', *Political Quarterly*, 83:2 (2012), 318–324.

27 CSPL, *Political Party Finance: Ending the Big Donor Culture*, Thirteenth Report (Cm 8208, 2011), pp. 108–111.

28 Office of the Deputy Prime Minister, *Response to the Political Party Finance Report*, 22 November 2011 (http://goo.gl/QHFpXx, accessed 19 March 2015).

29 CSPL, *Political Party Finance* (2011), pp. 59–62.

30 See Van Heerde-Hudson, J. and J. Fisher, 'Parties heed (with caution): public knowledge of and attitudes towards party finance', *Party Politics*, 19:1 (2013), 41–60.

31 Joseph Rowntree Trust, *State of the Nation 2010 Poll* (published online 20 February 2010), http://www.jrrt.org.uk/publications/state-nation-2010-poll, p. 3.

32 Funding Democracy, *Breaking the Deadlock: A Draft Bill for Consultation* (April 2013). The MPs were Andrew Tyrie (Con.) and Alan Whitehead (Lab.). The Liberal Democrat peer was Paul Tyler (report available at http://fundingukdemocracy.org/, accessed 19 March 2015).

33 Electoral Commission, *UK General Election 2010 – Campaign Spending Report*, February 2011, pp. 14–15.

34 Electoral Commission, *Briefing Note: Transparency of Lobbying, Non Party Campaigning and Trade Union Administration Bill 2013*, 13 December 2013 (http://goo.gl/DrX6rE, accessed 19 March 2015).

35 Renwick, A., *The Politics of Electoral Reform: Changing the Rules of Democracy* (Cambridge: Cambridge University Press, 2010).

12

Integrity issues in local government: the rise and fall of the Standards Board for England

Introduction

Local government is one area of British politics where, rightly or wrongly, there has long been a suspicion that sub-standard behaviour and perhaps even outright corruption was common. Since the 1970s, often under the pressure of such scandal or crisis, central government has imposed significant new controls to improve ethics at local level. In this it has paralleled broader patterns of central control over local government in many other ways.[1] The process reached a peak with the Local Government Act 2000 (LGA 2000). This chapter focuses on the procedures established by that Act, and on the reactions they engendered. The Act brought a redesigned statutory code of conduct for elected councillors. It also brought new standards committees charged with promoting high ethical standards. Alongside these changes came a new independent non-departmental agency, the Standards Board for England (SBE), to investigate alleged breaches of the code of conduct, and a separate Adjudication Panel to deal with the most serious cases which would be referred up to it by the SBE.[2]

The Act in its initial form did not last long. By 2008, the SBE was no longer a direct regulator but a strategic one. Originally it was the first destination for all complaints of breaches of the code. From 2008 it lost this role to the local standards committees. The moment of greatest centralisation passed quickly, and with it, after a delay, the SBE itself. In 2011, under the Localism Act, the SBE was abolished by the new coalition government as part of its 'bonfire of the quangos'.

The story is a story of failed institution building. The first two sections of the chapter examine the special complexities of ethics and propriety below the national level, and the antecedents of the LGA 2000. The chapter then considers how the SBE worked, how and why its framework had to be modified so quickly to that of a strategic regulator and ultimately why the institutions established failed to gain enough traction to survive a change of the party in power at national level.

Local-government ethics

Locally elected politicians are a large and diverse group. In 2012, across the 444 unitary and two-tier structures of local government in England, there were 18,431 elected representatives. There were a further 8,789 parish councils with the power to set minimal precepts (local additions to council tax) with an estimated 70,000 elected representatives. Local authority revenue expenditure in England in 2012/2013 was £154 billion (24 per cent of the UK's total managed expenditure), employing 1.56 million full-time equivalent staff.[3]

From this it can be readily understood that the main problems inherent in managing local government ethics are the political and institutional diversity found at this level, the relative public invisibility of many decision processes and the potential lack of professional experience in handling ethics and propriety issues, particularly in smaller authorities. Locally elected representatives are intrinsically less professionalised than national career politicians. Many will come to office with a poor understanding of legal procedures and little familiarity with public ethics. Some will have business backgrounds or own property in the community or have multiple affiliations to other local organisations. Inevitably these representatives bring latent conflicts of interest, pre-existing friendships, local ties and occasionally serious animosities. Local politicians in the United Kingdom since the 1970s have had to observe strict requirements concerning the registration of interests but it is difficult to impose on unpaid part-timers a requirement that they detach themselves from those interests entirely, as happens to ministers at national level. Local councillors can be required to remove themselves from *specific decisions* affecting such interests, but in close-knit communities it is inevitably harder to deal with trading-in-influence through hidden social or business links. Local government's multiple responsibilities involving contracting with local suppliers, as well as land-use and development, carry such risks permanently and endemically.

A robust system of ethics and propriety is also a function of wider governance arrangements. Standards of personal behaviour will reflect and be reflected in the efficiency with which an authority delivers services, the level of electoral participation, the willingness of individuals to serve as elected officials, and the level of confidence and trust citizens have in it. Successive governments in recent decades sought to make local government perform better through numerous initiatives: Compulsory Competitive Tendering (CCT) in 1980; more comprehensive auditing via the 1982 Audit Commission, and the 1999 'Best Value' initiative and its 2007 updated successor 'Value for Money' in the 2007 Comprehensive Spending Review.[4] Along the way, several local government finance acts detailing procedures for finance, contracting and capital-raising have added to the governance framework, as have softer programmes dealing with performance measurement and review. All these measures, and the local-level impact of other legislation like the Freedom of Information Act 2000, have affected the local ethical environment as well as its efficiency and effectiveness.

However central government has not stopped at these general governance improvements. It has also targeted directly both locally elected councillors and permanent professional officials. Paid officers have always had more to lose by improper behaviour than unpaid councillors and have been subject to clearer employment conditions and management regimes defining ethical duties and obligations. Elected councillors are subject to electoral accountability, and they must act within the law; but beyond that they have the potential to be the arbiters of their own ethical behaviour. Professional officials are in general seen as ethical safeguards, though relationships between officials and elected councillors vary a good deal with the competitiveness of local party politics and with the rate of party turnover in power. Some local authorities are thus likely to be highly sensitive to ethical issues while others remain fairly insensitive to them; and much will depend on contingent factors like the memory of a particularly difficult local case, the attitudes and temperament of key party leaders, and the longevity in power of particular party groups.[5]

Left to themselves elected councillors may struggle to develop high standards and their improprieties will dominate public attention, even if they are a minority of the local-government universe. This risk is not only to good governance locally, but to the reputation of local government generally. Central government therefore has a legitimate interest in the management of local government and in the ethical climate that prevails at that level.

The most persistent problem is conflict of interest. As we have seen in other chapters, the normal techniques for addressing conflict of interest are registers, declarations and withdrawal from decisions (recusal). There are several difficulties with these instruments at local level. First, there is proportionality; for roles less important than national elective office, they require a good deal of public intrusion into the lives of individuals. The definition of conflict of interest has expanded over time to cover private organisational membership (for example free masonry and trade union membership) and cause groups connected with, for example, the environment or planning, including organisations that may regularly interact with, or indeed be financed by, the individual's local authority. Secondly, some individuals have *personal* interests in outcomes that are identical to those of the voters they represent. Indeed, this may be a reason why they have been elected. Recusal is then problematic. It means voters go unrepresented. Thirdly, sanctions: some transgressions will be accidental and some will be motivated by political rather than personal objectives. Defining an appropriate scale of penalty is difficult – particularly for technical compliance failure. The United Kingdom's corruption laws deal with the exploitation of public office for clear personal – generally material – gain; but whether there should be a criminal penalty for an administrative failure such as failing to declare an interest is a more controversial question.

Beyond conflict of interest, the potential range of integrity issues can open out very broadly to cover matters as diverse as the maintaining of harmonious personal working relationships in the conduct of local-authority business, the treatment of confidential information obtained in the course of local-authority business and the observance of standards of personal, often private, behaviour, which sustain public respect for the integrity of both the office-holder and the office. Regulating in these areas is even more complicated than regulating conflicts of interest. Political debate can be robust and challenging; it is a subjective matter whether an individual has overstepped the mark in attacking an opponent, or in dealings with a permanent official. On the matter of confidentiality, there are clearly two opposing principles: disclosure in the public interest, versus confidentiality in the interest of effective working practices and obligations to commercial interests. Private behaviour is even harder. Individuals demand to stand for election for public office irrespective of aspects of their lifestyles or views, however distasteful to the majority. Conversely the public needs to have confidence in its elected officials, especially those working in sensitive areas like child welfare. Some lifestyles could test this confidence to breaking point. Here too, establishing what a code of behaviour should say, and who adjudicates it, will be challenging. It is a fine judgement whether failure, for example, to treat colleagues with respect, to engage in whistle-blowing or to follow a sober and respectable lifestyle should always be left to voter sanction.

Antecedents to the Local Government Act 2000

Local government has often experienced significant ethics failures, particularly in the decades before the First World War, and again from the

1970s onwards. It is difficult to say how serious these problems were. Some data on prosecutions was actually assembled in the 1970s, but prosecution data only ever reveals what has been detected. For what it is worth, between 1964 and 1972 ten councillors and twenty-two employees were convicted of corruption, and sixteen councillors were convicted of failing to declare pecuniary interests under prevailing Local Government Acts, mostly in isolated cases.[6] In general, however, before the 1970s, there was little debate about a *systemic* problem.

The Poulson affair changed this perception fundamentally. As we have seen in Chapter 2, the episode involved systemic collusion between John Poulson's international architect's practice and both national and local politicians and civil servants.[7] Construction contracts were won through bribery and planning procedures were extensively corrupted, both in the United Kingdom and abroad. Poulson and a handful of local politicians were sent to prison. The affair implicated politicians at the highest level, even forcing the resignation in 1972 of Conservative Home Secretary Reginald Maudling. Another Conservative MP, John Cordle, incautiously outlined in a letter to Poulson the extensive, if largely unsuccessful, ways in which he had used his influence to seek contracts in West Africa. It was mainly Poulson's obsessive record-keeping that brought the affair to light when his firm went bankrupt in the early 1970s.

The government response came in the Local Government Acts, 1972 and 1974. The first measure set out, in section 80, the grounds for ineligibility for elective office in local government: namely, publicly sourced conflict of interest (i.e. paid employment directly or indirectly by the authority in question) and conviction of an offence generating a custodial sentence of at least three months. Part III of the 1974 Act established a new office of Commissioner for Local Government to investigate complaints against local government. The Commissioner was given powers to declare a breach of the code to be incompatible with good administration and thus to make a finding of maladministration against an authority. It also established a *National Code of Local Government Conduct* (henceforth the '1974 Code') which, with a modification in 1989, remained in force for almost a quarter of a century.[8]

In 1986, the Widdicombe Report built on this foundation by introducing a statutory register of interests for elected members of local authorities.[9] The context was concern by the then Conservative government to strengthen local democracy and accountability in the face of growing partisanship at local level. Cases such as that of Labour's extreme left-wing Militant Tendency gaining control of Liverpool City Council gave the role of local government a new salience. Three new local government acts (1986, 1988 and 1989) introduced measures to prevent local authorities using authority resources for explicitly political purposes (for example advertising and the political appointments of staff) and tightened the declaration of interests. Section 19.2 of the 1989 Act made it a criminal offence for elected members to fail to make statutory declarations of interest. Section 5 established the new function of 'monitoring officer' (generally filled by a senior official or the chief executive) charged with steering elected representatives away from unlawful behaviour or violation of the code of conduct, though the workability of this provision was much disputed.[10]

By the 1990s therefore, substantial experience had accumulated of a stricter framework for local government. There were clear precedents. There was no recurrence of corruption on the scale seen in the Poulson affair; but in addition to the Liverpool episode there was another high-profile case (this time on the Conservative side) in the 'homes for votes' case in Westminster, and as we saw in Chapter 2 there was a serious case that started with falsified councillor expenses claims in Doncaster, and ran on for almost a decade. In that case, the Council was placed under commissioner rule for a period. It was also argued in the Audit Commission and the PAC reports that governance reforms introduced by the Conservative administrations in the 1980s had created conflicts of interests in relation to local-level privatisation and management-buyout schemes that developed out of the requirements for Compulsory Competitive Tendering.[11] So in the heightened concern over ethics issues during the mid-1990s, it was inevitable that concerns about local government would also re-surface.

The Local Government Act 2000 and the Model Code

When the Labour Party returned to power in 1997 it inherited a report on local-government ethics by the CSPL published shortly after the 1997 election, containing thirty-nine recommendations. These included a revised code of conduct, decriminalisation of the failure to register pecuniary interests (on grounds of unenforceability and impracticality), a compulsory *public* register of interests, a better definition of the circumstances under which elected representatives must withdraw from decision processes, abolition of the traditional penalty of surcharging (on grounds of unworkability), mandatory standards committees for all local authorities above parish/town level, and new forms of sanction against improper behaviour, including the power to suspend or disqualify councillors from office.[12]

The incoming government incorporated much of this in the Local Government Act 2000 and enabling statutory instruments.[13] Its central provision on local-level conflict of interest drew a distinction between *personal* interests (which, from a very low threshold, had to be registered and declared when relevant council business was being discussed) and *prejudicial* interests (where the representative had, except in certain defined circumstances, always to withdraw from discussions and decisions and not seek in any other way to influence decisions in these matters). The government's goal was a code of conduct capable of exercising some purchase over behaviour, the previous (1974) Code widely considered to have failed. Failure to register interests had been a criminal offence but the sanction was barely ever used. Inadvertent failures to register were too frequent, as were politically motivated and malicious allegations against councillors. Police willingness to prosecute was low. With *prejudicial* interests now added, it was feared criminalisation would become even more contentious. So in the new Code, failure to register interests and to withdraw in the case of prejudicial ones became a breach subject to administrative sanction, with, as we shall see, much greater probability of being invoked.

The new Code, which applied to family members as well as councillors, also contained a new range of non-pecuniary interests that had to be registered, applicable wherever membership of another body, whether public or private, might prejudice a councillor if the organisation had dealings with the local authority. Such non-pecuniary interests included housing associations, arts organisations, educational institutions, lobbying organisations and other interest groups. Further innovations spelled out in more detail undesirable and improper behaviour that local councillors were required to avoid. Several were contentious:

- The duty to promote equality 'by not discriminating unlawfully against any person'.
- The duty to treat others with respect.
- The duty to abstain from anything which compromises or is likely to compromise the impartiality of those who work for, or on behalf of, the authority.
- The duty of confidence whenever information has been given under conditions of confidentiality.
- The requirement to '*have regard for*' the advice of officials acting in pursuance of specific statutory duties, and to give reasons for particular classes of executive decision in accordance with any statutory requirement.
- The obligation to make a formal complaint to the SBE should the elected representative become aware that other members of their council have failed to comply with the Code.

A further innovation, and one where the government parted company quite radically with the CSPL, was the procedure for enforcement. The CSPL had argued that responsibility for enforcement should stay with local authorities.[14] It proposed that most decisions should be taken by the local authorities' own standards committees, though it envisaged a right of appeal upwards to a new regional tier of Local Authority Tribunals, responsible both for hearing appeals and monitoring each authority's code of conduct for compliance with basic requirements. A new *statutory* offence of misuse of public office (replacing the common law provision) would provide a higher tier of sanctions, but only for more serious cases and only where the full burden of proof required by the law was brought to bear.

The government feared that to set up new standards of behaviour, while allowing local authorities to interpret their precise meaning, would make it likely that the new Code would be interpreted inconsistently by local standards committees. Authorities with the weakest standards or greatest partisanship would deal with their problems as they chose.[15] Whether the government foresaw the downside risks of the centralisation that it adopted to deal with this concern is unclear. Its first white paper envisaged regional standards officers, and a central agency to hear appeals.[16] However, the Department for the Environment, Transport and the Regions's (DETR) 1998/1999 consultation process raised concerns about leaving the main enforcement mechanism at local authority level. A more radical model then emerged involving a full-blown agency – the SBE – to which *all* complaints about violations of the new code of conduct would initially be sent and the ambivalent regional model moved on to a completely new national institution.

For many at local-authority level the change was decidedly negative. There was to be a new expanded national code of conduct. For all practical purposes, it was imposed directly on local authorities. The Act contained a 'model' code but in practice most authorities simply adopted it unchanged, since the scope in the Act for local adaptation was so modest. The conflict of interest rules were supplemented with a range of new and untested behavioural requirements ('promoting equality, treating others with respect', etc.) Moreover, the Standards Committees that local authorities were required to establish had no immediate decisional role in complaints about breaches of the Code. Breaches would instead go directly to a centralised mechanism and sanctions would be imposed *at that level*. The emphasis in dealing with breaches fell squarely on administratively imposed sanctions, albeit ones that stopped short of the full burden of either criminal or civil law. So not only were there now apparently objective, if still loosely defined, *standards* by which to judge behaviour; there was also a new institutional framework for judging it, operating with standards considerably less onerous than that of a criminal court. And, compared to the previous system, there was a much greater probability of the rules being used.

The challenge for the government was thus to establish a new and untested institution for judging new and more demanding standards of ethical behaviour, against a background of considerable diffidence from the local authorities. To the public, political opponents, local-government employees, and all those with real and imagined grievances against their local authority or against individual members of it, the new mechanism had the potential to become a ready-made and relatively costless route for unlimited complaints. The combination of high set-up costs, a steep institutional learning curve, the overt hostility of many local authorities, and uncertain political support at national level all combined to make a protracted and difficult bedding-down process inevitable.

Procedure and practice

The SBE was a nine-member supervisory council appointed by the relevant Secretary of State, from individuals expert in local government, public finances and the law. Board members and the chair were non-executive directors exercising oversight. At its peak the executive staff was eighty-strong and the Board cost some £10 million per annum to run. The SBE had two roles: as direct regulator via its role as first-instance investigator of complaints and a strategic regulator, coordinating the development of the code of conduct by helping local authorities to disseminate it through their own Standards Committees. Until reformed by the Local Government and Public Involvement in Health Act 2007 (LGPIHA 2007), the vehicles of its direct-regulator role were the Referrals Unit and the Investigations Unit. Referrals assembled the information on which the Board itself took the preliminary decision on whether to pass the complaint on to one of its Ethical Standards Officers (ESOs). The ESO then conducted a full investigation, with four possible outcomes:

- No evidence of a Code violation.
- No action required (i.e. even if a violation had taken place, it was insufficiently serious to warrant further action of any kind).
- Referral back to the local authority monitoring officer (so-called 'local determination'), for decision by the local standards committee – again in cases that were less serious – the maximum penalty that could be imposed in the initial years being a three-month suspension.

- Referral to the Adjudication Panel for England, to be dealt with by an appointed tribunal (normally for the more serious matters). The Panel could impose sanctions ranging from short-term suspension to five years disqualification.

Following the LGPIHA 2007, the officer had a fifth option of a directive to improve certain procedural aspects of an authority's operation.

The enforcement dimension was at least as controversial as the behavioural requirements. It created a centralised mechanism with a complaints adjudication procedure substantially outside the local authority. From the beginning it had been envisaged that the local level would retain a role in the process by the repatriation of less serious offences to local determination. But no one could estimate how many complaints would be considered insufficiently serious to be redirected for local decision, and the controversy over continuing centralisation was exacerbated by the late approval of the statutory instruments required to facilitate greater local involvement which were only approved in 2003 and became operative only in November 2004.[17] The Standards Board therefore laboured for almost a full three years under the obligation to investigate all cases. This heavy centralisation stood in marked contrast to the situation in Scotland and Wales, where procedures were significantly different (in Scotland parish councils were not included; in Wales local determination was introduced immediately in 2001). In these two jurisdictions, delays in investigation from heavy workload were minimal.[18] The claim by the Office of the Deputy Prime Minister (ODPM), which had responsibility for drafting the amending legislation for the SBE, that the long delay was the result of the need to consult to get local determination right was therefore unconvincing. Indeed, the Select Committee covering the ODPM blamed the delays in referring and investigating squarely on the ODPM itself, observing that 'it was unreasonable to expect the Standards Board to function well within an incomplete statutory framework and without the necessary resources and powers'.[19] In the event, even after measures facilitating some local devolution, two-thirds of cases were still decided above the level of the local authority itself.

The new system certainly brought to light a large body of complaints. It is not clear whether the new Code's very existence increased the level of complaint, compared to its 1974 predecessor, because under the 1974 Code there was no way of monitoring the number of breaches nationally. In a majority of authorities there was not even a standing version of the Standards Committees to deal with complaints. So the first consequence of the new procedure was the appearance of a veritable avalanche of allegations of improper behaviour – around 300 allegations per month – assiduously recorded in the data made public by the Standards Board.

Assessing the experience of the early years of the Standards Board is complicated by the fact that in one very important sense, the Code and the new procedures *did* generate more impropriety. This was because the new requirements concerning declaration of interest at parish-council level were, for many individuals, either unexpected or unwelcome, or both. Research commissioned for the SBE by Mori in 2004 showed 26 per cent of parish and town councillors were hostile to the principle that they should sign a declaration to abide by the code of conduct.[20] Following the first elections (May 2002) under the new code, the SBE warned parish clerks and district and county monitoring officers that under Section 52 of the new Act councillors forfeited office if they did not sign a written undertaking to abide by their Code within two months of the Code being adopted.[21] There were as a result a large number of highly publicised cases of individuals refusing to cooperate or claiming to have been unaware of the new regulations, leading to 100 disqualifications.[22]

The raw data of the SBE's performance over the years 2002–2008, during which the first version of the Code was in operation, provide a picture of the workload of the Board, and the nature of the complaints process. Over this period, the Standards Board received some 21,307 complaints of a breach of the Code. After a rapid initial build-up, the number stayed remarkably constant at just over 300 per month (see Table 12.1).

About 60 per cent of these complaints came from members of the public, a handful (about 5 per cent) came from employees of the relevant authority, and the remainder came from fellow councillors on the authority (see Table 12.2).

The largest group of complaints were lodged against members of parish and town councils: numerically the largest group of councils. As a *proportion* of councillors in this category, however, it was in fact smaller than the proportion of councillors in districts and counties: complaints were proportionately more frequent, as is to be expected, where more was at stake (see Table 12.3).

The great majority of the complaints received were not, following preliminary investigation, referred for investigation, i.e. the Standards Board's Referrals Unit found most complaints to have been unfounded. The number referred for investigation was higher in the first year of the Board's operation, as the Board appeared to have opted (as regards the decision to investigate) for a precautionary principle weighted in favour of complainants; but in the light of experience – and faced with a heavy

Table 12.1 Complaints to the Standards Board for England, 2002–2008

	2002/ 2003	2003/ 2004	2004/ 2005	2005/ 2006	2006/ 2007	2007/ 2008	Total
Allegations	2,948	3,566	3,861	3,836	3,549	3,547	21,307

Source: The Standards Board, Cumulative Monthly Statistical Digests, available at: www. standardsboard.gov.uk/CaseInformation/MonthlyStatisticalDigest/Sourceofallegations/ Archive/.

Table 12.2 Source of complaints to the Standards Board, 2002–2008 (% of annual total)

	2002/ 2003	2003/ 2004	2004/ 2005	2005/ 2006	2006/ 2007	2007/ 2008
Council employees	6	6	8	5	5
Fellow councillor	40	23	28	31	27
Member of the public	51	60	64	62	67
Other	3	3	2	2	1

Source: The Standards Board, Cumulative Monthly Statistical Digests, available at: www. standardsboard.gov.uk/CaseInformation/MonthlyStatisticalDigest/Sourceofallegations/ Archive/.

case-load – the Referrals Unit appeared to have developed greater confidence to reject apparently unfounded claims at the early stage. Thus, as we see from Table 12.4, from in 2004–2005 onwards around a quarter of all complaints were forwarded for investigation.

The types of allegation investigated span a wide range of code provisions, and the recording procedure used by the Standards Board changed in 2004/2005, so the data is not fully comparable; but it resolves principally into six key types:

- bringing the authority into disrepute;
- failing to treat others with respect;
- failing to declare personal interests;
- disclosure of confidential information;
- failing to withdraw from business in the case of a prejudicial interest;
- using elective office to confer or secure an advantage or disadvantage.

As can be seen from Table 12.5, the distribution of referrals across these cases is fairly even, although, with greater familiarity with the Code, the instances of failure to declare a personal interest appeared to fall.

Table 12.3 Complaints to the Standards Board for England, 2002–2008 by type of local authority (% of total by year)

Authority type	2002/ 2003*	2003/ 2004	2004/ 2005	2005/ 2006	2006/ 2007	2007/ 2008
County council	21	5	3	6	4	4
District council	24	26	32	25	28	22
London borough		4	5	10	4	4
Metropolitan borough		7	8	8	10	9
Parish/town council	55	49	40	42	42	50
Unitary council		8	10	8	11	10
Other		1	2	1	1	1

Source: The Standards Board, Cumulative Monthly Statistical Digests, available at: www.standardsboard.gov.uk/CaseInformation/MonthlyStatisticalDigest/Sourceofallegations/Archive/.

* In 2003 the county recorded council figure includes all other categories than those listed seperately.

Table 12.4 Complaints to the Standards Board for England, 2002–2008: response of the Standards Board*

	2002/ 2003	2003/ 2004	2004/ 2005	2005/ 2006	2006/ 2007	2007/ 2008
% not referred	43	66	76	79	76	82
% referred	57	34	24	22	19	14
% other					5	4

Source: The Standards Board, Cumulative Monthly Statistical Digest, available at: www.standardsboard.gov.uk/CaseInformation/MonthlyStatisticalDigest/Sourceofallegations/Archive/.

* Percentages here refer to complaints referred on for investigation, or not referred. In 2006/2007 and 2007/2008, the Board had the option, in less serious cases, of referring the case back to the monitoring officer of the local authority for further action other than investigation itself.

After its first year of operation, the Board's investigation processes normally led to the referral to the Adjudication Panel of under one case in ten, the number thereafter eventually falling to 3 per cent in 2006/2007 and 2007/2008 (see Table 12.6).

The pattern that emerges from the above data confirms what turned out to be a stable and strikingly high level of complaints about breaches

Table 12.5 Complaints to the Standards Board for England, 2002–2008: nature of allegations referred for investigation

	2002/ 2003	2003/ 2004	2004/ 2005	2005/ 2006	2006/ 2007	2007/ 2008
Bringing authority into disrepute	16	16	21	24	24	11
Failure to disclose personal interest	17+17	12+13+14	16+2	12	11	10
Disclosure of confidential information				4	4	2
Failure to treat others with respect	14	13	13	12	12	11
Non-withdrawl with prejudicial; interest		13	23	25	25	25
Using position to confer advantage			12	12	12	12
Other	25	19	13	12	12	29

Source: The Standards Board, Cumulative Monthly Statistical Digest, available at: www.standardsboard.gov.uk/CaseInformation/MonthlyStatisticalDigest/Sourceofallegations/Archive/.

of the Code. The SBE's workload was high even though only around one in four complaints was eventually referred for investigation and one in twelve eventually judged sufficiently modest[23] to be referable to local authority monitoring officers for resolution. In fact it was the sheer volume of complaints, and the absence for three years of the local-determination safety valve, rather than the seriousness of the cases or the penalties eventually imposed, which caused the Standards Board most difficulty. The volume of work was excessive for a completely new organisation, struggling to recruit staff, establish working practices, clarify its principles, and find a balance between excessive zeal and excessive leniency. The result was a long delay in investigations: up to a year for many cases in the first two years of the SBE's operation. Such delays naturally added to the stress of being complained against. All concerned – the SBE, the ODPM, the CSPL – acknowledged that the situation was unacceptable.[24] There were frequent hostile questions in the House of Commons. The first three meetings of the Annual Assembly of Local Authority Standards Committees saw confrontations between delegates and the Standards Board representatives. The press regularly ran hostile articles about the SBE's alleged lack of efficiency, and the

Table 12.6 Complaints to the Standards Board for England, 2002–2008: outcome of referrals*

	2002/ 2003	2003/ 2004	2004/ 2005	2005/ 2006	2006/ 2007	2007/ 2008
No evidence of a breach	23	20	21	16	39	25
No further action	27	60	66	62	54	43
Refer to monitoring officer		8	5	5	4	5
Refer to APE	27	12	8	8	3	3
Other directions						24

Source: The Standards Board, Cumulative Monthly Statistical Digest, available at: www. standardsboard.gov.uk/CaseInformation/MonthlyStatisticalDigest/Sourceofallegations/ Archive/.

* Until 2003/2004 the investigating officer did not have the option of referring the case back to the local authority monitoring officer.

Tenth Report of the CSPL lent its authoritative weight to the growing campaign against the SBE.

Eventually, a combination of local determination, new staff and institutional learning reduced the delays and by 2005/2006 the Board was close to its own handling-time targets on most criteria.[25] Among local-authority monitoring officers at least there was evidence of broad satisfaction with the Board's performance.[26] But the reputational damage of the first four years was intense. When, in 2006, the government undertook a first quinquennial review of the Code, it was this damage which tipped the balance in favour of the policy advocated by the CSPL's Tenth Report for complete repatriation of case handling to local level. Having rejected the CSPL's advice in 2000, and delayed even limited local determination for three years, the measures introduced in the LGPIHA 2007 were a dramatic procedural U-turn.

Contested principles

Handling such a large case load was only a part of the SBE's difficulties, however. The complexity of the new code was the other. The environment in which the principles were worked out was now law-bound and litigious, and the SBE and the Adjudication Panel were called on to lead the process in a very public, highly scrutinised and contested light.

One of the major difficulties arose from the principle of a 'prejudicial interest'. The requirement to withdraw from discussion and decisions in circumstances where a councillor had such an interest proved hugely controversial. Moreover, it had an unexpected dual effect since it became linked to *pre-determination*: shorthand for the administrative law principle developed by the courts that a decision taken by a public body is unlawful if the decision-maker approaches the decision with a closed mind. Thus an individual who goes on record as being against a proposed planning development, even if as a matter of principle and public policy, rather than because of a personal interest, could be construed as eventually approaching the quasi-judicial decision to approve the planning proposal having 'pre-determined' the outcome. In such circumstances it could be argued that the outcome was flawed, the applicant not having received a fair hearing.

This point of administrative law had a long pedigree in English legal history, but it was given new life first by ambiguity over what constituted a prejudicial interest, and secondly by the possibility that an individual who, by failing to withdraw when holding such a prejudicial interest and thereby causing a planning procedure to be flawed, also brought the authority into disrepute. So even if a complaint for breach of the code could not be brought against the individual on grounds of personal and prejudicial interest, it could be brought on grounds of 'disrepute': having caused a planning procedure to fail. As we have already seen, however, the requirement to withdraw meant that voters could effectively be deprived of representation on critical issues.

In several landmark decisions, the Adjudication Panel determined that this was indeed so, and took the controversial decision to impose exemplary disqualifications. Prejudicial interests and withdrawal were in any case controversial wherever an elected representative could fairly claim that his or her voters' interests were at stake. The Adjudication Panel handled a number of such cases, devoid of any judicial complications about flawed proceedings, and here too it imposed disqualification penalties, apparently unmoved by the fact that the standard it set to demonstrate bias in its proceedings was significantly lower than that required to show predetermination in a court of law.

Disqualification is a controversial penalty, irrespective of the impropriety for which it is being imposed. To remove an elected representative, whether from an assembly or from executive office, is a major step and the standard of proof required to invoke it should be high. In most countries the criterion adopted is that used by a criminal court. The more important the role occupied by the disqualified individual, the more controversial the decision will be. When the directly-elected Mayor of

London was removed from office, as happened in the case of Ken Livingstone, in 2005, the controversy was intense. The case was provoked by remarks made to a journalist by Mr Livingstone, a local-government leader with a national profile and a populist political style. The remarks led to a complaint to the Standards Board, and somewhat controversially, to a reference on to the Adjudication Panel by the ESO who dealt with the case. This arose because it was impossible for the ESO to refer the issue back to the London Authority, that Authority having already informally (i.e. outside the complaints procedure) judged Livingstone, found him guilty of failing to treat others with respect, and asked him to apologise, which he promptly refused to do. To send the case back to the London Authority would therefore have led to Livingstone being judged by those who had already judged him.[27] Livingstone's case was especially colourful, but far from isolated: in the period down to March 2006 there were 308 referrals from the SBE to the Adjudication Panel, of which 180 resulted in disqualification, 61 full suspensions and 4 partial suspensions.[28]

What quickly became clear in these cases was the complexity of the iterative process required to give precision to the code. The SBE's Bulletin, its guidance and advice papers, its Annual Report, and particularly its Case Review, all published regularly from 2002 onwards, constitute powerful testimony to the effort required to make sense of the Code and ensure its even and effective application in a myriad of different cases and circumstances. The particularities of 20,000 cases of alleged breach of the code had to be turned into generalisable guidelines for transmission down to the local standards committees which were responsible for disseminating the conclusions of the case-work into meaningful guidance to councillors. There were difficulties concerning so-called 'disrespect' to fellow councillors, officers and the public (what for some was the rough and tumble of politics for others was bullying or offensive behaviour); the existence of a *general* disrepute clause linked to private behaviour (although used very sparingly by the Adjudication Panel, it hung over the Board in a way that further compromised its standing); the definition of 'personal interests', particularly as regards dual membership (where membership of one authority potentially compromised impartiality while serving on the other), and masonic connections;[29] and finally the issue of confidentiality, where public interest justifications clashed with the demands of confidential business practices.

Responding to this range of behavioural controversies and trying to fashion a form of case law was a huge challenge. The Board was also required to justify its choices to a very wide range of actors. Even excluding the case-based interaction with monitoring officers and standards committees, the list of representative agencies the Board had to interact with on a regular basis was formidable. It included: the Association of Council Secretaries and Solicitors, the Association of Larger Local Councils, the Association of National Parks Authorities, the Association of Police Authorities, the Local Government Association, the Local Government Ombudsman, the National Association of Local Councils, the Society of Local Council Clerks, the Society of Local Authority Chief Executives, and the Annual Conference of Local Authority Standards Committees. At national level, the Board interacted with the ODPM, with at least two parliamentary select committees, and with the CSPL. On top of this were the road-shows the SBE ran regularly to enhance understanding of the Code, the consultations leading to S.66 local determinations during 2003 and the Board's own reviews to test stakeholder satisfaction with its performance. The SBE also had to respond to parliamentary select committees and the CSPL in 2005 and to the Code Review initiated by the ODPM in 2006. These inquiries led to a much changed role for the Board, as set out in the LGPIHA 2007. The Act in turn entailed work to prepare local standards committees to take over the bulk of investigations at that point, and its own move from London to Manchester! If, as we saw in Chapter 5, IPSA faced a harrowing time in its early years the SBE's experience was a good deal worse; a more turbulent, transient and unstable start is hard to imagine.

The strategic regulator role 2008–2010

The change of role in 2008 followed hard on the heels of the Standards Board's own Code Review in 2004/2005, which overlapped with the ODPM Select Committee Report and the Tenth Report of the CSPL in 2005.[30] In the light of these reviews, the ODPM opened a consultation process to revise the Code, redefine the Standards Board's dual role, and open up discussions on other emerging issues: political restrictions on local government employees, the pay of political assistants in local government, and a code of conduct for employees. However on the central issue of the Board's dual role, the government signalled a clear U-turn from the outset. Initial assessment of all misconduct allegations should, it proposed, be undertaken by local standards committees, rather than the Standards Board. Local standards committees would likewise be responsible for investigating and determining most cases. The Standards Board would adopt a strategic, advisory and monitoring role, while retaining responsibility for investigating a handful of the most serious misconduct allegations.

To fulfil the new role, the ODPM argued, there would have to be improvements in the operation and composition of local standards committees, with independent chairs and committees including independent members. As for the Code itself, the ODPM proposed a 'clearer, simpler code of conduct, including changes to the rules relating to personal and prejudicial interests'. On this vexed issue of personal and prejudicial interests, a personal interest was redefined as one where a member's 'well-being or financial position' might be affected more than that of the majority of people in the ward affected. The change was intended to be permissive. It loosened a hitherto highly controversial restriction. Someone with the same interest as others was no longer automatically debarred from participating in a decision, and thus representing others equally affected. *Public-service interests* (where a member is also a member of another public body) had henceforth to be registered, but only needed to be declared if a member spoke on an issue.

The 'reasonableness test' (by which a personal interest translates into a prejudicial interest when a member of the public would reasonably regard it as strong enough to prejudice the judgment of the public interest) was henceforth bounded by tighter limits. A prejudicial interest was no longer deemed to arise unless a matter affected a member's financial position or involved approvals, licensing, or permissions. Nor would it arise over the setting of a council tax or precept. There was also some relaxation of the previous blanket ban on presence at meetings where interests preventing participation had been declared.

Beyond these changes, the new version of the Code removed the duty on councillors to report alleged breaches of the Code by colleagues (it had been encouraging precautionary or trivial allegations). On the matter of private behaviour, persuaded by the highly negative consequences of the Appeal Court's decision in the Livingstone case, the Code was amended so that only when acting in an official capacity (i.e. when conducting the business of the authority, or acting as its representative), must the member comply with the Code in respect of behaviour liable to bring the authority into disrepute. The exception to this was henceforth where the relevant conduct was a criminal offence for which the member has been convicted. A further step back occurred in the area of the so-called 'respect' agenda. Following an Adjudication Panel ruling that the Panel had no power to make a finding of 'unlawful discrimination', references to this were deleted. Instead, the Code simply said that members must not do anything which might cause their authority to breach any of the equality enactments. There was also an explicit prohibition on bullying – though no definition of what constituted bullying – related to efforts to address possible victimisation when members report alleged breaches of the Code. An explicit new clause sought to prevent intimidating a complainant or a witness or other person involved in considering the complaint, especially those who participate in local standards committees.

On confidentiality a public-interest defence of a breach of the obligations of confidentiality towards authority business was included in the new Code ('reasonable and in the public interest' and 'made in good faith and in compliance with the reasonable requirements of the authority'). The Consultation Paper stated that members should be able to disclose information where they reasonably believed that the disclosure would indicate evidence of a criminal offence; and where the authority was failing to comply with its legal obligations. Sensitive information exemptions on reporting personal interests were allowed, with the approval of the local authority monitoring officer, if disclosure created a serious risk that the member would suffer violence or intimidation, as for example where the individual was involved in sensitive scientific research.

As we have seen, the LGPIHA 2007 changed the role of the Standards Board to that of 'strategic regulator' and repatriated decisions on most complaints under the new Code to local standards committees. Henceforth the Board's role was to 'ensure that standards and conduct issues are properly integrated into corporate governance responsibilities ... to take responsibility for the Code of Conduct and advise government on any changes needed in light of experience ... issue appropriate guidance on case handling and Code-related issues ... and monitor the numbers and outcomes of cases, identifying trends and common problems'.

Under the new procedures standards committees at local authority level would be chaired by an independent member who was not a councillor and in the case of the smaller authorities would work with other standards committees. The Standards Board would monitor the effectiveness of local arrangements, in particular supporting authorities which were experiencing difficulties. It would also conduct those few investigations which, for reasons of conflict of interest, could be carried out locally.

The strategic regulation philosophy took the Board into areas best described as broader collateral conditions of good governance. It aimed henceforth to work closely in partnership with the Audit Commission on the incorporation of standards and conduct issues in the Comprehensive Performance Assessment. With the Commission and the Improvement and Development Agency for local government it planned what it described as an 'ethical governance toolkit', which it presented as part of its *Framework for Good Governance in Local Government*.

Abolition under the Localism Act 2011

Progress towards these new goals lasted barely two years: too short a period to assess effectively. The main visible impact was a substantial scaling back of the cost of the SBE and major restructuring as well as a substantial programme of redundancies within the referrals and investigation units. The Board also continued its developing programme of research on the impact of the framework introduced by the LGA 2000 and the LGPIHA 2007. Much of this research was outsourced to market research and academic teams and was based on intensive surveys of officers and councillors at local authority level and on some targeted authority-based research in selected communities.[31] The main project, outsourced to a team at Cardiff Business School, was originally intended to run over a five-year period to 2013 focusing both on local authorities where conduct issues had been significant and those where they had been relatively absent. The overall findings presented by this emerging if fragmentary research evidence, suggested that the conduct of councillors had improved, and that the ethical framework had made a significant contribution to this improvement. However, although the majority of those working as elected representatives or officers in local government believed standards of conduct had improved, this view had not filtered through to public perceptions. Indeed public confidence in local government ethics appeared over time to be deteriorating not improving.

It was perhaps questionable how far the optimism about rising integrity standards was actually found beyond the relatively narrow circle of local government ethics professionals who staffed the standards committees, provided monitoring officers, and paid close and engaged attention to the dialogues between the Standards Board and the local authorities that had become a permanent presence in the local government landscape. Although the investment of time and effort for these groups in keeping up with the constantly changing regulatory framework after 2000 was very high, it seems likely that, at this level at least, hearts and minds were won over. If so, it was a significant achievement. But higher up, on the Labour side of national politics, and in the CSPL, the tone of public statements was muted and equivocal. There was clearly continuing support for the general principle of a firm regulatory framework, but little willingness to go out and defend the Standards Board publicly, not least because it had initially been so unpopular and because at national level there had been recent disagreements over fundamental features of the design.

Only when, with swift and unapologetic speed, the Coalition announced that the Standards Board was to be abolished (along with its strategic partner the Audit Commission) did the CSPL break cover and emerge in stout defence of the Board.[32] In its submission to the Public Bill Committee handling the Localism Bill, and its exchange of letters with the Secretary of State for Communities and Local Government, the CSPL stressed its view about two fundamental failings in the new legislation: the absence of a mandatory code of conduct, and the complete repatriation to the local level of *all* ethical issues concerning elected representative behaviour.

The Localism Act abolished the entire standards regime including both the SBE, the First-Tier Tribunal that the Adjudication Panel turned into in 2009, and the Model Code of Conduct. Local authorities will remain under a duty to promote high standards of conduct though the only part which is *mandatory* will be the register of interests, with criminal sanctions attached to failure to declare interests. None of the Standards Board's function as strategic regulator will be transferred elsewhere. Local authorities will be under no obligation to adopt a code of conduct or to appoint standards committees. Parish councils will also be responsible for their own standards. There will still be a requirement, expressed as a duty, to promote high standards of conduct, but this will now be the function of the authority and not standards committees. Local authorities can create a voluntary code either by revising an existing code or adopting a new code to replace an existing one. But an authority can also withdraw an existing code without replacement. The authority can publicise what it has done about the code, or it can do nothing. Local authorities in England thus have a free hand in how they deal with complaints, other than suspension or disqualification which are expressly forbidden by provisions relating to how councils deal with failure to register or declare interests. Interests and criminal sanctions will be dealt by Regulations issued by the Secretary of State. The monitoring officer in the non-parish councils will be responsible for the registration of interests. New regulations will specify the interests to be registered, disclosure requirements, rules concerning withdrawal, sanctions and rules on access to the public register. Prosecutions in relation to failures to declare interests will be brought with the approval of the Director of Public Prosecutions. Sanctions on conviction will be a fine of up to £5,000 and/or disqualification for up to five years.

Although this comprehensive demolition of Labour's local government ethics framework had been signalled by successive Conservative local government spokesmen since 2005, the Localism Act was nevertheless an astonishingly swift and blunt execution of a work which had been in progress since 2002 and had developed a set of relationships and understandings which had cost formidable amounts of time and money. Despite the painstaking care which had gone into every rule and rule change involved in the code and into the procedures for implementing them, the new framework simply cut regulatory requirements back to the general one that authorities had to keep registers of interests, and that there would be severe court-based penalties for failing to make declarations and observe appropriate withdrawal requirements. There were no further inquiries or reviews, there was no consultation with the CSPL (which protested vigorously) and there was no consultation with local authorities.

Conclusion: failed institution-building

As we saw at the outset of this chapter, ethics in local government has two faces. From the perspective of an individual community, the challenge is to sustain high standards locally. From a national perspective, the challenge is to deliver high standards across many distinct communities, each with its own problems, standards, outlooks and political traditions. The central authorities must seek to do so without intruding too far into the autonomy of local government itself. The choice they face is the classic dilemma of ethics management more broadly: how to balance an externally imposed, rule-based system that sets clear standards and expectations, and an internally generated integrity-based system that allows the local authority to develop responsibility for its own values and behaviour.

In comparison to jurisdictions where the criminal law and the constitutional law are stronger and clearer, especially in the public law jurisdictions of Western Europe, the United Kingdom with the LGA 2000 chose to enter into extensive micro-management of the ethics environment. In 2011 it chose the opposite. The driver of change was the fear that even relatively isolated cases of doubtful propriety might undermine the authority and legitimacy of local government in an environment where levels of trust and support and electoral participation are already low. The chosen tools were soft law, codes of conduct, and a para-legal framework with consequences for poor behaviour, but not penal ones. The arrangements proved overly complex and had to be rapidly reviewed. Key decisional processes were repatriated to the local level, notwithstanding the government's fear that this could thwart the effectiveness of the entire process. Moreover, the values of the system, when revealed in detail exposed publicly what hitherto was largely hidden from view: namely that there can be real and irresolvable clashes of values in ethics and propriety in public life, and that however finely tuned, codes of conduct and sets of principles cannot generate a consensus that will apply to all situations that arise. The choice in 2011 was the polar opposite of the trajectory from 2000 onwards: hard law, almost complete local autonomy, with minimum direction and intervention from the centre.

Ultimately, as an exercise in building a robust and lasting institution for ethical regulation, the Standards Board experience was, by definition, a failure. It could be argued that the failure simply arose because the Board was the victim of Conservative Party policy, or even Conservative Party prejudice, but that would an unsatisfactory and only partial response. Successful institution-building creates broad public acceptance of the utility of the role being performed by the institution and thus at least some degree of political consensus on the need for that institution. That this never happened in the case of the Standards Board was the consequence of more than Conservative prejudice, or the Coalition's urgent need to save public money.

It was the consequence of a sequence of events, some avoidable and some probably very difficult to avoid. It is difficult to argue that the early difficulties, which led to serious delays in judging cases, and perceptions of gross inefficiency, were the consequence of poor resourcing, for the Standards Board was actually rather well resourced throughout most of its existence. Rather it was the combination of starting up without a clear sense of the likely workload, without, by definition, any previous experience of how to manage that workload, and without, in the early days, the possibility of off-loading the less serious cases back on to local authority standards committees because the secondary legislation permitting local determination, eventually approved in 2003/2004, was not initially in place. The Standards Board was therefore literally swamped at the outset. Blame for this can hardly be laid solely at the feet of the Board itself, or its line management. Responsibility seems to lie with Whitehall and Westminster as well as at Standards Board level. Within four years of its establishment, therefore, the Board's early controversial performance had made a mortal enemy at least of the Conservative Opposition at parliamentary level, and probably of a wider section of Westminster than just the Opposition since many of the attitudes that were being shaped were filtering up through party relationships between MPs and their elected colleagues in local government.

This made the necessary reviews, redrafts, and adjustments that the Board and the Code underwent from 2003 onwards particularly difficult. There was suspicion, if not hostility, all through the Code review of 2006. In particular, the CSPL persisted with its view that a fundamental strategic error had been made in the shape of over-centralisation of the initial design. The ODPM Select Committee did not share this view but its inbuilt Labour majority quickly found itself outflanked by its own government which, without ever acknowledging that it had itself been responsible for the extreme centralisation of the 2001 Act, assumed to itself the role of reformer in pushing through the Code review and the LGPIHA 2007. The shift to the status of exclusively strategic regulator after the 2007 reform was thus seen publicly almost as a punishment imposed of the Standards Board for its own failures.

However, the explanation for failure goes deeper still. The political isolation of the Standards Board was the consequence of the diffidence towards it of English local government as well. The Board overcame the overwhelming early years criticism coming from local authorities. Later surveys did indeed suggest, as the Standards Board had a strongly self interested reason to discover, that a large majority at least of monitoring officers and standards committees were fairly satisfied with its performance, and appreciated the iterative role it played in establishing ethical standards. Moreover, in sociological terms, the Board was the product of English local government. Many Board members and staff had extensive experience in local government and in this sense the system was not a new and alien tier of officialdom packed with individuals with little understanding or sympathy with the local government environment. Yet despite this, the Standards Board project never seemed to win the hearts and minds of local government, especially at the elective level. This is not surprising. The Board was, after all, set up in a potentially adversarial role. Elected councillors had a collective reputational interest in high ethical standards in local government, but for each of them individually the Standards Board framework also represented a regulatory burden. They were unlikely to love it for that reason alone, and also because of the iterative process by which challenging and stressful questions had to be worked through. Finding a national framework that improved on the very soft requirements of the 1974 Code of Conduct was never going to be easy and the search for a better solution, and one not dependent solely on criminal law enforcement, turned out to be a constant complication to local politics and policy-making, and a frequent irritant. Elected councillors might well recognise the need for a better framework, but it was unlikely to prevent them from regarding the process with great suspicion, if not hostility, when asked to implement it.

The Standards Board was therefore probably never going to have strong political allies or backers, however good a job it did and nor was the Code of Conduct. Even those at the very top – the senior executives and the Board members – were in no sense a strong and prestigious agenda-setting elite. They represented an extremely thin stratum of hard-pressed officials trying to tackle a complicated job no one had previously attempted.

The eventual institutional failure of the Board is of course a more important issue than the matter of exactly how well the Standards Board system managed ethics at local government level during its ten-year existence. However important and useful that painstaking work of investigating cases, unearthing complicated questions, reviewing the principles they raised, and establishing a case-law and disseminating awareness of it throughout local government, at major part of that work was destroyed with the abolition of the Board. It might be argued that ethical principles are ethical principles, and have a universality and a value which transcends any particular set of procedures, so if the work of the Board did lead to clearer understandings and greater awareness of key ethical principles, then this awareness will not be lost. But this argument looks naive. The Standards Board system was a complex one with a capacity for institutional memory and a set of networks in which knowledge and awareness could be communicated, even if it was too strong a claim to suggest they positively flourished. The new system involves a far simpler and cheaper set of solutions: a return to criminalisation of failures to register and declare interests, and complete autonomy for local authorities as to what, if any, local code of conduct they adopt. It is difficult to imagine, whatever view is taken about the taxpayer cost of regulatory agencies like the Standards Board, that abolition would not involve a loss of some of the capital built up during the decade of the Board's operation.

Notes

1 Lowndes, V., 'Between rhetoric and reality: does the 2001 White Paper reverse the centralising trend in Britain?', *Local Government Studies*, 28:3 (2002), 135–147; Ashworth, R., G. Boyne and R. Walker, 'Regulatory problems in the public sector: theories and cases', *Policy and Politics*, 30:2 (2002), 195–211; Chisholm, M. and S. Leach, *Botched Business: The Damaging Process of Reorganising Local Government 2006–2008* (Coleford: Douglas McLean, 2008). Chisholm, M. and S. Leach, 'Dishonest government: Local government reorganisation, England 2006–2010', *Local Government Studies* 37:1 (2011), 19–41.

2 In 2010, the SBE was renamed Standards for England, as some of its functions – relating to Welsh Police Authorities – were handed over under new devolution arrangements. Local government ethics in the devolved regions were in any case a devolved responsibility. Scotland and Wales created similar frameworks to that of the LGA 2000 though their experience followed a somewhat different trajectory thereafter, discussed briefly in this chapter and in more detail in Chapter 13. Northern Ireland had no similar arrangements.

3 Department for Communities and Local Government, *Local Government Financial Statistics for England No 24 2014*, London, pp. 9, 11, 21, 30.

4 Lowndes, 'Between rhetoric and reality', pp. 135–147. See also: DETR, *Modern Local Government: In Touch with the People* (London: DETR, 1998).

5 Cowell, R., J. Downe and K. Morgan, *Assessing the Impact and Effectiveness of the Ethical Framework in Local Government in England. First Interim Report to the Standards Board for England* (Centre for Local and Regional Government Research, 2009).

6 Committee on Local Government Rules of Conduct (1974), *Conduct in Local Government: Vol 1, Report of the Committee*, HMSO Cmnd. 5636, para 14.

7 Committee on Local Government Rules of Conduct (1974), *Conduct in Local Government: Vol 1, Report of the Committee*; Fitzwalter, R. and D. Taylor, *Web of Corruption* (London: Granada, 1981); Nicholls, C., T. Daniel, M. Polaine and J. Hatchard, *Corruption and Misuse of Public Office* (Oxford: Oxford University Press, 2006), 173–180.

8 CSPL, *Third Report of the Committee on Standards in Public Life: Standards of Conduct in Local Government in England, Scotland and Wales*, Cm 3702 (London: TSO, 1997), Appendix 1.

9 Committee of Inquiry into the Conduct of Local Authority Business, *The Conduct of Local Authority Business*, Cmnd 9800 (London: HMSO, 1986); Department of the Environment, *The Conduct of Local Authority Business: The Government's Response to the Report of the Widdicombe Committee of Inquiry*, Cm 997 (London: HMSO, 1988).

10 CSPL, *Third Report of the Committee on Standards in Public Life: Standards of Conduct in Local Government in England, Scotland and Wales*, Cm 3702 (London: TSO, 1997), pp. 40–41.

11 Audit Commission, *Management Paper 6* (London: HMSO, 1990); Committee of Public Accounts, *Eighth Report: The Proper Conduct of Public Business*, HC 154 (London: HMSO, 1994); Doig, A., 'No reason for complacency? Organisational change and probity in local government', *Local Government Studies*, 21:1 (1995), 99–114; Doig, A. and C. Skelcher, 'Ethics in local government: evaluating self-regulation in England and Wales', *Local Government Studies*, 27:1 (2001), 89–90.

12 CSPL, *Third Report of the Committee on Standards in Public Life: Standards of Conduct in Local Government in England, Scotland and Wales*, Cm 3702 (London: TSO, 1997).

13 The new framework was set out in Part III of the Local Government Act 2000, and subsequent Statutory Instruments. See Statutory Instrument 2001, No. 3537, *The Local Authorities (Model Code of Conduct) (England) Order 2001*; Statutory Instrument 2001, No. 1401, *The Relevant Authorities (General Principles) Order*.

14 CSPL, *Third Report of the Committee on Standards in Public Life*, p. 3.

15 DETR, *Local Leadership, Local Choice*, Cm 4298 (London: DETR HMSO, 1999), 4.19–4.36.

16 DETR, *Modern Local Government: In Touch with the People* (London: DETR HMSO, 1998), pp. 38–50.

17 Statutory Instrument 2003, No. 1483, *The Local Authorities (Code of Conduct) (Local Determination) Regulations 2003*; Statutory Instrument 2004, No. 2617, *The Local Authorities (Code of Conduct) (Local Determination) (Amendment) Regulations 2004; 2001*).

18 CSPL, *Getting the Balance Right: Implementing Standards of Conduct in Public Life*, Cm 6407 (London: TSO, 2005) pp. 50–53.

19 Select Committee on the Office of the Deputy Prime Minister: Housing Planning, Local Government and the Regions, *The Role and Effectiveness of the Standards Board for England* (HC2004–200) HC60-1. Communities and Local Government Committee, *The Role and Effectiveness of the Standards Board for England: The Government's Response to the Committee's Seventh Report of Session 2004–2005* (HC2005–2006) HC 988.

20 Mori, *Satisfaction with the Standards Board for England's Guidance to Key Stakeholders*, p. 3.

21 Standards Board for England (SBE) (2002) *Bulletin*, issue 4, p. 2.

22 Adjudication Panel for England, 2005, *Annual Report*, p. 10. APE decisions, as reported on the website of the then Ministry of Justice Tribunals website, showed that in 2003 between two and ten councillors in about twenty parish councils were disqualified by APE judgements. See www.adjudicationpanel.tribunals.gov.uk/Public/Decisions.aspx (accessed 1 April 2011).

23 The criteria used by the SBE for reference back for local determination was that the behaviour would not be sufficiently serious to warrant any of the more serious penalties for which only the Adjudication Panel had authority, nor were they part of a pattern of recurring (if less serious) misbehaviour by the councillor in question. SBE, *Bulletin*, 21, 2004, 2.

24 SBE, *Bulletin*, 19, 2004, 1.

25 SBE, Annual Report 2006/2007, 4.

26 Macauley, M., *Supporting Monitoring Officers*, Research report conducted by Teesdale Business School for the Standards Board, 2004, p. 5; SBE, *Bulletin*, 16, 2.

27 Minutes, London Assembly, 14 February 2005, pp. 2–4 and appendix C. Livingstone was initially suspended from his post for a period of two weeks but was later exonerated even from this token gesture by a decision of the Appeal Court overturning the decision of the Panel.

28 Adjudication Panel for England *Annual Report*, 2006, p. 40.

29 SBE, *Annual Report*, 2004, pp. 2–4.

30 Committee on Standards in Public Life, Tenth Report, *Getting the Balance Right: Implementing Standards of Conduct in Public Life*, 2005; HC 60-I, Select Committee on the ODPM: Housing Planning, Local Government and the Regions, *The Role and Effectiveness of the Standards Board*, 6 April 2005.

31 SBE, *The Components of an Ethical Environment*, 2006; Standards Board for England, *Public Perceptions of Ethics*, July 2007; BMG Research, *Satisfaction with the Standards Board for England and Attitudes to the Ethical Environment*, Final Report June 2007; Cowell, R., J. Downe and K. Morgan,

Assessing the Impact and Effectiveness of the Ethical Framework in Local Government in England. First Interim Report to the Standards Board for England (Centre for Local and Regional Government Research, 2009).

32 CSPL, *Localism Bill: Submission to the Public Bill Committee*, January 2011 (accessed via UK Government web archive [1 January 2015], www. public-standards.gov.uk/Library/31012011___Localism_Bill_Submission_ to_Public_Bill_Committee.pdf).

13

Integrity issues and devolution

The advent of devolution, which brought a new layer of governance to Scotland, Wales and Northern Ireland in the late 1990s, has generated somewhat different provisions for regulating standards across the three jurisdictions. In this chapter we explore the divergent integrity arrangements in the several parts of the United Kingdom and evaluate the effects of these institutional arrangements.

The CSPL was set up before devolution occurred and its remit initially covered the whole of the United Kingdom. However, as the devolved authorities bedded down, this situation became anomalous, not least because the CSPL reported to the UK prime minister and had no provision for ensuring that the devolved areas were represented fully in its deliberations. The Cabinet Office review of 2013 therefore recommended that in future the CSPL should not investigate matters relating to the devolved bodies unless asked to do so.[1] In 2014 the CSPL was indeed invited to comment on the review of the Northern Ireland Assembly's Code of Conduct and the CSPL duly emphasised the importance it attached to common standards and principles. Whether the freedom from CSPL oversight will produce greater variety in future remains to be seen; but there is the potential for a dilution of the common approach so valued by the CSPL. And, as was seen in relation to an expenses scandal which erupted in Northern Ireland in late 2014, the removal of CSPL oversight from the devolved areas may have been premature given the absence of strong local integrity bodies.

Devolution formed part of the ambitious constitutional agenda of the Blair government after 1997. In a short space of time it brought greater political autonomy and new institutional arrangements to Scotland, Wales and Northern Ireland. The timing of the establishment of the devolved systems (which were set up at the end of a decade in which 'sleaze' was high on the national agenda) made them keenly aware of the salience of integrity issues. Each of the devolved systems therefore created machinery to ensure that high ethical standards were enforced in such matters as legislative and ministerial conduct, public appointments and local government. Initially the devolution legislation empowered the Secretaries of State for the devolved areas to make standing orders for the legislature but the assumption was that these standing orders would provide only a framework and that the detail of procedures and provisions would be fleshed out later. However, the Scottish Parliament was empowered to set its own Code of Conduct while initially those of the National Assembly for Wales (NAW) and the Northern Ireland Assembly (NIA) were imposed by Westminster. These Codes were then revisited by the Assemblies as they sought to take ownership of their standards machinery. And, although each of the three areas faced the need to frame appropriate codes of conduct and registers of interests and to make arrangements for their members' pay, pensions and expenses, the manner and timing of their addressing these issues varied considerably. Codes of conduct had also to be set for ministers in the new executives in Scotland, Wales and Northern Ireland and each devolved government confronted familiar questions about how to handle lobbying, revolving door issues and the general promotion of high standards across their administrations. Devolution thus multiplied the arenas where integrity issues had to be addressed and the introduction of new elections for the devolved legislatures made the regulation of political donations and campaign finance regulation more complex.

The salience of the public ethics debate in the 1990s created a pre-sumption that strict ethical regimes would be put in place in the new polities, not least to draw a contrast with the politics of the United Kingdom as a whole. Whether this contrast was accurate is debateable but enhanced transparency and accountability became a part of the narrative of Scottish and Welsh politics despite the fact that both Scotland and Wales historically had experienced corruption and graft especially in the cities. In Northern Ireland the situation was more complex as its history of violence and sectarian politics had created a culture of secrecy and distrust and there was a long tradition of corruption in public life on both sides of the border.

Devising new integrity machinery posed challenges to the devolved systems. Not only was the task of building new institutions time-consuming; in some cases it was hampered by the institutional structure of the devolution legislation itself. Thus the absence of primary legislative powers from the Welsh Assembly limited its flexibility to respond to a changing ethics agenda. In Scotland an early lobbying scandal imposed a degree of urgency to crafting new arrangements for regulating parliamentary conduct. In Northern Ireland the goal of restoring devolved government and keeping it functioning was given priority over standards regulations and indeed may have encouraged the tolerance of practices which would elsewhere have been prohibited.

In all three devolved areas new offices for handling complaints and securing accountability were put in place but on a piecemeal basis without immediate regard to the coherence of the system as a whole. This incrementalism in turn produced subsequent reappraisals, most dramatically in Scotland where, following a series of reviews from 2005 onwards, the regulatory architecture was radically restructured. This restructuring culminated in 2010 in legislation to bring key regulatory bodies together in a single Commission for Ethical Standards in Public Life in Scotland.[2]

The creation of new political sub-systems also provided opportunities to experiment with new solutions to familiar regulatory problems. The devolved authorities did not simply adopt procedures which replicated United Kingdom wide ones. Although sometimes their arrangements did reflect UK practice, as time went on there was a conscious desire to take a distinctively radical line. Thus in Scotland there was a determination to ensure that any changes to the rules on lobbying were more consensual and comprehensive than Westminster's legislation and indeed in 2015 the Parliament issued a report on the topic which foreshadowed new legislation.

The self-conscious promotion of a 'new politics' for their areas created institutions that were different in ethos and style from Westminster. In Scotland especially there was a strong emphasis on the role of the Parliament as the legitimate focus of political life. Indeed one of the hallmarks of the Scottish approach to scrutiny issues was the establishment by the Scottish Parliament of a series of Commissioners with responsibility to oversee such matters as Standards, Public Appointments and Human Rights. This Commissioner model at one point appeared to offer an alternative to the executive-appointed bodies set up to perform similar tasks in the United Kingdom as whole.[3]

Devolution also provided an opportunity to rethink the handling of complaints and citizen protection especially the various ombudsmen services. In Wales, four individual ombudsmen were integrated into a 'one-stop shop' in a way which was very different from the ombudsmen services in the United Kingdom as a whole.[4]

The values of openness and accountability were heralded as central to the ethos of the Scottish Parliament and the National Assembly for Wales. Northern Ireland by contrast lagged behind somewhat and a legacy of secrecy remained. An 'Open Stormont' movement was launched by the *Belfast Telegraph* in March 2008 to challenge the system's lack of transparency on such issues as expenses, interests and party donations.[5] The new representative bodies were all keen to show themselves to be more constituent-friendly than Westminster and encouraged greater access for the media and the public, not least by electronic means. Certainly the legislative process in Scotland was far from being a mirror image of Westminster's; it was more consultative, more transparent and more committee-dominated and adopted different legislative procedures (and terminology) from Westminster's. A pattern of experiment thus marked all three jurisdictions as they wrestled with procedures for handling ethical and accountability issues.

There were similarities between the arrangements each devolved region introduced to promote high administrative and ethical standards and a good deal of self-conscious learning both from the United Kingdom as a whole and from thinking in the other regions, for example about the scope and operation of legislative codes of conduct. Nevertheless differences naturally emerged. This was inevitable given that devolution was designed to encourage responses to local agendas. Nor were the devolution arrangements static. The powers available to the devolved governments were changed. The Welsh government and the National Assembly for Wales became separate entities and gained enhanced legislative authority. Devolved powers were expanded for Scotland. In Northern Ireland additional responsibilities were transferred, especially the important powers of policing and law and order.[6] The expansion of powers in all three cases changed the context for their integrity arrangements and prompted reviews of their ethics regimes.

A new style of government

Constitutional powers and governance arrangements for the devolved areas were not symmetrical. In Scotland a Parliament was established with wide-ranging primary legislative powers.[7] In Wales the Assembly (which was set up initially as a body corporate with no clear distinction between the executive and the legislative arms) was given no primary legislative powers. It did, however, have the powers to amend secondary legislation. From the beginning Wales saw a determination to push beyond the constraints of the original design both in relation to legislative authority and in relation to the role of the executive. Legislation in 2006 brought major changes to the governance of Wales and in 2011 a referendum cleared the way to give the Assembly direct legislative power.[8] In Northern Ireland, in contrast, devolved government formed part of a complex peace process and its operation has been unstable and susceptible to disruption by political crises.[9] Northern Ireland's troubled history and pattern of religious discrimination and a constitutional framework based on consociational theory gave the NIA its own distinctive character. Not surprisingly therefore the NIA's operations have been more marked by tension and uncertainty than those of the Scottish and Welsh administrations. Indeed the NIA was suspended and direct rule reintroduced on a number of occasions after 1998, including one long period between 2002 and 2007. However, the Third Assembly (2007–2011) ran its full term. Establishing settled legislative and administrative processes in Northern Ireland has not been easy and this obviously affected the working of its standards machinery. Thus a Commissioner for Standards was recommended in 2001 but was not properly established until 2012 when Douglas Bain was appointed as Parliamentary Standards Commissioner.[10] In between an interim Assembly Commissioner for Standards had to deal with complaints on a case-by-case basis and had to navigate the problems occasioned by the Assembly's periods of suspension.[11] Both the NIA and its executive are thus still engaged in something of a catching up exercise with regard to many aspects of its arrangements for ethical regulation.

Part of the reason why provisions for the regulation of standards in the devolved assemblies could not be simply adapted from the national arrangements was constitutional. The formal constitutional position of the devolved administrations was statutory. This created basic differences from Westminster in the regulatory machinery and the handling of integrity issues. Regulation of parliamentary behaviour at Westminster is still predominantly in the hands of each chamber, although the system has been augmented with new institutions and the important matters of pay, expenses and pensions have been transferred to a wholly external body. The Scottish Parliament and the Assemblies of Wales and Northern Ireland did not inherit parliamentary privilege as understood at Westminster and could not base their regulation of their members' conduct on it. Rather the rules governing members' conduct were dependent on the founding statutes of each devolved system.

The dependence of the Scottish Parliament, of the NAW and the NIA on their respective statutes has the important consequence that the proceedings and acts of these legislative bodies are subject to judicial review.[12] And in all three cases serious breaches of the legislative code of conduct were made criminal matters which might become the subject of police inquiry. (For example in the wake of two BBC television documentaries in late 2014 alleging the misappropriation of expenses in the Northern Ireland Assembly it was reported that the police were investigating the claims.[13]) As the Scottish Parliament's Standards Committee pointed out in 2000, MSPs were subject to 'comprehensive statutory requirements in relation to their interests and conduct' as well as being subject to parliamentary regulations including the Code of Conduct.[14] This dependence on statute was reinforced by the passage of the 2006 Interests of Members of the Scottish Parliament Act which established a regime for the declaration of interests and made failure to declare an interest a criminal offence. The Scottish Parliament's dependence on statutory provision as well as on convention and on parliamentary procedures has meant that breaches of the parliamentary rules governing conflict of interest in Scotland are potentially breaches of the criminal law and a matter for the police not just for internal disciplinary committees. Although the Scotland Act of 2012 gave the Scottish Parliament more flexibility in relation to the sanctions it could impose in cases of misconduct, this aspect of the regime has not yet changed, although it could be modified in future.

Other factors have enhanced the role of law in the devolved areas. The provisions of the Humans Rights Act 1998 made much of the European Convention of Human Rights applicable in Scotland, Wales and Northern Ireland *before* it was implemented in the United Kingdom as a whole. The devolved assemblies and the Scottish Parliament are also public bodies for the purposes of the Human Rights Act 1998 and for legislation such as the Corruption Acts of 1889–1916, whereas the Westminster Parliament is not.

Once established, therefore, the separate systems of governance for Scotland, Wales and Northern Ireland followed their own paths, although there are numerous formal and informal mechanisms for keeping them in touch with each other and with central government. These arrangements have included informal networks of officials concerned with standards in the various assemblies as well as consultative visits such as the NIA's visit to the Scottish Parliament in 2014 in connection with the revision of Stormont's Code of Conduct.

Scotland, Wales and Northern Ireland have their own political cultures as well as their own institutional arrangements and political elites. For much of the twentieth century both Scotland and Wales had been areas of strong Labour dominance; but by the time devolution came this dominance had been eroded and in both countries there was a national party presence in the form of the SNP and Plaid Cymru. After devolution the party system in Scotland and Wales became markedly different from that of Westminster, reflecting the use of the mixed member electoral system. The party system in Northern Ireland had become increasingly detached from that of the mainland since 1974 but it was further transformed by the fragmentation of the Ulster Unionist Party and the rise both of the Democratic Unionist Party (DUP) and of Sinn Fein.

The mixed-member system was in part designed to prevent single-party domination of the devolved systems of Scotland and Wales. The four sets of elections to the devolved systems thus far – in 1999, 2003, 2007 and 2011 – have shaped the emergence of their constitutional politics. Initially Scotland operated coalition government, although after the 2007 Scottish parliamentary elections the SNP became the largest single party. It took office first without an overall majority, and then with one in 2011. This achievement of a majority by the SNP changed the terms of the devolution debate in Scotland, placing the issue of independence firmly on the agenda. Although independence was decisively rejected in a referendum in September 2014, the referendum triggered further debate about the appropriate constitutional powers for Scotland and about the constitutional arrangements for other parts of the UK.

In Wales Labour had operated minority government after the first elections; but Labour went into partnership with the Liberal Democrats in 2000 and again after the second round of elections in 2003. After the third set of elections in 2007, Labour again took office as a minority government. Welsh Labour formed the government after the 2011 Assembly elections. In Northern Ireland the Good Friday Agreement imposed a form of power-sharing and from 2007 a four-party executive, including the DUP and Sinn Fein, existed until 2015.

The areas tend increasingly to spawn their own interest groups and lobbying firms. In Scotland many UK-based public affairs firms established Edinburgh offices in the run-up to devolution and the organisation of Edinburgh-based lobbying began to develop in earnest once the Parliament was up and running.[15] Although the growth of lobbying companies has been slower in Cardiff and Belfast, both areas have seen a growth of the lobbying industry and concomitant concern about special interest influence in policy-making. Apart from the early 'Lobbygate' scandal in Scotland there was there was a major scandal in 2008 Northern Ireland as Ian Paisley, Jr was forced to resign from the executive in the wake of a property lobbying scandal.[16]

The devolved areas have their own newspapers, some of which have no equivalent in England, and their own broadcasting networks. Although the existence of regional media adds much to the political life of the devolved regions and can, as in the case of the *Belfast Telegraph* or *The Scotsman*, expose official misconduct, political and administrative issues in those regions is likely to be less closely covered by the national media in the United Kingdom.

Local government is organised on rather different lines from that in England. In Scotland there are thirty-two unitary authorities (councils) while in Wales there are twenty-two unitary areas.[17] In Northern Ireland there are twenty-six districts exercising more limited local government functions than in the rest of the United Kingdom, although local government reform means that this number will be reduced to eleven in 2015.

Inevitably, politics in the devolved areas is more local and small-scale than in the United Kingdom as a whole which, together with long periods of single-party rule in many authorities, makes it more susceptible to cronyism, personalism, and clientelism. Historically, corruption at the local government level has been extensive in Scotland and Wales. In Northern Ireland the long period of Unionist hegemony prior to 1974 had created political enclaves in which there was little opportunity to challenge decisions and discrimination on the basis of religion and political affiliation had been deeply entrenched. As a result of this history, allegations of discrimination are especially sensitive in Northern Ireland and form an important sub-group of ethical concerns. In addition the strongly sectarian politics, combined with the history of paramilitary organisation, has created a distinctive political culture. For example, fraud related offences – both fraud by the public against the authorities, and that involving office holders – have been generally higher in Norther Ireland than in the rest of the UK. Some of the cases that have emerged recently have been very serious. Thus in 2012 convictions were secured in a case which exposed corrupt financial payments to Ministry of Defence officials in an effort to influence the procurement of closed-circuit television (CCTV) contracts.[18]

Scotland's ethics regime

The Scotland Act of 1998 established a 129-member Scottish Parliament elected by a mixed system with 73 MSPs elected by the first-past-the-post method and the remainder by proportional representation in the regions. The Scottish Parliament was given power to determine the content of its own Code of Conduct whereas Wales and Northern Ireland had to begin life with codes imposed by Westminster. The basic framework for the Scottish Parliament was laid down by a Consultative Steering Group, which acted a 'bridge between the major component organizations of the movement for the parliament and the new institution itself'.[19] Its various working parties addressed a number of key ethical issues such as the appropriate disciplinary mechanism for the new Parliament and its approach to the regulation of lobbying.

How to manage integrity issues became a major problem early in the life of the Scottish Parliament. In September 1999 the *Observer* revealed how a public relations firm, Beattie Media, was soliciting business by claiming it had privileged access to Scottish ministers.[20] The affair implicated Jack McConnell, then the Finance Minister and later First Minister, as well as Kevin Reid, son of the then Secretary of State for Scotland, John Reid. Scotland's 'Lobbygate' scandal forced integrity issues up the political agenda, making the young Scottish Parliament prioritise a Code of Conduct for MSPs.

'Lobbygate' also highlighted the regulation of interest groups in Scotland. The traditional Westminster practice had been to set rules for legislators but 'Lobbygate' raised the question of whether regulation of the lobbying industry itself was required, which has moved closer with the report from the Scottish Parliament's Standards Procedures and Public Appointments Commission (SPAA) which recommended a more radical approach than that adopted in the UK.[21] (The Report proposed a Register which will cover all significant lobbying including in-house lobbyists and details of the lobbying activity taking place.) Improving the self-regulation of the industry is, however, the preferred option for many lobbying groups. In 1999 the supervisory bodies in the public relations industry (such as the Association for Scottish Public Affairs) were relatively new and did not cover the whole of Scotland's lobbying industry. Thus Beattie Media, the firm at the centre of the Lobbygate affair, was not a signatory of any code at the time.

'Lobbygate' clearly influenced the framing of new standards machinery for Scotland. The Scottish Parliament's Standards Committee (a mandatory as opposed to a subject committee) had the responsibility for devising a Code of Conduct (which it did in 2000) and a Register of Interests which it had done by 2003. However the Committee itself was initially the body which had responsibility for devising a mechanism for lodging complaints against MSPs and for investigating those complaints.[22]

When the Standards Committee was faced with the 'Lobbygate' inquiry, it encountered formidable procedural difficulties. The Scottish Parliament's lack of parliamentary privilege meant that it had no inherent power to summon witnesses or send for papers. The Committee at that stage sometimes met in secret, prompting the *Scotsman* to file for judicial review to force it to meet in public.[23] The availability of sanctions was another major problem as there was no clear provision for the Scottish Parliament to discipline its members. Above all the time-consuming nature of such inquiries troubled the Standards Committee.

The inquiry ultimately cleared Jack McConnell of wrong-doing but the procedural and practical difficulties exposed during the proceedings increased pressure for a dedicated investigating official to handle alleged breaches of the rules. The Scottish Parliamentary Standards Commissioner Act 2002 introduced an independent Parliamentary Standards

Commissioner for Scotland and made Scotland the first of the three devolved regions to set up this machinery. (This office survived as an independent entity until April 2011 when as part of a major reorganisation of bodies with responsibility for standard setting its functions were transferred to a new Commission for Ethical Standards in Public Life in Scotland.) The role of the Scottish Parliamentary Standards Commissioner (SPSC) is to investigate any complaint that an MSP has breached the Code of Conduct for MSPs or the Interests of Members of the Scottish Parliament Act 2006 or other provisions. The Commissioner reports to the Scottish Parliament which effectively now means to the SPAA as the earlier Standards Committee was renamed. The Commissioner does not decide on sanctions which remain a matter for the Parliament itself. Nor does he give advice on standards issues which are the responsibility of the clerks to the SPAA. There are other areas outside his remit including complaints about behaviour in the Chamber, complaints about staff or complaints about ministerial action.

The Commissioner does not have jurisdiction over expenses. Pay, pensions and expenses for the Scottish Parliament are supervised by the Scottish Parliamentary Corporate Body (SPCB) which is the functional equivalent of the House of Commons Commission, although in the UK matters relating to pay, pensions and expenses are now handled by IPSA. The Commissioner's initial remit was however broader than in some jurisdictions because the Code incorporates provisions about service to constituents. Initially the Code of Conduct provided that complaints about the level of service would be made to the Parliamentary Commissioner for Standards but this was changed between 2003–7 and the 2007–11 Sessions because so many of the complaints were trivial. Such complaints normally now go to the Presiding Officer of the Assembly but were a serious complaint to arise it could be considered by the Commissioner. When s.8 of the Code was reviewed in 2008 a change was made to allow complaints to go to any of a constituent's representatives whether the MSP had been elected on a regional list or for a constituency. (Previously only constituency MSPs had been able to take up local cases.[24]) Currently the relevant sections of the Code state as one of the key principles that members 'should be accessible to the people of the areas for which they have been elected and to represent their interests conscientiously'.[25] S.8 of the Code deals in detail with the complaints procedure. The provision relating to constituency service still generates a significant number of the complaints which the Parliamentary Commissioner receives even though they are outside his jurisdiction, forming the largest category in the three years 2011/2012, 2012/2013 and 2013/2014. The investigation of alleged misconduct is, as in Westminster, a multi-stage process which is conducted on an inquisitorial rather than an adversarial basis. Stage One determines whether the complaint is admissible and then, if it is admissable, Stage Two is the conduct of an inquiry into the facts which are reported to the SPAA. Stage Three of the procedure is the consideration by SPAA of the Commissioner's findings (which may be rejected). The final Stage (Four) is the determination of sanctions.

The number of complaints handled by the SPSC is relatively small and the majority of all complaints made to the Commissioner were found to be inadmissible.

Several features of the parliamentary regulation process have remained problematic. One is the inability of the SPSC (as in the Welsh and Northern Ireland Assemblies) to offer members advice. This advice is given by the clerks, not the Commissioner. However, if an MSP relies on the advice of the clerks and it turns out to be in error or the SPSC takes a different view, this does not automatically constitute a defence, although it will be taken into account. The Code of Conduct suggests that MSPs may wish to take other professional advice, especially in relation to financial matters.

Also problematic is the overlap with the criminal law. As mentioned earlier the statutory basis of the regulations governing the conduct of MSPs means that, once it appears to the SPSC that an offence has been committed, he must cease his investigation and turn it over to the Procurator Fiscal. There is no discretion in the SPSC's office and no public interest test to determine how an offence should be handled. All of this makes the regulatory process cumbersome and disproportionate.

The SPSC does not have the same heavy workload as the PCS at Westminster. The SPSC may initiate inquiries without waiting for a complaint to come to him. One of the regular duties of the SPSC is to review the Code of Conduct each Parliament. In 2010, following an extensive inquiry into the registration of interests, the SPAA proposed reducing the categories of interests which had to be registered from eight to five and improving the clarity of the definitions involved. The Committee also recommended some minor changes such as fixing the threshold for the registration of gifts at the beginning of a session and removing the Electoral Expenses because MSPs already returned that information to the Electoral Commission. Those changes were implemented in 2011. And in 2012 there was a further review of the Code which focused especially on s.7 which covers general conduct in the Chamber and in Committee, including confidentiality requirements and the treatment of other MSPs and their staff.[26]

More wide-ranging consultation on a new Members' Interests Bill occurred in April 2013 following the passage of the Scotland Act 2012 which gave the Scottish Parliament greater freedom to restructure its integrity machinery. However, the SPAA agreed to retain and strengthen the existing criminal offences for a failure to register or declare financial interests and to promote legislation to that effect.

Pay and expenses. The level of pay and pensions and allowances for the new Scottish Parliament was determined initially on recommendations from the Senior Salaries Review Body (SSRB) which produced an initial report and then a further review in December 2001.[27] The pay of MSPs and members of the Scottish executive had initially been linked to that of Westminster MPs calculated as a proportion (87.5 per cent) of Westminster salary. Maintaining a coherent approach to MSPs pay was complicated by the fact that the different jobs undertaken both by MSPs and members of the executive had evolved even since 1998 and the relationship between pay at Holyrood and at Westminster had been undermined by changes to the Westminster pay arrangements. In December 2013, following IPSA's controversial recommendation of an 11 per cent pay rise for Westminster MPs, the Presiding Officer announced that the link between MSPs' pay and Westminster's would be broken and that MSPs would limit themselves to a 1 per cent pay increase.[28]

The expenses regime which was to prove such a problem for Westminster was handled differently in Scotland and, although it has generated some allegations of abuse, there have not been large-scale scandals. Although it was recognised that MSPs might have to obtain accommodation in Edinburgh, only limited subsidy was available for the additional accommodation. Initially mortgage interest relief could be claimed but no provision was made for subsidising furniture and fittings. Expenditure would only be reimbursed on the basis of receipts.[29]

Notwithstanding these somewhat stricter administrative arrangements, criticisms of the expenses regime at Edinburgh soon surfaced. There was especially criticism of the provision for subsidised purchase of accommodation in Edinburgh which allowed MSPs to profit from buying and selling property at public expense. There was also criticism of allowing MSPs to reclaim money spent on council tax and television licences.

A 2007 review of allowances under Sir Alan Langlands suggested radical change.[30] It recommended ending tax relief on mortgage interest. It controversially recommended that different levels of staffing allowances should be paid to the two different categories of MSPs (constituency-elected and list-elected) because constituency MSPs would have a higher workload than MSPs elected in the regions. This proposal was rejected by the Scottish Parliament, which endorsed a uniform staff salary allowance set at that time at £54,562.[31]

The explosion of the expenses scandal at Westminster in 2008/2009 caused the Scottish Parliament to initiate another full-scale inquiry into its own expenses regime. This review (chaired by Sir Neil McIntosh, a former Electoral Commissioner) reported in December 2009 with thirteen recommendations which were all approved by the SPCB and the Parliament on 24 March 2010.[32] The most notable recommendations were the phasing out of employment of family members by 2015 and the introduction of a binding commitment by MSPs to pay capital gains tax on houses purchased at public expense through the mortgage interest subsidy.

The publication of the details of Scottish MPs' expenses claims has led to difficulties for some MSPs. David McLetchie, the Conservative leader at Holyrood, was forced to resign in 2005 after it was revealed that he claimed some £11,000 for taxi expenses and much of this expense had been for party rather than constituency business.

The Executive and the Scottish Ministerial Code. Scotland has its own ministerial code, although the First Minister remains the final judge of conduct. The first Scottish Ministerial Code was published by the new Scottish executive in August 1999 to provide a code of conduct and guidance on procedure for Scottish ministers. It covered a range of matters including the conduct of governmental business, dealings with the Scottish Parliament, the responsibilities of ministers, how private interests should be handled, the presentation of policies, appointments and relationships with civil servants, the role of special advisers, constituency and party interests, engagement with planning matters and rules governing travel. The Scottish Ministerial Code explicitly tried to go further than the UK Code (although it replicated many of its provisions) by embracing the culture of 'openness and partnership with Parliament' which had suffused the thinking about the Scottish devolved system.[33] The Code required the publication of material about special advisers, and engagements including meetings with the media and travel. Like the United Kingdom Code it was not intended to operate as a rulebook. Rather, it was designed as a guide to the principles which should apply to ministers. The Code has to be seen in the context of a system where legal rules are more important than convention and discretionary decisions: 'the code should be read against the overarching duty on Ministers to comply with the law, including international law and treaty obligations, and to uphold the administration of justice and to protect the integrity of public life.' A new Code is promulgated in each Parliament.

From the 2008 revision of the Code the investigation of breaches of the Code has been the responsibility of a panel of independent advisers on ministerial interests on whom the First Minister can draw when needed. The findings are published after they have been reported to the First Minister. The panel of advisers has included George Reid, Lord Steel, Lord Fraser, Dame Elish Angiolini, Sir David Bell and James Hamilton. Having a panel rather than a single official has the advantage of flexibility and can be useful if for any reason a member has to recuse himself from an inquiry. On the other hand critics have suggested that the panel procedure allows the First Minister to handpick the person who will be in charge of the process. Thus far six inquiries have occurred and all have been referred to the panel by the First Minister himself who has in fact also been the subject of the complaint in all cases. The subject matter has been diverse but has included the alleged misleading of the Scottish Parliament by the First Minister, a nomination for an honour and the alleged abuse of Bute House for the entertainment of personal guests by the First Minister in an affair known as 'biscuitgate'.

In Scotland and Wales (though not Northern Ireland) the civil service remained integrated with the United Kingdom as a whole, although officials working in Edinburgh and Cardiff owe their loyalty to the devolved governments. The UK Civil Service Code was revised in 1999 to take account of devolution. Regulation of the take up by officials of positions in the private sector after public sector work also continued to be regulated at a national level by ACOBA.

Non-departmental public bodies and local government. One of the first statutes passed by the new Scottish parliament provided an ethical framework for local authorities and devolved NDPBs. The Ethical Standards in Public Life etc (Scotland) Act 2000 established new machinery in the form of two legal bodies – the SPSC and the Standards Commission for Scotland. The legislation also required ministers to promulgate two codes of conduct one for councillors and one for NDPBs. Both Codes came into effect in 2003. The SPSC investigates allegations of breaches of the Codes. The Commission then decides whether to hold a hearing on an alleged breach.

The establishment of a statutory framework for NDPBs was a departure from the then practice in the United Kingdom where Nolan had retained a non-statutory framework for NDPBs. The Scottish executive did not believe that a statutory system would deter applicants from taking up appointments to NDPBs (an important factor in Nolan's preference for non-statutory means). As the research paper on the subject noted, the Scottish executive thought that 'by providing a clear and strong framework of control, backed by transparent and readily understood sanctions', the reformed system would 'offer greater reassurance to members of public bodies themselves'.[34]

The Commission started work in 2002. By May 2003 it had put in place the required codes including a Code of Conduct for councillors and individual codes of conduct for the many public bodies which fell within its jurisdiction including health boards, colleges of further education and Area Tourist Boards.

The 2000 legislation said nothing about the process for *appointment* to public bodies. In 2003 this gap was remedied by the Public Appointments and Public Bodies etc. (Scotland) Act 2003 which established a Commissioner for Public Appointments. The Commissioner is not a crown servant or subject to direction by MSPs, the Scottish government or the SPCB. The SPAA receives its reports as part of a process of information sharing, not accountability. Indeed the Commissioner has been concerned to protect the independence of the office from the Scottish Parliament as much as from the executive.

The Public Appointments Commissioner regulates a large number of appointments to public bodies. As with the UK Commissioner the focus is on the openness of the process of appointment which must conform to a Code of Practice which was introduced first in 2006 and amended in 2011. As at the national level the emphasis has been on ensuring transparency of appointment procedures. The Appointments Commissioner has also promoted a substantive diversity agenda in an attempt to ensure that minorities receive fair treatment. However, there has been criticism that the new safeguards may make the appointments process time-consuming and cumbersome.

Revision of the architecture. The piecemeal creation of a number of different offices for maintaining standards in the Scottish public sector resulted in a fragmented and somewhat unwieldy system which suffered paradoxically both from overlaps and gaps in coverage. There was also concern that, while some of the scrutiny bodies were supported by the SPCB, others reported to ministers. After 2005 there were reviews of these bodies and their governance arrangements. A review was commissioned from Audit Scotland in 2005 and this was followed by a review from the Parliament's Finance Committee in 2006. In 2006 also the Scottish executive initiated a review chaired by Professor Lorne Crerar who had a wide-ranging brief to examine the arrangements for inspecting, regulating, audit and handling complaints about Scottish public services. Following the Crerar Report the government launched five action groups to take its proposals forward. And in 2008 the Scottish Parliament initiated an ad hoc review of all SPCB (i.e. parliamentary) supported bodies.

As a result of these inquiries a new integrated body (the Commission for Ethical Standards in Public Life) was established. It now brings together the work of the Commissioner for Public Appointments, the former Parliamentary Standards Commissioner and the Chief Investigating Officer. A new Public Standards Commissioner can investigate complaints against MSPs, against local councillors and against devolved public bodies. If this integration succeeds it may provide a model for emulation in the other devolved areas.

The machinery in Wales

Devolution in Wales was originally conceived of as a modest exercise compared to devolution to Scotland, reflecting the limited support for devolution within Wales. The sixty-member NAW was initially set up as a corporate body with a combination of legislative and executive functions, a model which resembled the traditional version of local government where executive ministers and representatives served on committees organised on a functional basis.

This original Welsh model of devolution proved problematic from the start and its legitimacy was further weakened by the forced resignation of the First Minister Ron Davies early in the life of the devolved Assembly.[35] There was a demand to give formal separation to the executive and in 2002 the Richard Commission was established. Its recommendations urged changes to give the NAW substantive legislative powers.[36] The 2005 Better Governance for Wales white paper and Government of Wales Act 2006 presaged extensive constitutional changes which were confirmed by referendum in 2011.[37] In July 2011 an independent Commission chaired by Paul Silk was established to investigate the financial and constitutional arrangements for Wales. It reported on financial accountability in November 2012 and on legislative powers in March 2014.[38] There has thus been incremental change in the role of the Welsh Assembly as it has moved from a weak body primarily focused on pure representation to a body with more law-making and policy framing powers.

The original architecture had profound effects on the handling of integrity issues. As Diana Woodhouse pointed out in her 2002 review of the operation of the standards machinery in Wales, this constitutional position meant that the NAW had an 'unusually large' number of documents prescribing rules of conduct.[39] In addition to the various documents relating to the Assembly's representative business there were documents specifically related to its executive functions – namely a Code of Conduct for Assembly Ministers, a protocol between the NAW, the South Wales Police Force and CPS and a Civil Service Code. The Assembly was required to have standing orders to ensure that financial interests were registered and declared. As in Scotland under the 1998 Act the legislative status of the Code meant that breaches were potentially criminal offences.

The Code was expanded during the early years of the Assembly's life and the Woodhouse Review marked a turning point in the standards machinery. Although an adviser had existed from early in the life of the NAW, the Woodhouse Review wanted to strengthen its independence by putting it on a statutory basis. The Commissioner for Standards Measure 2006 broadened the scope of the office and the Commissioner now has a range of duties including the investigation of alleged breaches of the rules by members of the NAW and managing the rules on the registration of interests. There has been remarkably little misconduct in the NAW. In 2013–2014 the Commissioner reported that no admissible complaints about misconduct by NAW members had been received. A major review of lobbying in 2013 found little evidence of wrong-doing and, while it did not rule out tighter measures in the future, saw no need for substantive change.[40]

The Executive and the Ministerial Code. The first separate Ministerial Code for Welsh Ministers was published in 2007, although there had previously been a code for NAW ministers, which was introduced in 2002. A new ministerial code is issued with each Assembly. The Code itself is divided into an ethical part and a procedural part. As in Scotland the First Minister is ultimately the person responsible for compliance with the code.

As yet there is no separate office to give independent advice to the First Minister on alleged breaches of the ministerial code. However, a debate, supported by the Welsh Liberals and many academics, has now emerged about the need for such an independent office and it seems unlikely that this demand will disappear.

Public appointments. Although Welsh government ministers make appointments to sixteen Welsh Sponsored Government Bodies (WSGBs) and to Welsh health authorities, there is no separate Public Appointments Commissioner to scrutinise these appointments. Rather they fall under the remit of the PAC for England and Wales. There are, however, three important posts (the Children's Commissioner for Wales, the Older People's Commissioner for Wales and the Welsh Language Commissioner) which do not fall under the England and Wales PCA; and there are a range of other appointments within the gift of Welsh ministers which are outside the jurisdiction of the England and Wales PCA. The somewhat patchy situation in relation to quangos has increasingly been criticised both because of the accountability gap and because of a demand for greater participation in appointments by the NAW. Although pre-appointment hearings have become more common in Westminster and in Scotland, the NAW has lagged behind the innovative use of procedures to allow parliamentary participation in key nominations. NAW participation is somewhat greater in relation to three key posts which have direct links into the Assembly – the Auditor General for Wales, the Commissioner for Standards, and Public Services Ombudsman for Wales – but only in relation to the appointment of the Commissioner for Standards is there provision for a pre-appointment hearing. However, calls for greater use of pre-appointment hearings have grown and it is likely that the scope for such NAW participation will be expanded.

Salaries and expenses. As was the case with other devolved bodies, the initial provisions for pay, pensions and allowances were set by the SSRB in April 1998 and pegged as a percentage of that of a Westminster MP (in the case of Wales this was 74.3 per cent, a figure that was increased in subsequent reviews). The initial idea was thus to link the pay of NAW members with Westminster and with the other devolved legislatures. However, following the Westminster expenses scandal a major review of pay and expenses was set up under Sir Roger Jones.[41] In 2009 this report broke the linkage with Westminster salaries, set up an Independent Remuneration Board and made radical changes to the system of allowances, including cutting the availability of mortgages on second homes. The employment of new family members on the payroll was banned.[42] This tough and innovative approach appears to have proved successful as a way of avoiding the expenses scandals which plagued Westminster. Indeed the Assembly's Commissioner for Standards in his 2013 report noted how little misconduct had been found in the Assembly. It may be, however, that an extension of legislative power for the NAW may bring with it some further problems, especially a growth of interest from lobbyists, which have surfaced elsewhere.

The machinery in Northern Ireland

The integrity machinery in Northern Ireland has a special sensitivity as a result of the sectarian divisions and turmoil which brought Northern Ireland's first long period of devolution to an end and ushered in a period of direct rule from 1974 until 1998. Since then, although devolved government has been established, it has been fragile.

The regulation of standards in the NIA is governed by Standing Order. There is a Committee of Standards and Privileges and Members of the Assembly are required to comply with its Code of Conduct and Guide to the Rules Relating to the Conduct of Members which covers the registration of interests, declaration of interests, the advocacy rule and the procedure for complaints.[43] Both the Code and the Register have gone through several versions; as of 2015 the most recent edition of the Code was 2009 and the Register was 2012. The Register of Interests for the NIA does not have to be published.

Efforts to appoint an independent Commissioner of Standards began early in the life of the NIA, although later than in Scotland and Wales. From 2007 the Ombudsman Dr Tom Frawley acted as an interim Assembly Commissioner for Standards on the invitation of the Assembly Standards Committee.

In 2009 the Committee on Standards and Privileges initiated an inquiry into enforcing the Code and the appointment of a separate Commissioner to handle breaches of it. Following consultation the Committee concluded that an independent Commissioner should be established with the power to undertake investigations to determine whether a breach had occurred and that the role, powers and independence of the office should be set out on a statutory basis. However, not until 2011 did legislation produce an independent Standards Commissioner who can initiate inquiries and require witnesses to give evidence or provide documents. The Commissioner holds office for one five-year term.[44]

In 2014 the NIA announced a review of the 2009 Code of Conduct. This review reflected the desire by both the Standards and Privileges Committee of the NIA and the Assembly Commissioner for Standards to improve the Code in the light of Northern Ireland's own experience as well as recommendations about best practice from the CSPL and indeed from international bodies, most notably the Council of Europe where GRECO devoted its fourth evaluation round to preventing corruption in legislatures as well as in relation to the judiciary and prosecutors.[45]

Pay and expenses. The pay and expenses of the NIA have proved controversial. There is widespread suspicion that within the Assembly a culture of maximum claiming for expenses was flourishing and, as has been brought out in television documentaries, that public money was being channelled to individuals and organisations without proper accountability or transparency. The 1998 legislation explicitly precluded the Assembly from delegating matters of remuneration to another body. When the St Andrews Agreement was signed in 2006 a number of changes were made to the operation of Stormont including an increase in office allowances for Members of the Legislative Assembly (MLAs) from £48,000 per annum to £68,000 per annum. In June 2010, however, the Assembly Commission published a major report looking at all aspects of its members and in 2011 Westminster passed legislation to allow the delegation. A new independent panel to review pay, pensions and expenses was established in 2011.[46] And in a major report in 2012 it argued for an

11 per cent rise in MLAs' salaries, which would be compensated for by a cut in expenses. This increase brought the annual salaries of ordinary MLAs from just £43,000 in 2012 to £48,000 in 2013.[47] The panel also set in motion a major review of pensions and a review of constituency office rental arrangements by MLAs. As mentioned earlier, however, controversy continued to surround the use which some MLAs make of their allowances, especially in relation to office rentals where it seems money is being siphoned off to political parties.

The Ministerial Code in Northern Ireland. From the beginning the Northern Ireland Act of 1998 stipulated that there should be a Ministerial Code of Conduct to provide a framework of rules and procedures and a pledge of office for ministers and junior ministers in the Northern Ireland Executive. The latest version was promulgated in 2011. The Code covers both the conduct expected of ministers and the structures and functions of the Executive Committee (which is the Northern Ireland executive). It also covers of the relationships between Northern Ireland's ministers and the North-South Ministerial Council and the British Irish Council.

The Code's effectiveness has been criticised from a number of quarters. There is no published record of ministerial meetings with outside interests as in the UK, and there is no code governing either the role of special advisers or permanent civil servants. Nor is there an independent investigator who can undertake inquiries into breaches. When the First Minister Peter Robinson was involved in allegations about the conduct of his wife in a scandal which became known as 'Irisgate' there were numerous inquiries including one in which he appointed a lawyer to investigate the affair; but the report (which exonerated him) was not published. This non-publication was firmly criticised by the CSPL.

Conclusions

The integrity machinery for the three devolved regions has been subject to continuing review since the advent of devolution, reflecting changed thinking about how best to secure standards in the territories and experience of working machinery established earlier. When GRECO commented on the devolved legislatures in its fourth evaluation it noted that the devolved bodies differed from Westminster most markedly because in all three areas breach of the system for registering and declaring interests along with paid advocacy were criminal offences.[48] It found some slight differences between the system for registering interests of members themselves and of relatives. And it noted that the thresholds for registration in the devolved assemblies, as in Westminster, were high. That said,

GRECO noted the steps that had been taken to strengthen parliamentary procedures at all levels in recent years. Certainly the reports of the various committees charged with investigating complaints against members of the devolved legislatures seem to reveal a relatively small number of admissible cases although more seem to appear in Northern Ireland than in Scotland and Wales.

What seems clear is that both Scotland and Wales have devoted a good deal of attention to refining their standards machinery and that both are confident that their integrity institutions are robust and fit for purpose. The same cannot be said of Northern Ireland. Not only have a range of serious problems surfaced but there is doubt about whether the machinery which currently exists is sufficiently strong to be able to handle them. To some extent the weaknesses in Northern Ireland's approach to integrity issues are a product of its troubled history and political culture and improvements may take a correspondingly longer time to achieve.

Notes

1 *Report of the Triennial Review of the Committee on Standards in Public Life* (2013) Recommendation e and paragraphs 40–43.
2 Parliamentary Commissions and Commissioner etc Act 2010.
3 On this see the discussion in Public Administration Committee, *Ethics and Standards: The Regulation of Conduct in Public Life* HC 121-1 2007 especially ch. 4; and Gay, O. and B. Winetrobe, *Parliament's Watchdogs: The Crossroads* (London: SPG & Constitution Unit, 2008).
4 See Public Services Ombudsmen (Wales) Act 2005 which merged the Welsh Administration Ombudsman, the Local Government for Wales Ombudsman, the Health Service Ombudsman and the Social Housing Ombudsman. On the role of ombudsmen more generally see Gregory R. and P. Giddings, *The Ombudsman, the Citizen and Parliament: History of the Office of the Parliamentary Commissioner for Administration and Health Service Commissioner* (London: Politico, 2002).
5 See *Spinwatch*, 21 April 2008.
6 The executive and legislative elements of the Wales were formally separated in the Government of Wales Act 2006.
7 Scotland Act 1998; Scotland Act 2012.
8 Government of Wales Act 1998; Government of Wales Act, 2006.
9 See Northern Ireland Act 1998 and Northern Ireland (St Andrews Agreement) Act, 2006.
10 See Assembly Members (Independent Financial Review and Standards) Act (Northern Ireland) 2011 and Northern Ireland Assembly Press Release 18 June 2012.
11 *Final Report* to the Committee on Standards and Privileges from Dr T. Frawley, (former) Interim Assembly Commissioner for Standards, 2012.

12 Scotland Act; Wales Act; see also Northern Ireland Assembly, Research and Library Service, Parliamentary Privilege Paper 27/11 January 2011.

13 See McDonald, H., 'Northern Ireland police investigating Stormont expenses scandal', *Guardian*, 26 November 2014

14 Standards Committee, Fourth Report, *Models of Investigation of Complaints*, 2000 SP Paper 186.

15 McCade, I.C., 'Focus Scotland –Scotland's false start' *Public Affairs*, 30 July 2008. For a general discussion see Schlesinger, P., D. Miller and W. Dinan, *Open Scotland: Journalists Spin Doctors and Lobbying* (Edinburgh: Polygon, 2001).

16 On the Paisley case see Gordon, D., *The Fall of the House of Paisley*, revised edition (Dublin: Gill & Macmillan, 2010).

17 Local Government (Wales) Act 1996.

18 Serious Fraud Office, *Sentencing in Northern Ireland Contracts Corruption*, 30 March 2012.

19 Bonney, N., 'The Scottish parliament and participatory democracy: vision and reality', *The Political Quarterly* 74:4 (2003), 459–467.

20 See Dean, N. and B. Laurance, 'Exposed: lobbygate comes to Scotland', *Observer*, 26 September 1999.

21 See Standards Procedures and Public Appointments Committee (SPAA)e, *Proposal for a Register of Lobbying Activity*, SPAA/4, 15 February 2015.

22 The remit of the Standards Committee was extended in 2005 to cover public appointments but in Session 3 (2007–2011) it merged with the Procedures Committee.

23 For a discussion see Schlesinger *et al.*, *Open Scotland*, p. 236.

24 Standards, Procedures and Public Appointments Committee. Session 3 (2008) 9th Report s.8 of the Code of Conduct. SP 176.

25 Scottish Parliament, *Code of Conduct edition 5* (2011) s.3.1.5.

26 See SPAA 8th Report 2012 (Session 4) *Review of s7 of the Code of Conduct*. SP 223.

27 See SSRB Report 42 *Initial Pay and Allowances, Pensions and Severance Arrangements for Members of the Scottish Parliament, National Assembly for Wales and Northern Ireland Assembly*, March 1999 and SSRB Report No 43 *Devolution Salaries for Ministers and Office Holders, Support for Members and Parliamentary Development Recommendations*, March 1999. See also Review Body on Senior Salaries: Report No 50, *Scottish Parliament: Review of Pay and Allowances* (Chair Sir Michael Perry), December 2001.

28 Carrell, S., 'Scottish Parliament to reject Westminster-style pay increases', *Guardian*, 9 December 2012.

29 Reimbursement of Members Expenses Scheme Scotland 2001, www.scottish.parliament.uk/Allowancesandexpensesresources/Members_Expenses_Scheme.pdf (accessed January 2014).

30 Independent Review of Parliamentary Allowances: Report to the Scottish Parliamentary Corporate Body on the Reimbursement of Expenses for Members of the Scottish Parliament, March 2008.

31 See SPICe briefing, *Parliamentary Pay and Expenses*, 8 September 2010 10/56.
32 The Scheme for the Reimbursement of Members Expenses (December 2009). For an overview see SPICe Briefing Parliamentary pay and expenses 8 September 2010 10/56.
33 See Shephard, M. in Fleming, J. and J. Holland (eds), *Motivating Ministers to Morality* (Aldershot: Ashgate, 2001).
34 Scottish Executive, *Ethical Standards in Public Life etc Bill (SP Bill 9 – PM Session 1) (2000): Policy Memorandum* (paras 9–10) (Edinburgh, 2000). See also Scottish Parliament Research Paper (SPICE) 005, *Ethical Standards in Public Life* (Edinburgh, 2000).
35 For overviews of the early period of devolution see Jones, B. and D. Balson, *The Road to the National Assembly for Wales* (Cardiff: University of Wales Press, 2000) and Morgan, K. and G. Munghen, *Redesigning Democracy: The Making of the Welsh Assembly* (Bridgend: Seren, 2000).
36 Commission on the Powers and Electoral Arrangements of the National Assembly for Wales (Chair Lord Richard) Spring 2004.
37 HMSO, *Better Governance for Wales*, Cm 6582, June 2005.
38 Commission on Devolution in Wales, *Empowerment and Responsibility: Financial Powers to Strengthen Wales* (November 2012) and *Empowerment and Responsibility: Legislative Powers to Strengthen Wales* (March 2014).
39 See report of the Review of Standards of Conduct of the National Assembly for Wales STD 04-02 (03).
40 Report 0–13 *Lobbying and Cross Party Groups in the Assembly* (2013).
41 National Assembly for Wales, *Getting it Right for Wales: An Independent Review of the Current Arrangements for the Financial Support of Members*, June 2009.
42 National Assembly for Wales (Remuneration) Measure 2010.
43 For an early discussion of the NIA see Wilford, R. and R. Wilson, *A Democratic Design? The Political Style of the Northern Ireland Assembly* (Belfast: Democratic Dialogue, May 2001).
44 Northern Ireland Assembly, Assembly Members (Independent Financial Review and Standards) Act 2011.
45 CSPL, 14th Report Standards Matter; GRECO Fourth Evaluation Report on the United Kingdom.
46 Northern Ireland Assembly, Assembly Members (Independent Financial Review and Standards) Act 2011.
47 Report of the Independent Financial Review Body, *Northern Ireland Assembly Members' Salaries, Allowances, Expenses and Pensions*, March 2012 (www.ifpr.org.uk, accessed 1 January 2015).
48 GRECO Fourth Evaluation Report on the United Kingdom.

14

Conclusions: higher standards, lower credibility?

This book has traced the great lengths to which the United Kingdom has gone since the mid-1990s in defining and regulating behaviour that, while not criminal, receives widespread disapproval if not condemnation. Having lost its old confidence that standards in public life were clear, widely understood, and followed by all public office-holders, there was a determined effort to return to a golden age of high standards, whether or not such an age had ever really existed. The direction has been set by a body – the CSPL – which has few parallels elsewhere. The Committee has been engaged in continuous probing of a widening circle of public life, and regular review of areas where it has previously made recommendations. Much of its work covers behaviour where the precise definition of right and wrong is elastic and hard to pin down.

The fact that there is potentially so much of this type of behaviour, compared to the occasional instances of outright criminality, means that such disputes are easily exploited for partisan purposes and rarely come to clear conclusions. They are politicised between the major parties, and they feed anti-party and anti-politics sentiments in the public and the press. Regulation has therefore fed an appetite for more ethics intervention, but without ever properly satisfying it. The consequence of sensitising the media and public to ethics issues is that (non-criminal) impropriety is not just defined by non-criminal codes and rules, but increasingly by whatever the media and the public decide they do not much like, even when there are no rules proscribing it.

Predictably this trend has had its strongest impact on political actors who are most prominent in the public mind: elected representatives. Comparing the laxity of the ethics regimes of the House of Commons or House of Lords two decades ago, before the arrival of their codes of conduct and registers of interests, few would advocate going back to that era of loose self-regulation. On most counts, the regime that has applied since 1995 has probably helped raise standards of behaviour, resolve conflicts of interest in the public's favour, and made most if not quite all MPs and peers much more conscious of the dangers of running even appearance-standard ethical risks. In any case the clock cannot be turned back. On the contrary, the more tightly the underlying demands of accountability and transparency bear down on office-holders, the greater the demands seem to grow for absolute integrity.

However, transparency not only makes the public aware of egregious failings like those involved in the expenses scandal, where few dispute what is right and wrong, but seems also to breed public intolerance in areas where right and wrong are more evenly balanced, such as the admissibility of outside earnings for MPs. The 2015 cases of the two former foreign secretaries, Jack Straw and Sir Malcolm Rifkind, caught in a media sting seeking advisory roles (*after* leaving office in the former case, and *during* office in the latter case), are clear instances. Neither had apparently broken any formal rules, and outside earnings are certainly not impermissible once MPs leave the House of Commons, yet both were suspended from their parliamentary parties, both felt forced to refer their cases to the PCS, and in Sir Malcolm's case, the affair forced his resignation from a select committee chair, and deterred him from running for a further term as an MP. The goalposts have clearly moved. Public expectations are fundamentally different from a generation earlier, as are party sensitivities to exposure in these areas.

It would be wrong to pretend, however, that the *only* change is a change in sensitivities, masking an absolute increase in ethical standards. Both these matters are certainly a part of the story we have traced in this book, and in many areas the ethical performance of office-holders *has* greatly improved. But there is another dimension too. Changes in context expose elected representatives to new risks. Thus parliamentary careers at younger ages, fewer safe seats, better post-parliamentary career opportunities, and much increased lobbying of legislatures mean that MPs and peers are more aware of the pecuniary rewards that may flow from their having been, or in the case of peers being, in Parliament: directorships, consultancies and remunerated advisory roles. The explosive growth of APPGs, and the potential access this gives lobbying companies, as evidenced in Chapter 10, is another case, as is the shift in the basis of party finance from membership fees and dues to individual donations from very wealthy individuals. Right across the expanded public service, moreover, the role of money, rewards and incentives raises difficult questions about proper procedures and appropriate checks. The widening wealth gap in the United Kingdom in the last two decades has had the effect of pushing up top salaries in many areas of public and semi-public senior management; but how exactly salaries are set in these areas, how compensation packages are agreed in payoffs and dismissals, how pension arrangements determined, and even in some cases how tax-efficient payment vehicles are arrived at, all run the risk of collusive or improper practices. The politics of envy is closely related to the politics of outrage, and the cases examined in this book are testimony to the growing risks that modern governments face as the boundary between public and private, and the nature of the public sector, change. Faced with these stormy waters, what can be done to ensure the best possible arrangements?

This study started from the premise that ethics regulators cannot operate effectively without strong support from those most closely involved in their creation. Regulation is most likely to bed down effectively along an optimal path of consensus about mission and resources where there is agreement on how a regulator should be operated, audited and assessed, where there is good public understanding of the problems in the field, and where there is strong buy-in from the leadership of institutions being regulated. Where a regulator is born without wide support, is subjected to regular and intense forms of scrutiny, starved of resources, contested by those it seeks to regulate, and brought to public attention only in the case of its shortcomings, the outcome will be unsatisfactory.

We also postulated that over time there is a natural tendency for regulation to use detailed codes of conduct rather than general principles. Problems arise where general principles are ambiguous, where ethics training is difficult to deliver, and where its effectiveness is hard to demonstrate. These difficulties stem from the potentially vulnerable position of regulators themselves. They are likely, if they rely on principles-based regulation, to have difficulty demonstrating their own effectiveness, especially in the face of periodic controversies over lapses within their sphere of competence. The CSPL, ever mindful of the vulnerability of ethics regulators, and of the need for proportionality, warned in 2013 that: 'over-elaboration can lead to codes being resented or ignored or encourage creative compliance' and noted positively in at least some areas a process of simplification rather than further elaboration.[1] It is certainly the case that as rules become more precise the task of assembling adequate resources and skill sets to enforce them efficiently and fairly becomes more challenging. There is rarely enough money for what is aimed at, and teams capable of dealing with complex rules are difficult to build. All these factors, as we have seen in parts of our account of what happened from 1995 onwards, can affect regulator reputation.

UK regulation in areas such as energy, transport services, education or banking has frequently revealed such imperfections. Poor regulatory performance may arise from weak preparation and design, inadequate resources, or simply a failure of political will to make regulation work. Regulation may, as memory of past problems fades, quickly come to seem outdated, and there is evidence of this in UK ethics regulation even over as short a period as the two decades since 1995. The issue of paid advocacy in the House of Commons seemed by the end of the 1990s to have been solved only to return with a vengeance in the Parliament elected in 2010. Regulatory burden has a strong tendency to reflect the most recent experience.

A final distinctive and important premise of ethical regulation in the explicitly political arena is that the targets of regulation are office-holders themselves: the very group who design regulations in the first place. If office-holders do not abide by the rules they set themselves, public controversy will be especially acute. This brings a further difficulty. If elected office-holders behave improperly, to whom are they to be accountable: to voters, as in the traditional British political narrative, or to regulators? Efforts to address this dilemma in the last two decades have created a new framework that has become increasingly complex, poorly understood and in many quarters accepted with bad grace.

The complexity of the post-1997 regime is more striking than any obvious deleterious change in the behaviour of office-holders. With more rules to break there will certainly be more transgressions and with them the impression that things are getting worse, not better. Since the mid-1990s, public office-holders have become embroiled in controversy about ethical matters with much greater frequency than in the past, and sleaze, cronyism and spin seem to be *seen* as a far greater problem than before the 1990s began. But this looks less like the consequence of a sharp deterioration in real public standards than the vector of more complex sources.

The first of these is credit-claiming under an (until recently) two-party system: incoming governments have an understandable tendency to respond to past ethical issues by claiming that they stand for reform. In 1997 'New' Labour's desire to occupy the moral high ground, and claim the credit for innovation in the ethical field, made it vulnerable to failure once in office. Something similar happened after 2010, though by then public expectations were lower, and the fall of the incoming government was less precipitous. But two changes of power over thirteen years and the very dramatic parliamentary expenses scandal in 2009 left the major parties vulnerable to the perception that parties in general were unworthy of public trust.

The second vector is the independence/accountability nexus. Under British conditions, this makes any shift away from adversarial accountability difficult. When power has resided for so long in the political executive and the parliamentary majority, rather than in fully independent regulators, it is difficult for the groups involved, or the public, to get used to new arrangements.

The third vector is design and implementation failures. Our study shows an accumulation of many new agencies, some potentially in conflict with each other, some endowed with multiple and conflicting objectives. It also shows widespread difficulty in following through high-profile public initiatives with timely enactment legislation, with adequate resources, and with lasting political support.

The fourth is the changing ethics agenda: the sensitisation of the public to judgements about the acceptability or appropriateness of behaviour by public figures – in politics, administration, business and finance, local government, the media, entertainment and sport – together with the immediacy of contemporary information about this behaviour, have fed uninhibited probing of ethics in more and more areas of public life and its hinterland.

In the following sections we expand on what each of these issues means, and how they interact with each other.

Credit-claiming, incumbency and the moral high ground

In the 1990s, as a result of the headline-catching scandals thrown up by the cash-for-questions affair, the Conservatives appeared the original sinners and Labour cast itself as the saviour. Labour's rapid fall from grace after 1997 was therefore a serious problem for the credibility of the entire political class. Its occupation of the moral high-ground before 1997 made it vulnerable to even modest ethical slips. The party in power is responsible for public standards. Having promised an ethics revolution, and behaviour in office that would be 'whiter than white', Labour's huge parliamentary majority meant that it could not avoid full responsibility to deliver on its pledge. It failed. In office a continuing endemic propensity to ethical controversies was always likely. The difference was not so much between parties but between past and future. After 1997 there would be a more vigilant press, a sensitised public and the more stringent regulatory rules that Labour had itself enthusiastically supported in opposition. So Labour was quite likely, periodically, to be entrapped by regulations of its own making. As we saw with the Ecclestone and Hinduja affairs, the traps emerged almost as soon as it came to office.

Labour was also iconoclastic about some of the conventions in British political life. The boundary between the political class and public administration was changed on several fronts, starting with the higher civil service. The appointment of special advisers, and the new roles they were allowed to play, together with the uncomfortable political roles some senior civil servants were drawn into, compromising their obligations of political neutrality, suggested an ends-justifies-means cast of mind. Issues also arose in relation to lower-tier supervisory public appointments, most notably, soon after 1997, in the area of hospital trusts, where the extraordinary explosion of Labour-affiliated appointees to public agencies like hospital trusts – ostensibly in the name of 'diversity' – had the same effect. The accusations of cronyism stuck and while the element of impropriety in this behaviour was probably extremely modest, it did the Labour Party's reputation no favours. The government's policy of appointing figures with Labour affiliations to a range of public appointments generated fears that a practice common in other democracies, but hitherto relatively limited in the UK, was on the increase.

Finally, there was a narrow dividing line between perceptions of *spin* and perceptions of *sleaze*. Successive surveys by the CSPL suggested that from 2006 onwards British voters had become seriously worried about honesty among public office-holders driven by a strong belief that they were not being told the truth, or at least were not being informed fairly and objectively, about policies, outcomes and achievements. In its early years in power, Tony Blair's government showed an iron determination to retain control of the political agenda, to maintain party discipline, and to tailor information and news presentation to sustain a coherently tailored political narrative. Here too, the extent of a serious ethical failure may be debated (though in relation to the case for war in Iraq that debate has been fierce) but what matters is as much perception as reality. Governments face a daily choice between complete frankness, and construing events and outcomes to present themselves in a favourable light. In that daily choice, personal and departmental reputations are at stake. Establishing a reputation for complete frankness might be in the long-term public interest in enhancing public trust, but the immediate cost of personal and departmental reputations, and of the government's short-term standing, is likely to far outweigh this.

These imperatives and others – notably the need to secure increasing levels of party funding – bear heavily on all parties. The Conservatives were in power when public perceptions of standards in public life first turned negative and Labour happened to be in power for most of the period when that negative turn was entrenching itself. Both parties faced problems of news and information management. Both parties needed finance, and both were short of money. Without turning to the taxpayer, they could not easily resist a growing reliance on major donors. Out of this reliance came the steady trickle of dubious appointments to the House of Lords, of questionable soft loans, and of post-employment opportunities to retiring politicians to cement party–business relationships. Both parties were vulnerable to the claim of a growing professional political class recruited from a narrow training ground of public relations, think-tanks, lobbies, and advisers.

Most seriously of all, both parties were deeply implicated in the consequences of the expenses scandal, which came just before a further change of power. Whatever efforts were being made by the Brown government from 2007 onwards to distance Labour from the tarnish of the Blair era were blown away in 2009 by the expenses scandal and its legacy. Yet the Conservatives could not escape an equal share of the blame. They made some efforts to cleanse their own parliamentary ranks ahead of the 2010 election, and the Conservative leader David Cameron promised to be tough on the growing issue of lobbying. But given the pre-1997 history of sleaze, given the Conservative performance on parliamentary expenses, and given the party's natural hostility to regulation, the Conservative Party had neither the disposition, nor the inclination, to make a strong stand on ethical issues. Nor, given its growing advantage over Labour in terms of financial donors, did it have any financial interest in doing so. Unsurprisingly, therefore, even if the issue of parliamentary expenses did not resurface again in the acute form experienced in 2009 the same range of controversial behaviour from ministers, MPs, special advisers, party fund-raisers, funders and lobbyists continued to flow throughout the life of the 2010–2015 coalition. It is often argued, in favour of the UK's traditional two-party alternating-government model, that it sacrifices representativeness for clarity and accountability. Voters can hold the party in power responsible for what happens. By the time the coalition came to power, and certainly by the time it completed its term of office, that no longer held as regards standards in public life. Both parties appeared equally tarnished.

Ethics, accountability and adversarial politics

In the last two decades, through initiatives including devolution, the Human Rights Act, the creation of the Supreme Court, and Freedom of Information legislation, the United Kingdom has taken modest strides towards a partial constitutionalisation of what was hitherto a system decidedly lacking in formal checks and balances. However, the impact of the majoritarian system has continued to impose pressures that make life difficult for the new independent regulatory agencies, stoking an enduring argument over exactly how much independent regulation there should be, and how vigorously it should be enforced.

At central government level, even where new ethical procedures have been introduced suggesting a less politicised approach to resolving controversies, the authorities have been unwilling to give way completely and cede influence to neutral arbiters. The result has been conflict over arbitration of the ministerial, parliamentary and civil service codes between a government (or Parliament in the case of the legislative code) that wants to keep matters under its control, and others who want more robust regulation, independently operated.

Moreover, independence in regulation is often laid out as a principle as if its contents were self-evident, or as if the only way of describing independence were institutional. The 2007 PASC report defined an independent regulator as a body whose members were appointed by parliamentary resolution for a fixed, probably non-renewable term, only removable on address from both chambers, and a body which enjoyed statutory protection, adequate resources beyond the control of the executive, its own staffing, accommodation and access to the facilities necessary for its operation and *operational* independence.[2] In practice, the effectiveness of institutional and operational independence will also depend on a hinterland of support for the individual or agency exercising this independence. That does not necessarily mean agreement about every individual decision but it does require a strong inter-institutional consensus around the principle of operational independence.

This issue, as we have seen, is particularly acute for regulators that sit at the rule-making and rule-implementing end of a spectrum. That spectrum runs from agencies with an advisory or at most audit function, to those that carry out tangible tasks with real and immediate effects and in some cases penalties. In this book we have seen how the need for inter-institutional support has affected in particular the EC, IPSA, and the now defunct SBE. The EC was blamed for failing to act resolutely over the loans affair at the time of the 2005 general election, and more generally for getting the balance wrong in allocating its efforts and resources between its regulatory and administrative remit and its wider role in encouraging electoral participation and educating citizens. The SBE was widely criticised for administrative inadequacies even though much of the administrative difficulty the SBE faced in the early years was generated by inadequate legislative follow-up by government. Eventually the Board paid the price, first by being stripped (by statute) of many of its functions, secondly by exile to Manchester, and finally by abolition. Independence is especially difficult to balance with accountability whenever the administrative roles of the agency in question are extensive and potentially controversial, as with IPSA. As we saw in Chapter 5, this caused serious problems for IPSA, even if not the fatal ones involved with the SBE. IPSA dealt with the circumscribed areas of parliamentary expenses; full independence in that area, given the expenses scandal, was unavoidable. However, the broader and more important issues inherent in the parliamentary code of conduct, especially the ban on paid advocacy, and in the register of interests, proved too sensitive to be handed over to independent supervision. The result was an unhappy halfway house between independence and self-regulation, with standards commissioners performing investigative roles, but with the House authorities themselves, including eventually those in the Lords too, retaining the final say.

Implementation and follow-up

Further risk factors in ethics regulation lie at the implementation stage. Implementation difficulties are likely to arise if, ahead of legislating, the authorities have not fully decided what a regulator is to do it, how it will do it, or what resources it will enjoy. Given that much regulatory architecture is introduced in response to a crisis, and therefore in haste, precision is rather unlikely. The importance of a solid basis of agreed support when regulators are established is borne out in several case studies presented here. This imperative places a heavy responsibility on both government and Parliament to consider with care, and ahead of time, what will be involved in achieving a settled understanding of mission, purposes, resources and duration. If there is more work to be done on these questions after the regulator has started work, there is a serious risk of drawing it into unhealthy political controversy. Moreover, whether or not regulatory agencies are endowed with a statutory base, they should as far as possible be seen as long-term quasi-constitutional projects, in which an underpinning of prior cross-party agreement has been established. Such agreement is vital to ensure that the proper accountability to which all regulators must be subject is not overlain by continuing political controversy. Accountability which is overlain by partisan arguments not about performance, but about the more fundamental issues of the mission and resources of the regulator, are likely to damage the regulator's effectiveness. Good-quality public servants will not commit to an organisation that may have a limited life, and is constantly facing unjustified criticism. Recruitment and retention of staff, poor morale, and endemic arguments over priorities and procedures, can seriously damage performance.

IPSA, the Standards Board, and the Office of the Parliamentary Commissioner for Standards present different aspects of this general pattern of difficulty. The weakness might be forgivable in the case of IPSA – which was established in haste – but even where there was less need for haste, as in the case of the Standards Board, the authorities could be said to have failed in the requirement of a clear idea of quite how they intend to proceed. The government was unsure how far it wanted to allow local determination of cases at authority level, and prevaricated for long enough to seriously jeopardise the Board's operating capacity and its reputation.

A changing ethics agenda

A final striking element of the last twenty years of ethics regulation is the injection into political consciousness of the values captured formally in the Seven Principles of Public Life and their gradual extension to many areas that were either assumed already to be regulated, or lay beyond the strictly public sphere. This has slowly added new issue areas to the ethics agenda. Police behaviour, for example, has attracted intense attention in part because of major episodes of long-suppressed misconduct such as the Hillsborough football tragedy and the mishandling of the Stephen Lawrence murder, and in part because of long-standing generalised doubts about police susceptibility to corruption in various forms including misuse of office and bribery. Freedom of Information has gradually revealed the scale of the problems. In 2013 the coalition government's legislation to enhance police accountability by creating elected police commissioners under the Police Reform and Social Responsibility Act 2011 may well have been intended to strengthen public confidence. But the low turnout in the first (2012) elections for these crime commissioners coupled with revelations that a high proportion of those elected had been the subject of Independent Police Complaints Commission investigations inevitably generated scepticism about the new arrangements. In addition there was widespread criticism of the manipulation or 'gaming' of crime statistics. Not surprisingly the controversy surrounding the framework for policing in England and Wales prompted an inquiry into police governance by the CSPL in 2014. This inquiry followed a major review of the new system's financial implications from the NAO and a review by the Home Affairs Committee of the whole experience of elected police commissioners.[3] It was paralleled by a series of other inquiries including a review of police leadership by the College of Policing, a review of the disciplinary and of the complaints system and of police forces' anti-corruption capability and a consultation on whistle-blowing. The sheer range of inquiries underlines the multi-faceted and deep-seated problems associated with policing (and some other law enforcement institutions including prisons). Creating a culture where appropriate values are embedded within the police forces of the UK is likely to be a long-term exercise requiring sustained political support and attention as well as resources.

Corruption and misconduct in the police force of course has a history which pre-dates the 2011 legislation although that reform has given the problems a new character. Alterations in the way the state delivers some of its other key services and shifts in the boundary between the public and private sector have raised many new challenges for the maintenance of ethical standards. In Chapter 2 we explored some of the issues associated with the advent of privatisation and new public management. More recently a new generation of integrity issues has come to the fore as a result of experiments in private/public cooperation. Thus the proposal to allow general practitioners to commission medical service has created the potential for a new and expanded sphere of decision-making with potential for conflict of interest if not outright corruption. The example of GP commissioning and private/public partnerships raises the question of whether the definition of 'public life' in the early years of the debate about standards in the UK was somewhat artificial. Not only is the public/private sector boundary porous and flexible but there are many areas where private actors may have a major impact on the quality of public decisions and confidence in the integrity of its processes. We have seen how political parties, although voluntary organisations, have slowly and increasingly been brought within the framework of regulation; and opinion has shifted also on the extent to which lobbying organisations need to be subject to some kind of oversight. Equally problematic from the perspective of integrity in public life was the media, where the discovery of hacking by News International provoked intense disquiet about the practices of British newspapers and a call for regulation of the media which has not been resolved.

Political parties, pressure groups and the media, although technically voluntary actors or players in the private sector, have a vital role in the political system of any democracy and their ethical standards will be seen as crucial to the health of its public life. All this points to three inter-related concluding points. The first is that, whatever the original definition of 'public life' in the minds of those who established the CSPL, the ground itself has shifted as a result of changing policies, governmental strategies and organisational experiments, and the public's view of what constitutes public ethics is unlikely to fit into any neat constitutional construct. Secondly, while these demands form an expanding agenda in which something must be done to cure an increasing variety political improprieties, it should not be assumed that there will be any obvious or immediate payback in terms of enhanced trust in the political system or faith in its integrity. Finally, despite the somewhat pessimistic prospect of a future in which the public demands more and more intervention but is increasingly dissatisfied with what is achieved, we suggest that there is much to learn from the twenty-year period since the CSPL was established. Indeed, while it is likely that various forms of misconduct will continue to spatter and stain British public life, we have to learn to live with ever rising expectations about all office-holders and key actors public and private. But in that process it would be unforgivable not to try to learn the lessons of ethical regulation as they emerge. We hope we have made a contribution to that process in this book.

Notes

1 Committee on Standards in Public Life, *Standards Matter: A Review of Best Practice in Promoting Good Behaviour in Public Life*, Cm 8159, 2013, p. 28.
2 Public Administration Select Committee, *Ethics and Standard: The Regulation of Conduct in Public Life*, HC 121, April 2007.
3 National Audit Office, *Police Accountability: Landscape Review*, HC 963 Session 2013–2014, 22 January 2014; Home Affairs Committee, 16th Report of Session 2013–2014. *Police and Crime Commissioners: Progress to Date*, HC 757, May 2014; see also Committee on Standards in Public Life, *Local Policing – Accountability, Ethics and Leadership* (Issues and questions paper), November 2014.

Select bibliography

This book cites a large number of official and semi-official publications. To make the bibliography manageable references are provided here only to the major documents and substantive reports but some material is omitted (e.g. government responses to select committee reports.

Official publications and reports

Audit Commission, *Protecting the Public Purse; Probity in the Public Sector: Combatting Fraud and Corruption in Local Government 1993* (London: HMSO, 1993).

Cabinet Office, *Introducing a Statutory Register of Lobbyists* January 2012 (Cm 8233) and *Responses to the Cabinet Office's Consultation Document* July 2012 (Cm 8412).

Cabinet Office, *Report of the Triennial Review of the Committee on Standards in Public Life* February 2013.

Committee on Standards in Public Life, First Report, *MPs, Ministers and Civil Servants, Executive Quangos* 1995 (Cm 2850).

Committee on Standards in Public Life, Second Report, *Local Spending Bodies* 1996 (Cm 3270).

Committee on Standards in Public Life, Third Report, *Standards of Conduct in Local Government in England Scotland and Wales* 1997 (Cm 3702).

Committee on Standards in Public Life, Fourth Report, *Review of Standards of Conduct in Executive NDPBs, NHS Trusts and Local Public Spending Bodies* 1997.

Committee on Standards in Public Life, Fifth Report, *The Funding of Political Parties in the United Kingdom* (Cm 4057).

Committee on Standards in Public Life, Sixth Report, *Reinforcing Standards* 2000 (Cm 4557).

Committee on Standards in Public Life, Seventh Report, *Standards of Conduct in the House of Lords* 2000 (Cm 4903).

Committee on Standards in Public Life, Eighth Report, *Standards of Conduct in the House of Commons* 2002 (Cm 5663).

Committee on Standards in Public Life, Ninth Report, *Defining the Boundaries within the Executive: Ministers, Special Advisers and the Permanent Civil Service* 2003 (Cm 5775).

Committee on Standards in Public Life, Tenth Report, *Getting the Balance Right: Implementing Standards in Public Life* 2005 (Cm 6407).

Committee on Standards in Public Life, Eleventh Report, *Review of the Electoral Commission* 2007 (Cm 7006).

Committee on Standards in Public Life, Twelfth Report, *MPs' Expenses and Allowances: Supporting Parliament, Safeguarding the Taxpayer* 2009 (Cm 7724).

Committee on Standards in Public Life, Thirteenth Report, *Political Party Finance: Ending the Big Donor Culture* 2011.

Committee on Standards in Public Life, Fourteenth Report, *Standards Matter: A Review of Best Practice in Promoting Good Behavior in Public Life* 2013 (Cm 8519).

Committee on Standards in Public Life, *Public Attitudes Survey* 2012.

Committee on Standards in Public Life, *Public Attitudes Survey* 2010.

Committee on Standards in Public Life, *Public Attitudes Survey* 2008.

Committee on Standards in Public Life, *Public Attitudes Survey* 2006.

Gay, O. and R. Kelly, *The Code of Conduct for Members: Recent Changes* March 2015, House of Commons SN/PC/05/05127.

GRECO *First Evaluation Report: Evaluation of the United Kingdom (Greco Eval I Rep (2001) 8E Final)* (Strasbourg: Council of Europe, 2001).

HMSO Parliamentary Privilege April 2012 Cm 8318.

House of Commons, Resolution of the House 19 July, 1995: Code of Conduct and Resolution of the House 24 July 1995: Code of Conduct.

House of Commons, *The Green Book: A Guide to Members Allowances* (revised edition, July 2009).

Joint Committee on Parliamentary Privilege Session 1998–99 HL 43I-III and HC 214 I-III.

Joint Committee on Session 2013–2014 (July 2013) HL30; HC100; see also Government Response to the Joint Committee on Parliamentary Privilege Cm 8771 December 2013.

Kelly, R. and H. Armstrong, *Repeal of s141 of the 1983 Mental Health Act* House of Commons SN 6168 February 2014.

Members Estimates Committee, *Review of Allowances* HC 578-I, 2007–2008.

Members Interests Committee (Declaration) Report, HC57 1969–1970 (Strauss Report).

Parliamentary Commissioner for Standards, *Annual Report* (2002–2003) HC 905.

Parliamentary Commissioner for Standards, *Annual Report* (2009–2010) HC 418.

Parliamentary Commissioner for Standards, *Annual Report* (2010–2011) HC 1328.

Parliamentary Commissioner for Standards, *Review of the Guide to the Rules relating to the Conduct of Members*, consultation paper January 2012.

Parliamentary Commissioner for Standards, *Annual Report* (2013–2014) HC 354.

Public Accounts Committee, *The Proper Conduct of Public Business*, Eighth Report, January 1994, HC 153, 1993–1994.

Public Administration Committee, *Government by Appointment: Opening Up the Patronage State*, HC 165-1, 2002–2003.

Public Administration Committee, *Ethics and Standards: The Regulation of Conduct in Public Life*, HC 121, 2006–2007.

Public Administration Committee, *Lobbying: Access and Influence in Whitehall*, HC 36, 2008–2009.

Public Administration Committee, *Business Appointment Rules*, HC 1762, 2012–2013.

Royal Commission on Standards of Conduct in Public Life (Salmon) 1976 (Cmd 6524).

Standards Committee, *Mr Tim Yeo*, HC 849, 2013–2014.

Standards Committee, *Reflections of the Lay Members on their First Year in Post January 2013–January 2014*. Published April 2014.

Standards and Privileges Committee, *Complaint from Mr Mohamed Al Fayed, The Guardian and Others Against 25 members and Former Members* Vols 1–1V, HC 30, 1997–1998.

Standards and Privileges Committee, *A New Code of Conduct and Guide to the Rules*, April 2002, HC 763, 2001–2002.

Standards and Privileges Committee, *Guidance for Chairmen and Members of Select Committees*, HC 1292, 2002–2003.

Standards and Privileges Committee, *Pay for Select Committee Chairmen*, HC 1150, 2002–2003.

Standards and Privileges Committee, *Reviewing the Code of Conduct*, HC 472, 2004–2005.

Standards and Privileges Committee, *Complaints about Alleged Misuse of Parliamentary Dining Facilities*, HC 431, 2006–2007.

Standards and Privileges Committee, *Conduct of Mr Julian Brazier*, HC 682, 2006–2007.

Standards and Privileges Committee, *Handling of Future Complaints About Misuse of Parliamentary Dining Facilities*, HC 683, 2006–2007.

Standards and Privileges Committee, *Conduct of Mr Derek Conway*, HC, 2007–2008.

Standards and Privileges Committee, *Conduct of Mr George Osborne*, HC 560, 2007–2008.

Standards and Privileges Committee, *Dual Reporting and Revised Guide to the Rules*, February 2009, HC 208, 2008–2009.

Standards and Privileges Committee, *Mr David Curry*, HC 509, 2009–2010.

Standards and Privileges Committee, *Mr. David Tredinnick*, HC 66, 2009–2010.

Standards and Privileges Committee, *Mr Stephen Byers*, HC 110, 2009–2010.

Standards and Privileges Committee, *Power of the Parliamentary Commissioner for Standards to Initiate Investigations*, HC 578, 2010–2011.

Standards and Privileges Committee, *Sir John Butterfill, Mr. Stephen Byers, Ms Patricia Hewitt, Mr. Geoff Hoon, Mr. Richard Caborn and Mr. Adam Ingram*, HC 654-1, 2010–2011.

Standards and Privileges Committee, *Registration of Income from Employment*, HC 749, 2010–2012.

Standards and Privileges Committee, *Review of the Code of Conduct for Members of Parliament: Consultation Paper*, 7 March 2011.

Standards and Privileges Committee, *Former Members Sentenced to Imprisonment*, HC 1215, 2010–2012.

Standards and Privileges Committee, *The Code of Conduct and the Guide to the Rules*, November 2014.

Standards Review Sub-Committee, *The Standards System in the House of Commons*, Oral evidence of Lord Bew, Richard Thomas and Peter Riddell, HC 383, 24 June 2014.

Transparency International, *Corruption Perceptions Index 2013* (Berlin: Transparency International, 2013).

Articles

Allen, N. and S. Birch, 'Political conduct and misconduct: probing public opinion', *Parliamentary Affairs*, 64:1 (2011), 61–81.

Allington, N. and G. Peele, 'Moats, duck houses and bath plugs: members of parliament, the expenses scandal and the use of web sites', *Parliamentary Affairs*, 63:3 (2010), 385–406.

Beyers, J., R. Eising and W. Maloney, 'Researching interest group politics in Europe and elsewhere: much we study, little we know?', *West European Politics*, 31:6 (2008), 1103–1128.

Bradley, A.W., 'Parliamentary privilege and the common law: *R v Greenway* and others', *Commonwealth Law Bulletin*, 24:3–4 (1998), 1317–1324.

Brown, A.J. and B.W. Head, 'Consequences, capacity and coherence: an overall approach to integrity system assessment', in B. Head, A.J. Brown and C. Connors (eds), *Promoting Integrity: Evaluating and Improving Public Institutions* (Farnham: Ashgate, 2008), pp. 285–307.

Carter, D., 'The powers and conventions of the House of Lords', *Political Quarterly*, 74:3 (2003), 319–321.

Coghill, K., P. Holland, K. Rozzoli and G. Grant, 'Professional development programmes for Members of Parliament', *Parliamentary Affairs*, 61:1 (2008), 73–98.

Doig, A., 'Mixed signals? Public sector change and the proper conduct of government business', *Public Administration*, 73:2 (1995), 191–212.

Doig, A., 'No reason for complacency? Organisational change and probity in local government', *Local Government Studies*, 21:1 (1995), 99–114.

Doig, A., 'Cash for questions: Parliament's response to the offence that dare not speak its name', *Parliamentary Affairs*, 51:1 (1998), 36–50.

Doig, A. and C. Skelcher, 'Ethics in local government: evaluating self-regulation in England and Wales', *Local Government Studies*, 27:1 (2001), 87–108.

Dunbabin, J.P.D, 'British local government reform: the nineteenth century and after', *The English Historical Review*, 92:365 (1977), 777–805.

Faccio, M., 'Politically connected firms', *American Economic Review*, 96:1 (2006), 369–386.

Fox, R. and M. Korris, 'A fresh start? The orientation and parliamentary commissioner induction of new MPs following the 2010 election', *Parliamentary Affairs*, 65:3 (2012), 559–575.

Gilbert, B.B., 'David Lloyd George and the great Marconi scandal', *Historical Research*, 62:149 (2007), 295–317.

Johnson, M., 'Measuring the new corruption rankings: implications for analysis and reform', in A. Heidenheimer and M. Johnson (eds), *Political Corruptions: Concepts and Contexts* (New Brunswick:Transaction Publishers, 2000), pp. 865–885.

Kelly, J., 'The Audit Commission: guiding, steering and regulating local government', *Public Administration*, 81:3 (2003), 459–476.

Kelso, A., 'Reforming the House of Lords: navigating representation, democracy and legitimacy at Westminster', *Parliamentary Affairs*, 59:4 (2006), 563–581.

Kelso, A., 'Parliament on its knees: MPs expenses and the crisis of transparency at Westminster', *Political Quarterly*, 80:3 (2009), 329–338.

Lawton, A. and A. Doig, 'Researching ethics for public service organizations: the view from Europe', *Public Integrity*, 8:1 (2005–2006), 11–33.

Leopold, P., 'Standards of conduct in the Lords', in O. Gay and P. Leopold (eds), *Conduct Unbecoming: The Regulation of Parliamentary Behaviour* (London: Politico's, 2004), pp. 299–330.

Lock, G., 'The Hamilton affair', in O. Gay and P. Leopold (eds), *Conduct Unbecoming: The Regulation of Parliamentary Behaviour* (London: Politico's, 2004), pp. 29–58.

Nagel, J.H. and C. Wlezien, 'Centre-party strength and major party divergence in Britain 1945–2005', *British Journal of Political Science*, 40:2 (2010), 279–304.

Norton, P., 'Cohesion without discipline: party voting in the House of Lords', *Journal of Legislative Studies*, 9:4 (2003), 57–72.

Norton, P., 'Reform of the House of Lords: a view from the parapets', *Representation*, 40:3 (2004), 185–199.

Oliver, D., 'Regulating the conduct of MPs: the British experience of combatting corruption', *Parliamentary Affairs*, 45:3 (1997), 539–558.

Oliver, D., 'The politics-free dimension to the UK constitution', in M. Quortrup (ed.), *The British Constitution: Continuity and Change* (Oxford: Hart, 2013), pp. 69–92.

Peele G. and R. Kaye, 'Regulating conflicts of interest: securing accountability in the modern state', in I. Erendira Sandoval (ed.), *Contemporary Debates on Corruption and Transparency: Rethinking State, Market and Society* (Washington, DC: World Bank and National Autonomous University of Mexico, 2011), pp. 155–187.

Percival, J., 'Lobbyist to have security pass withdrawn', *Guardian* (26 June 2008).

Pinto-Duschinsky, M., 'Corruption in Britain: the Royal Commission on standards of conduct in public life', *Political Studies*, 25:2(1977), 274–284.

Platt, D.C.M., 'The commercial and industrial interests of Ministers of the Crown', *Political Studies*, 9:3(1961), 267–290.

Porter, A., 'MPs face fury over vote to keep lavish "John Lewis list" expenses', *Daily Telegraph* (4 July 2008).

Riddell, P., 'In defence of politicians: in spite of themselves', *Parliamentary Affairs*, 63:3 (2010), 545–557.

Rubenstein, W.D., 'The end of "Old Corruption" in Britain 1780–1860', *Past and Present*, 101:1 (1983), 55–86.

Russell, N., 'Nice work if you can get it: MPs keep their perks', *Independent* (4 July 2008).

Ryle, M., 'Disclosure of financial interests by MPs –the John Browne case', *Public Law* (1990), 313–323.

Saint-Martin, D., 'The Watergate effect or why is the ethics bar constantly rising', in C. Trost and A. Gash (eds), *Conflict of Interest in Public Life: Cross National Perspectives* (Cambridge University Press, 2008), pp. 35–55.

Syal, R. and J. Ball, 'One in five passholders in House of Lords linked to lobbying', *Guardian* (8 November 2011).

Taylor, J., 'Commercial fraud and public men in Victorian Britain', *Institute of Historical Research*, 78:200 (2005), 230–252.

White, M., 'The sinking of Hamilton', *Guardian* (26 October 1994).

Wright, A., 'What are MPs for?', *Political Quarterly*, 81:3 (2010), 298–308.

Wright, O. and M. Newman, 'Watchdog to investigate Lord Blencathra over lobbying for Cayman Islands', *Independent* (18 April 2012).

Wright, O. and M. Newman, 'The murky world of interests peers don't think you need to see', *Independent* (20 June 2012).

Books

Baldwin, N.J. and D. Shell (eds), *Second Chambers* (London: Frank Cass, 2001).

Baldwin, R. and C. McCrudden, *Regulation and Public Law* (London: Weidenfeld & Nicolson, 1987).

Baldwin, R., M. Cave and M. Lodge (eds), *The Oxford Handbook of Regulation* (Oxford: Oxford University Press, 2010).

Baldwin, R., M. Cave and M. Lodge, *Understanding Regulation: Theory, Strategy and Practice* (Oxford: Oxford University, 2nd edition, 2011).

Ballinger, C., *The House of Lords 1911–2011* (London: Hart, 2011).

Barchard, D., *Asil Nadir and the Rise and Fall of Polly Peck* (London: Gollancz, 1992).

Baston, L., *Sleaze: The State of Britain* (London: Channel Four Books, 2000).

Baumgartner, F., J. Berry, M. Hojnacki, D. Kimball and B. Leech, *Lobbying and Policy Change: Who Wins, Who Loses and Why?* (Chicago: University of Chicago Press, 2009).

Bell, M., *An Accidental MP* (London: Penguin Books, 2001).

Bell, M., *The Truth That Sticks: New Labour's Breach of Trust* (London: Icon Books, 2007).

Bell, M., *A Very British Revolution: The Expenses Scandal and How to Save Our Democracy* (London: Icon, 2009).

Blick, A., *People Who Live in the Dark: A History of the Special Adviser in British Politics* (London: Politico's, 2004).

Bourne, J.M., *Patronage and Society in Nineteenth Century England* (London: Edward Arnold, 1986).

Bower, T., *Fayed: The Unauthorised Biography* (Basingstoke: Macmillan, 1998).

Brooke, H., *The Silent State: Secrets, Surveillance and the Myth of British Democracy* (London: Heinemann, 2010).

Butler, D. and D. Kavanagh, *The British General Election of 1997* (Basingstoke: Palgrave, 1997).

Butler, D. and D. Kavanagh, *The British General Election of 2001* (Basingstoke: Palgrave, 2002).

Campbell, C. and G.K. Wilson, *The End of Whitehall: Death of a Paradigm* (Oxford: Blackwell, 1995).

Campbell-Smith, D., *Follow the Money: The Audit Commission, Public Money and the Management of Public Services* (London: Allen Lane, 2008).

Camplin, J., *The Rise of the Plutocrats: Wealth and Power in Edwardian England* (London: Constable, 1978).

Chafetz, J., *Democracy's Privileged Few* (New Haven: Yale University Press, 2007).

Clarke, M., *Business Crime: Its Nature and Control* (London: Polity, 1990).

Clarke, M., *Regulation: The Social Control of Business between Law and Politics* (London: Palgrave, 2000).

Coglianese, C. and A. Kagan (eds), *Regulation and Regulatory Processes* (Farnham: Ashgate, 2007).

Cook, R., P. Tyler, T. Wright and G. Young, *Reforming the House of Lords: Breaking the Deadlock* (London: Constitution Unit, 2005).

Crick, M., *Jeffrey Archer: Stranger than Fiction* (London: 4th Estate, revised and updated edition, 2000).

Critchley, J. and M. Halcrow, *Collapse of Stout Party: The Decline and Fall of the Tories* (London: Indigo, 1997).

Cullen, T., *Maundy Gregory Purveyor of Honours* (London: Bodley Head, 1974).

Denning, L., *The Denning Report the Profumo Affair* (London: Pimlico, 1963, 1992).

Dimoldenberg, P., *The Westminster Whistleblowers: Shirley Porter, Homes for Votes and Twenty Years of Scandal in Britain's Rottenest Borough* (London: Politico's, 2006).

Dobel, J.P., *Public Integrity* (Baltimore: Johns Hopkins University Press, 2002).

Doig, A., *Corruption and Misconduct in British Politics* (Harmondsworth: Penguin, 1984).

Doig, A., *Westminster Babylon* (London: Allison and Busby, 1990).

Doig, A., *Fraud* (Farnham: Gower, 2012).

Donaldson, F., *The Marconi Scandal* (London: Harcourt Brace, 1962).

Ewing, K., *The Cost of Democracy: Party Funding in Modern British Politics* (Oxford and Portland: Hart, 2007).

Fitzwalter, R. and D. Taylor, *Web of Corruption* (London: Granada, 1981).

Gay, O. and P. Leopold (eds), *Conduct Unbecoming: The Regulation of Parliamentary Behaviour* (London: Politico's, 1994).

Giddings P. and M. Rush, *Parliamentary Socialisation: Learning the Ropes or Determining Behaviour?* (Basingstoke: Palgrave, 2011).

Gillard, M., *Nothing to Declare* (London: John Calder, 1980).

Ginsberg, B. and M. Shefter, *Politics by Other Means: Politicians, Prosecutors and the Press from Watergate to Whitewater* (London: Norton, 1999).

Gordon, R. and M. Jack, *Parliamentary Privilege: Evolution or Codification?* (London: Constitution Society, 2014).

Gould, P. *The Unfinished Revolution* (London: Little Brown, 1998).

Grant, W., *Business and Politics in Britain* (Basingstoke: Macmillan, 2nd edition, 1993).

Greenslade, R., *Maxwell's Fall* (London: Simon & Schuster, 1992).

Greer, I., *One Man's Word: The Untold Story of the Cash for Questions Affair* (London: Deutsch, 1997).

Hall, P. (ed.), *Governing the Economy: The Politics of State Intervention in Britain and France* (Oxford: Oxford University Press, 1993).

Hall, P. and D. Soskice (eds), *Varieties of Capitalism: The Institutional Foundations of Comparative Advantage* (Oxford: Oxford University Press, 2001).

Head, B., A.J. Brown and C. Connors (eds), *Promoting Integrity: Evaluating and Improving Public Institutions* (Farnham: Ashgate, 2008).

Heath, A.F., R. Jowell and J. Curtice (eds), *The Rise of New Labour: Party Politics and Voter Choices* (Oxford: Oxford University Press, 2001).

Heidenheimer, A. and M. Johnston, *Corruption: Concepts and Contexts* (New Brunswick and London: Transaction Books, 2002).

Hennessy, P., *Whitehall* (London: Secker & Warburg, 1989).

Herrick, R., *Fashioning the More Ethical Representative* (Westport: Praeger, 2003).

Hollingsworth, M., *MP's for Hire* (London: Bloomsbury, 1991).

Hood, C., *The Blame Game: Spin Bureaucracy and Self-Preservation in Government* (Oxford and Princeton: Princeton University Press, 2010).

Hood, C. and D. Heald, *Transparency: The Key to Better Governance?*(Oxford: Oxford University Press, 2006).

Hood, C. and H. Margetts, *The Tools of Government in the Digital Age* (Basingstoke: Macmillan, 2007).

Hood, C., H. Rothstein and R. Baldwin, *The Government of Risk* (Oxford: Oxford University Press, 2001).

Hood, C., C. Scott, O. James and T. Travers, *Regulation Inside Government: Waste Watchers, Quality Police and Sleaze Busters* (Oxford: Clarendon Press, 1999).

Hosken, A., *Nothing Like a Dame: The Scandals of Shirley Porter* (London: Granta, 2006).

Huberts, L.W., J. Maesschalk and C. Jurkiewicz (eds), *Ethics and Integrity of Governance: Perspectives across Frontiers* (Cheltenham: Edward Elgar, 2008).

Jones, P., *From Virtue to Venality: Corruption in the City* (Manchester: Manchester University Press, 2013).

Jordan, G. (ed.), *The Commercial Lobbyists: Politics for Profit in Britain* (Aberdeen: Aberdeen University Press, 1991).

Kavanagh, D., *Thatcherism and British Politics: The End of Consensus?* (Oxford: Oxford University Press, 1990).

Kavanagh, D., *The Reordering of British Politics: Politics after Thatcher* (Oxford: Oxford University Press, 1997).

Kaye, R., *Regulating Westminster* (DPhil Thesis, Oxford, 2002).

King, A. and I. Crewe, *The Blunders of Our Governments* (London: Oneworld, 2013)).

Leigh, D. and E. Vulliamy, *Sleaze: The Corruption of Parliament* (London: 4th Estate, 1997).

Leys, C., *Market Driven Politics* (London: Verso, 2003).

Macmillan, G., *Honours for Sale: The Strange Story of Maundy Gregory* (London: Richards, 1954).

Maloney, K., *Rethinking Public Relations: PR Propaganda and Democracy* (London: Routledge, 2006).

Mancuso, M., *The Ethical World of British MPs* (London: McGill-Queen's University Press, 1995).

Mann, T. and N. Ornstein, *It's Even Worse Than It Looks: How the American Constitutional System Collided with the New Politics of Extremism* (New York: Basic Books, 2012).

Miller, D and W. Dinan, *A Century of Spin: How Public Relations became the Cutting Edge of Corporate Power* (London: Pluto Press, 2008).

Moran, M., *The British Regulatory State* (Oxford: Oxford University Press, 2003).

Nicholls, C., T. Daniel, M. Polaine, and J. Hatchard, *Corruption and Misuse of Public Office* (Oxford: Oxford University Press, 2006).

Office of the Civil Service Commissioners, *Changing Times: Leading Perspectives on the Civil Service in the 21st Century and its Enduring Values* (London, 2005).

O'Leary, C., *The Elimination of Corrupt Practices in British Elections, 1868–1911* (Oxford: Clarendon Press, 1962).

Osler, D., *New Labour PLC: New Labour as a Party of Business* (Edinburgh: Mainstream Publishing, 2002).

Parvin, P. *Friend or Foe? Lobbying in British Democracy: A Discussion Paper* (London: Hansard Society, 2007).

Perkin, H., *The Rise of Professional Society, England since 1880* (London: Routledge, 1989).

Phythian, M., *The Politics of British Arms Sales since 1964: 'To Secure Our Rightful Share'* (Manchester: Manchester University Press, 2000).

Pimlott, B., *Harold Wilson* (London: HarperCollins, 1992).

Preston, N. and C. Sampford with C.A. Bois, *Ethics and Political Practice: Perspectives on Legislative Ethics* (London: Routledge, 1998).

Rawnsley, A., *The End of the Party: The Rise and Fall of New Labour* (London: Viking, 2010).

Ring, A.J. and D. Frantz, *Full Service Bank: How BCCI Stole Millions Around the World* (London: Pocket Books, 1992).

Russell, M., *House Full: Time to Get a Grip on Lords Appointments* (London: The Constitution Unit, 2011).

Russell, M., *The Contemporary House of Lords: Westminster Bicameralism Revived* (Oxford: Oxford University Press, 2013).

Russell, M. and M. Sciara, *The House of Lords in 2005: A More Representative and Assertive Chamber?* (London: Constitution Unit, 2006).

Sampford, C., A. Shacklock, C. Connors and F. Galtung, *Measuring Corruption* (Aldershot: Ashgate, 2006).

Schattschneider, E., *The Semi-Sovereign People: A Realist's View of Democracy in America* (Austin: Holt, Rinehart and Winston, 1960).

Searle, G., *Corruption in British Politics 1895–1930* (Oxford: Oxford University Press, 1987).

Seldon, A. (ed.) *Blair's Britain, 1997–2007* (Cambridge: Cambridge University Press, 2007).

Seldon, A. and L. Baston, *Major: A Political Life* (London: Weidenfeld & Nicolson, 1977).

Shell, D., *The House of Lords* (Manchester: Manchester University Press, 2007).

Skidelsky, R. (ed.), *Thatcherism* (Oxford: Blackwell, 1989).

Smith, D.C., *Follow the Money: The Audit Commission Public Money and the Management of Public Services* (London: Allen Lane, 2008).

Stapenhurst, R., R. Pelizzo and N. Johnston, *The Role of Parliament in Curbing Corruption* (Washington, DC: World Bank, 2006).

Thompson, D., *Ethics in Congress: From Individual to Institutional Corruption* (Washington, DC: Brookings Institution, 1995).

Tomkinson, M. and M. Gillard, *Nothing to Declare* (London: John Calder, 1980).

Transparency International, *Does the United Kingdom Need an Anti-Corruption Agency?* (Policy Paper, 4 October 2012).

Trost, C. and A. Gash (eds), *Conflict of Interest in Public Life: Cross National Perspectives* (Cambridge: Cambridge University Press, 2008).

Van Heerde-Hudson, J. (ed.), *The Political Costs of the 2009 British MPs' Expenses Scandal* (Basingstoke: Palgrave, 2014).

Vinen, R., *Thatcher's Britain: The Politics and Social Upheaval of the 1980s* (London: Simon & Schuster, 2009).

Vogel, D., *National Styles of Regulation: Environmental Policy in Great Britain and the United States* (Ithaca: Cornell University Press, 1986).

Wade Baron, S., *The Contact Man: The Story of Sidney Stanley and the Lynskey Tribunal* (London: Secker & Warburg, 1966).

White, F. and K. Hollingsworth, *Audit, Accountability and Government* (Oxford: Clarendon Press, 1999).

Whyte, D. (ed.), *How Corrupt is Britain?* (London: Pluto Press, 2015).

Winnett, R. and G. Rayner, *No Expenses Spared* (London: Bantam Press, 2009).

Wootton, G., *Pressure Groups in Britain 1790–1970* (London: Allen Lane, 1975).

Index

Note: 'n' after a page reference indicates the number of a note on that page.

accountability 2, 11, 14, 17–20, 22–24, 26, 31, 32, 38, 39, 45–46, 52, 56, 61–63, 75, 85, 105, 113–118, 153–154, 157, 174–175, 230, 242, 244, 270–272, 283–285, 287, 293, 295–296, 298–301

Adjudication Panel for England 249, 267n.22
  see also local government

Additional Costs Allowance (ACA) 104, 106, 117

administrative ethics 167–183

Advisory Committee on Business Appointments (ACOBA) 18, 22, 159, 185–196, 201
  Chair of 186
  and civil servants 185–196
  conditions imposed by 186
  and ministers 185–196
  rules of 186
  and special advisers 191

Advisory Committee on Civil Service Appointments 185

Afriye, Adam 114–115

Aitken, Jonathan 43

All–party Parliamentary Groups 85, 97, 202–203

Al Yamamah Deal 41

Angiolini, (Dame) Elish 282

Anti–Fraud Authority 168

Armstrong Memorandum (1985) 169

Ashby, Robin 136

Association of Council Secretaries and Solicitors 257

Association of Larger Councils 257

Association of National Parks Authorities 257

Association of Police Authorities 257

Association for Scottish Public Affairs 277

Attlee, Clement 36

Audit Commission 12, 39, 56, 242, 245, 259, 261

Audit of Political Engagement 6–9

Audit Scotland 283

Bain, Douglas 273

Ballot Act (1872) 32

Baldwin, Stanley 36

Bank of Credit and Commerce International (BCCI) 40

Banking, Independent Commission on (Vickers) 13

Banking Standards, Parliamentary Commission on 13

Barber, (Sir) Michael 173

Bearwood Corporate Services Ltd 228

Beattie Media 276–277

Beckett, Margaret 233

Belcher, John 36

Belfast Telegraph 272, 275

Bell, David 282

Bell, Martin 43, 93

Berlinsky, Samuel 155

Berlusconi, Silvio 158

Best Value (1999) 242

Bew, Paul (Lord Bew) 54

Bhatia, Amir (Lord Bhatia) 141

Bill of Rights (1689) 56–57

Blair, Tony 43, 187
   government of 53, 189–190, 297
Blencathra, Lord 147
blind trust 157
Blunkett, David 1, 158, 161, 186
Boothroyd, Betty (Lady Boothroyd) 93
Bourn, (Sir) John 162
BPP 200
Bribery Act (2010) 55
bribery law 199
British Irish Council 288
British National Party (BNP) 9
British United Industrialists 219
Brittan, (Sir) Leon 156
Brown, Gordon 162, 175, 187, 190
   government of 53, 98, 298
Brown Report 189–190, 194
BSkyB 200
Budd (Sir) Alan 161
Butcher, Herbert 37
Butler, (Sir) Robin (Lord Butler) 42, 157,
   159, 174
   Review of Intelligence (2004) 174
Byers, Stephen 187, 200

Cable, (Sir) Vincent 155
Cabinet Office 13, 22, 53–54, 114,
   162–163, 173, 176, 186, 188, 199
   Triennial Review of the Committee on
   Standards in Public Life (2000) 65
   Triennial Review of the Committee on
   Standards in Public Life (2013)
   54, 269
Cabinet Secretary 159–160, 175–176
Cameron, David 91, 199–200, 298
   government of
Campbell, Alastair 173
'cash for questions' scandal 41, 42, 46, 52,
   57, 69, 73, 75 76, 89–90, 93, 200
Chamberlain, Neville 36
Children's Commissioner for Wales
Civil Service 168–183
   appointments in 170–183
   Change Programme (2010) 176
   Civil Service Act 171
   Civil Service Commission 21, 172,
   175, 178
   Civil Service Clerical Union 89
   First Civil Service Commissioner
   178, 179
   Management Board 174

Management Code 21, 170, 201
Modernising Government (1999) 174
and post–employment questions
   171, 293
reform of 170–183
see also code(s) of conduct
Clarke, Anthony (Lord Clarke of
   Hampstead) 140–141
Coalition Government (2010–2015)
   176, 190
code(s) of conduct 13, 20, 25, 48, 59–60,
   63, 75, 77, 80, 133–134, 177,
   206–209, 262, 270, 282, 292,
   294, 300
   for lobbyists 177, 206–209
   for local government 240, 245–250,
   257–258, 261, 265
   for special advisers 179
   in devolved government 273, 281
   see also House of Commons, House
   of Lords, Ministerial Code, Civil
   Service
Code of Practice for Public Appointments
   177, 179
College of Policing 301
Commission for Ethical Standards in
   Public Life etc (Scotland) Act
   2000 271
Commission for Ethical Standards in
   Scotland 278, 283
Commissioner for Local Government
   244, 257
Commissioner for Public Appointments
   177–178
   Office of 178–180
Commissioner for Public Appointments
   (Scotland) 283
Commissioner for Standards (House of
   Lords) 139–152
Committee on Standards in Public Life
   (CSPL) ix–x, xii, 2, 5–8, 14–17, 22,
   32–34, 42–43, 52–71, 78, 84, 92,
   107–109, 113, 117, 126, 132–135,
   138, 142, 146, 148, 160–161, 164,
   175, 177–179, 186, 188–189, 192,
   201, 218, 220–223, 229, 231,
   233–235, 237, 245, 247, 253–254,
   257, 260–263, 269, 287–288, 292,
   294, 297, 301–303
and local government 245–253, 260
and MPs' expenses 107–109

Committee on Standards in Public Life
(CSPL) (*cont.*)
and parliamentary ethics 75–97
and the Civil Service 188
and the Electoral Commission 117
and the House of Lords 133–135
and the Ministerial Code 160–164
surveys of public attitudes 7–9, 98
Comprehensive Spending Review (2007) 242
Comptroller and Auditor General (CAG)
12, 32, 55, 91, 162, 230
conflict(s) of interest vii, 2, 3, 20, 27n.5,
35, 39, 44–45, 55, 60–61, 71,
72–73, 82, 85, 125, 129, 131, 155,
157, 161, 163–164, 167–168, 170,
181n.1, 184–185, 187, 189, 202,
241–244, 246, 247, 259, 293, 302
Conservative Party 40–41, 43–44, 177,
187, 216–239, 263, 298
see also Conservatives
1922 Committee 115
Conservatives 9, 35, 39, 44–45, 74, 107, 176,
219–221, 232, 236, 239n.25, 296–298
see also Conservative Party
Constitutional Reform and Governance
Act 2010 (CRGA2010) 84,
108–109, 114, 116, 171, 175, 177
Conway, Derek 76
Cooper, Yvette 136
Cordle, John 37, 244
Corrupt and Illegal Practices Act
(1883) 32
corruption ix–x, 1–4, 9–10, 20, 27n.9,
30, 33–34, 36, 38–39, 47, 52–56,
67n.14, 71–72, 77, 104, 159, 168,
203, 216–217, 240, 243–245, 270
276, 287, 301, 302
Corruption Perceptions Index (CPI) 4
Council of Europe 31, 46, 287
Group of States against Corruption
(GRECO) 46
Crerar, Lorne 283
Critchley, (Sir) Julian 40
Crown Prosecution Service (CPS) xii,
142, 227
Cruddas, Peter 200
Curry, David 90

Daily Mirror 41
Daily Telegraph 76, 104, 107

Davies, Ron 284
Democratic Unionist Party (DUP) 274
devolution 54, 269–291, 298
devolved elections 275
see also National Assembly for Wales,
Northern Ireland Assembly,
Scottish Parliament
Department of the Environment (DOE) 39
Department for Trade and Industry
(DTI) 42
Director of Public Prosecutions (DPP) 141
Dispatches (Channel Four) 76
Doncaster Council 20
Downey, (Sir) Gordon 42, 70, 92
Draper, Derek 44–45

Eagle, Angela 95
Eames, Robin (Archbishop Eames)
137–140
Eames Report 138–140
see also Leader's Group Report
Eden, (Sir) Anthony 36
Ecclestone, Bernie 44, 221, 296
Electoral Administration Act (2006)
227–229
Electoral Commission 19–20, 22, 55,
116–117, 219–239, 299
Chair 55
Ethical Standards in Public Life etc
(Scotland) Act (2000) 282
Eurobarometer 5
European Convention on Human Rights
(ECHR) 97, 274
European Court of Human Rights 97
European Social Survey 5
Evans, Nigel 84
expenses scandal (House of Commons,
2009) *see* House of Commons

Fawley, Tom 287
Fayed, Mohamed al 41–42
Filkin, Elizabeth 93, 98
Financial Aid to Political Parties (1976),
Committee on 219
financial interests declaration (MPs) 109
Financial Times 231
Flinders, Matthew 178–179
'flipping' (of MPs' second–home
declarations) 105–106
Formula 1 221

Fox, Liam 1, 163, 173, 200
freedom of information 53, 76, 77, 106

general elections
  1997: 42–44, 173, 198, 220–221,
    223, 245
  2001: 233
  2005: 35, 123n, 299
  2010: 28n.25, 56, 70, 77, 80, 109–110,
    155, 162, 187, 199–200, 213n.15,
    223, 231, 233, 237, 238n.19, 298
  2015: 119–120, 177, 205, 235
Gershon, Peter 173–174
Gladstone (government of) 35
Good Friday Agreement 275
Government of Wales Act (2000) 284
Goudie, Mary (Lady Goudie) 141
Graham, (Sir) Alastair 65, 160
GRECO xii, 46, 47, 287–289
  Fourth Evaluation Round 146–147
Green Party 9
Greer, Ian, 40–43
  Ian Greer Associates 40–43
Gregory, Maundy 35
Griffiths, Hugh (Lord Griffiths) 132
  Griffiths Report 133–135
Grylls, (Sir) Michael 42
Guardian 41, 76, 148

Hamilton, James 282
Hamilton, Neil 41–43
Hammond, (Sir) Anthony 161
Hancock, Michael 84
Hanningfield, (Lord) 142, 145–146, 148
Hansard Society 5–8, 202, 219
Healey, John 136
Heald, Oliver 233
Her Majesty's Revenue and Customs
    (HMRC) 55, 113, 191
Hewitt, Patricia 187, 200
Hillsborough Tragedy 301
Home Office 55
Hinduja affair 45, 296
'homes for votes' affair 20, 39
Honours (Prevention of Abuses) Act
    (1925) 35, 225
Hoon, Geoff 187, 200
Hordener, Peter 42
Houghton Committee *see* Financial Aid to
    Political Parties (1976), Committee on

House of Commons 14, 18
  allowances 74, 104, 106, 110, 112, 117
  Clerks of the House 108
  Code of Conduct 75, 79, 80–85, 91,
    109, 118, 158, 294
  Commission of 114, 278
  declarations of interest 78
  Disqualification Act (1957) 77
  education and training in 79
  exclusive cognisance 57, 75
  expenses scandal x, 1, 19, 26n.1,
    28n.25, 34, 57, 66, 70–71, 73–74,
    77, 90, 98, 104–124, 130, 147, 298
  Fees Office 75, 106
  Guide to the Rules 69, 72–73, 84–85
  Leader of the House 113
  paid advocacy 89, 200
  Register of Interests 85
  Register of Financial Interests 37, 41,
    85–89, 91
  Select Committees
    chairs of 78
    Home Affairs 219, 301
    Members' Allowances
      Committee 115
    Members Estimates 76, 106, 114
    Members' Expenses 114, 116–118
    Members' Interests 37, 42, 90
    MPs' Personal Interests (1896) 35
    Political and Constitutional Affairs
      117, 223, 231
    Political and Constitutional
      Reform 199
    Privileges 90
    Public Accounts (PAC) 32, 39, 116
    Public Administration (PASC) 2, 64,
      89, 160–162, 175, 186–196
    Standards 58, 77, 90, 91, 93, 96, 109
    Standards and Privileges 78, 85,
      90–91, 97, 108
    Trade and Industry 42
  Speaker 78, 115
  Standards Review Sub Committee 71
House of Lords 35, 85, 125–152, 190, 300
  Allowances 129, 140–141, 144–146
  'cash for amendments' ('Ermingate)
    130, 140

House of Lords (*cont.*)
  Chairman of Committees 144
  Clerk of the Parliaments 140–141
  Code of Conduct 128–152
  Leader's Group 137–139
  Leader's Group Report 138–140
  Lord Speaker 143
  Members' Reimbursement Scheme 141
  Peers, hereditary 125
  Peers, life 125
  Principal Deputy Chairman of
    Committees 144
  Register of Lords' Interests 130–133,
    135, 138–140, 143, 147
  Select committees
    Privileges 90, 130, 135, 137, 141, 149
    Privileges and Conduct 139, 145
    Procedure 130–133
  Sub–Committee on Lords Conduct
    139, 142–143
  Sub–Committee on Lords Interests 135,
    137, 139–140, 147
House of Lords Act (1999) 78, 131
House of Lords Appointment Commission
    127–128, 179
House of Lords (Reform) Act 2014 126,
    146, 149
Hudson, Kathryn 78, 93
Human Rights Act1998 274, 298
Hunt, Jeremy 155, 159, 163, 200
Hutton Inquiry 174

Ian Greer Associates 40–3
Independent Adviser on Ministerial
    Interests 162–163
Independent Commission on Banking
    Standards 13
Independent Parliamentary Standards
    Authority (IPSA) 19, 21–22, 58,
    70, 77 80, 84, 93, 98, 104–124,
    125, 148, 230, 257, 299–300
  budget 114
  chair 115
  Commissioner for Investigations 108–109
  Compliance Officer 93, 108–109
  London Area Living Payment 112
  London costs allowance 106
  pay and pensions 120
  scheme for expenses 108, 110–113, 119
  staffing 112

Independent Police Complaints
    Commissioner 301
Information Commissioner 55
Insolvency Service 39
Institute for Democracy 46
Interests of Members of Scottish
    Parliament Act (2006) 274, 278
Interests of Members of Scottish
    Parliament Bill (2013) 279
interest groups 197–215
  In devolved areas 275
'Irisgate' affair 288
Isaacs, Rufus 35

Jinman, Peter 91
Joint Committee on Parliamentary
    Privilege 57
Jones, (Sir) Roger 286
Jowell, Tessa (Lady Jowell) 158, 161
Judges 202
Judicial Appointments Commission 179

Kagan, Joseph (Lord Kagan) 37
Kelly (Sir) Christopher xi, 54
Kernaghan, Paul 130, 144

Labour Party 9, 43, 44, 120, 127, 175,
    187, 216–239, 245, 296–297
Labour government(s) 34, 36, 62, 107,
    173–174, 188, 193, 207, 232
Laird, John, (Lord Laird) 145, 147
Lang, Ian (Lord Lang) 190, 193
Langland Review (Scottish Parliament
    Expenses System) 280
Lawrence, Stephen 301
Legal Aid, Sentencing, and Punishment of
    Offenders Bill (2011)147
Legg Audit 97
Legg, (Sir) Thomas 106–107
Leigh, David 40
Leopold, Patricia 133
Leveson Inquiry 13, 28n.20, 165n.2
Levy, Michael (Lord Levy) 44
Liberal Democrats 9, 84, 93, 176, 176,
    221, 226, 234, 275
Liddle, Roger 44
Liverpool City Council 244
Livingstone, Ken 255–256, 258
Lloyd George, David 35
  trafficking in honours 35, 38

loans to parties 225–229
'loans for peerages' affair 2, 35, 162
lobbying 64, 73–89, 125–152, 184–196,
     197–215, 293, 298
  and civil servants 197–215
  and Ministers 197–215
  multi–client lobbying firms 72
  regulation of lobbying 80, 85, 89, 93,
     204, 207, 210, 276
local government 240–268
  Code of Conduct (Local Government
     Act 2000) 38, 244, 246, 264
  Code of Conduct for Councillors
     (Scotland) 283
  complaints against
     councillors 250–253
  conflict of interest in 20
  Ethical Standards Officers 248, 256
  Improvement and Development
     Agency 259
  Local Government Act (2000) 64
  local self–determination 64
  National Code of Conduct in Local
     Government (1974) 38, 244, 246, 264
  personal and prejudicial interests (of
     councillors) 251–258
  local standards committees 247–248,
     261, 264
  annual assemblies of local standards
     committees 253, 257
  structure of local government 241
  tribunals of local government 247
  see also codes of conduct, Standards
     Board, Adjudication Panel for
     England
Local Government Acts: (1972) 38, 244
  (1974) 38, 244
  (1986) 244
  (1988) 244
  (1989) 244
  (2000) 64, 240, 243, 245–247, 260–262
Local Government Association 257
Local Government and Public
     Involvement in Health Act
     2007(LGPIHA) 248–249, 254,
     257–259, 264
Local Government Ombudsman
     see Commissioner for Local
     Government
London, Mayor of 255–256

Lucas, Ben 44
Lynsky, Tribunal 36
Lyon, John 93, 96, 174

McConnell, Jack 277
Macdonald, Ramsay 36
Mackenzie, Brian (Lord Mackenzie of
     Framwellgate) 144–145, 147
Macmillan, Harold 36
Maitland, Olga (Lady Maitland) 42
Major, John 1, 31, 41–43, 53, 176, 219
  government of 53, 62, 173
Malik, Shahid 162–163
Malone, Gerald 42
Mandelson, Peter (Lord Mandelson) 45,
     158, 161, 164
Marconi scandal 35
Maude, Francis (Lord Maude) 177
Maudling, Reginald 37, 244
Maxwell, Robert 41
Mawer (Sir) Philip xi, 70, 93 162
McIntosh Review (of Scottish Parliament
     expenses system) 281
McNally, Tom (Lord McNally) 139
Members of Parliament (MPs) x, 69–124,
     201, 206, 263, 293, 298
  bribery of 58
  code of honour 75
  entrapment of 76
  families of 111–112
  financial interests 77, 78, 85–89, 107
  outside earnings 106
  paid advocacy 76, 80, 89–90, 107
  recusal 78
  salaries and pensions 104–106, 109,
     119–120
  staff 106
  see also House of Commons, code of conduct
Mendelson, Jon 44
Mental Health Act (1983) 78
Mercer, Patrick 95–96, 148
Michel, Frederic 200
Millenium Dome Project 155
Miller, (Sir) Eric 37
Miller, Maria 90–91, 95, 149, 158
Ministerial Code 18, 60, 80–81, 157–164,
     187, 201
  in Northern Ireland 288
  in Scotland 281–282
  in Wales 285–286

Ministers 153–164
  relationships with civil servants
    154–156, 167–183
  resignations 155
Ministry of Defence (MOD) 39, 163,
    188, 276
Ministry of Justice (MOJ) 55, 107
Moonie, Lewis (Lord Moonie)
    130, 136–137
Moore, Jo 159
Mulgan, Geoff 173

National Assembly for Wales 270,
    272, 284–286
  Auditor General for Wales 286
  Children's Commissioner for Wales 285
  Code of Conduct 270–271
  Commissioner for Standards Measure 285
  Commissioner for Standards Wales 286
  expenses 286
  Independent Remuneration Board 286
  Ministerial Code 285
  pay 286
  Public Services Ombudsman for
    Wales 286
  Richard Commission 284
  Silk Commission 284
  Woodhouse Review 284
National Association of Local Councils 257
National Audit Office (NAO) 39,
    112–113, 115–118, 301
National Code of Local Government
    (1994) see local government
National Health Service (NHS) x, 39, 55,
    59, 112, 178–179, 181
Neill, Patrick (Lord Neil of Bladon) 65, 142
New Public Management (NPM) 39, 46,
    177–178, 302
Nolan, Michael (Lord Nolan) 42, 65, 132
Normington, (Sir) David 178
Northcote–Trevelyan Report (1854) 169
Northern Ireland Act (2000) 288
Northern Ireland Assembly 269, 273
  Conduct 269–270, 286–287
  Commissioner for Parliamentary
    Standards 273, 287
  expenses 287–288
  Guide to the Rules 286–288
  Independent panel to review pay and
    expenses (2011) 287
  Ministerial Code 288
  pay 287–288
  Ombudsman 288
  Register of Interests 286–287
  Standards and Privileges
    Committee 286
North–South Ministerial Council 288

O'Donnell, (Sir) Gus (Lord
    O'Donnell) 175
Office of the Deputy Prime Minister
    (ODPM) 234, 249, 253, 257–258
  Select Committee on 249
Older People's Commissioner for Wales 286
Organisation for Economic Cooperation and
    Development (OECD) 31, 46–47
  Anti–Bribery Convention 55

Paisley, Ian, Jr 275
Panorama 145
Parliament Act (1911) 125
Parliament Act (1949) 125
Parliamentary Commissioner for
    Standards 21, 42, 69, 73, 83,
    89, 90–94, 108, 158–159, 162
    278, 300
parliamentary privilege 56, 57, 73, 75
  see also House of Commons – exclusive
    cognisance
parliamentary staff 74
Parliamentary Standards Act (2009) 84
party funding ix, 3, 21, 34, 53, 55, 61, 63,
    169, 201, 216–240, 297
patronage 30, 32, 35, 154, 169–170,
    172, 177–179
Paul, Swraj (Lord Paul) 141
Peachey Properties 37
personal and prejudicial interest see local
    government
Phillips Review 232–236
Plaid Cymru (PC) 202, 301–302
police 202, 301–302
Police Reform and Social Responsibility
    Act (2011) 301
Political Parties, Elections and
    Referendums Act, 2000 (PPERA)
    19, 87, 218–236
Polly Peck 40–41
Porter, (Dame) Shirley 39
Poulson affair 20, 33, 37–38, 75, 244–245

Powell, Jonathan 173
Power, Greg, 96
post–employment conflict of interest 61,
    189, 208, 270, 298
press regulation 13, 155, 165n.2
Prevention of Corruption Acts (1906
    and1916) 33–34, 274
Prime Minister's Office (10 Downing St)
    173, 179
Profumo affair 30, 36
Public Affairs Council 198
Public Appointments and Public Bodies
    (Scotland) Act2003 283
Public Bodies Corrupt Proceedings Act
    (1889) 33–34, 274
Public Honours Scrutiny Committee 37
Public Service Agreements 174

Questions of Procedure for Ministers
    157, 201
    see also Ministerial Code

Redcliffe-Maud Committee 37–38
Reid, (Sir) George 282
Reid, John 277
Reid, Kevin 277
register of interests see House of
    Commons
Riddick, Graham 41, 43
Rifkind, (Sir) Malcolm 73–74, 93, 96,
    148, 293
Roberts, Albert 37
Robinson, Peter 288
Rowntree State of the Nation Report
    (2010) 234
Royal Commission on Standards in Public
    Life (1976, Salmon Commission)
    37–38, 58
Royall, Janet (Lady Royall of Blaisdon) 137
Rumbold, (Dame) Angela 43
R v Chaytor and others (2010) 57

Sainsbury, David (Lord Sainsbury) 44, 160
St Andrews Agreement 288
Schattschneider, E.E. 197, 211
Scotland Acts (1998) 276
    (2000) 282
    (2003) 283
    (2012) 274, 279
Scotsman, The 275

Scotland, Patricia (Lady Scotland of
    Asthal) 137
Scottish National Party (SNP)
    9–10, 274–275
Scottish Parliament 270, 276–284
    code of conduct 270, 274, 276–277, 279
    Consultative Steering Group 276
    Corporate Body (SPCB) 278, 281, 283
    expenses 278, 280–281
    Finance Committee 283
    First Minister 282
    lobbying in 276–277
    Parliamentary Standards
        Commissioner 283
    pay 280–281
    Presiding Officer 278
    Scottish Parliamentary Standards
        Committee 273
    Standards Procedures and Public
        Appointments Committee
        (SPAA) 277
Scottish Parliamentary Standards
    Commissioner Act (2002) 277
select committees see House of Commons
    – select committees; House of
    Lords – select committees
Senior Salaries Review Body 113, 144, 280
Serious Fraud Office 55
Serious Organizaed Crime Agency 55
Seven Principles of Public Life 15–16, 21,
    59, 80, 134, 146, 152, 157, 301
Shadow Cabinet 73
Short Money 114, 219
Sinn Fein (SF) 274–275
'sleaze' ix, 41, 43, 48, 53, 219, 269,
    295, 297–298
Smith, Adam 159, 200
Smith, Jacqui 158
Smith, Tim 42
Snape (Lord) 130, 136–137
SOCA 55
Society of Local Council Chief
    Executives 257
Society of Local Council Clerks 257
Speaker 113, 115
special advisers 20, 64, 156, 159,
    171–175, 179, 184, 191, 193, 200,
    208, 217, 220, 281, 288, 297–298
Speaker's Committee on the Electoral
    Commission 230–231

Speaker's Committee on Independent
    Parliamentary Standards Authority
    (SCIPSA) 113–119
Standards Board for England (SBE) 12,
    22, 56, 240–268, 299–300
Starmer, (Sir) Keir 141
Steel, David (Lord Steel) 282
Stoddart, David (Lord Stoddart of Swindon)
Strauss Committee 75, 77
Sunday Times 41, 76, 78, 126, 135–137,
    140, 145, 187
Supreme Court 73, 298
Swinton Committee 135, 137

Taylor, Thomas (Lord Taylor of
    Blackburn) 130, 136–137
Taylor, John (Lord Taylor of Warwick)
    142, 148
Thatcher, Margaret 40, 156
    Thatcher years 38, 40, 43
They work for you.com 76, 110, 201
third party organisations 228
Thomas, Jimmy 36
Thompson, Dennis 73–74
Tower Hamlets 21
Transparency International 4, 46, 55
Transparency of Lobbying, Non–party
    Campaigning and Trade Union Act
    (2014) 89–90, 235
transparency 11, 14, 18, 21–22, 31,
    45–46, 52, 59–62, 74, 76, 85, 97,
    105, 107, 110–113, 119, 142,

    163, 199, 201–210, 216–217,
    221–232, 236, 270, 272, 283,
    287, 293
Tredinnick, David 41, 43
Truscott, Peter (Lord Truscott) 130, 136–137
trust 5–10, 15, 56, 62, 72, 82, 85, 164,
    211, 255, 262, 295, 297, 303
Turnbull, (Sir) Andrew (Lord Turnbull) 174

Uddin, Pola (Lady Uddin) 141, 148
UKIP 9
Ulster Unionist Party (UUP) 274

Vesty, William 35
Vulliamy, Ed 40

Waller, Gary 43
Werrity, Adam 173, 200
Welsh Language Commissioner 285
Welsh Sponsored Governmental Bodies
    (WSGBs) 285
Westminster Communications 40
Who's Lobbying? 201
Wicks, (Sir) Nigel 64–65
Widdicombe Report (1986) 244
Williams, Gareth (Lord Williams of
    Mostyn) 134
Wilson, Harold 37
Wilson, (Sir) Richard (Lord Wilson) 174
World Bank 46

Yeo, Tim 43, 78–79, 93